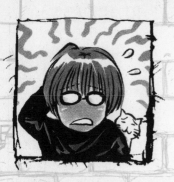

Agh! Sorry about springing this on you all out of the blue! But my schedule for this volume was tighter than ever before, so I couldn't work on any empty pages, even though I promised in volume 5 that "I will fill every empty page." In any case, I did my best on the main body and the cover drawing, so please forgive me.

—Kentaro Yabuki, 2004

Kentaro Yabuki made his manga debut with *Yamato Gensoki*, a short series about a young empress destined to unite the warring states of ancient Japan and the boy sworn to protect her. His next series, *Black Cat*, commenced serialization in the pages of *Weekly Shonen Jump* in 2000 and quickly developed a loyal fan following. *Black Cat* has also become an animated TV series, first hitting Japan's airwaves in the fall of 2005.

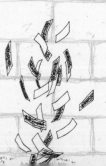

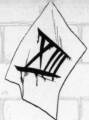

BLACK CAT VOL. 17
The SHONEN JUMP Manga Edition

STORY AND ART BY
KENTARO YABUKI

English Adaptation/Kelly Sue DeConnick
Translation/JN Productions
Touch-up Art & Lettering/Gia Cam Luc
Design/Courtney Utt
Editor/Jonathan Tarbox

Editor in Chief, Books/Alvin Lu
Editor in Chief, Magazines/Marc Weidenbaum
VP, Publishing Licensing/Rika Inouye
VP, Sales & Product Marketing/Gonzalo Ferreyra
VP, Creative/Linda Espinosa
Publisher/Hyoe Narita

Printed in the U.S.A.

Published by VIZ Media, LLC
P.O. Box 77010
San Francisco, CA 94107

SHONEN JUMP Manga Edition
10 9 8 7 6 5 4 3 2 1
First printing, November 2008

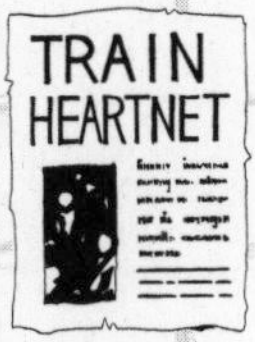

www.viz.com

THE WORLD'S
MOST POPULAR MANGA

www.shonenjump.com

PARENTAL ADVISORY
BLACK CAT is rated T+ for Older Teen and is recommended for ages 16
and up. This volume contains tobacco use and graphic, realistic violence.
ratings.viz.com

BLACK CAT

ブラック・キャット

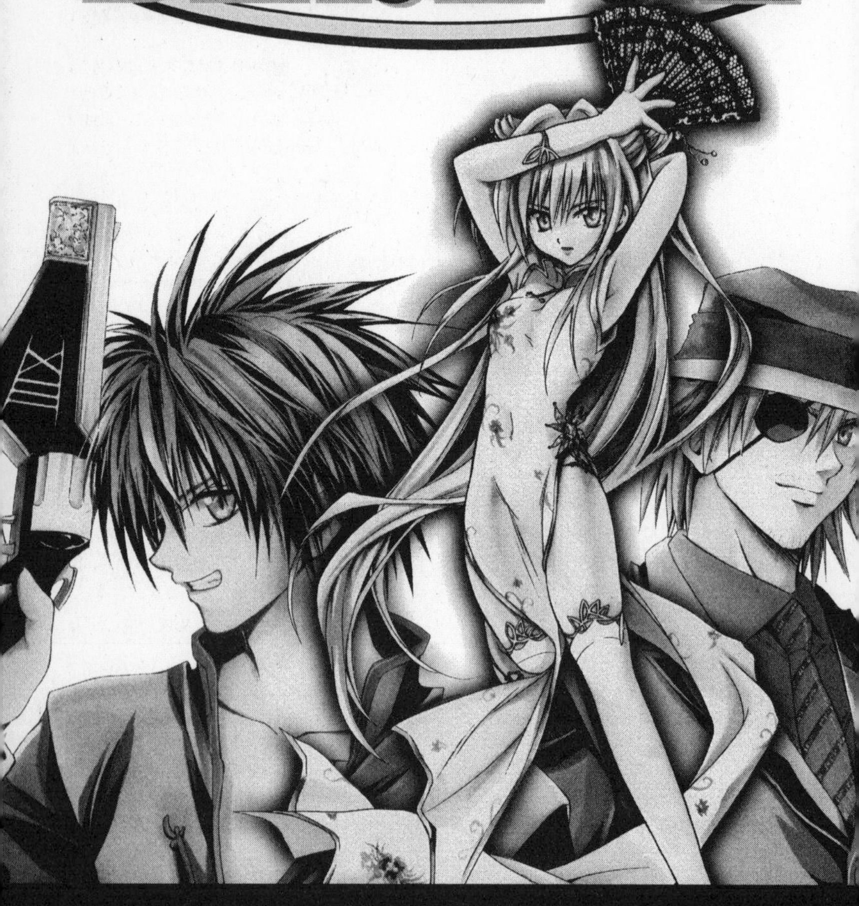

VOLUME 17

COMING THROUGH!

STORY & ART BY KENTARO YABUKI

SVEN VOLLFIED

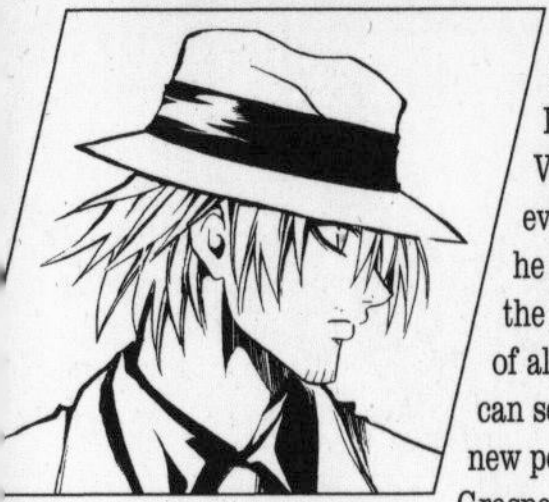

Train's partner Sven, a former IBI agent. His Vision Eye has evolved, and now he can slow down the movement of all objects he can see with his new power, the Grasper Eye.

SEPHIRIA ARKS

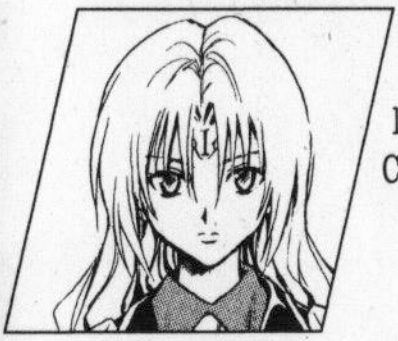

As Number I, Sephiria is the leader of the Chrono Numbers.

BELZE ROCHEFORT

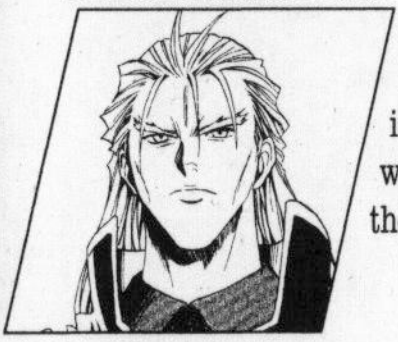

As Chrono Number II, Belze is equally adept with the pen and the sword.

JENOS HAZARD

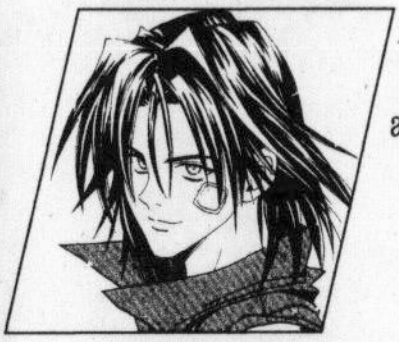

Chrono Number VII manipulates wires... and women.

LIN SHAOLEE

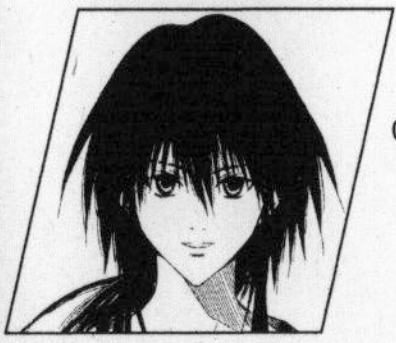

Chrono Number X is a master of disguise.

TRAIN HEARTNET

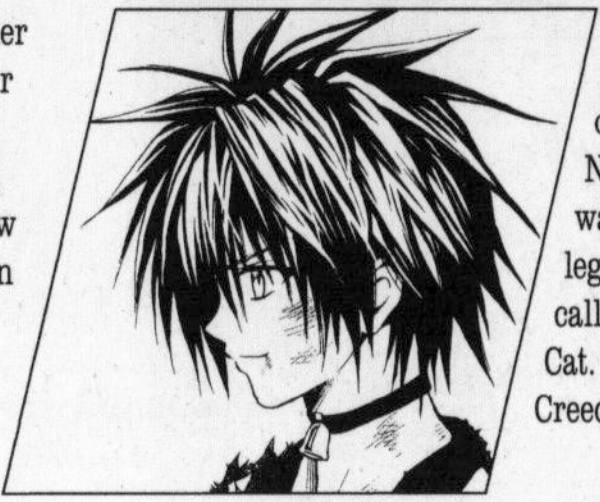

Formerly Number XIII of the Chrono Numbers, Train was once a legendary eraser called the Black Cat. He now pursues Creed as a sweeper.

EVE

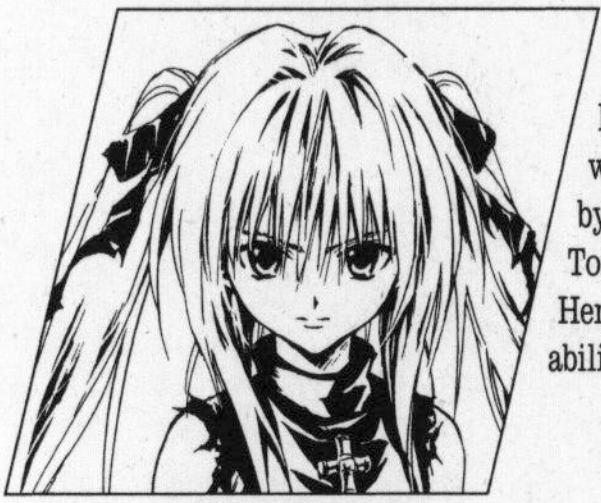

Part bio-weapon and part little girl, Eve was manufactured by weapons dealer Torneo Rudman. Her power lies in her ability to transform.

RINSLET WALKER

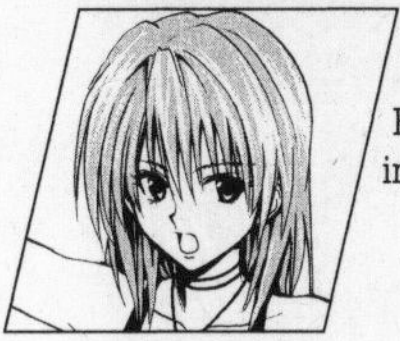

A self-styled thief-for-hire, Rinslet is fiercely independent.

RIVER ZASTORY

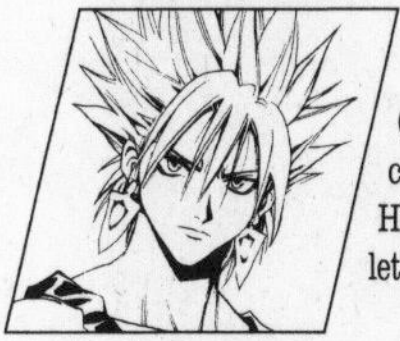

River is a sweeper and a master of the Garbell Commando combat technique. His fists are lethal weapons.

SAYA MINATSUKI

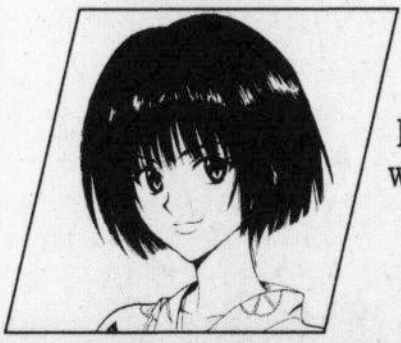

Saya is an important woman from Train's past who was fatally wounded by Creed.

A fearless "eraser" responsible for the deaths of countless men, Train "Black Cat" Heartnet was formerly an assassin for the crime syndicate Chronos. Train betrayed Chronos and was supposedly executed for it, but now, two years later, he lives a carefree wanderer's life, working with his partner Sven as a bounty hunter ("sweeper") and pursuing Creed Diskenth, the man who murdered his dear friend Saya Minatsuki.

Creed finally turns up, determined to lead a revolution against Chronos. He tries to convince Train to join his Apostles of the Stars, but fails at that and escapes once again.

Train decides Creed must be stopped, and for the first time, he tells his friends the story behind Creed and Saya. In an effort to close the door on Train's past, he, Sven and Eve head out with a new resolve. They hook up with an elite band of bounty hunters to form a Sweeper Alliance and infiltrate Creed's island hideout. Once there, they confront formidable Apostles wielding the power of Tao.

Shiki unmasks himself and unleashes his true Tao power against Train and River. Train, in turn, plays his new trump card, the Black Cat's Claws!

CREED DISKENTH

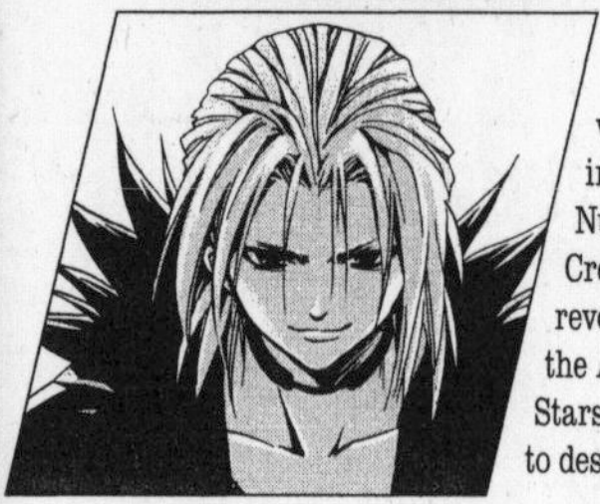

Though he and Train were associates in their Chrono Numbers days, Creed now heads the revolutionary group the Apostles of the Stars, whose goal is to destroy the world.

DOCTOR

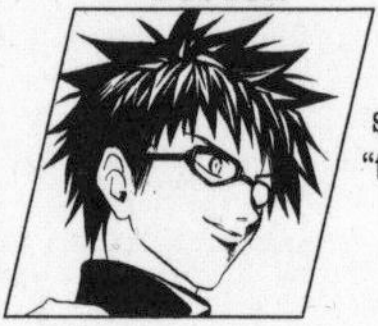

Little is known about Creed's spokesman, "the Doctor."

SHIKI

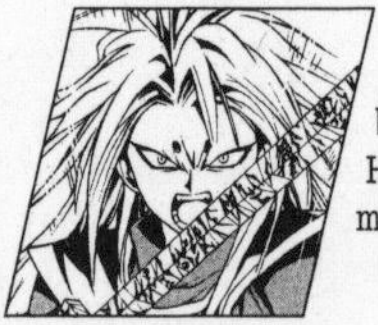

Shiki hails from Itairiku, the birthplace of the Tao. He has the power to manipulate insects.

ECHIDNA PARASS

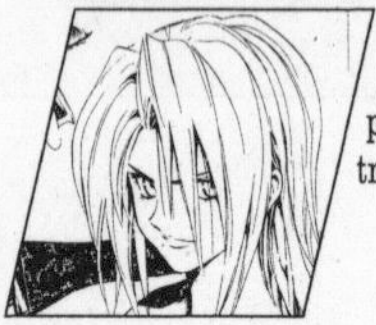

Echidna has the power to create portals in space and travel through them.

BLACK CAT

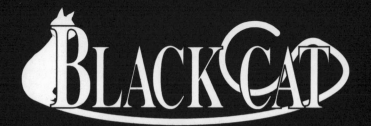

VOLUME 17 COMING THROUGH!

CONTENTS

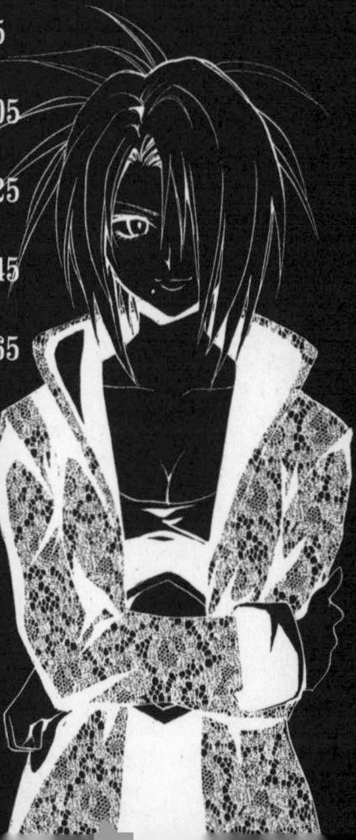

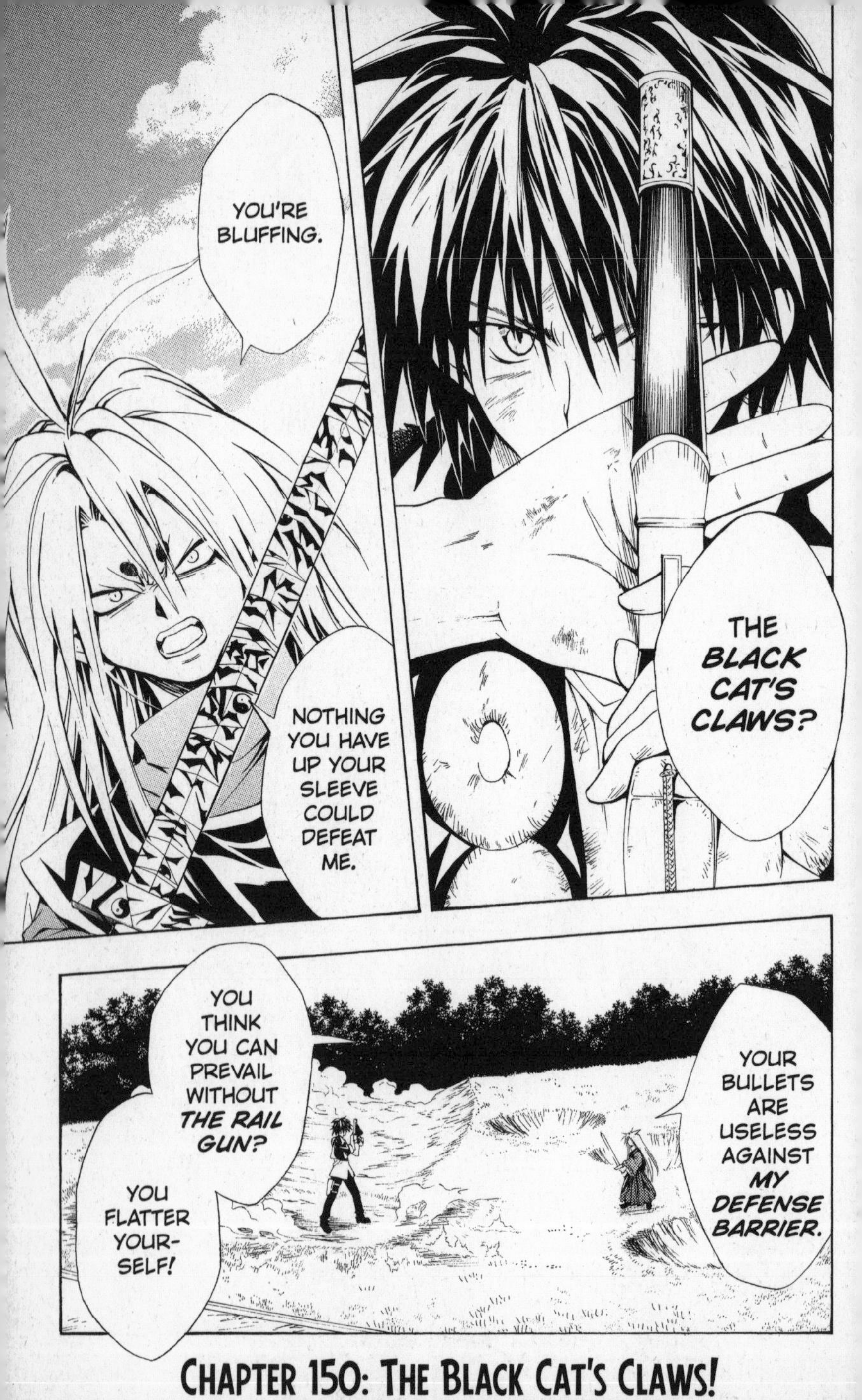
THE *BLACK CAT'S CLAWS?*
YOU'RE BLUFFING.
NOTHING YOU HAVE UP YOUR SLEEVE COULD DEFEAT ME.
YOUR BULLETS ARE USELESS AGAINST *MY DEFENSE BARRIER.*
YOU THINK YOU CAN PREVAIL WITHOUT *THE RAIL GUN?*
YOU FLATTER YOUR-SELF!

Chapter 150: The Black Cat's Claws!

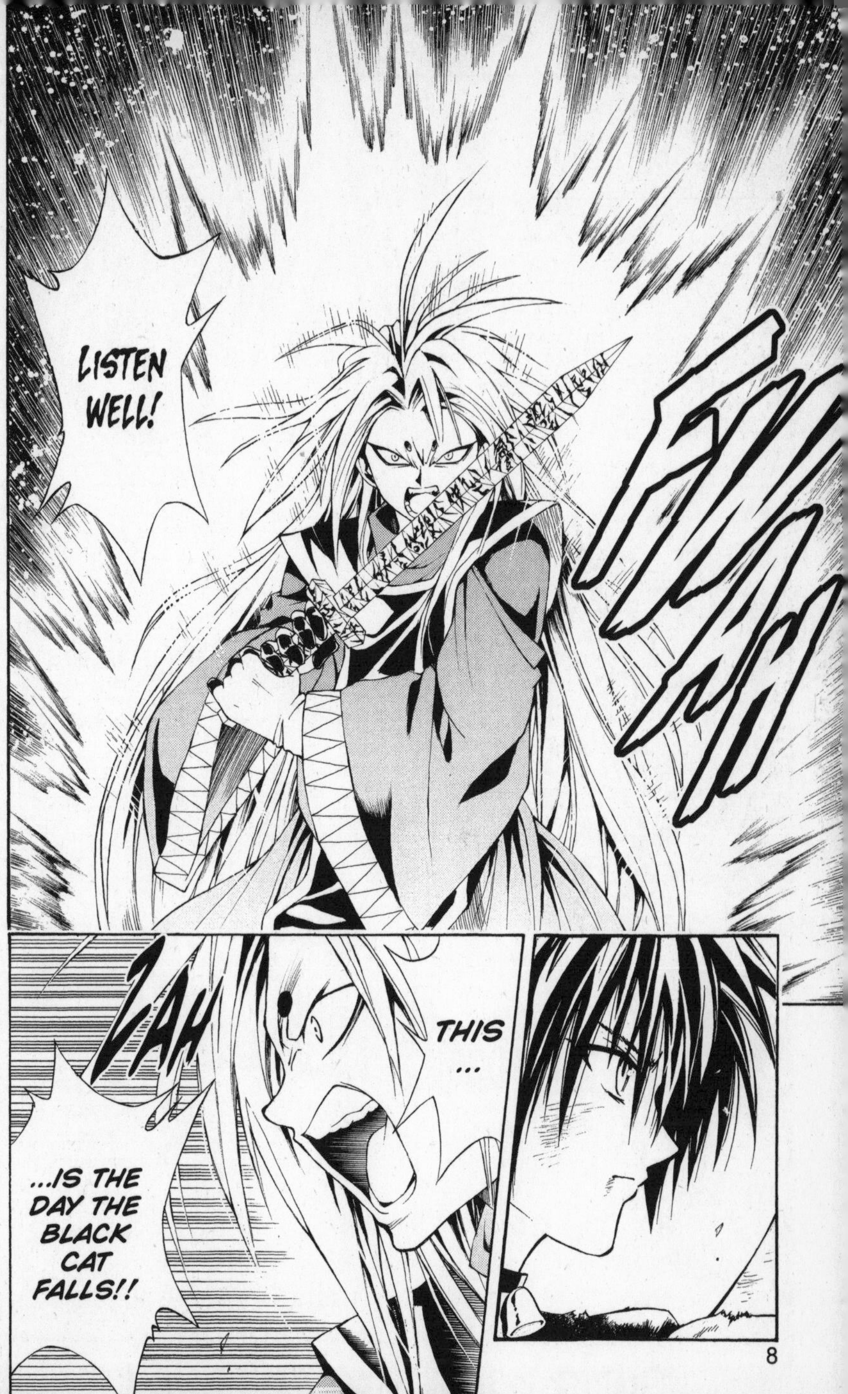
LISTEN WELL!
THIS ...
ZAH
...IS THE DAY THE BLACK CAT FALLS!!

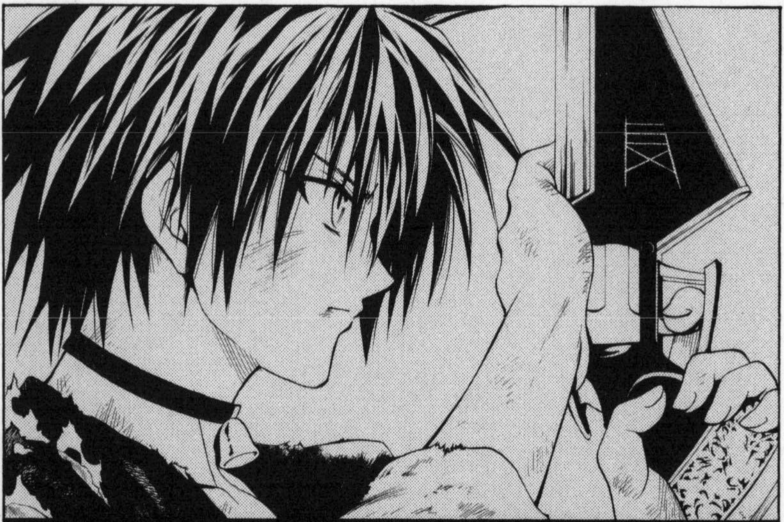

Chapter 150: The Black Cat's Claws!

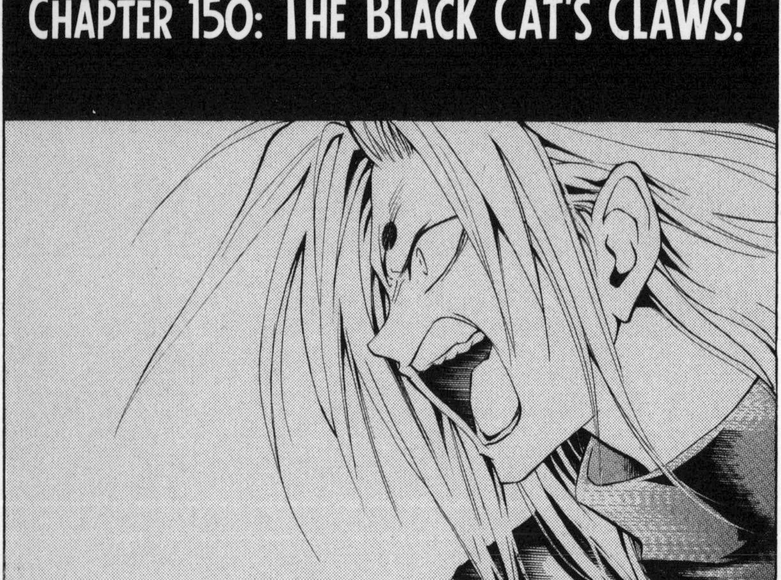

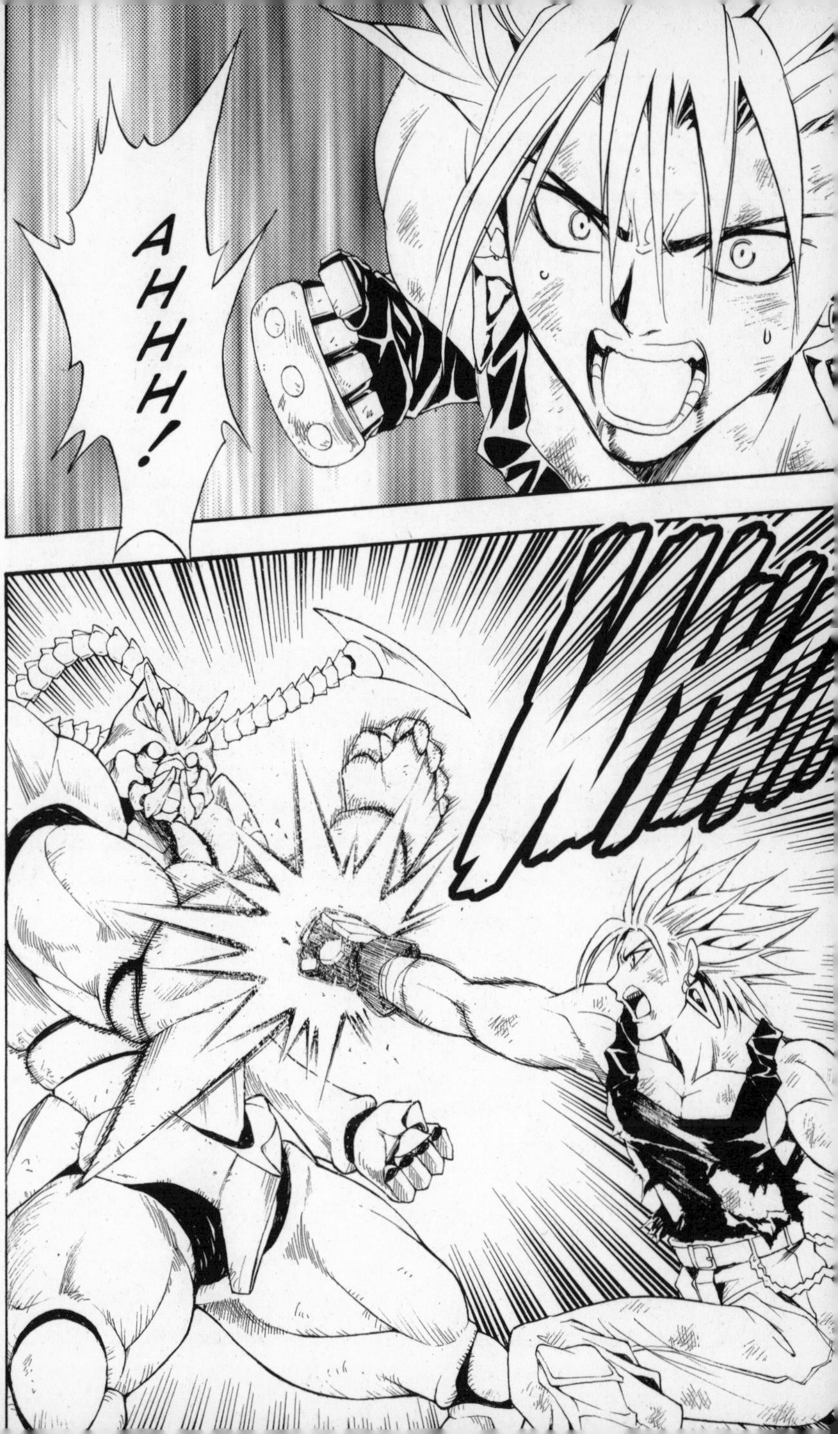
AHHHH!

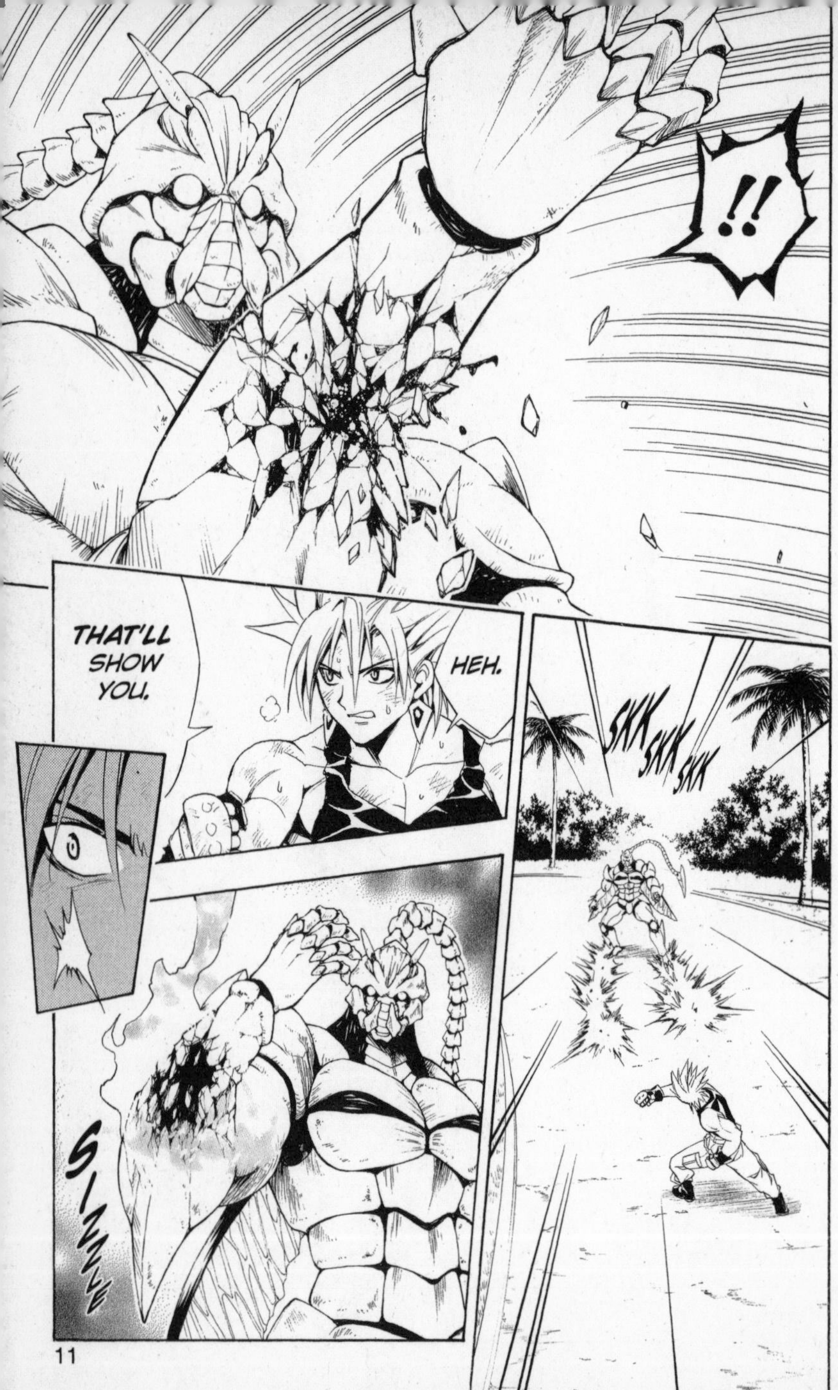
!!
SKK SKK SKK
HEH.
THAT'LL SHOW YOU.
SIZZLE

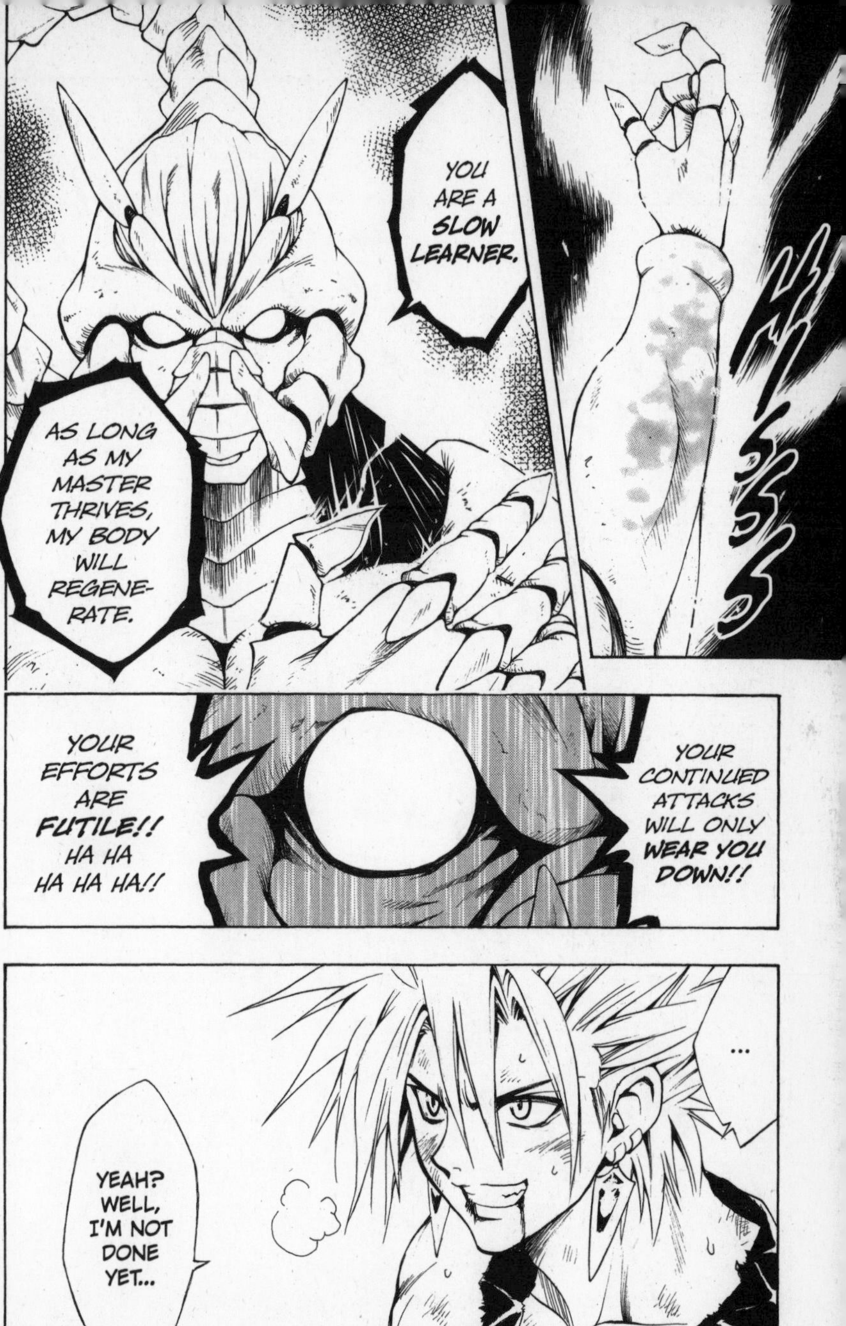
HISSSS
YOU ARE A SLOW LEARNER.
AS LONG AS MY MASTER THRIVES, MY BODY WILL REGENERATE.
YOUR CONTINUED ATTACKS WILL ONLY WEAR YOU DOWN!!
YOUR EFFORTS ARE FUTILE!! HA HA HA HA HA!!
...
YEAH? WELL, I'M NOT DONE YET...

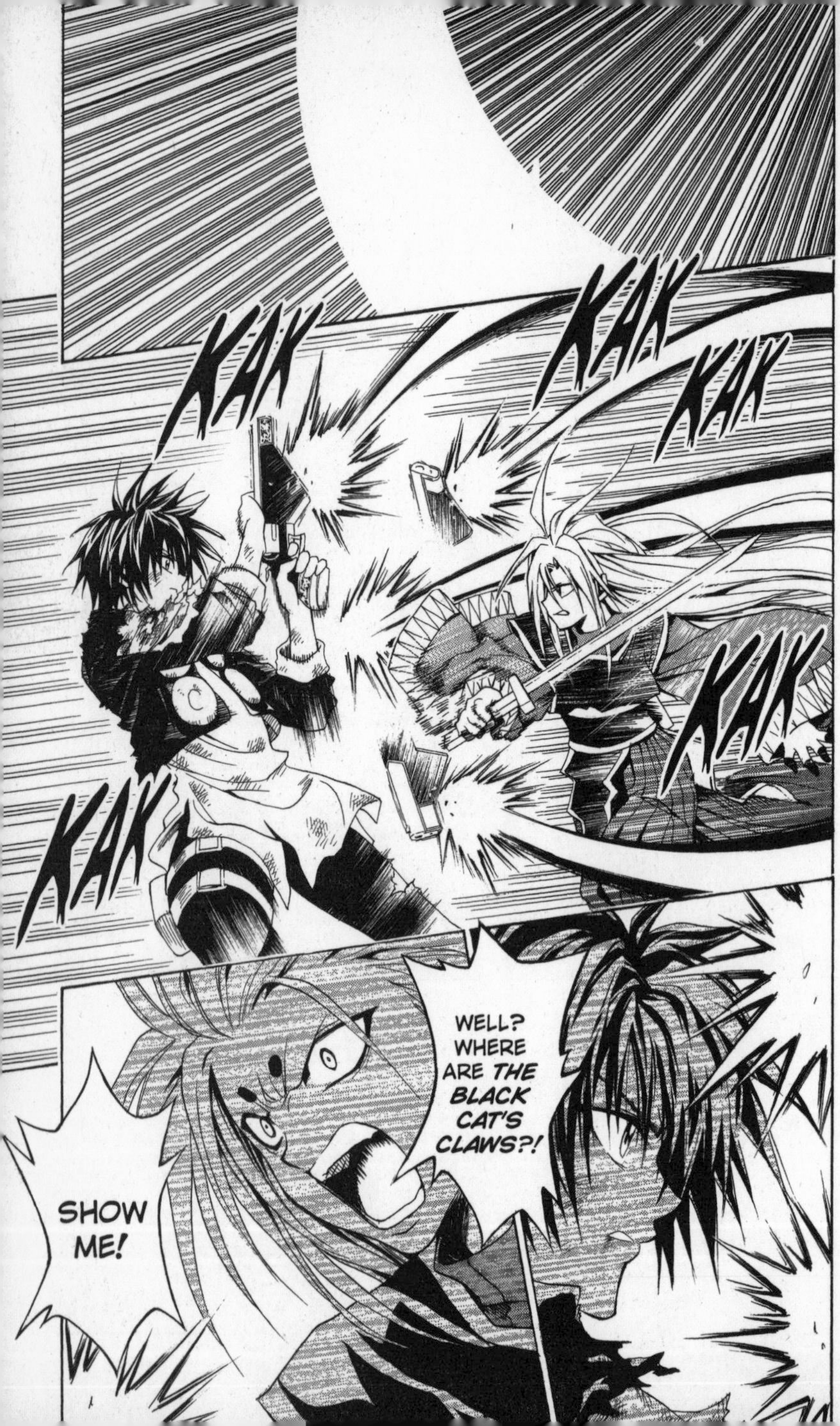
KAK
KAK
KAK
KAK
KAK
WELL? WHERE ARE THE BLACK CAT'S CLAWS?!
SHOW ME!

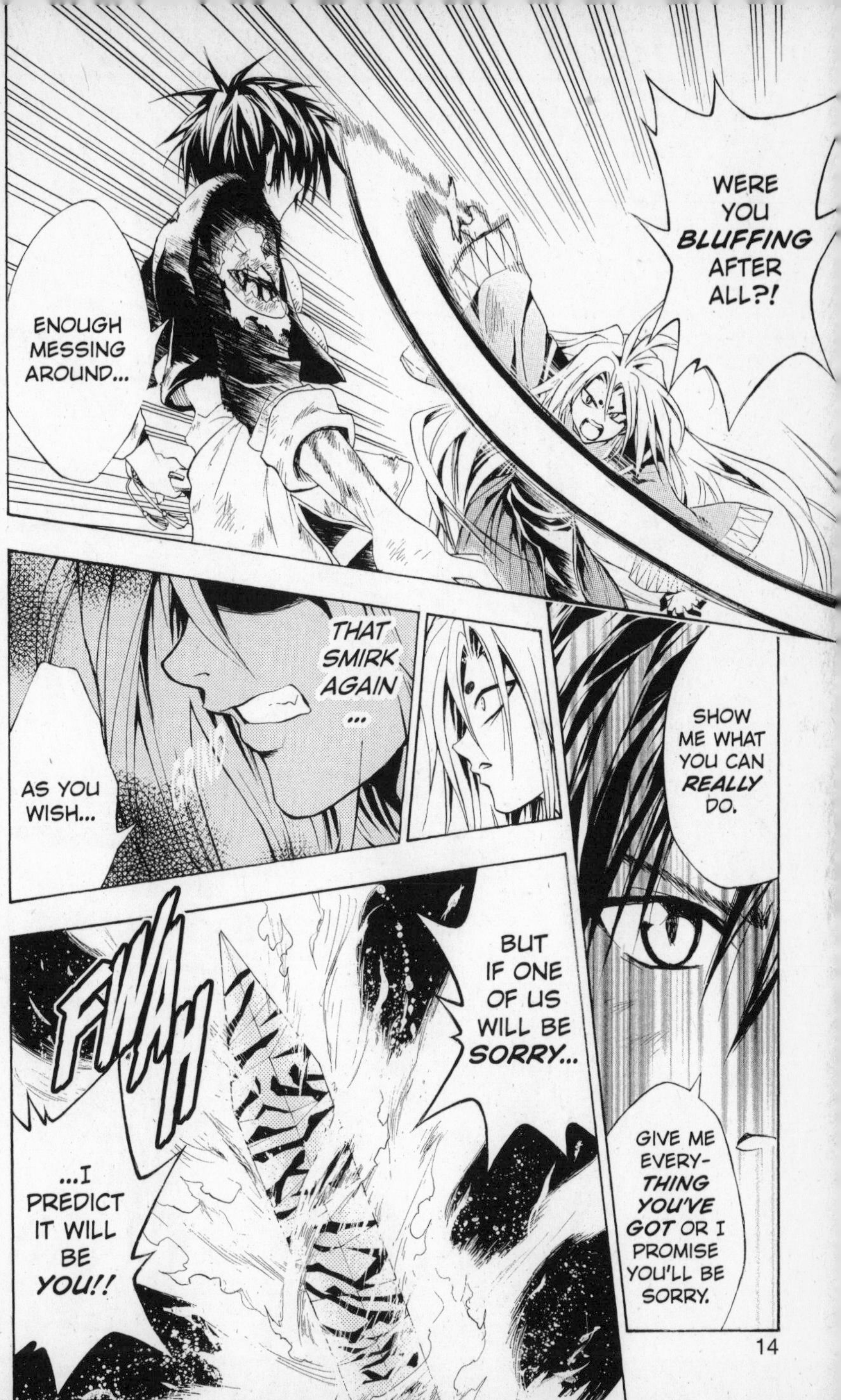
WERE YOU *BLUFFING* AFTER ALL?!
ENOUGH MESSING AROUND...
SHOW ME WHAT YOU CAN *REALLY* DO.
GIVE ME EVERY-THING *YOU'VE GOT* OR I PROMISE YOU'LL BE SORRY.
THAT SMIRK AGAIN ...
AS YOU WISH...
BUT IF ONE OF US WILL BE *SORRY...*
FWAH
...I PREDICT IT WILL BE *YOU!!*

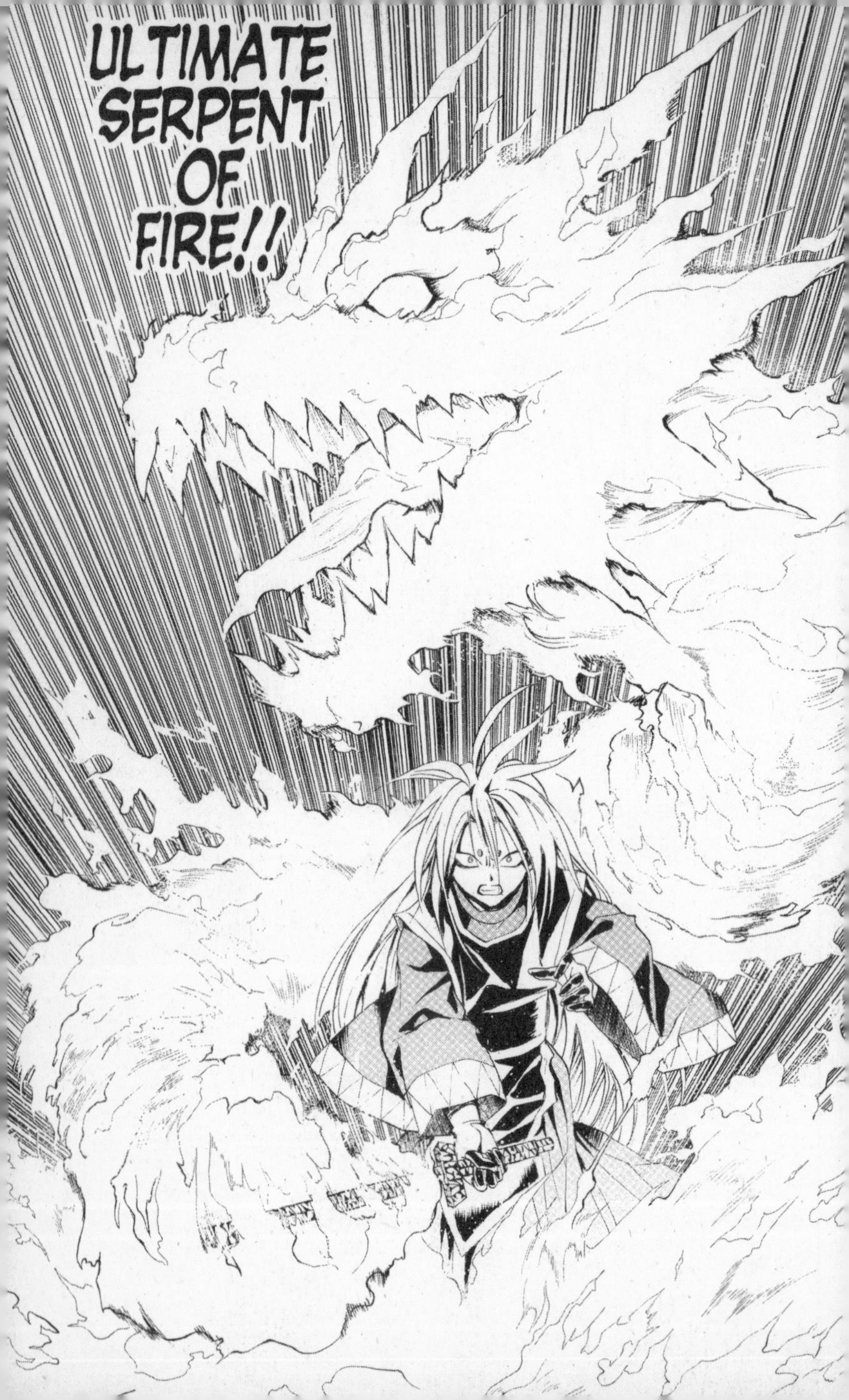
ULTIMATE SERPENT OF FIRE!!

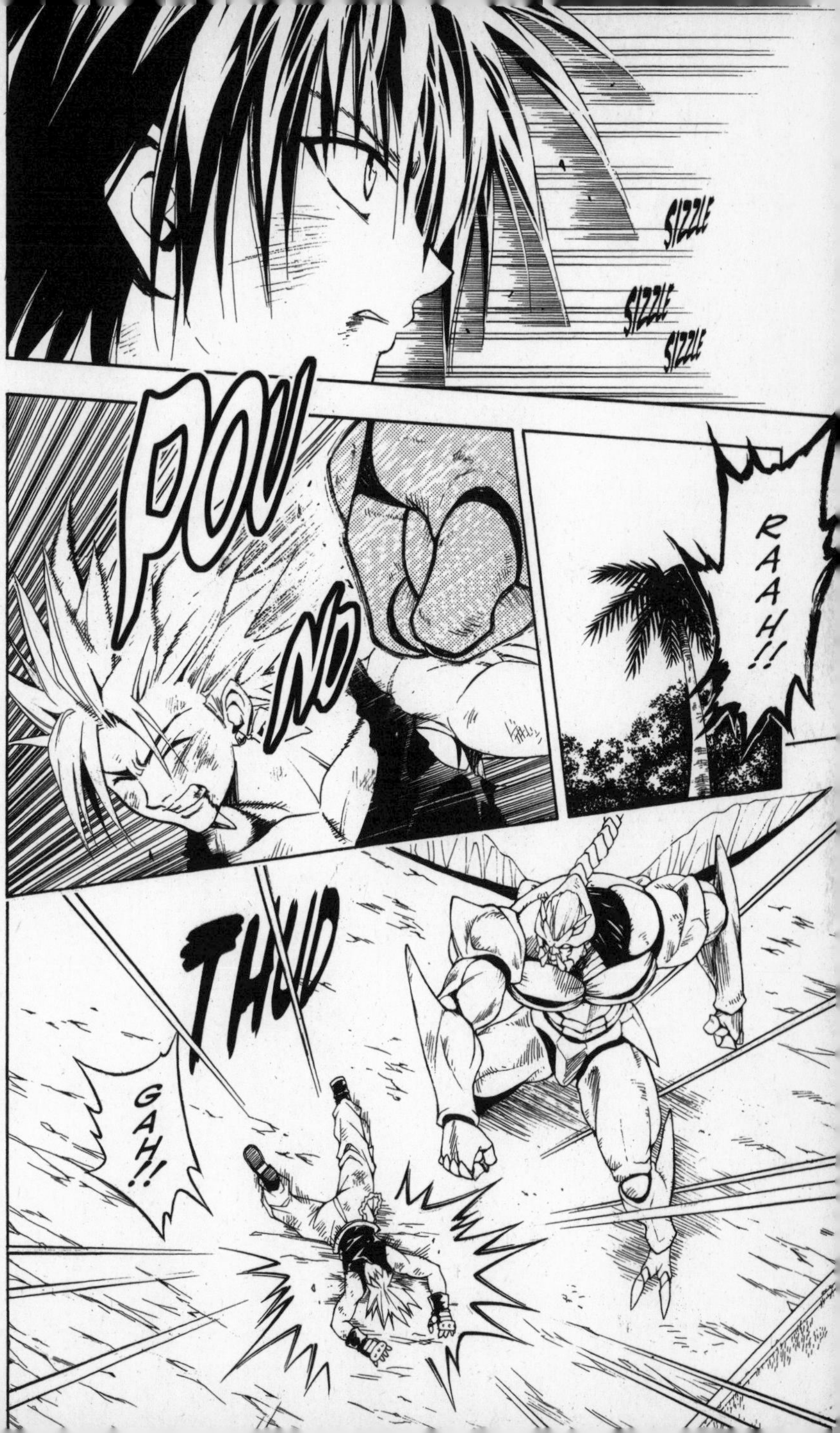
SIZZLE
SIZZLE
SIZZLE
RAAAH!!
POW
NG
THUD
GAH!!

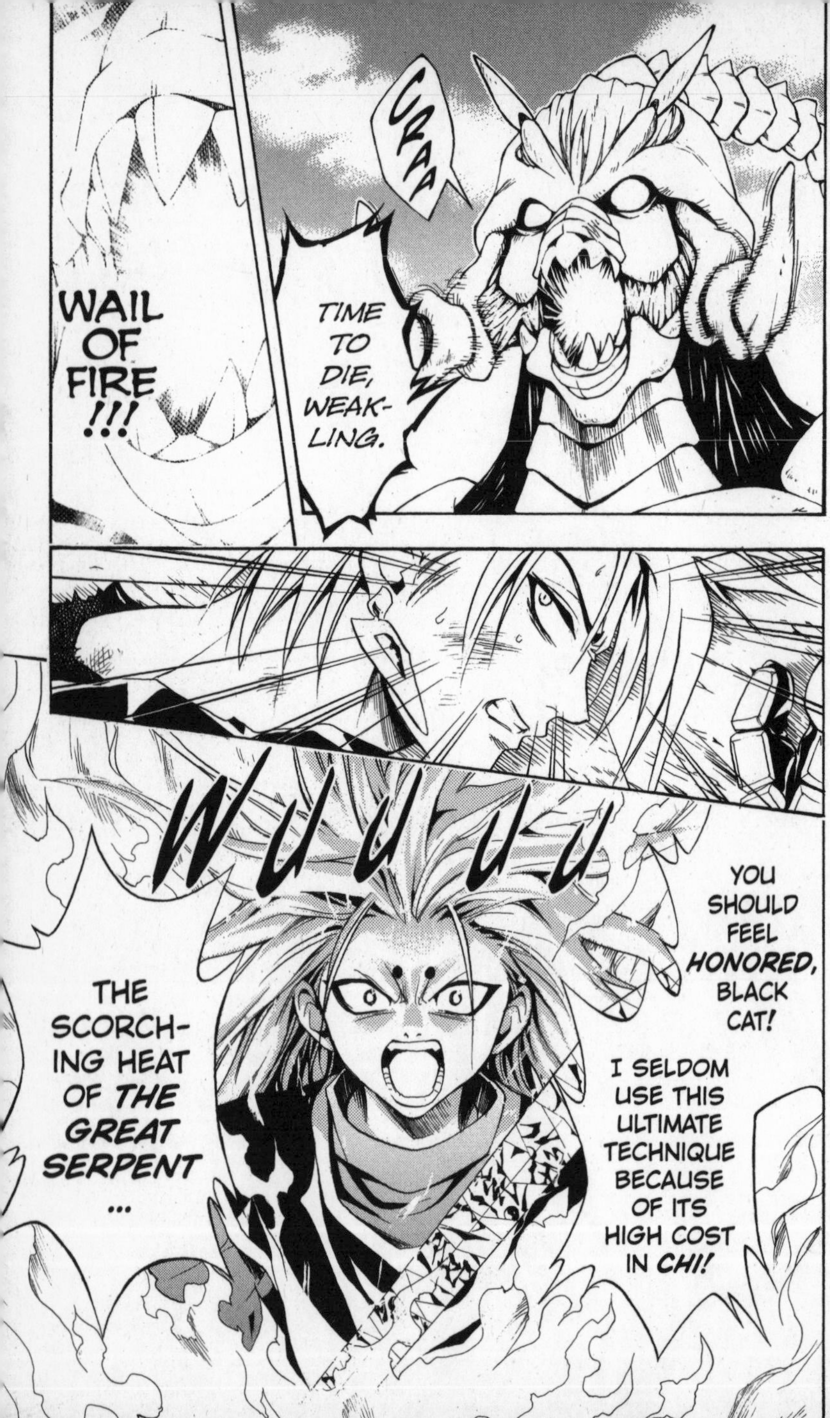
CRAAA
TIME TO DIE, WEAK-LING.
WAIL OF FIRE!!!
WUUUUU
YOU SHOULD FEEL HONORED, BLACK CAT!
I SELDOM USE THIS ULTIMATE TECHNIQUE BECAUSE OF ITS HIGH COST IN CHI!
THE SCORCH-ING HEAT OF THE GREAT SERPENT...

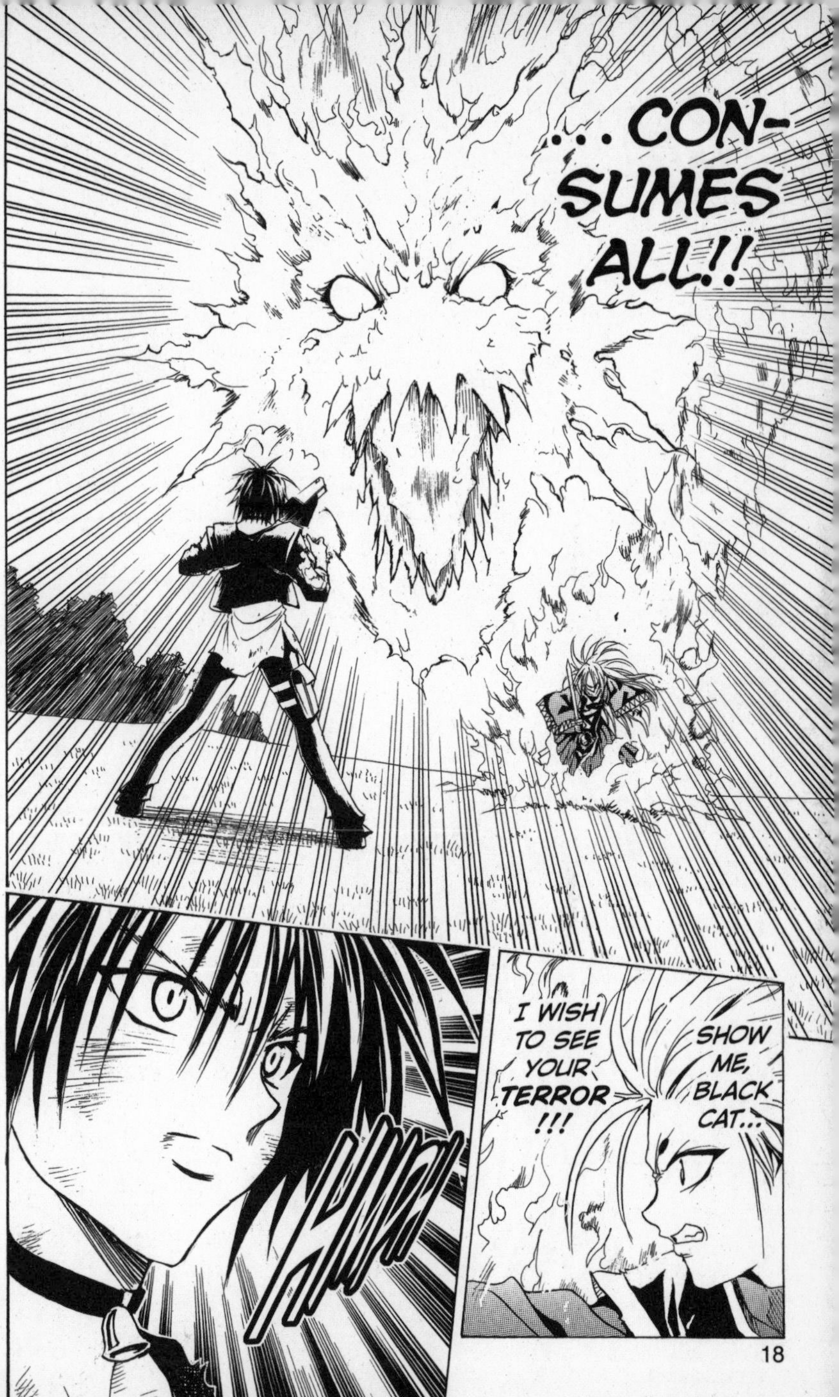
...CON-SUMES ALL!!
SHOW ME, BLACK CAT...
I WISH TO SEE YOUR TERROR!!!

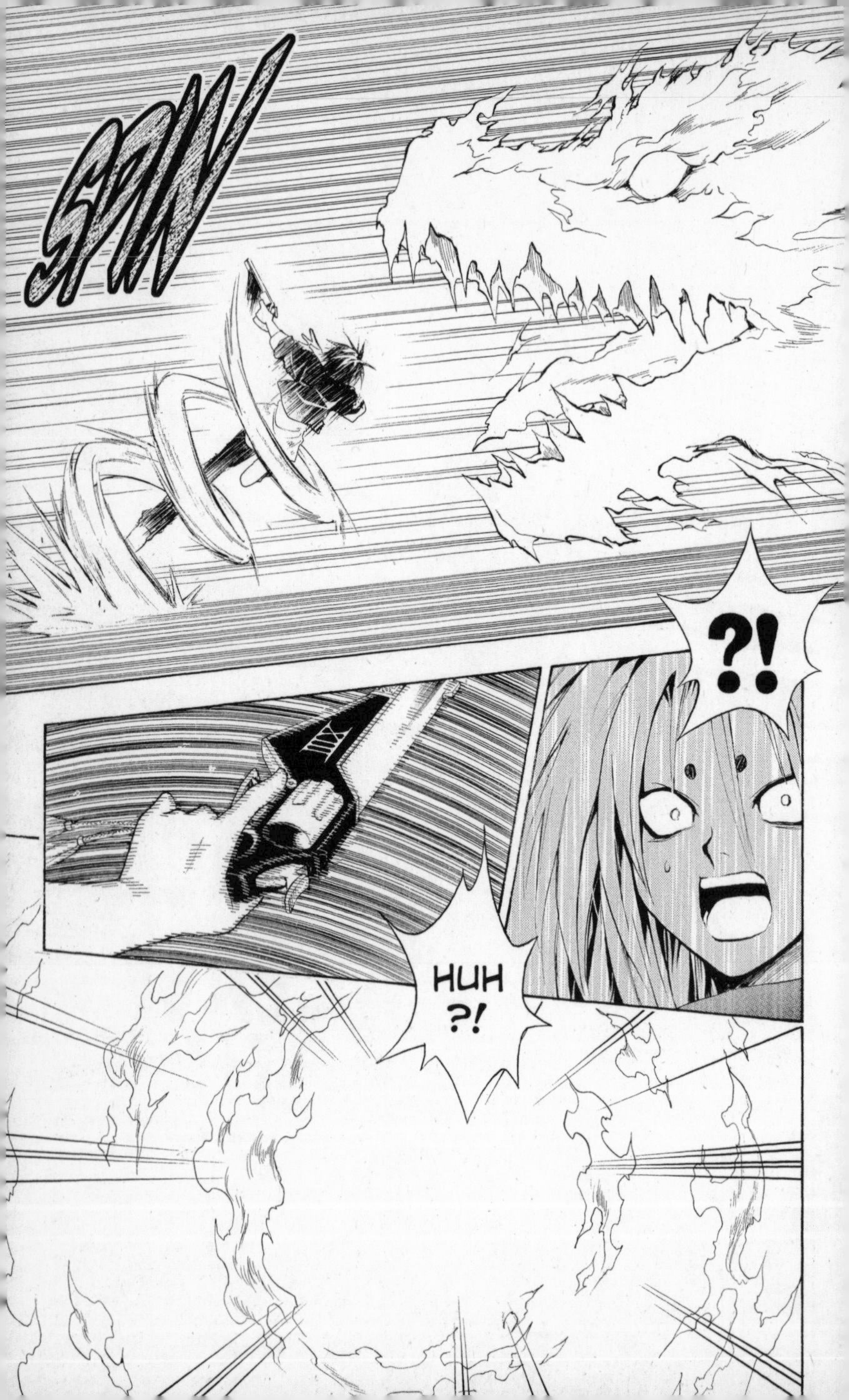
SPIN
?!
HUH ?!

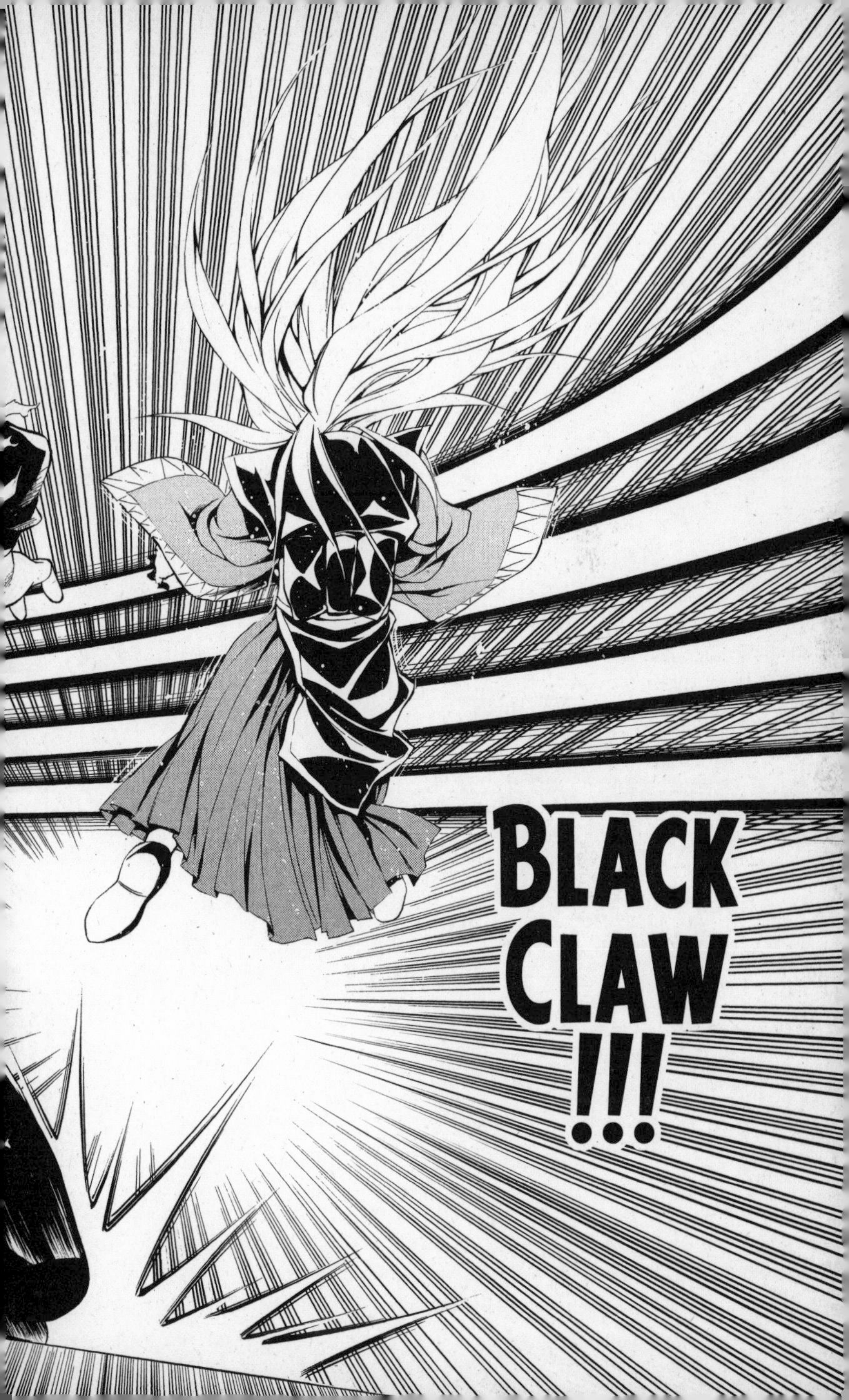
BLACK CLAW !!!

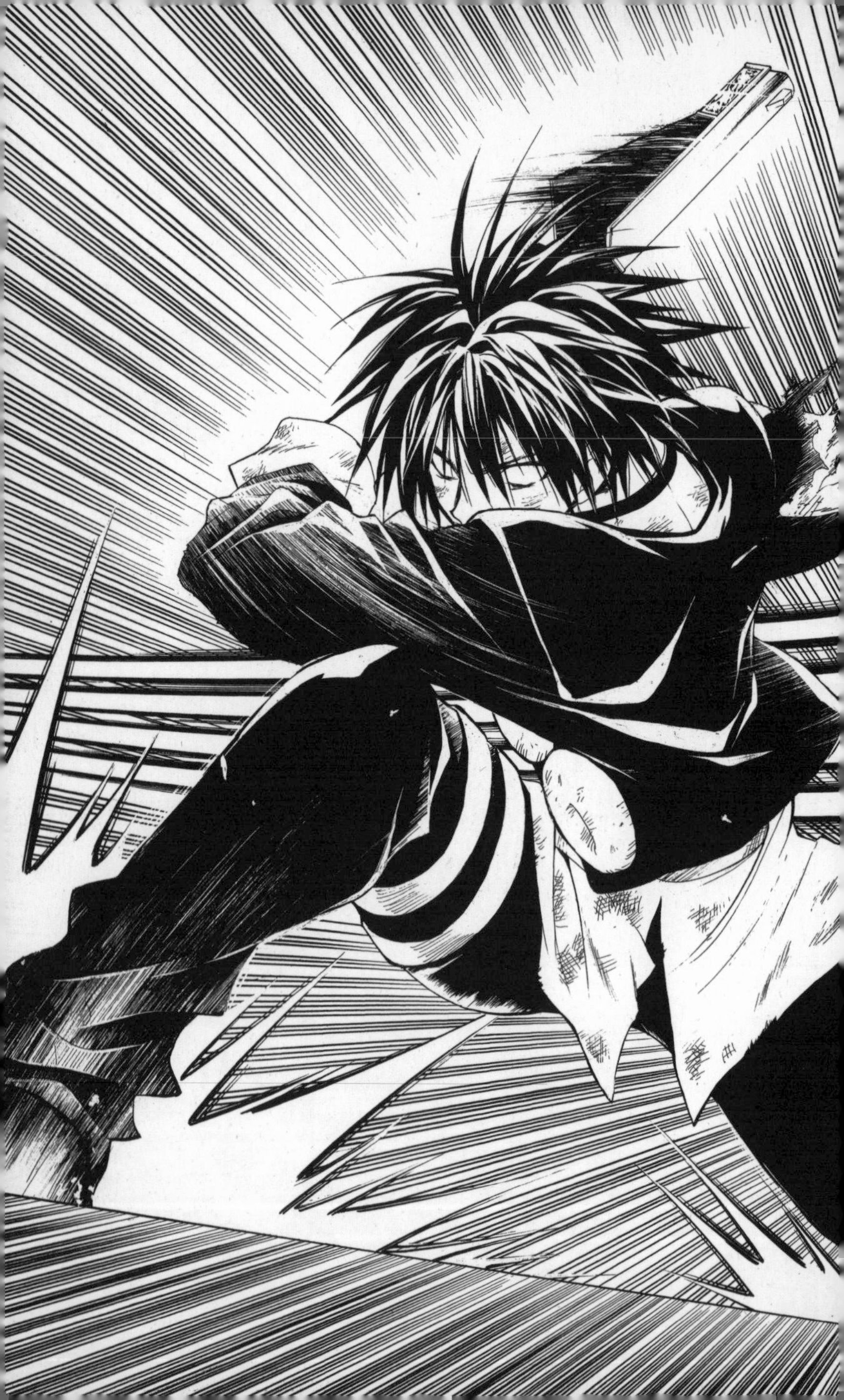

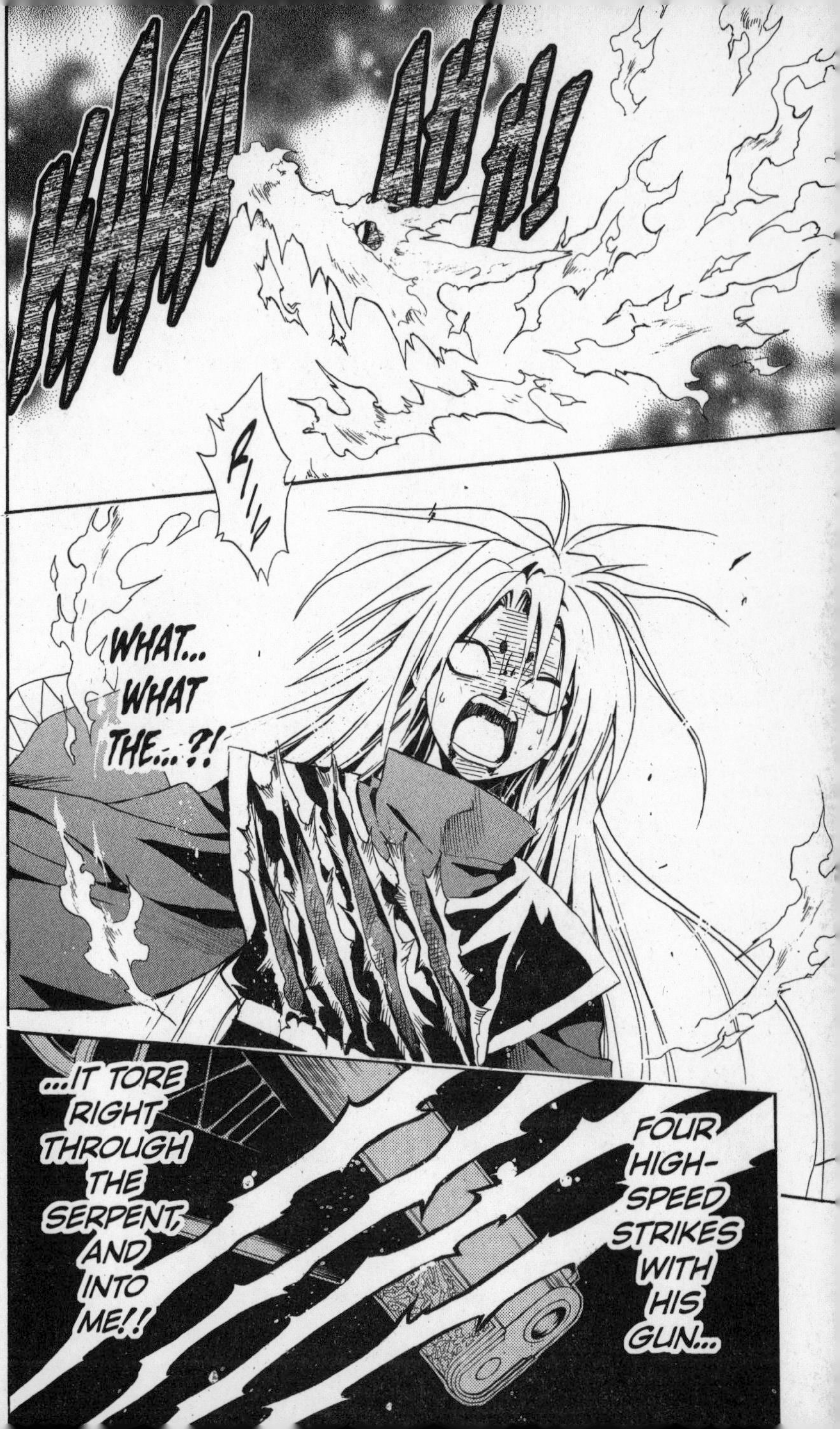
WHAT... WHAT THE...?!
FOUR HIGH-SPEED STRIKES WITH HIS GUN...
...IT TORE RIGHT THROUGH THE SERPENT, AND INTO ME!!

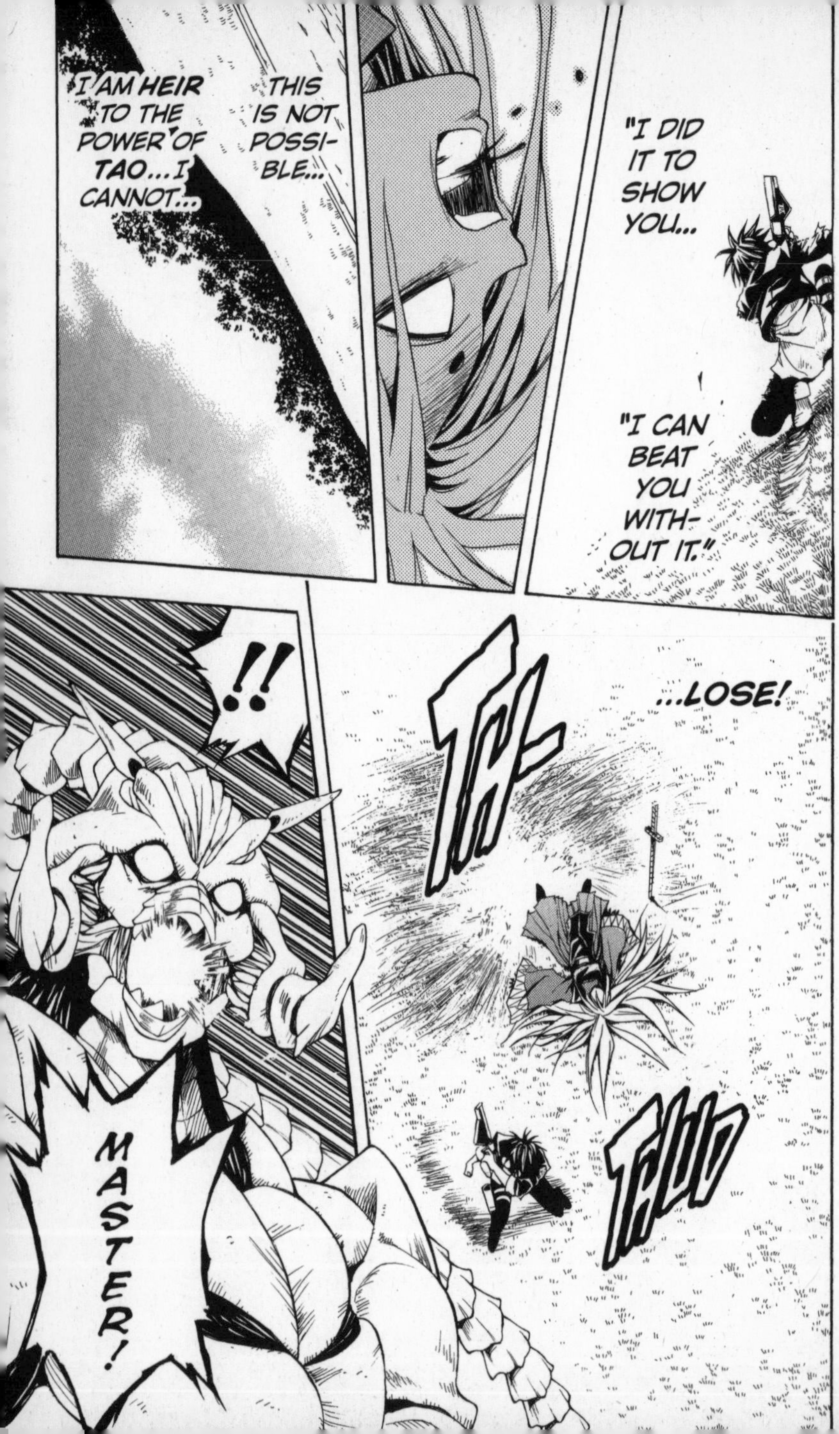
"I DID IT TO SHOW YOU...
"I CAN BEAT YOU WITH-OUT IT."
THIS IS NOT POSSI-BLE...
I AM HEIR TO THE POWER OF TAO... I CANNOT...
...LOSE!
!!
MASTER!

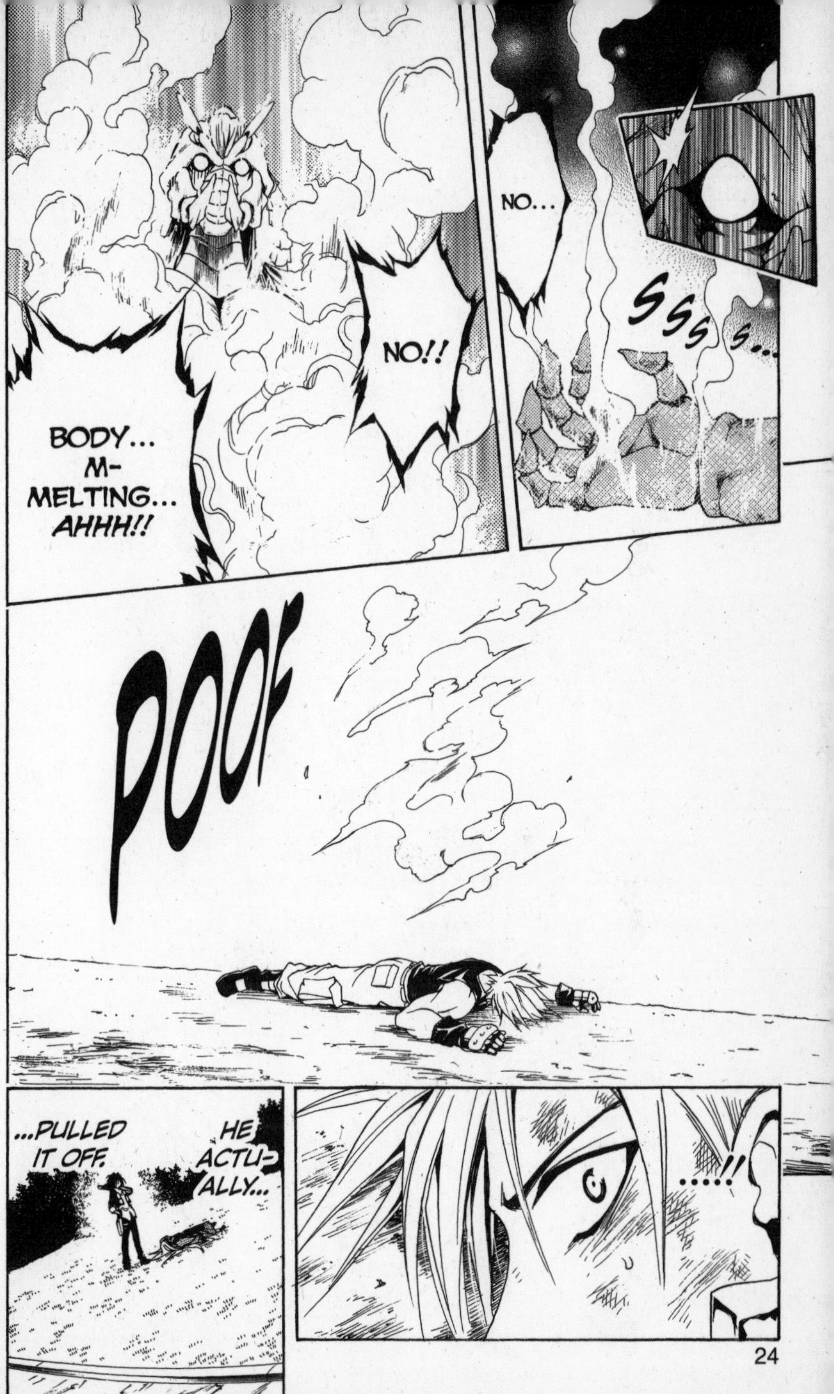

NO...
SSSS...
NO!!
BODY... M-MELTING... AHHH!!
POOF
.....!!
HE ACTU-ALLY...
...PULLED IT OFF.

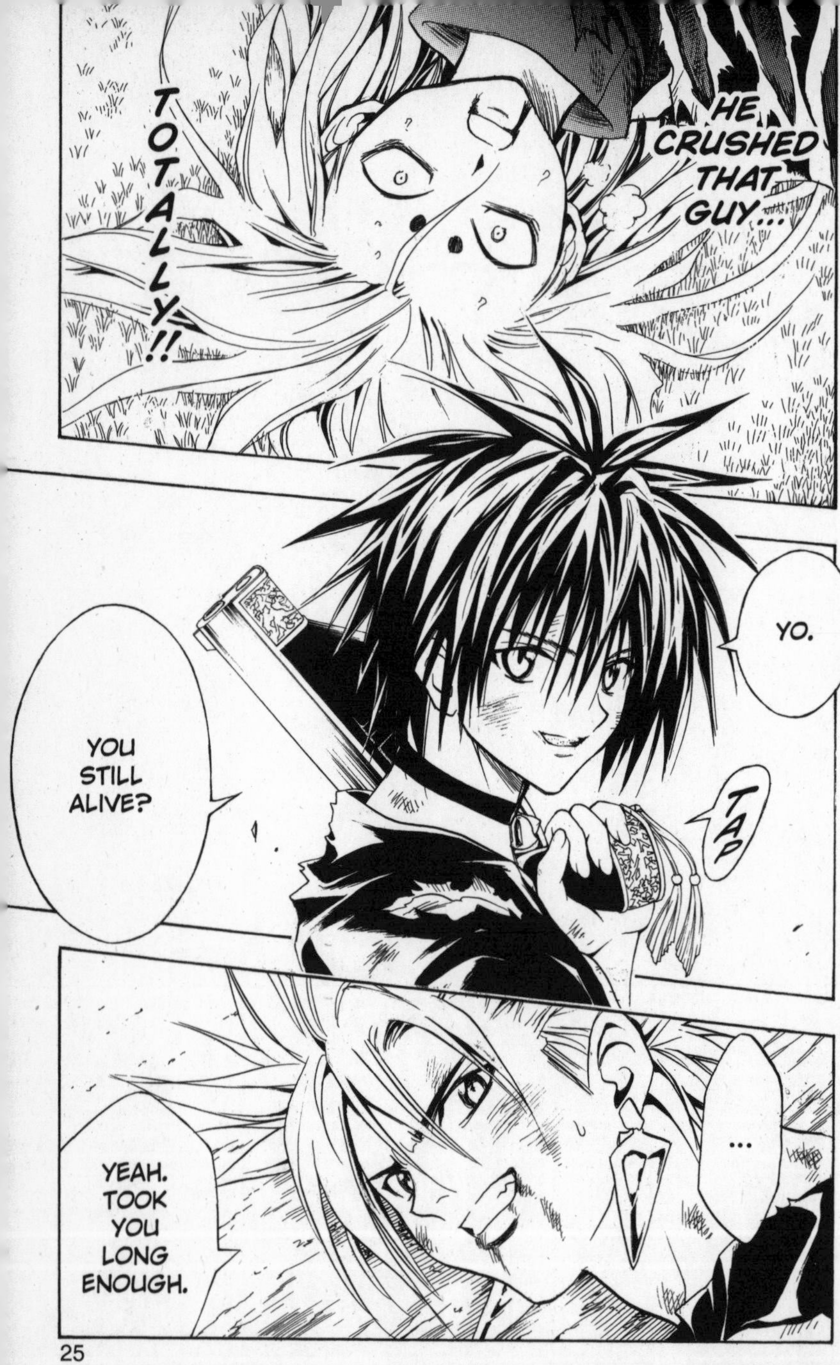
HE CRUSHED THAT GUY...
TOTALLY!!
YO.
TAP
YOU STILL ALIVE?
...
YEAH. TOOK YOU LONG ENOUGH.

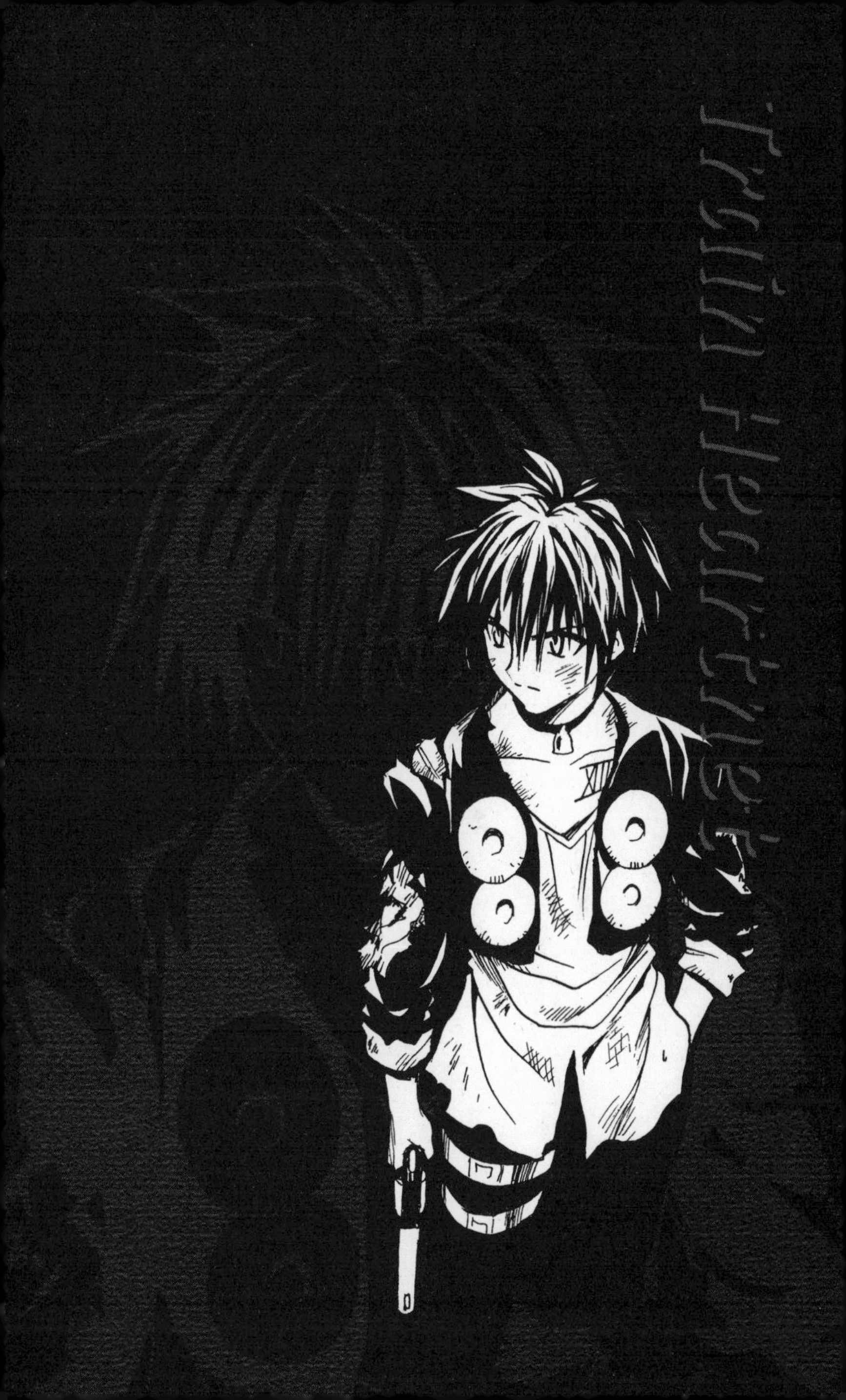

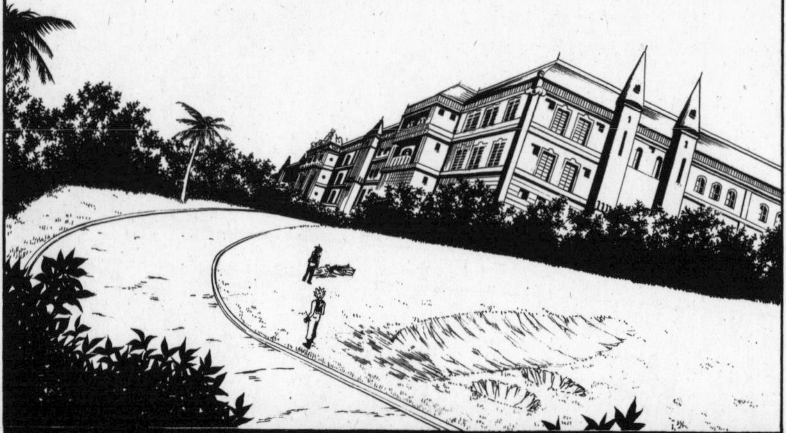

Chapter 151: Two Thoughts

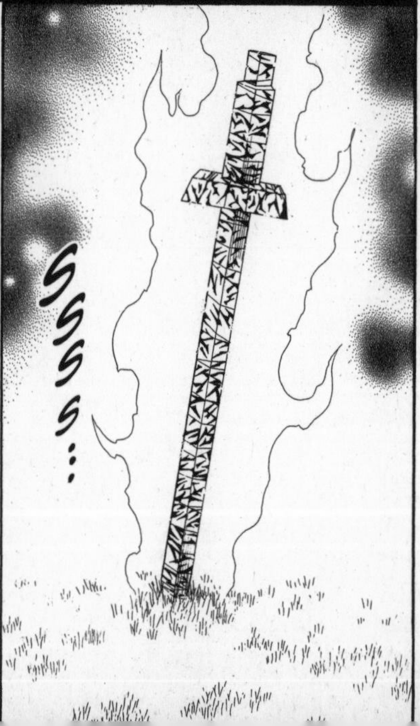
SSSS...

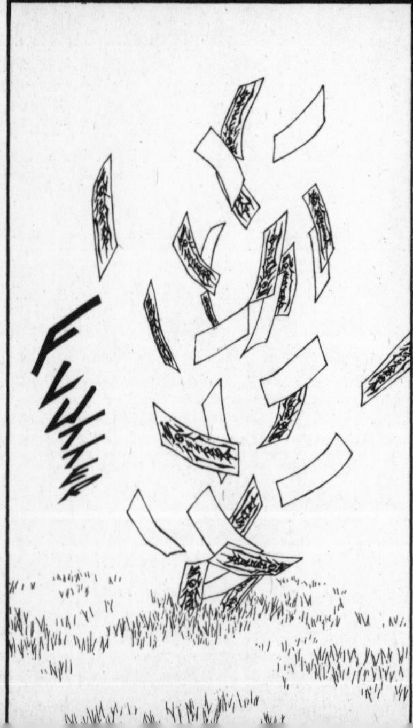

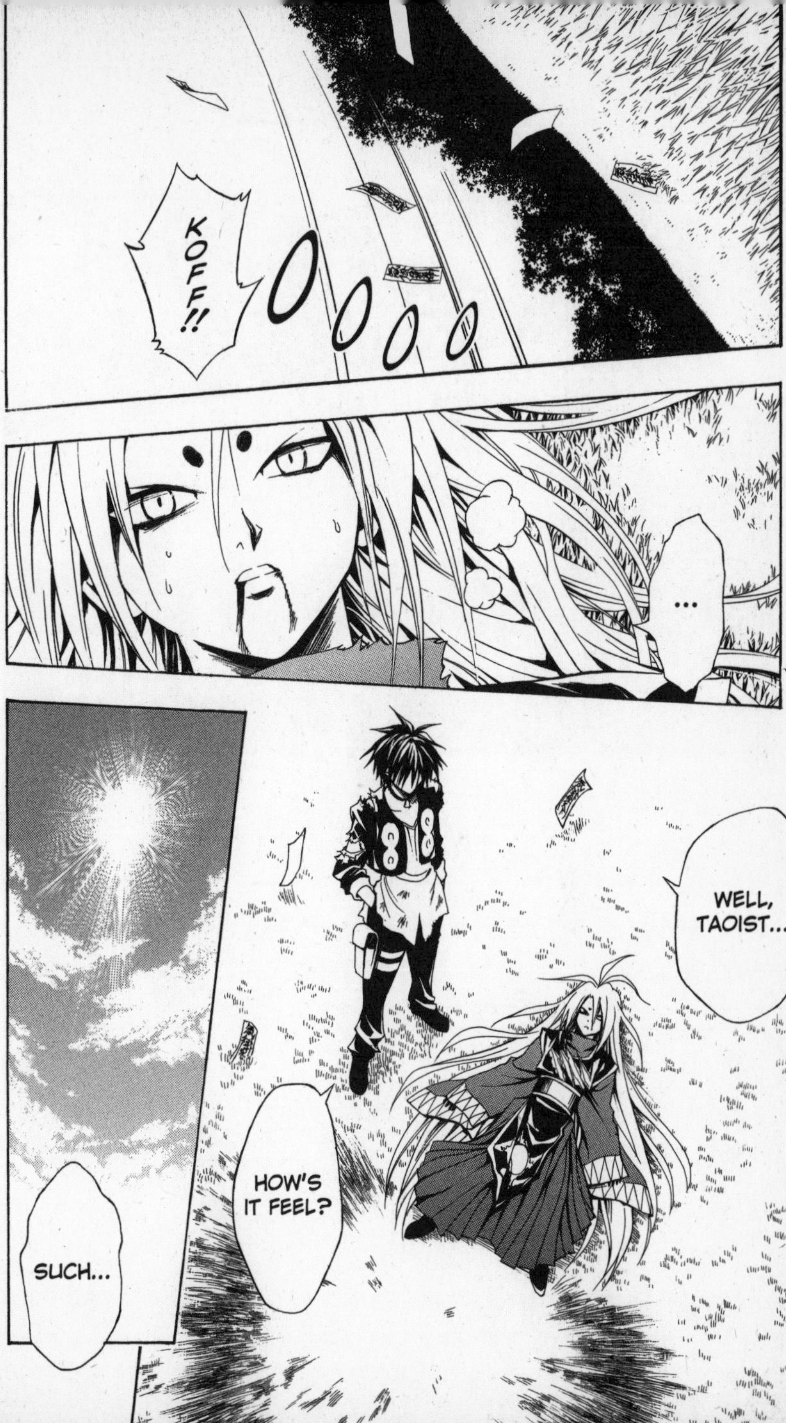
KOFF!!
...
WELL, TAOIST...
HOW'S IT FEEL?
SUCH...

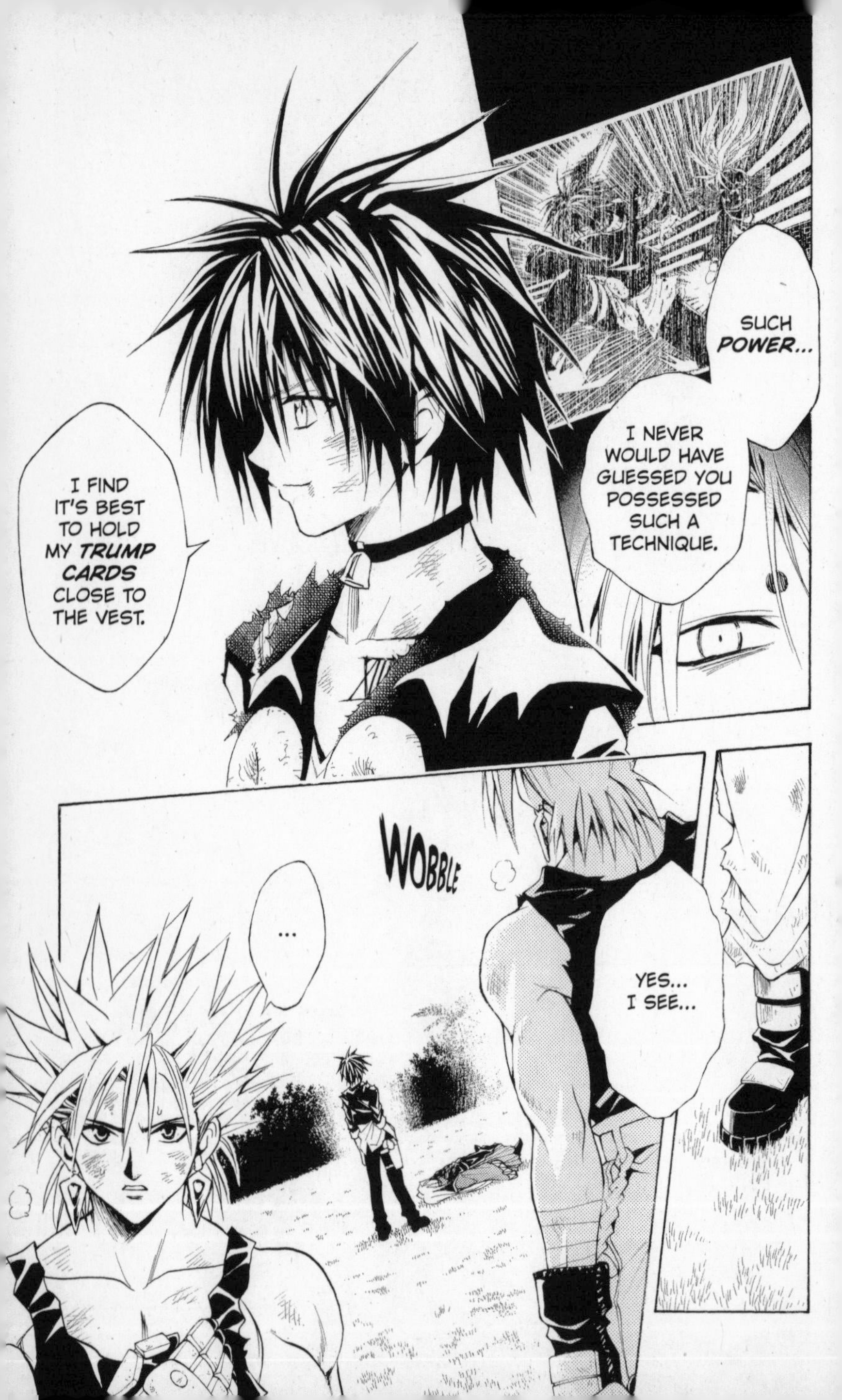
SUCH POWER...
I NEVER WOULD HAVE GUESSED YOU POSSESSED SUCH A TECHNIQUE.
I FIND IT'S BEST TO HOLD MY TRUMP CARDS CLOSE TO THE VEST.
WOBBLE
YES... I SEE...
...

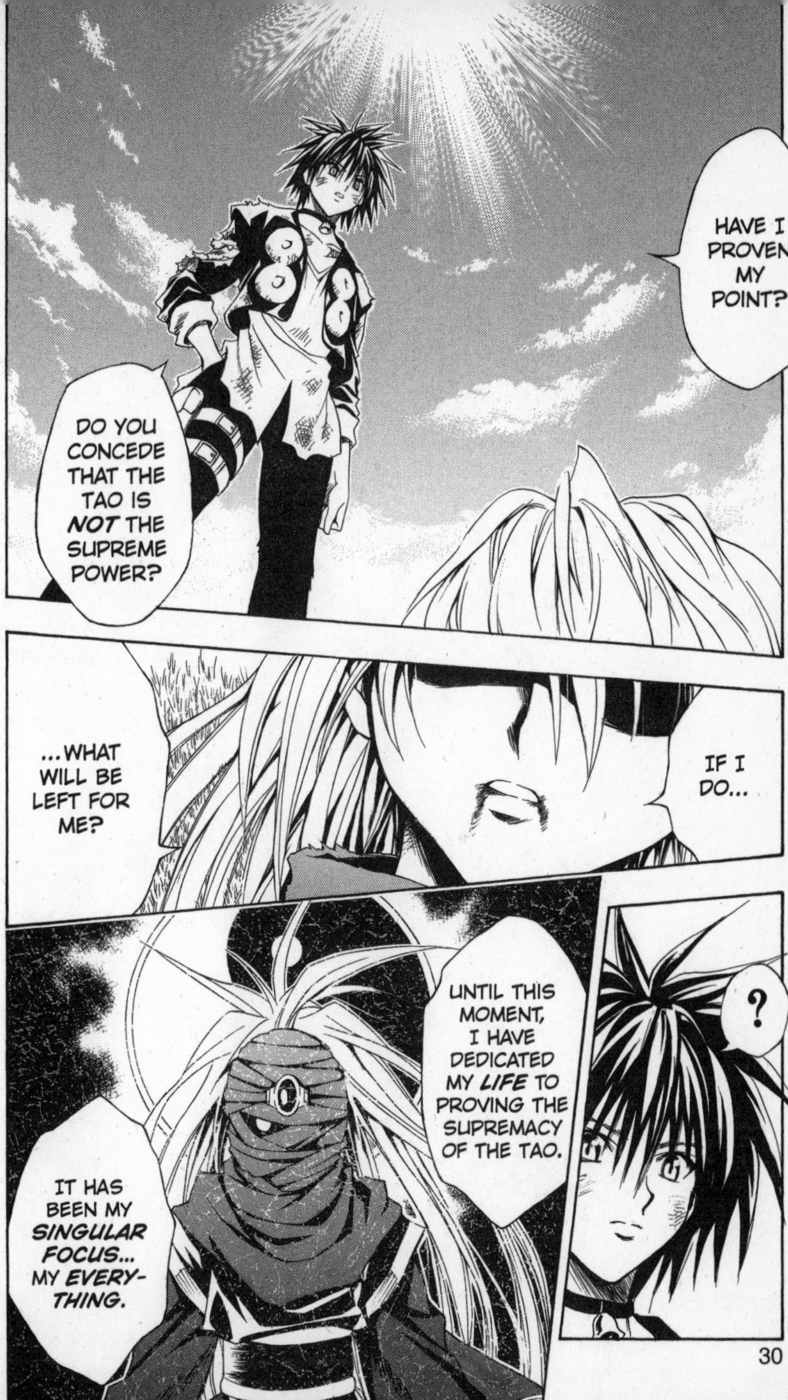
HAVE I PROVEN MY POINT?
DO YOU CONCEDE THAT THE TAO IS NOT THE SUPREME POWER?
IF I DO...
...WHAT WILL BE LEFT FOR ME?
?
UNTIL THIS MOMENT, I HAVE DEDICATED MY LIFE TO PROVING THE SUPREMACY OF THE TAO.
IT HAS BEEN MY SINGULAR FOCUS... MY EVERY-THING.

READ THIS WAY

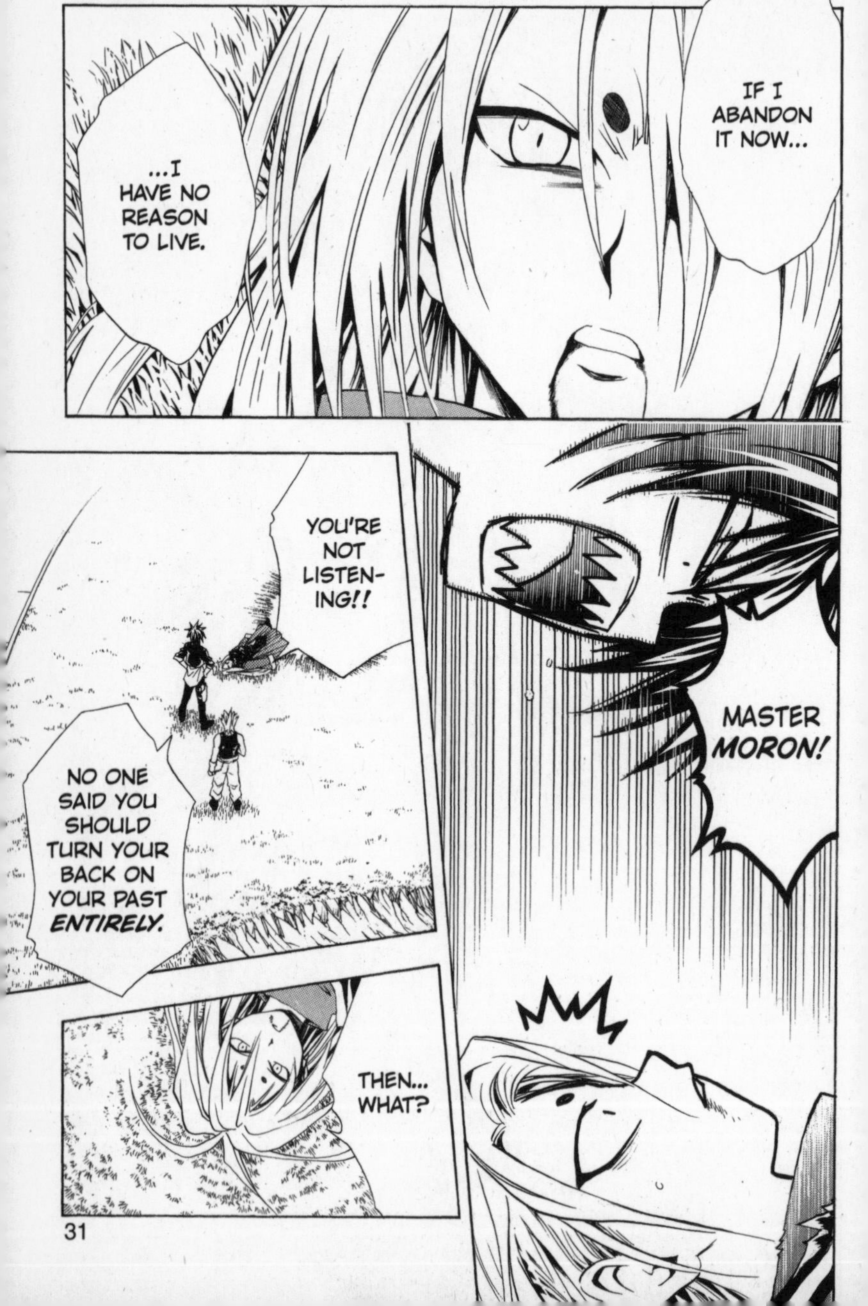
IF I ABANDON IT NOW...
...I HAVE NO REASON TO LIVE.
MASTER *MORON!*
YOU'RE NOT LISTENING!!
NO ONE SAID YOU SHOULD TURN YOUR BACK ON YOUR PAST *ENTIRELY.*
THEN... WHAT?

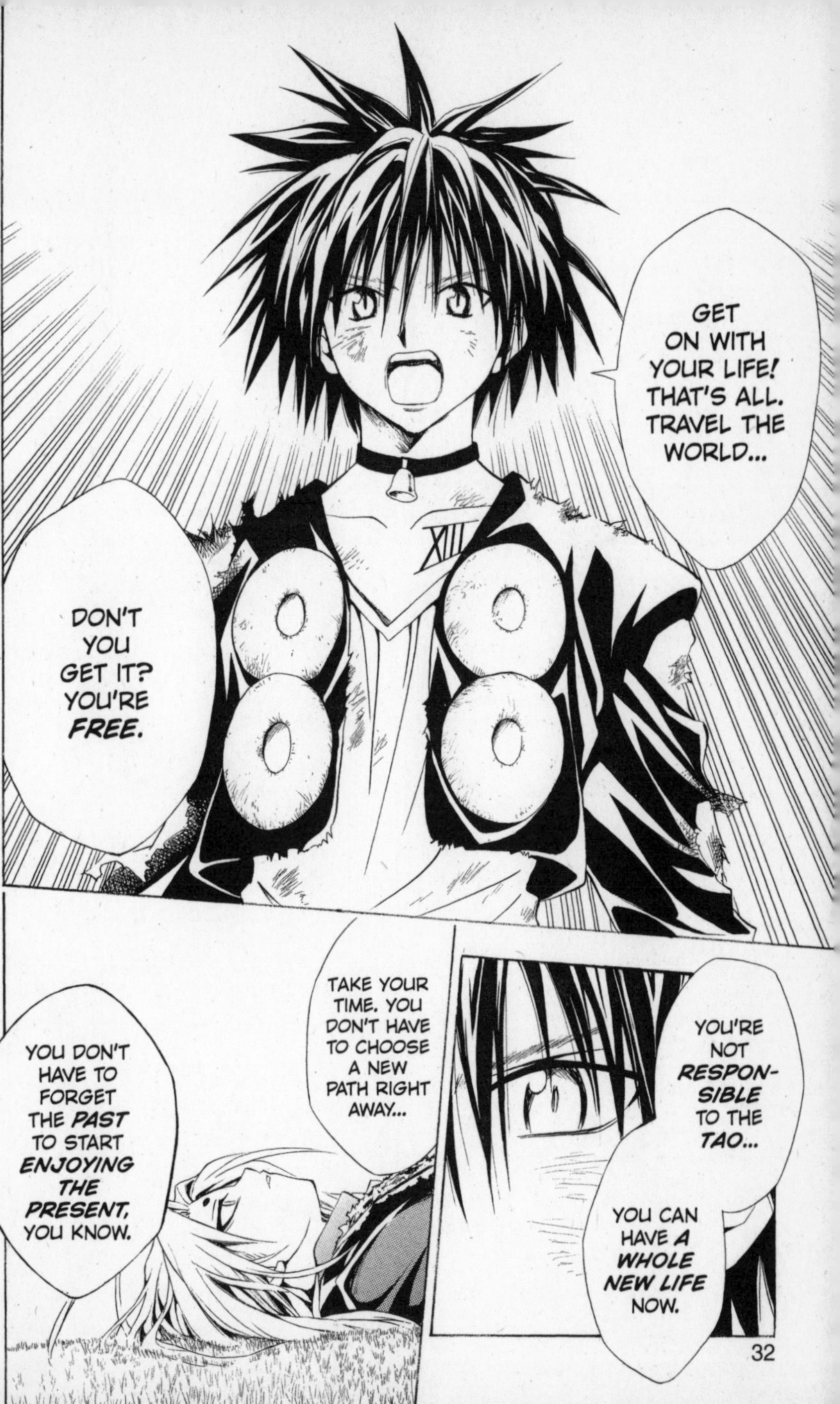
GET ON WITH YOUR LIFE! THAT'S ALL. TRAVEL THE WORLD...
DON'T YOU GET IT? YOU'RE FREE.
YOU'RE NOT RESPON-SIBLE TO THE TAO...
YOU CAN HAVE A WHOLE NEW LIFE NOW.
TAKE YOUR TIME. YOU DON'T HAVE TO CHOOSE A NEW PATH RIGHT AWAY...
YOU DON'T HAVE TO FORGET THE PAST TO START ENJOYING THE PRESENT, YOU KNOW.

READ THIS WAY

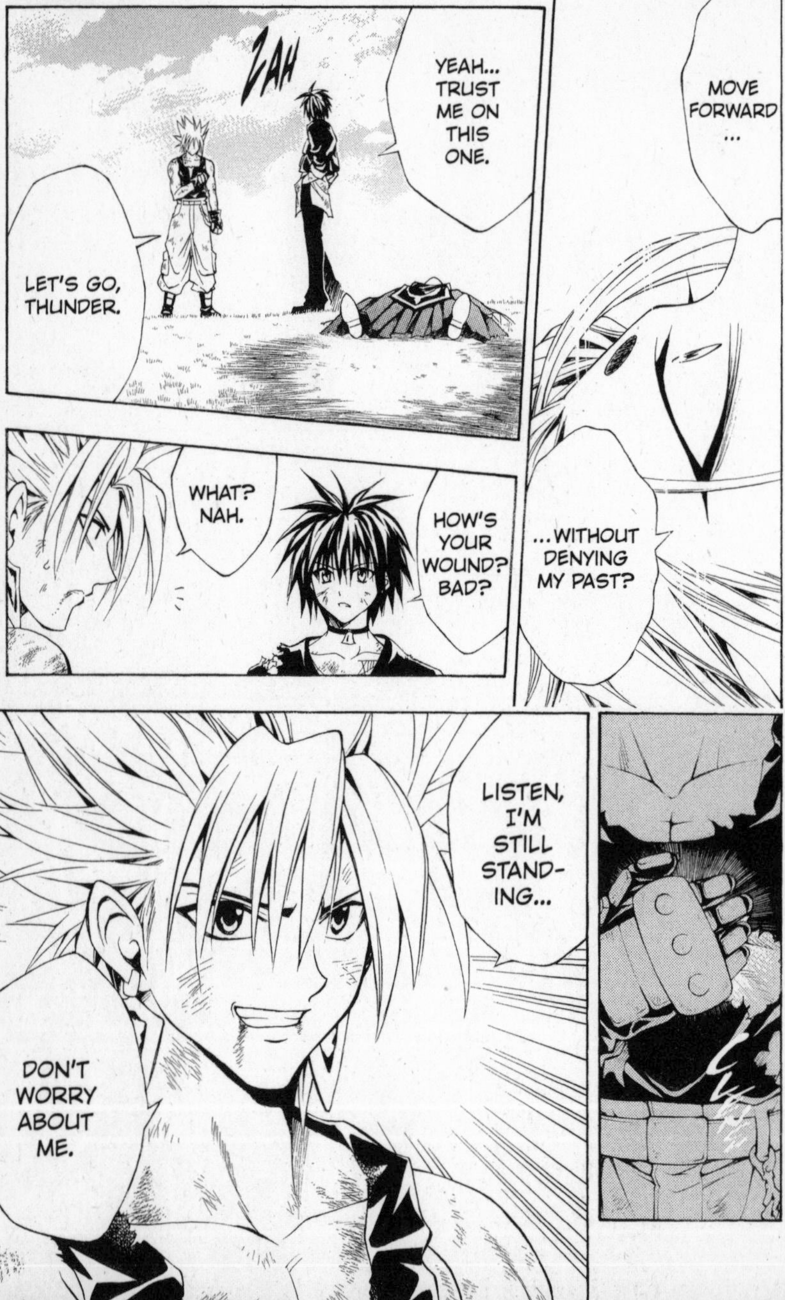

MOVE FORWARD ...
...WITHOUT DENYING MY PAST?
YEAH... TRUST ME ON THIS ONE.
ZAH
LET'S GO, THUNDER.
HOW'S YOUR WOUND? BAD?
WHAT? NAH.
LISTEN, I'M STILL STAND-ING...
DON'T WORRY ABOUT ME.

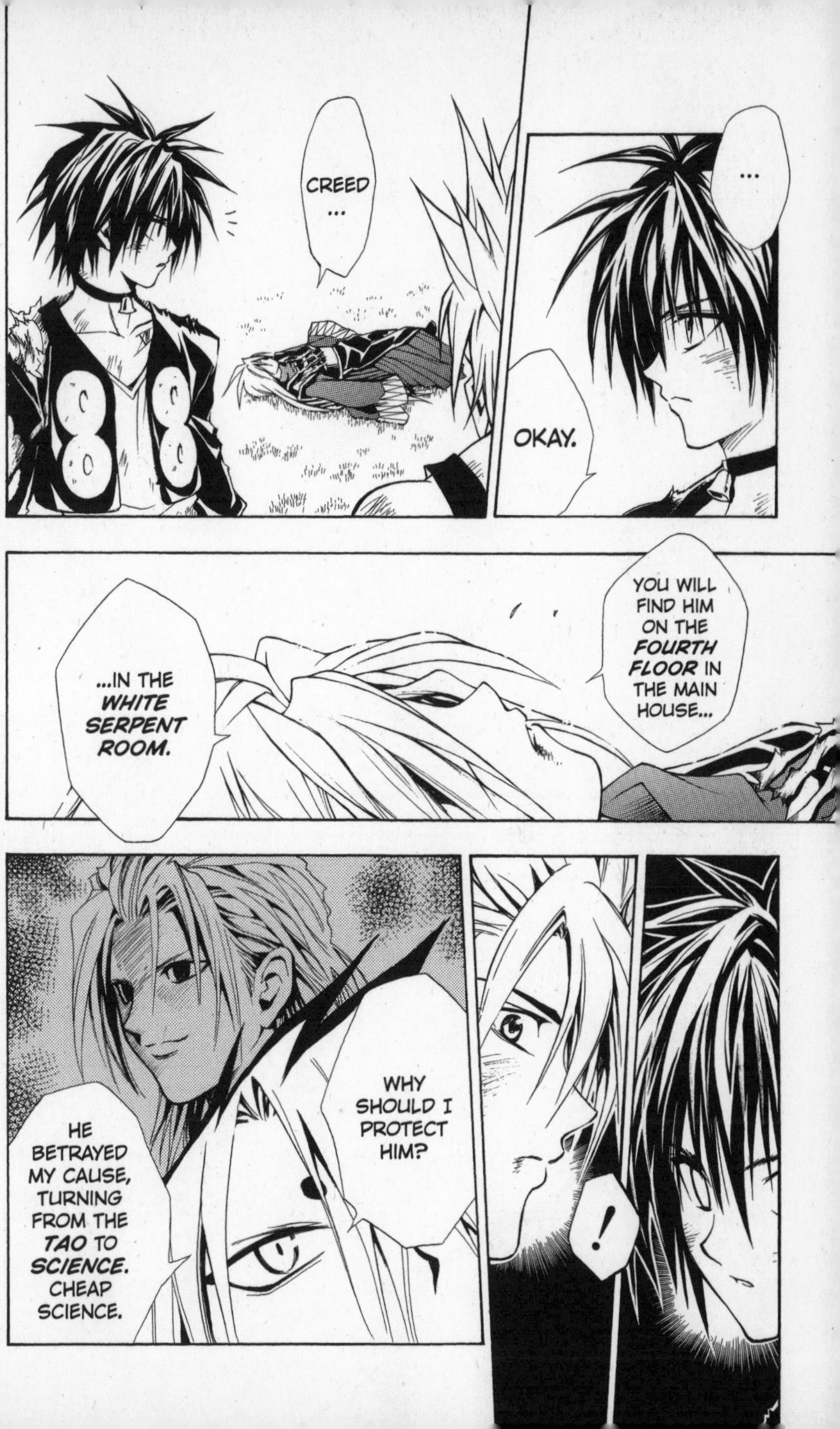
...
OKAY.
CREED ...
YOU WILL FIND HIM ON THE FOURTH FLOOR IN THE MAIN HOUSE...
...IN THE WHITE SERPENT ROOM.
!
WHY SHOULD I PROTECT HIM?
HE BETRAYED MY CAUSE, TURNING FROM THE TAO TO SCIENCE. CHEAP SCIENCE.

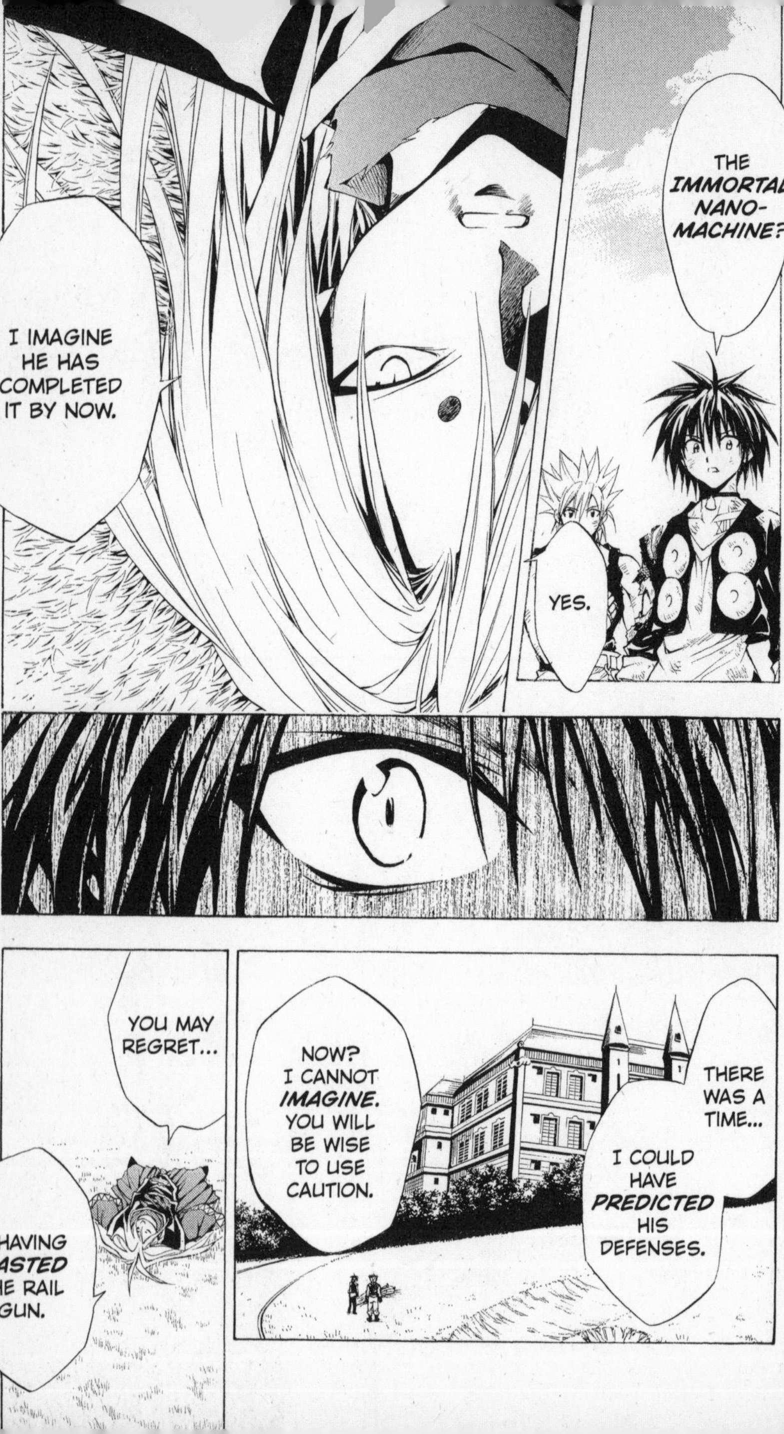
THE IMMORTAL NANO-MACHINE?
YES.
I IMAGINE HE HAS COMPLETED IT BY NOW.
THERE WAS A TIME...
I COULD HAVE PREDICTED HIS DEFENSES.
NOW? I CANNOT IMAGINE. YOU WILL BE WISE TO USE CAUTION.
YOU MAY REGRET...
...HAVING WASTED THE RAIL GUN.

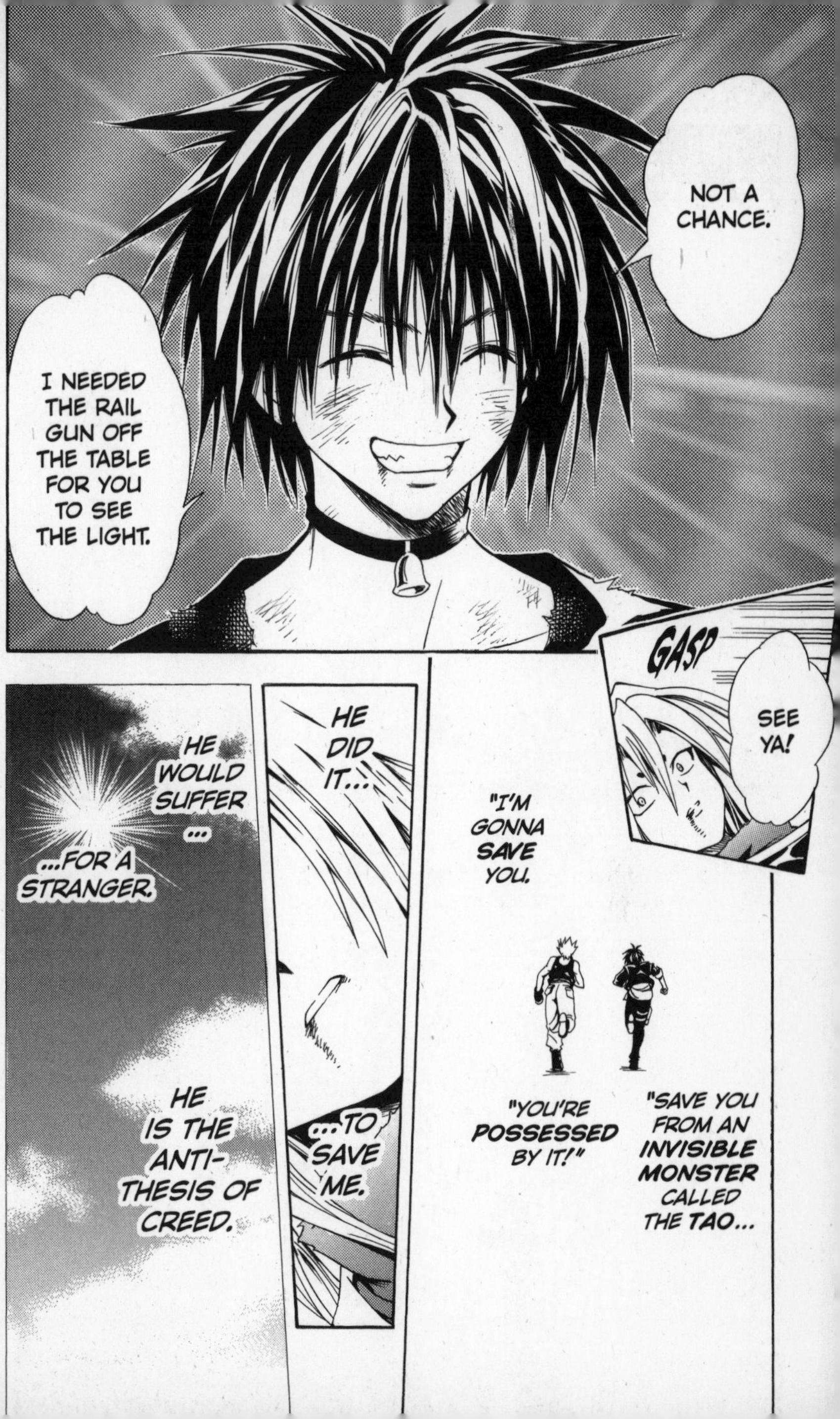
NOT A CHANCE.
I NEEDED THE RAIL GUN OFF THE TABLE FOR YOU TO SEE THE LIGHT.
GASP
SEE YA!
"I'M GONNA SAVE YOU.
"SAVE YOU FROM AN INVISIBLE MONSTER CALLED THE TAO...
"YOU'RE POSSESSED BY IT!"
HE DID IT...
...TO SAVE ME.
HE WOULD SUFFER ...
...FOR A STRANGER.
HE IS THE ANTI-THESIS OF CREED.

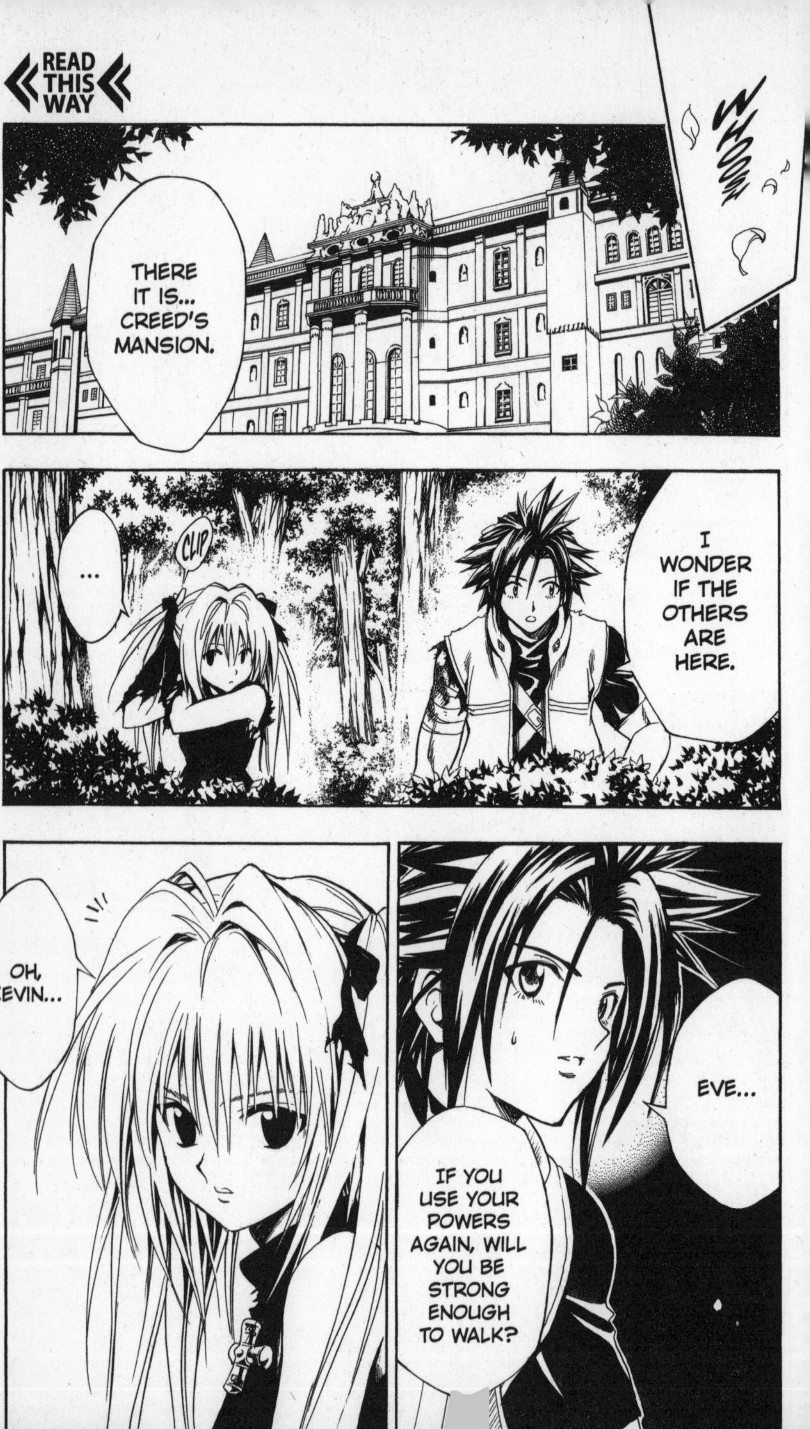
READ THIS WAY
WHOOM
THERE IT IS... CREED'S MANSION.
I WONDER IF THE OTHERS ARE HERE.
CLIP
...
EVE...
IF YOU USE YOUR POWERS AGAIN, WILL YOU BE STRONG ENOUGH TO WALK?
OH, KEVIN...

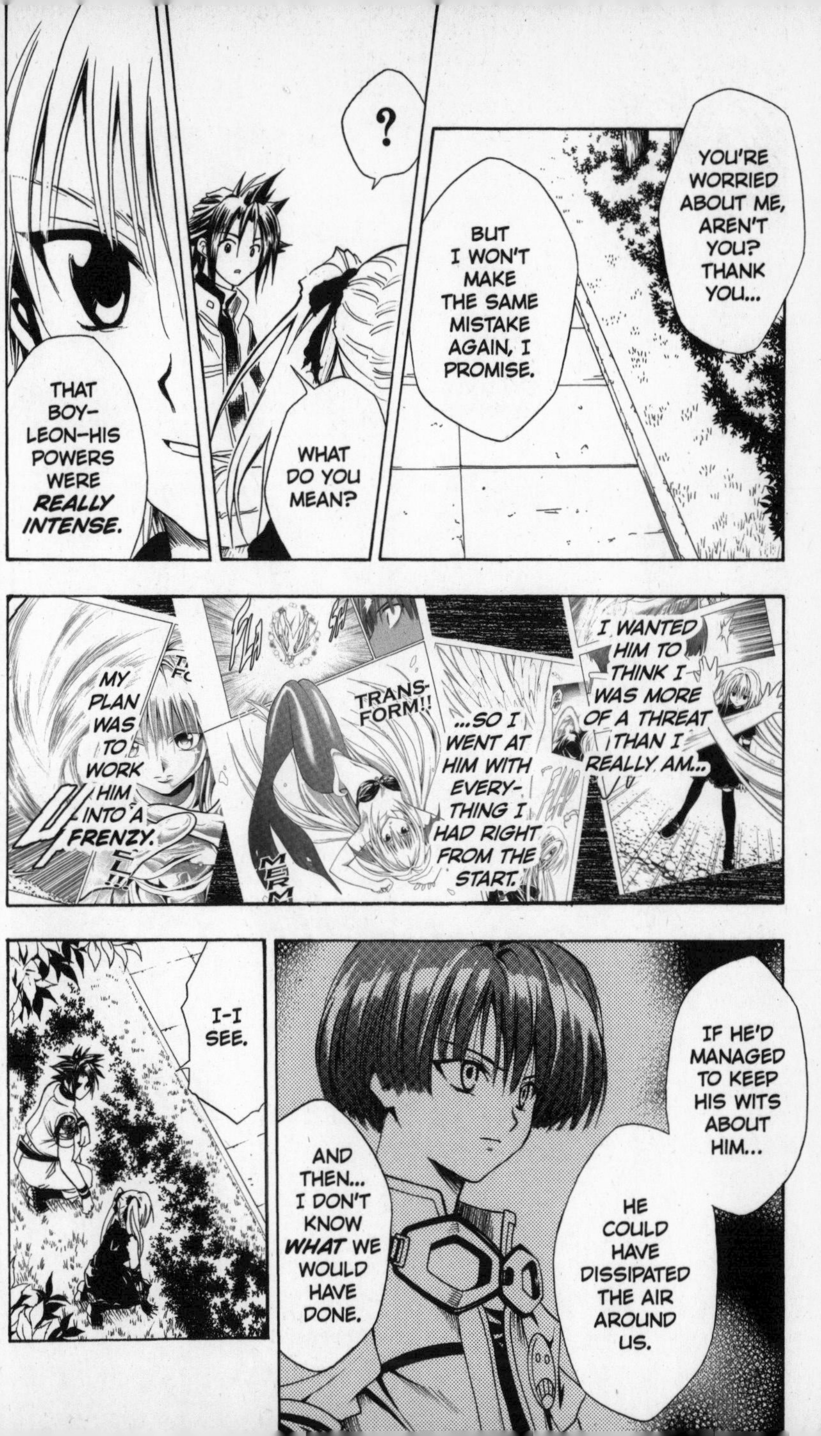
YOU'RE WORRIED ABOUT ME, AREN'T YOU? THANK YOU...
BUT I WON'T MAKE THE SAME MISTAKE AGAIN, I PROMISE.
?
WHAT DO YOU MEAN?
THAT BOY—LEON—HIS POWERS WERE *REALLY INTENSE.*
I WANTED HIM TO THINK I WAS MORE OF A THREAT THAN I REALLY AM...
...SO I WENT AT HIM WITH EVERY-THING I HAD RIGHT FROM THE START.
TRANS-FORM!!
MY PLAN WAS TO WORK HIM INTO A FRENZY.
IF HE'D MANAGED TO KEEP HIS WITS ABOUT HIM...
HE COULD HAVE DISSIPATED THE AIR AROUND US.
AND THEN... I DON'T KNOW *WHAT* WE WOULD HAVE DONE.
I-I SEE.

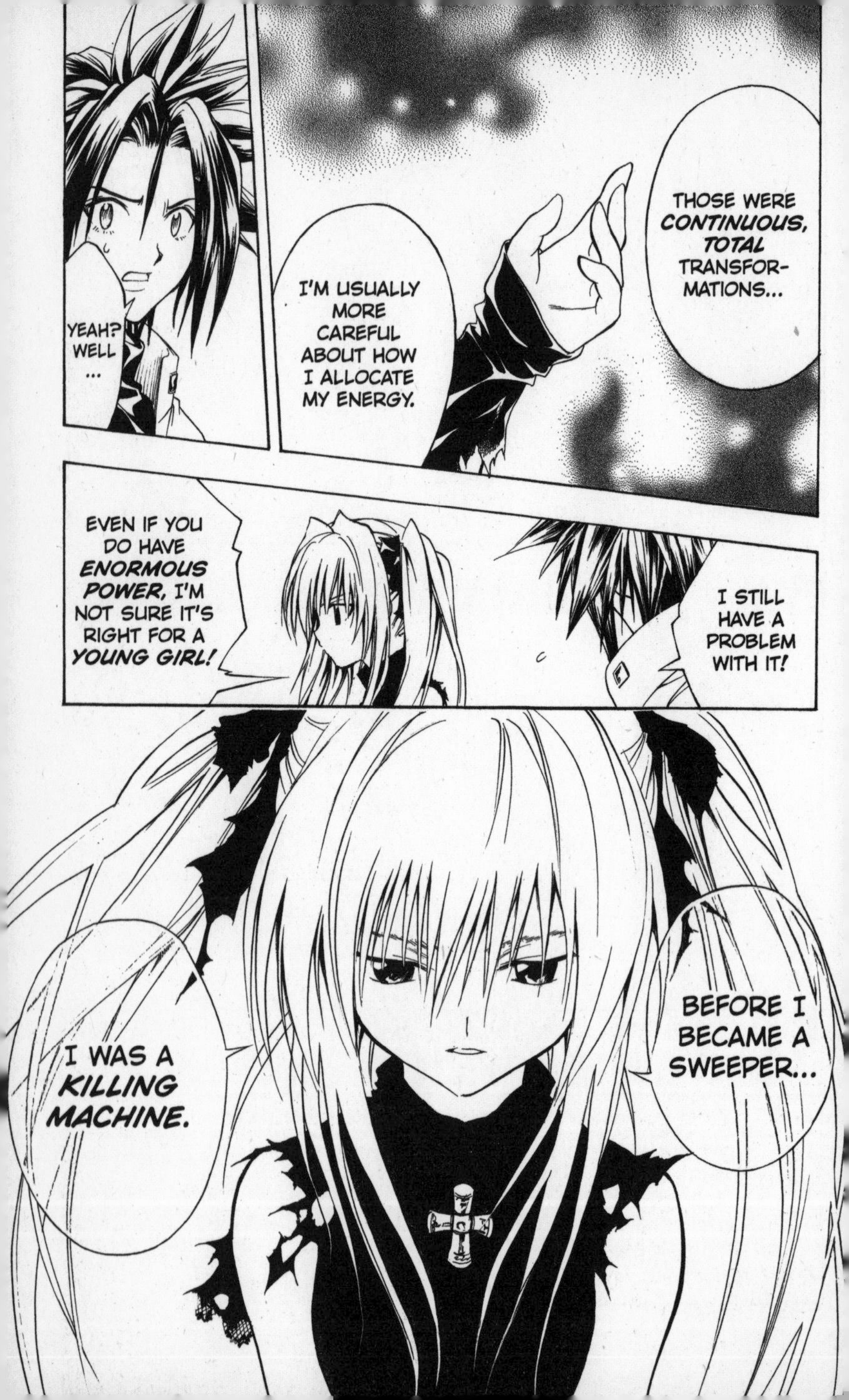
THOSE WERE *CONTINUOUS, TOTAL* TRANSFORMATIONS...
I'M USUALLY MORE CAREFUL ABOUT HOW I ALLOCATE MY ENERGY.
YEAH? WELL ...
EVEN IF YOU DO HAVE *ENORMOUS POWER,* I'M NOT SURE IT'S RIGHT FOR A *YOUNG GIRL!*
I STILL HAVE A PROBLEM WITH IT!
BEFORE I BECAME A SWEEPER...
I WAS A *KILLING MACHINE.*

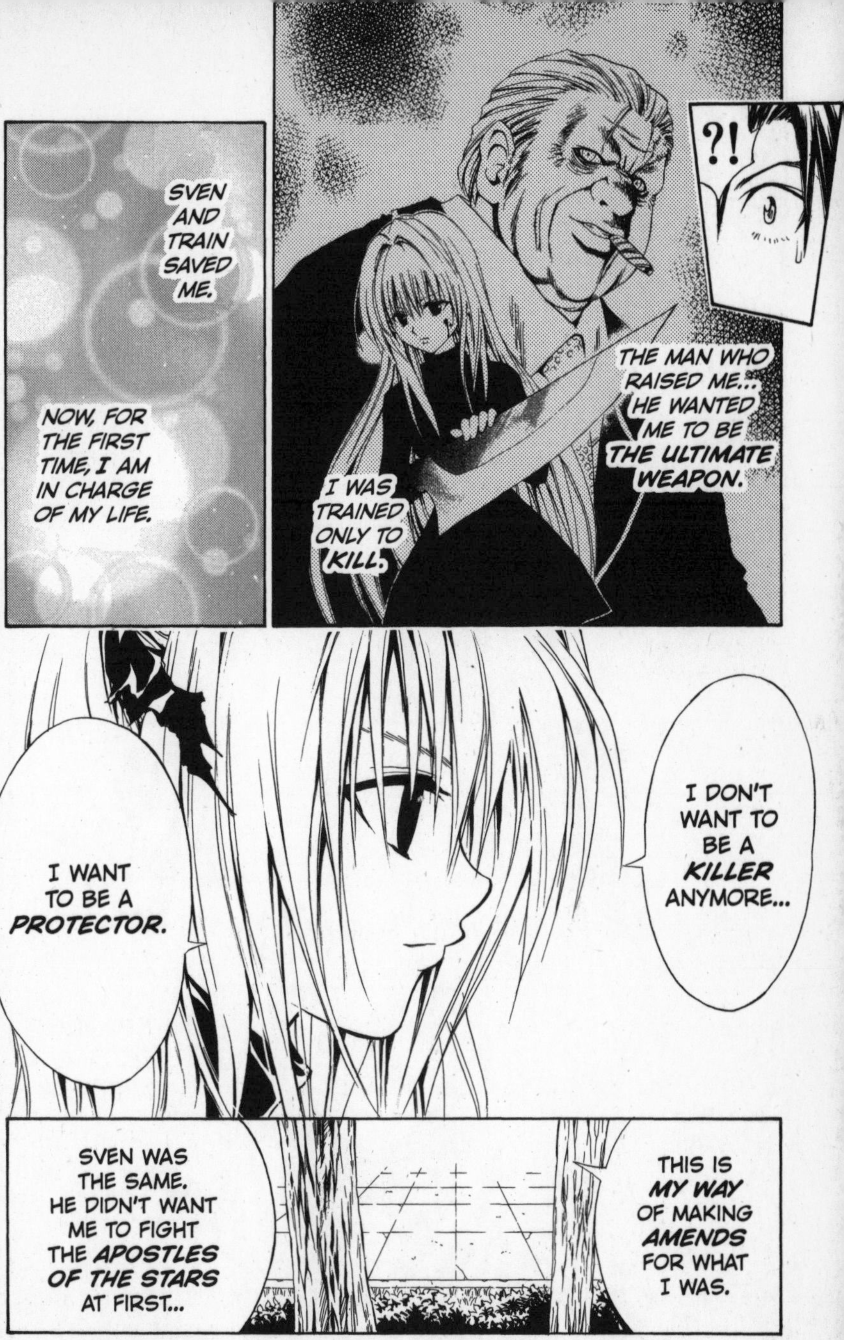
?!
THE MAN WHO RAISED ME... HE WANTED ME TO BE THE ULTIMATE WEAPON.
I WAS TRAINED ONLY TO KILL.
SVEN AND TRAIN SAVED ME.
NOW, FOR THE FIRST TIME, I AM IN CHARGE OF MY LIFE.
I DON'T WANT TO BE A KILLER ANYMORE...
I WANT TO BE A PROTECTOR.
THIS IS MY WAY OF MAKING AMENDS FOR WHAT I WAS.
SVEN WAS THE SAME. HE DIDN'T WANT ME TO FIGHT THE APOSTLES OF THE STARS AT FIRST...

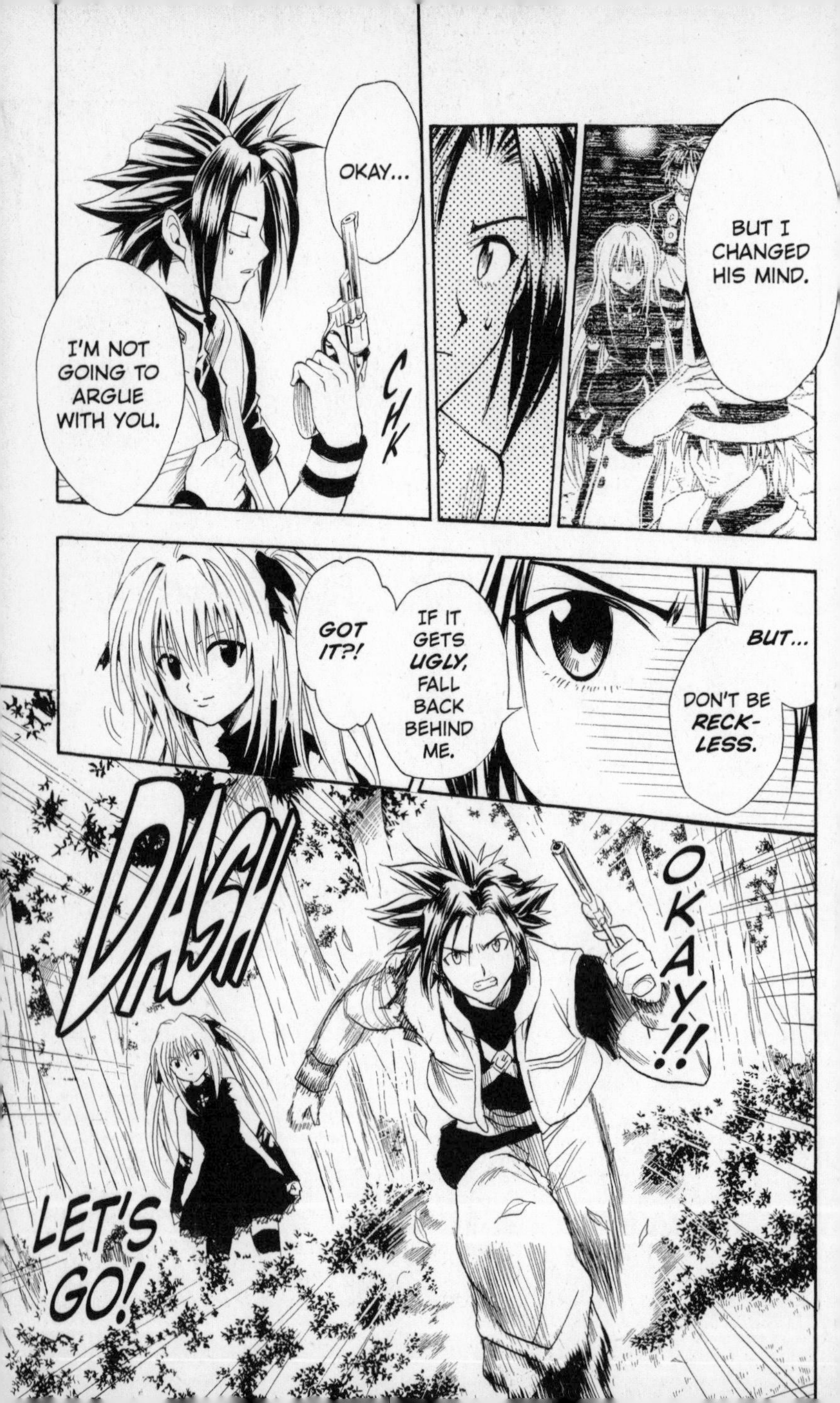
BUT I CHANGED HIS MIND.
OKAY...
CHK
I'M NOT GOING TO ARGUE WITH YOU.
BUT...
DON'T BE RECKLESS.
IF IT GETS UGLY, FALL BACK BEHIND ME.
GOT IT?!
OKAY!!
DASH
LET'S GO!

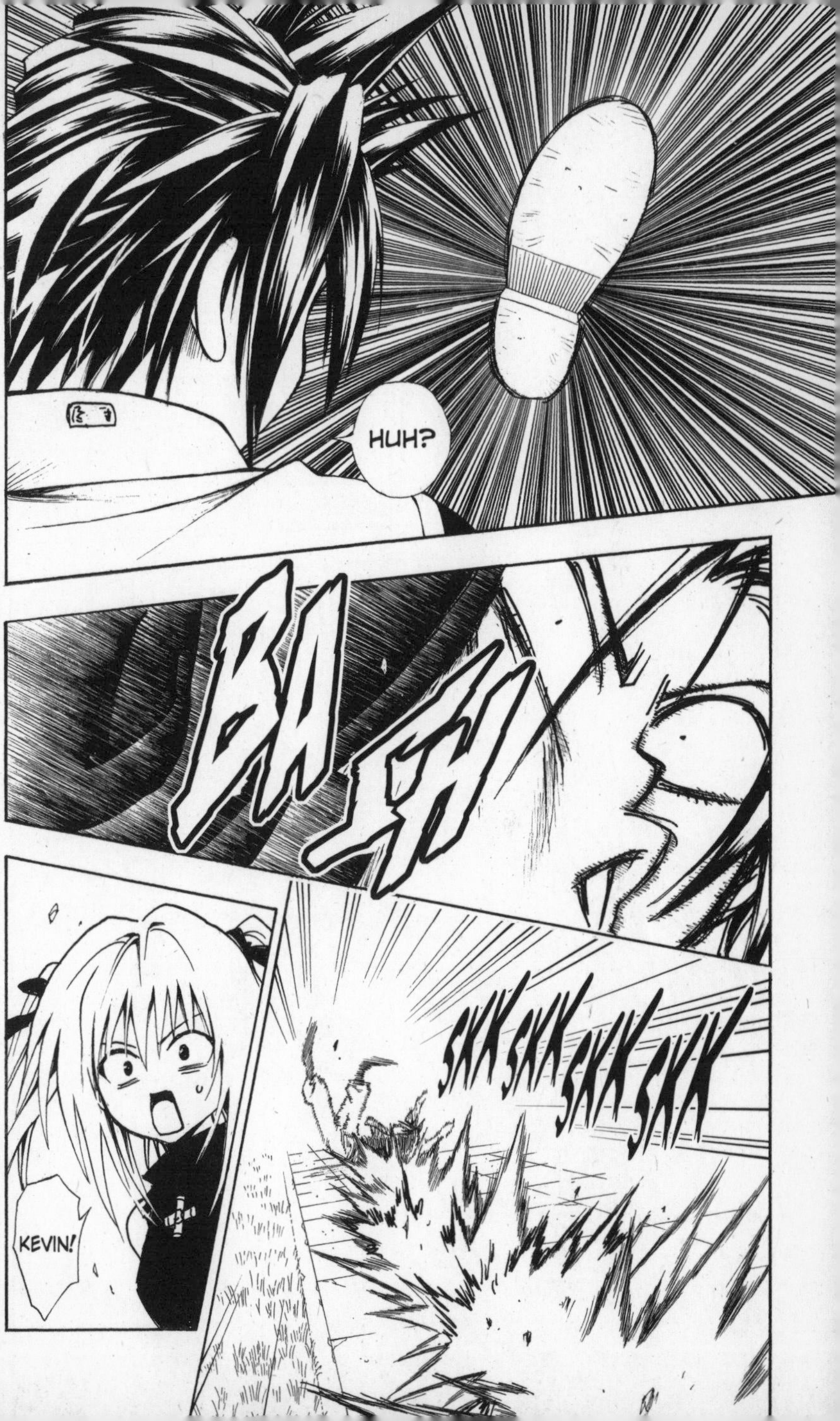
HUH?
BASH
SKK SKK SKK SKK
KEVIN!

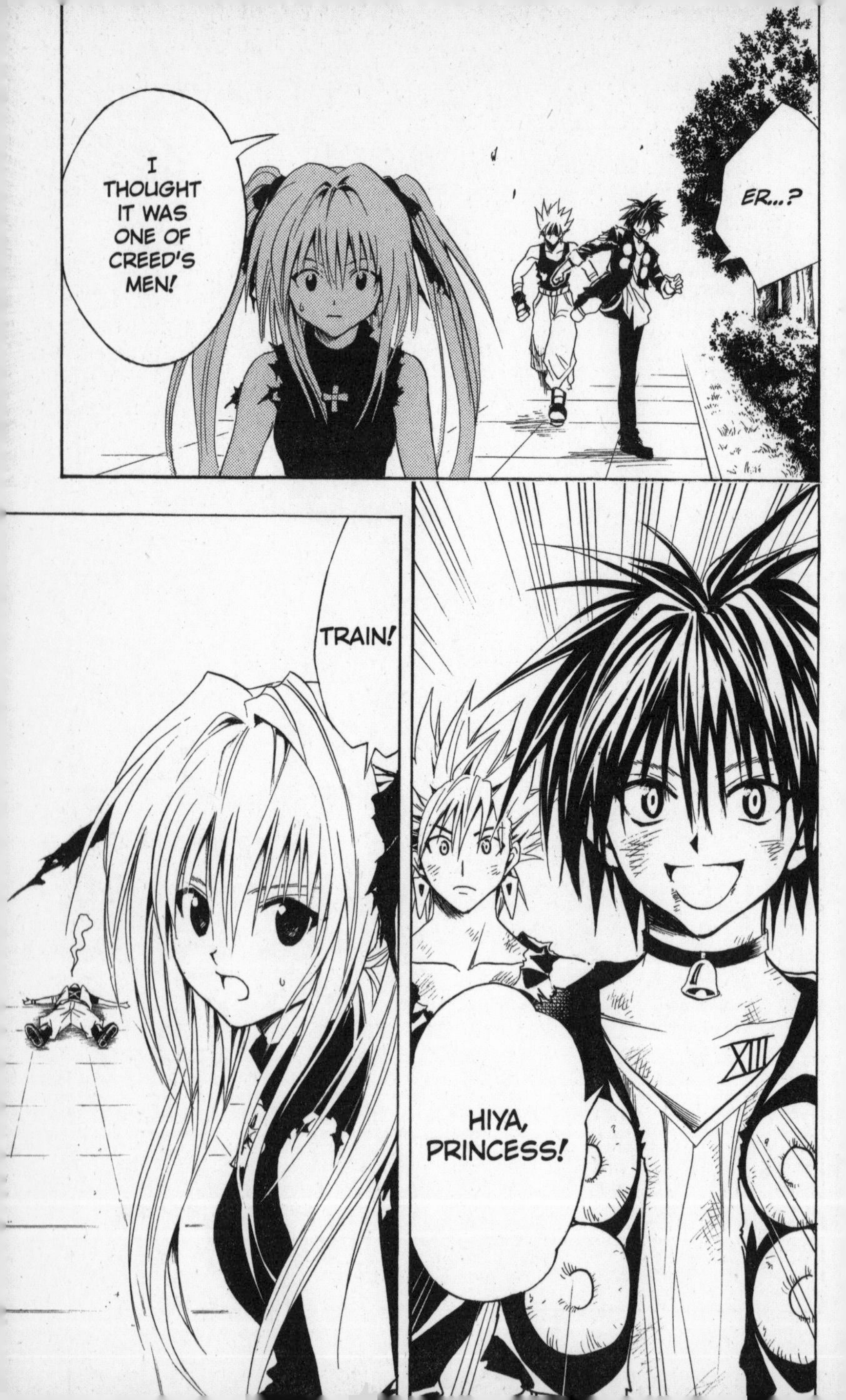
ER...?
I THOUGHT IT WAS ONE OF CREED'S MEN!
HIYA, PRINCESS!
TRAIN!

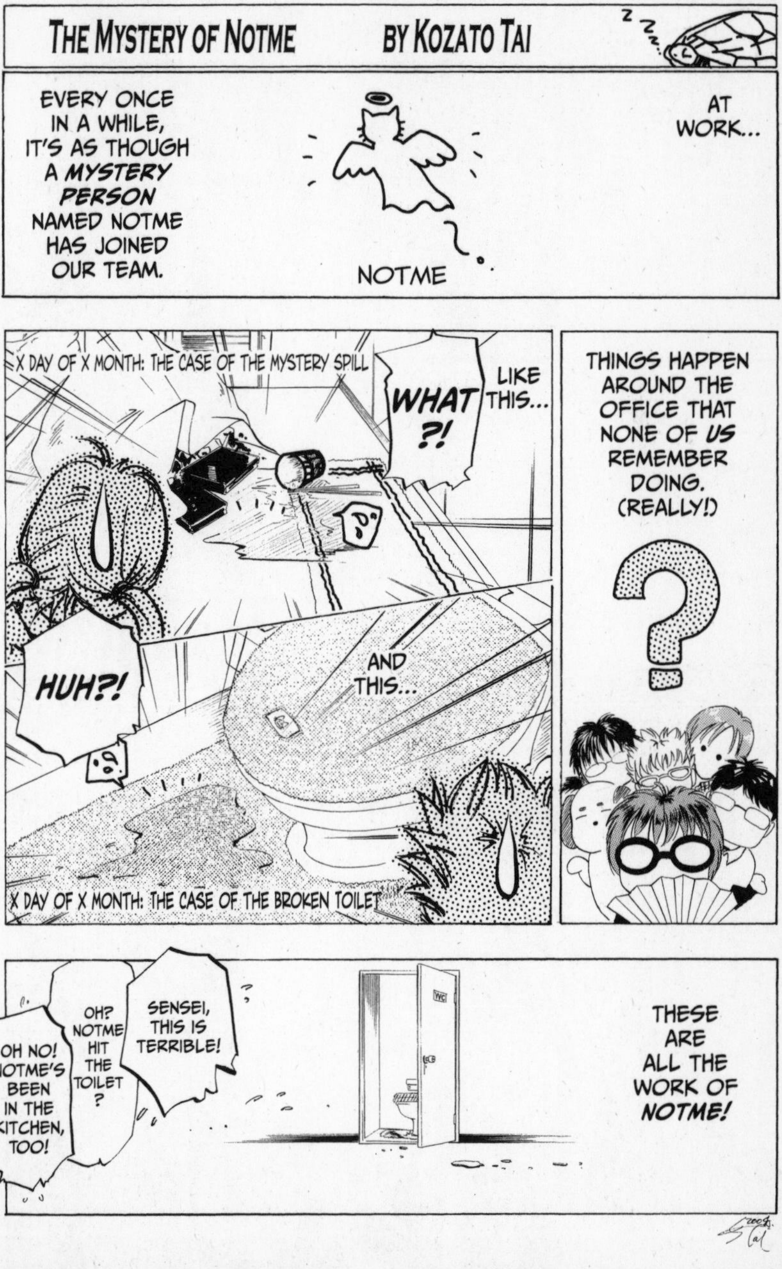
THE MYSTERY OF NOTME
BY KOZATO TAI
Z Z Z...
AT WORK...
EVERY ONCE IN A WHILE, IT'S AS THOUGH A MYSTERY PERSON NAMED NOTME HAS JOINED OUR TEAM.
NOTME
THINGS HAPPEN AROUND THE OFFICE THAT NONE OF US REMEMBER DOING. (REALLY!)
LIKE THIS...
WHAT?!
X DAY OF X MONTH: THE CASE OF THE MYSTERY SPILL
AND THIS...
HUH?!
X DAY OF X MONTH: THE CASE OF THE BROKEN TOILET
THESE ARE ALL THE WORK OF NOTME!
WC
SENSEI, THIS IS TERRIBLE!
OH? NOTME HIT THE TOILET?
OH NO! NOTME'S BEEN IN THE KITCHEN, TOO!

Chapter 152: The Power of the Alliance!

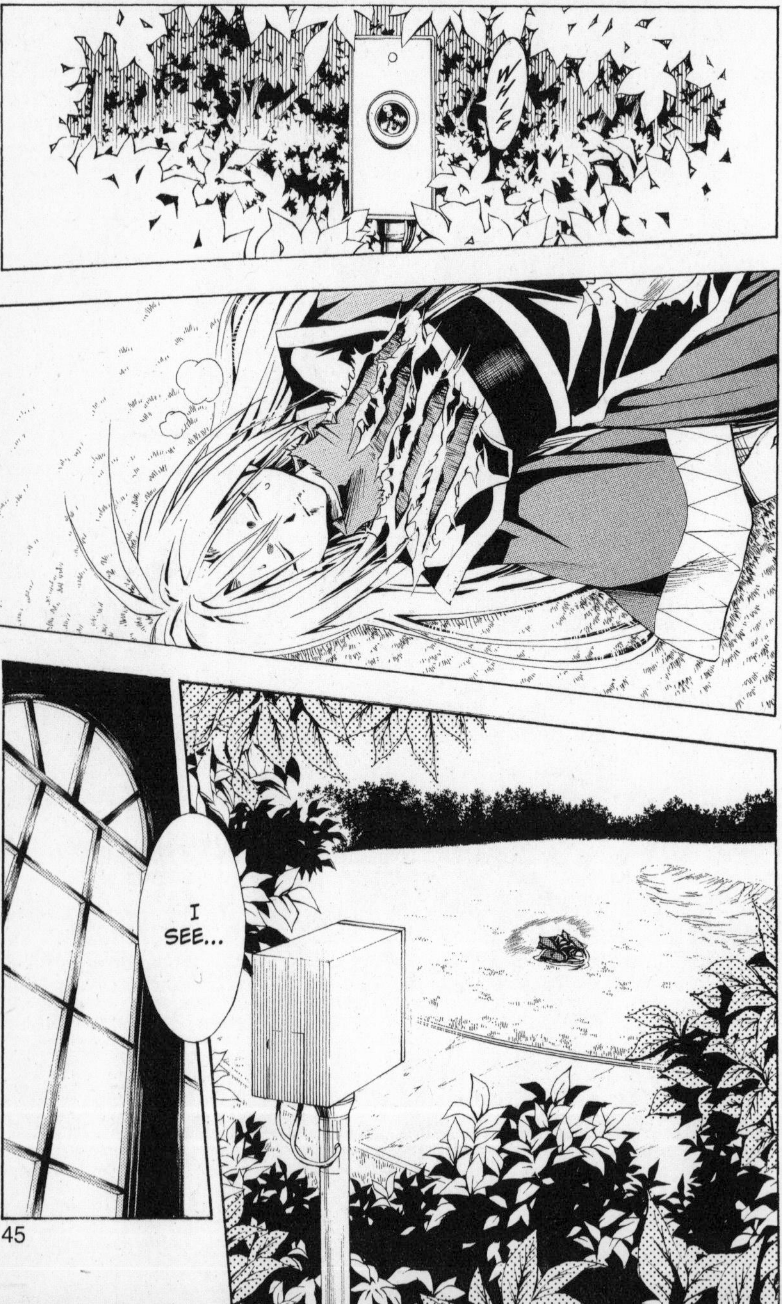
WHIFF
I SEE...

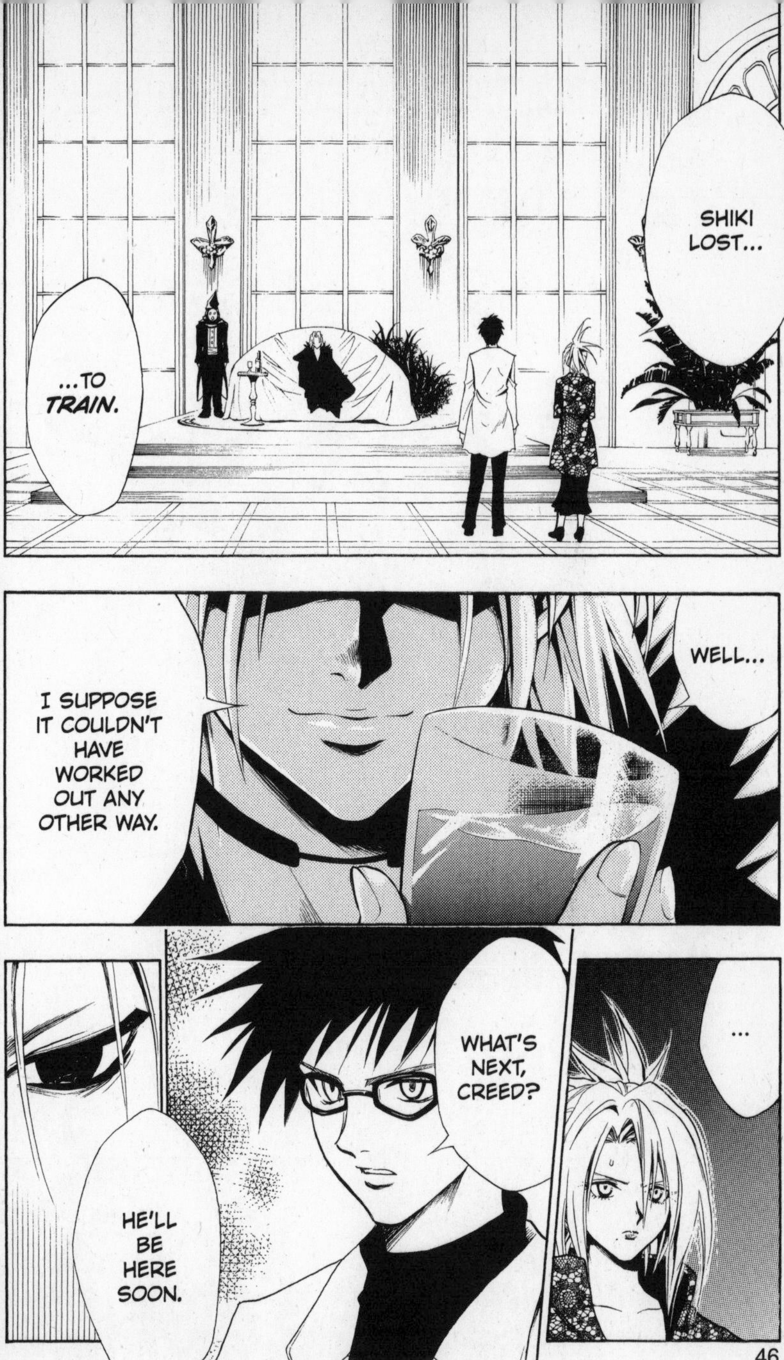
SHIKI LOST...
...TO TRAIN.
WELL...
I SUPPOSE IT COULDN'T HAVE WORKED OUT ANY OTHER WAY.
...
WHAT'S NEXT, CREED?
HE'LL BE HERE SOON.

Chapter 152: The Power of the Alliance!

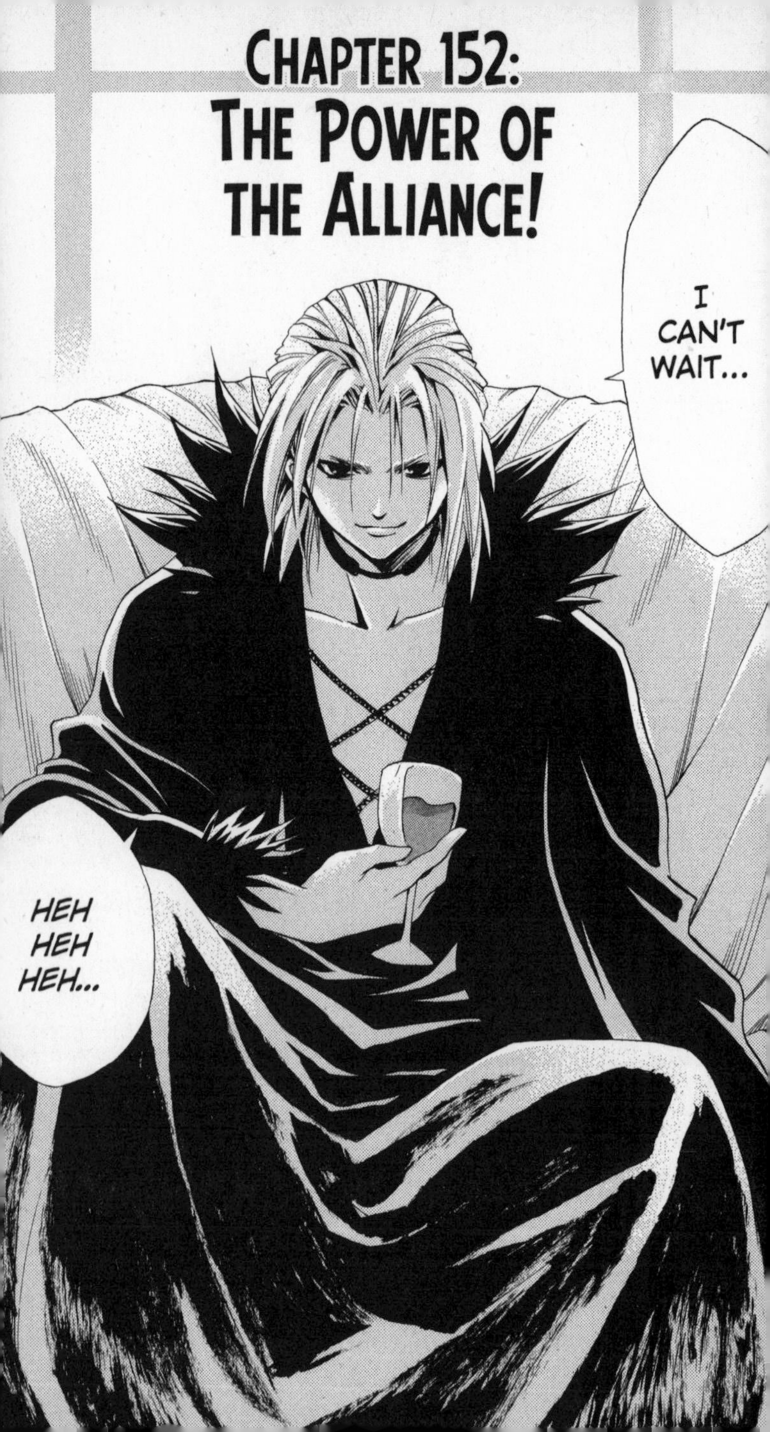
I CAN'T WAIT...
HEH HEH HEH...

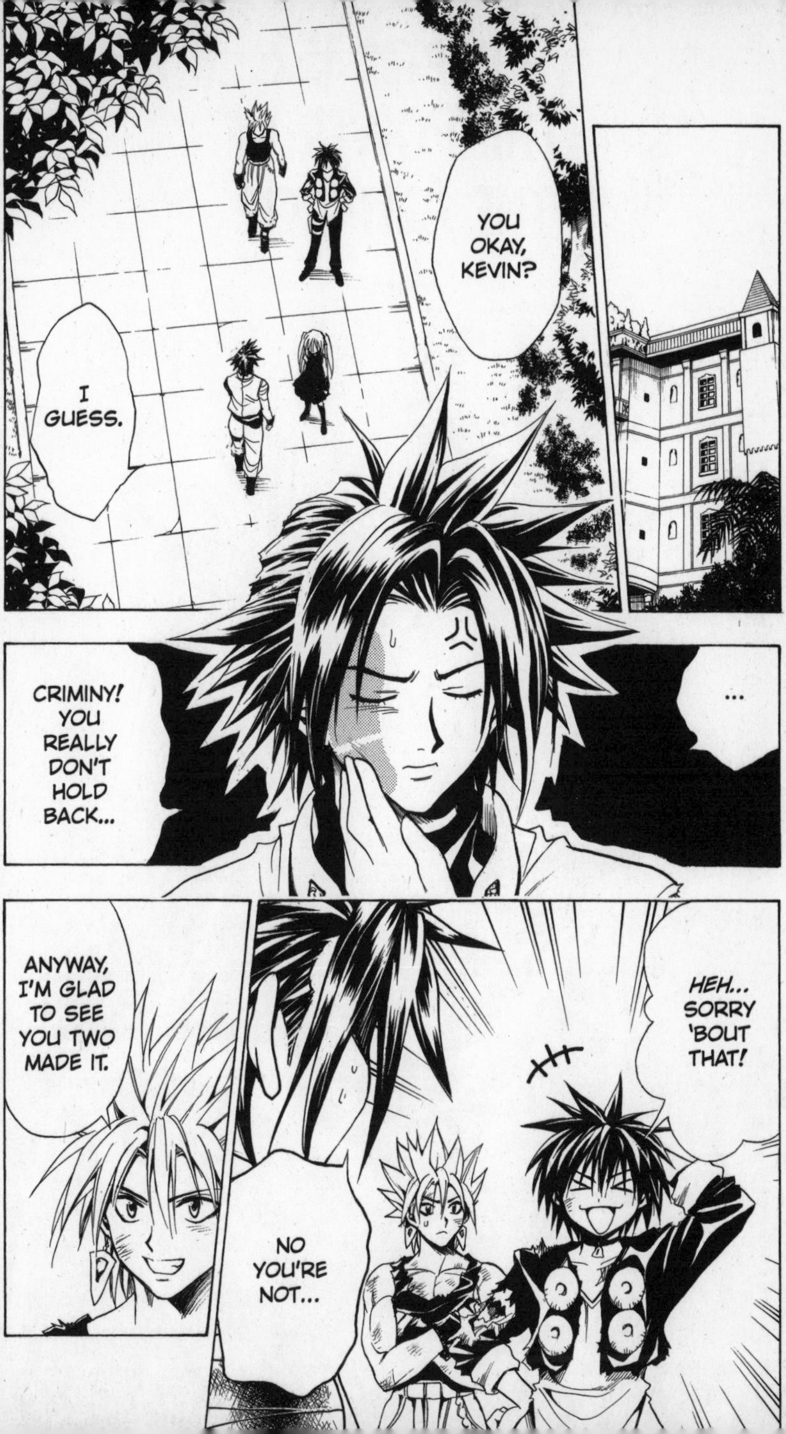
YOU OKAY, KEVIN?
I GUESS.
...
CRIMINY! YOU REALLY DON'T HOLD BACK...
HEH... SORRY 'BOUT THAT!
NO YOU'RE NOT...
ANYWAY, I'M GLAD TO SEE YOU TWO MADE IT.

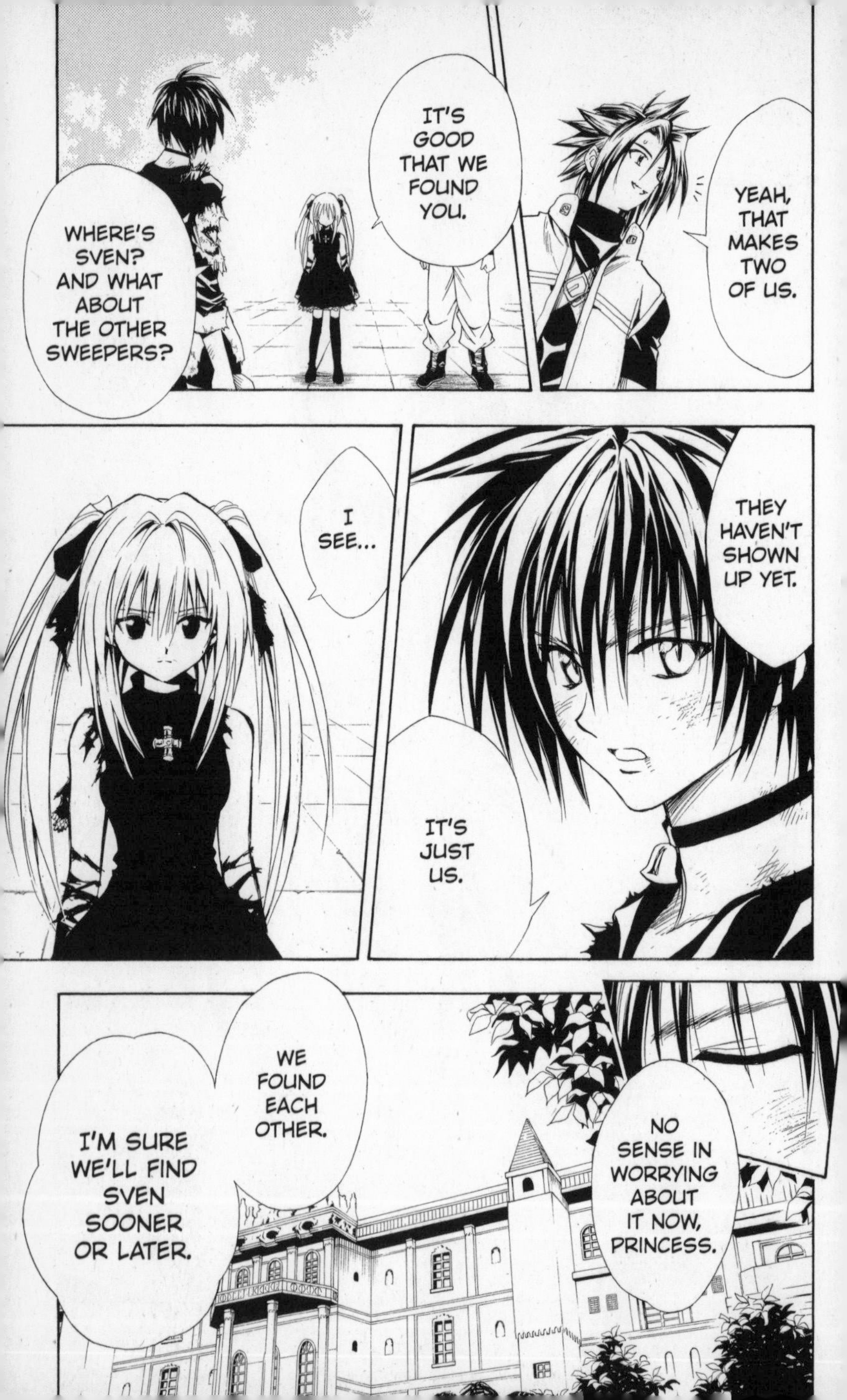
YEAH, THAT MAKES TWO OF US.
IT'S GOOD THAT WE FOUND YOU.
WHERE'S SVEN? AND WHAT ABOUT THE OTHER SWEEPERS?
THEY HAVEN'T SHOWN UP YET.
IT'S JUST US.
I SEE...
NO SENSE IN WORRYING ABOUT IT NOW, PRINCESS.
WE FOUND EACH OTHER.
I'M SURE WE'LL FIND SVEN SOONER OR LATER.

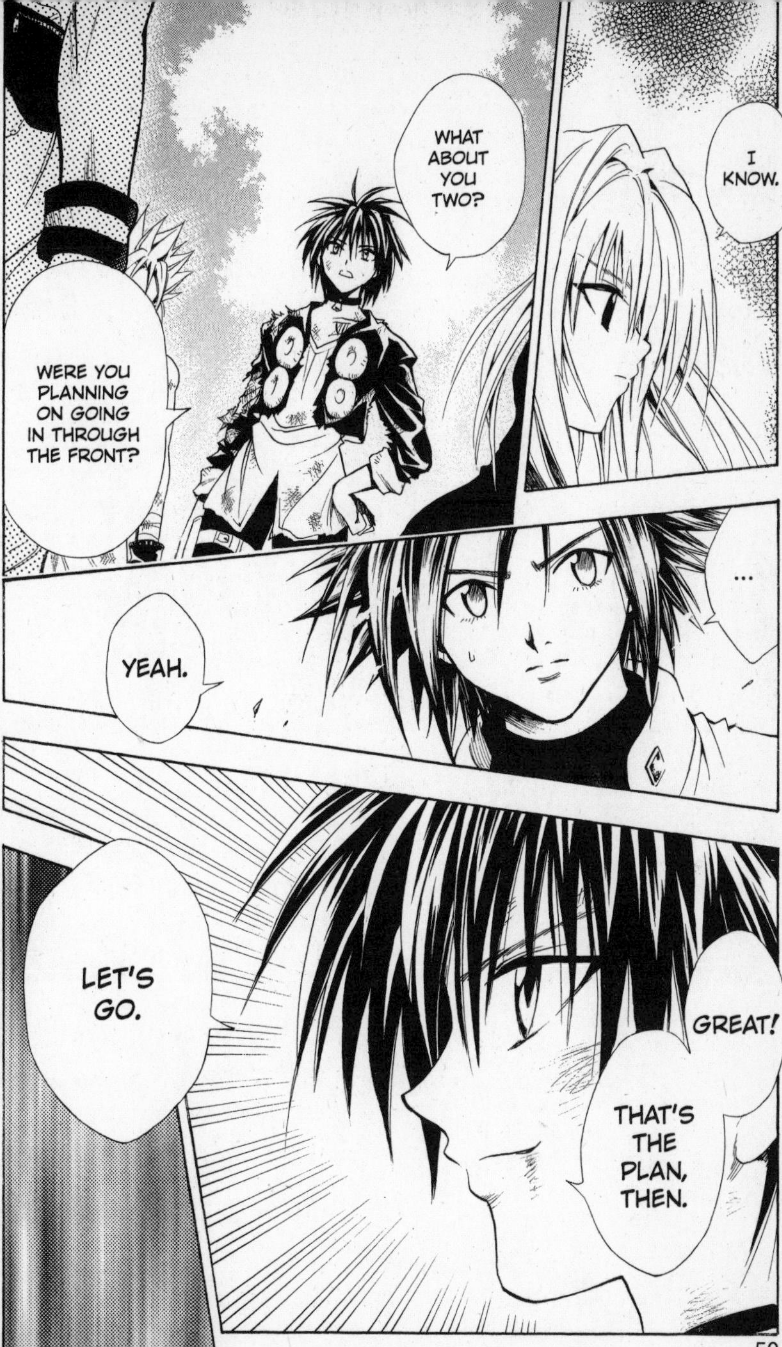
I KNOW.
WHAT ABOUT YOU TWO?
WERE YOU PLANNING ON GOING IN THROUGH THE FRONT?
...
YEAH.
GREAT!
THAT'S THE PLAN, THEN.
LET'S GO.

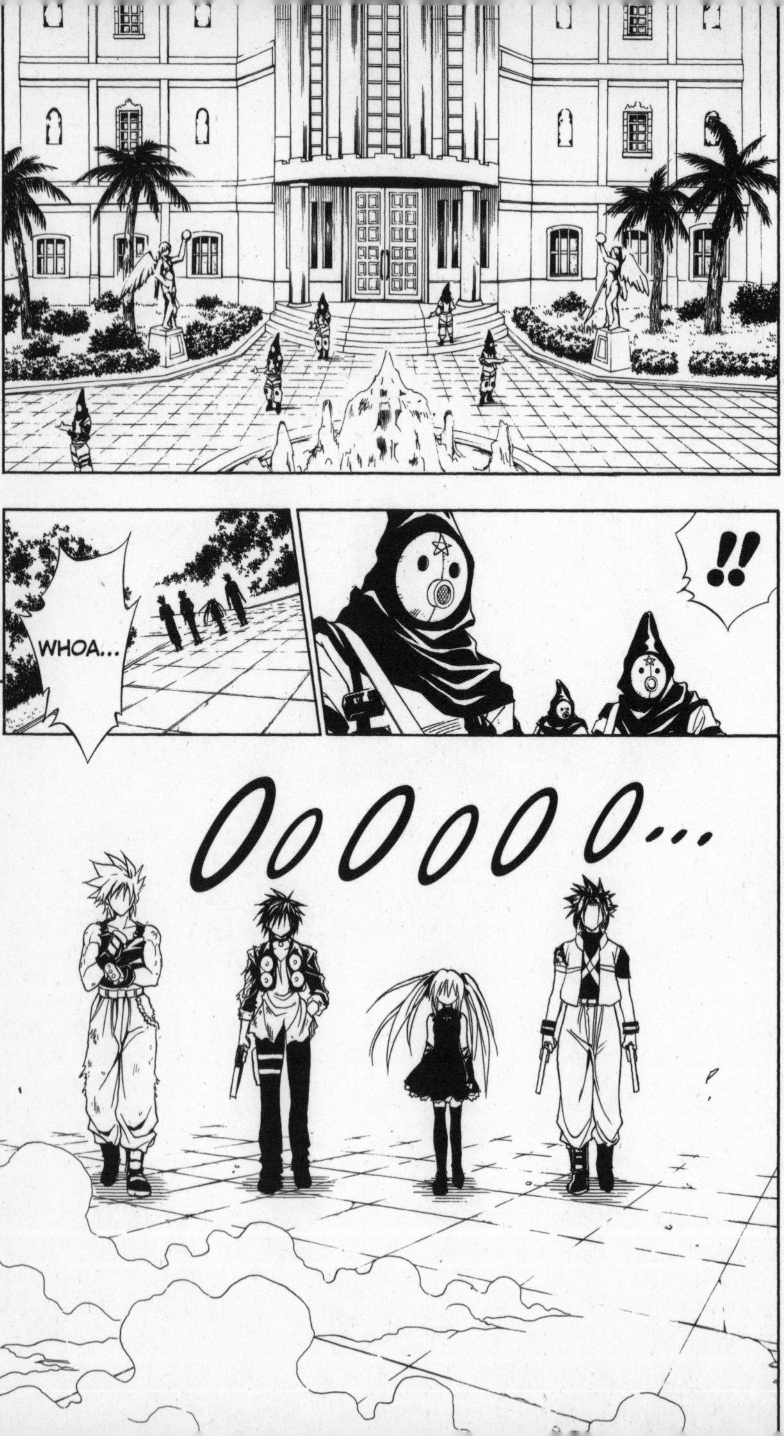
!!
WHOA...
OOOOOO...

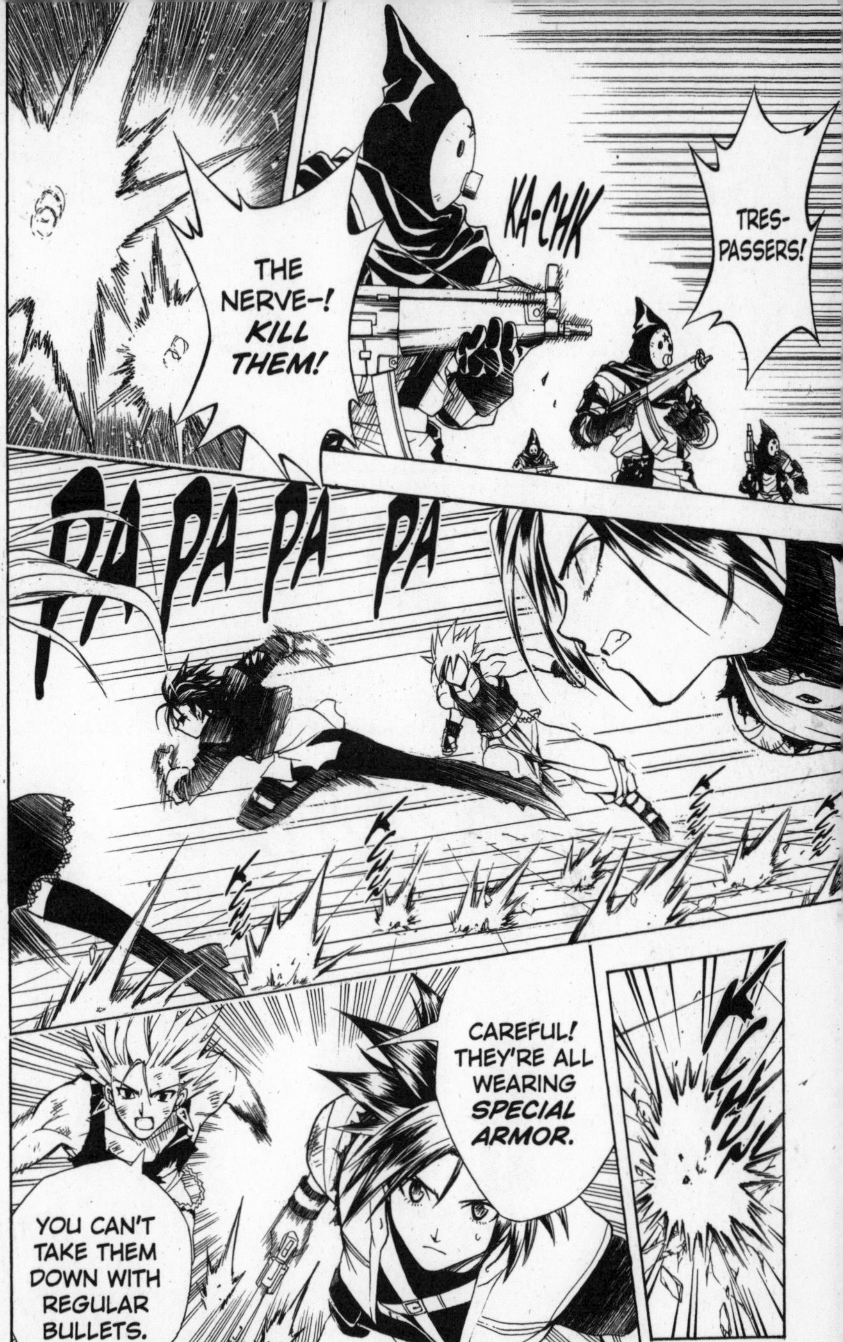
TRES-PASSERS!
KA-CHK
THE NERVE–! KILL THEM!
PA PA PA PA
CAREFUL! THEY'RE ALL WEARING SPECIAL ARMOR.
YOU CAN'T TAKE THEM DOWN WITH REGULAR BULLETS.

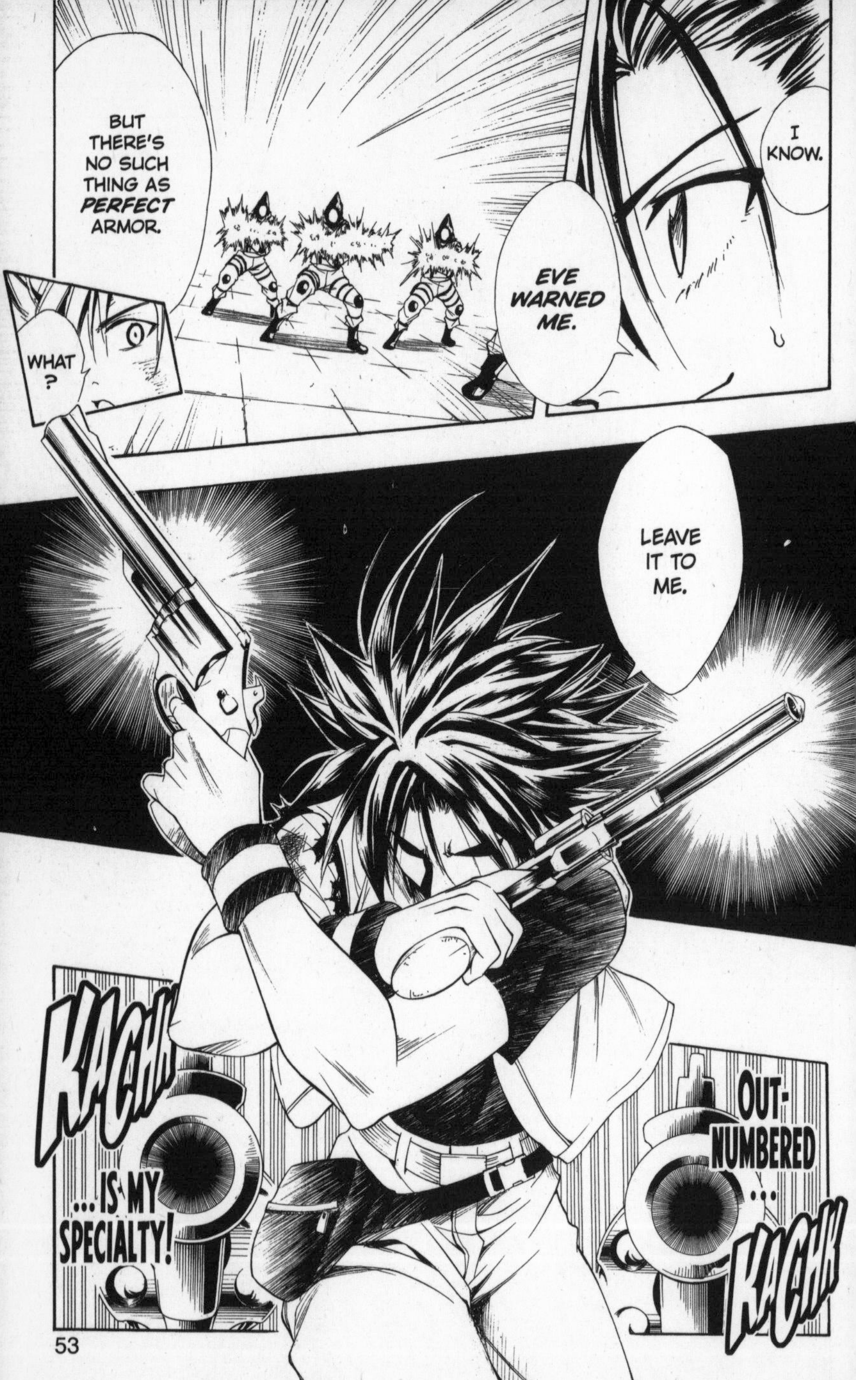

I KNOW.
EVE WARNED ME.
BUT THERE'S NO SUCH THING AS *PERFECT* ARMOR.
WHAT?
LEAVE IT TO ME.
OUT-NUMBERED...
KACHK
...IS MY SPECIALTY!
KACHK

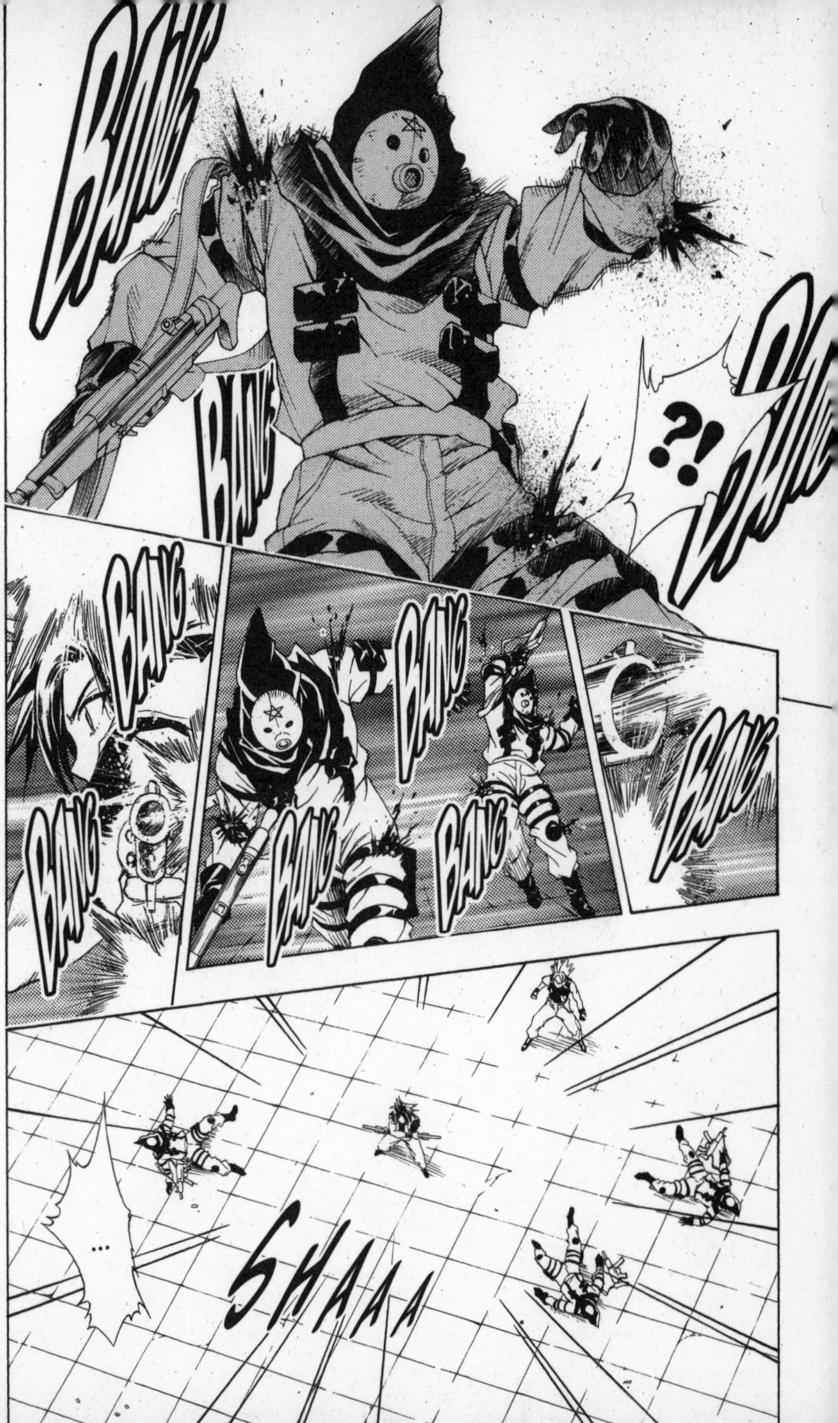
BANG
?!
BANG
BANG
BANG
BANG
BANG
BANG
BANG
BANG
SHAAA
...

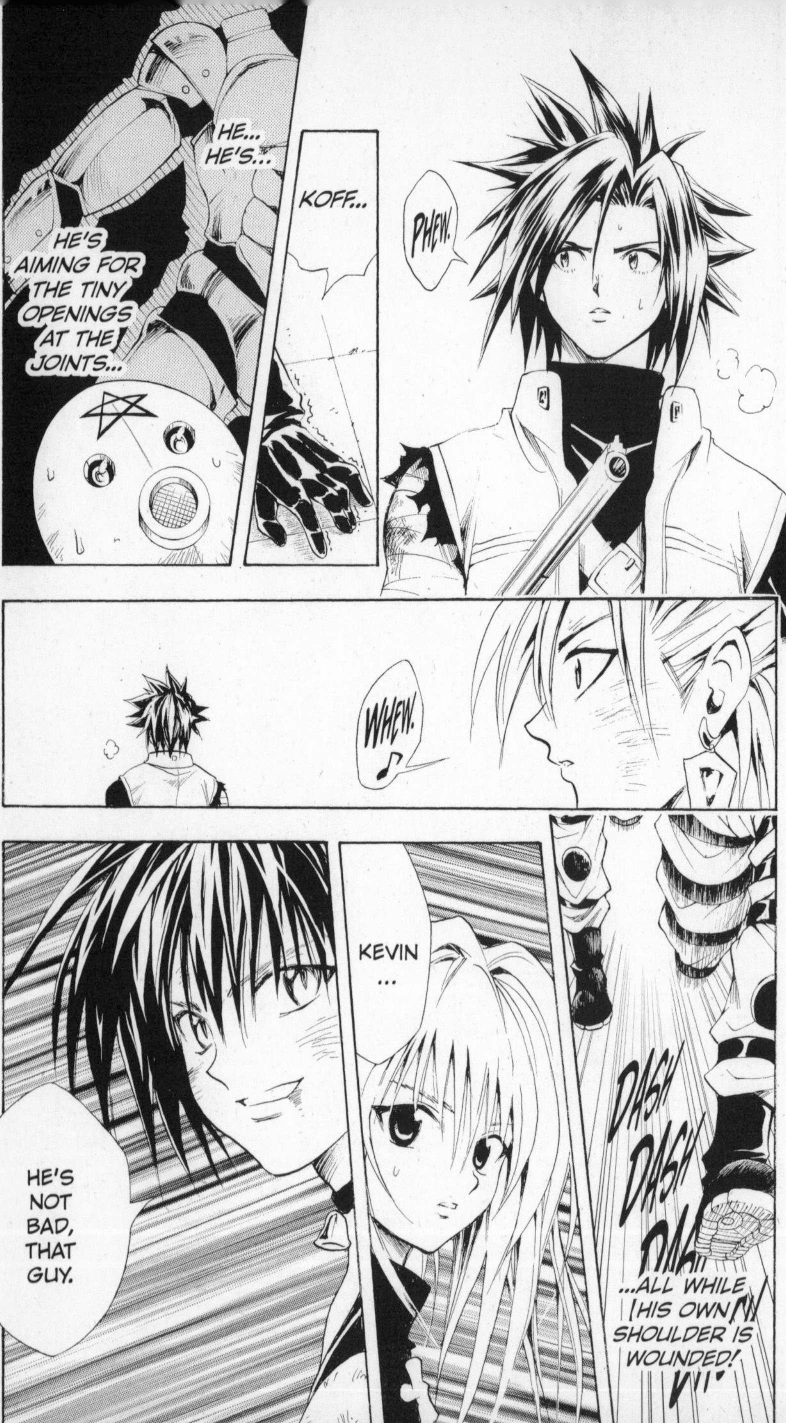
PHEW.
KOFF...
HE... HE'S...
HE'S AIMING FOR THE TINY OPENINGS AT THE JOINTS...
WHEW. ♪
DASH DASH DASH
...ALL WHILE HIS OWN SHOULDER IS WOUNDED!
KEVIN ...
HE'S NOT BAD, THAT GUY.

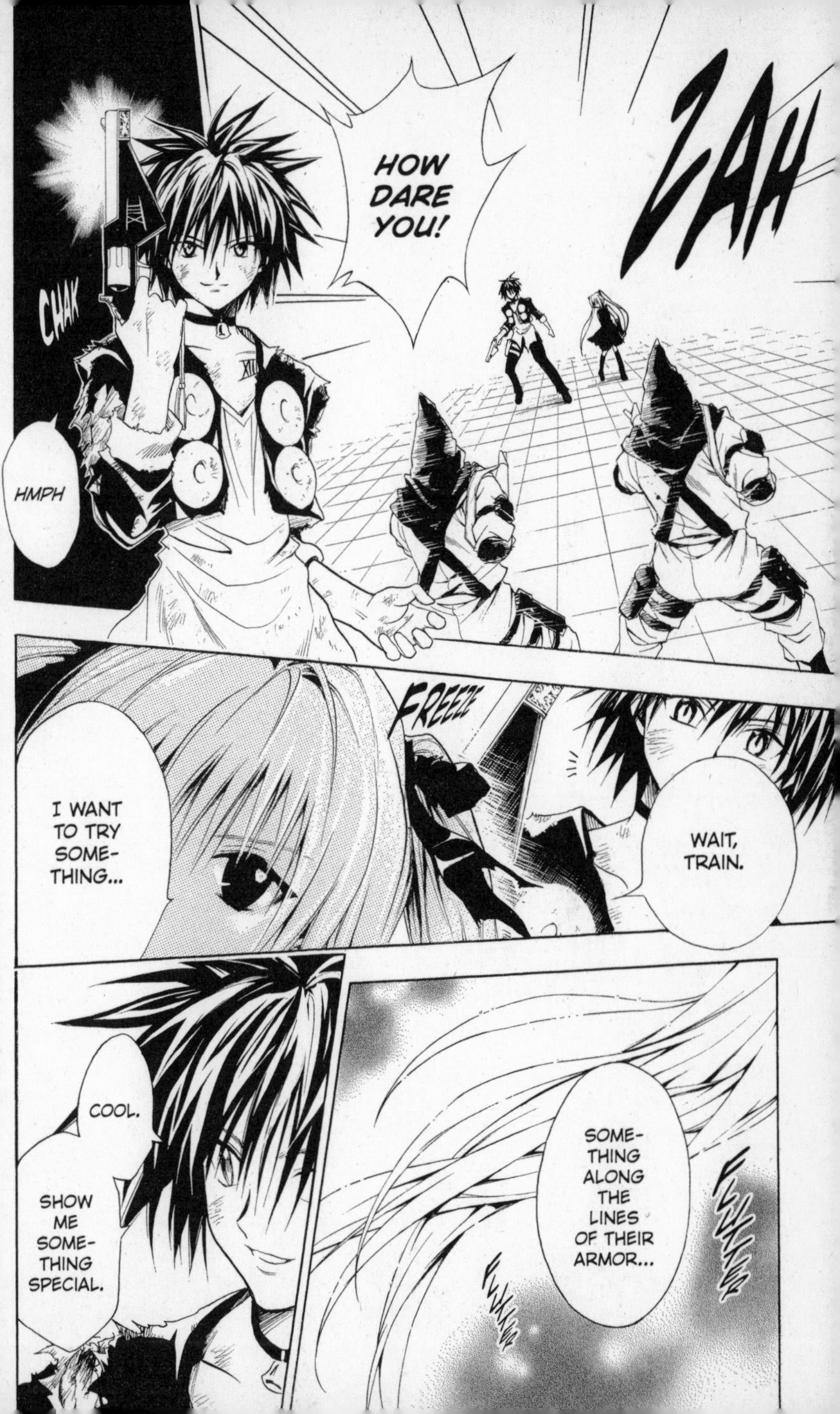
ZAH
HOW DARE YOU!
CHAK
HMPH
WAIT, TRAIN.
FREEZE
I WANT TO TRY SOMETHING...
SOMETHING ALONG THE LINES OF THEIR ARMOR...
COOL.
SHOW ME SOMETHING SPECIAL.

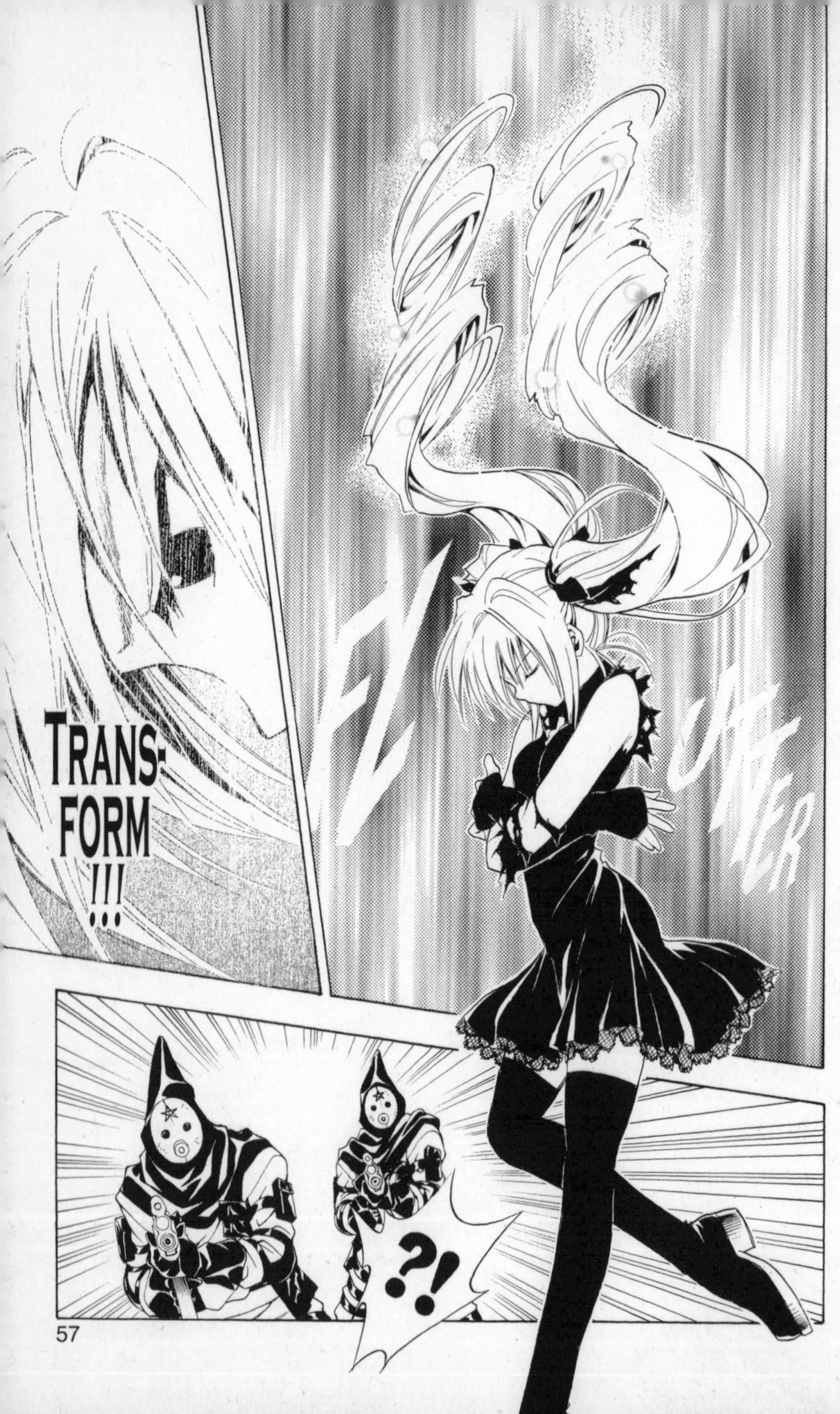
TRANS-
FORM
!!!
?!

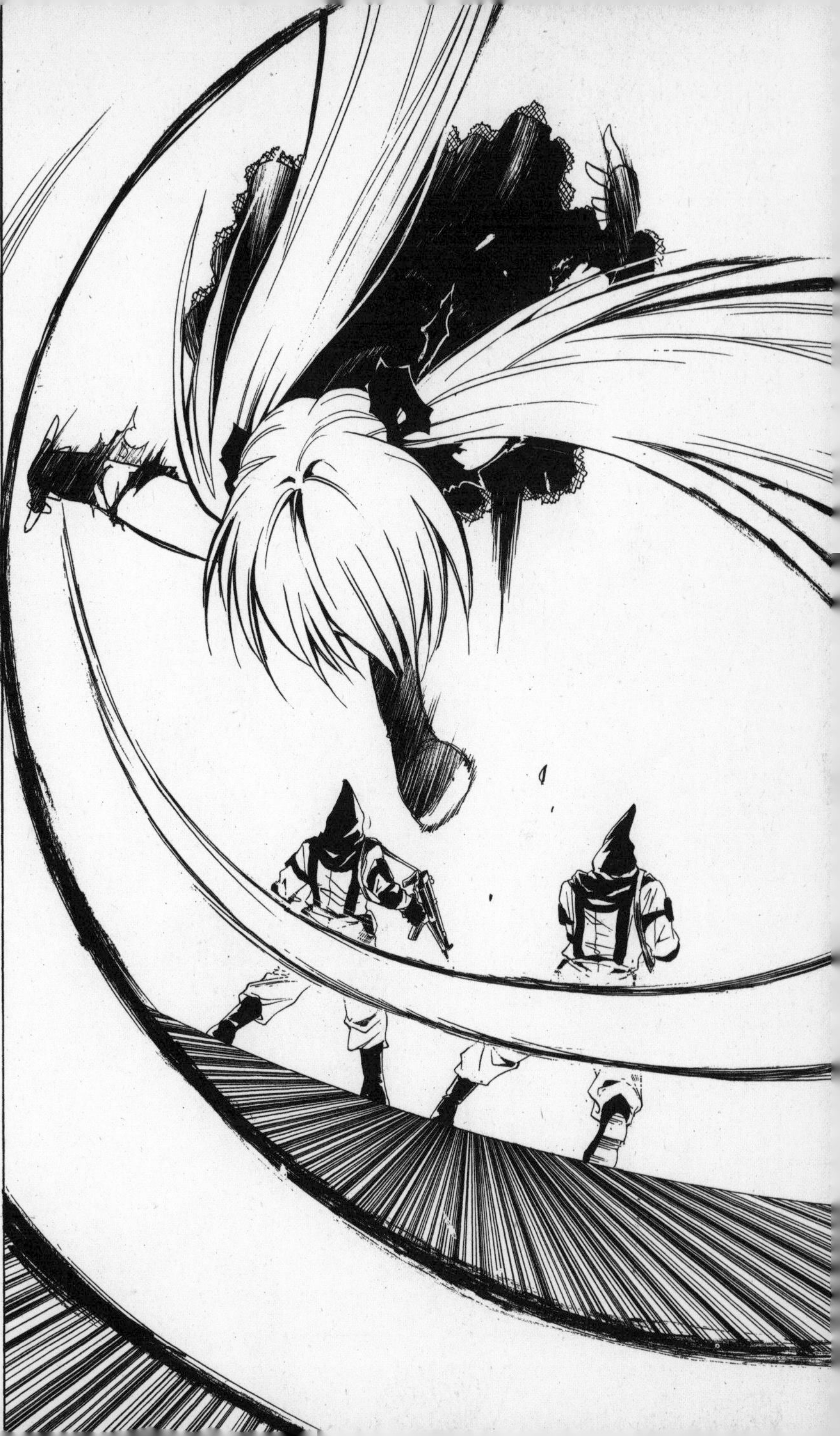

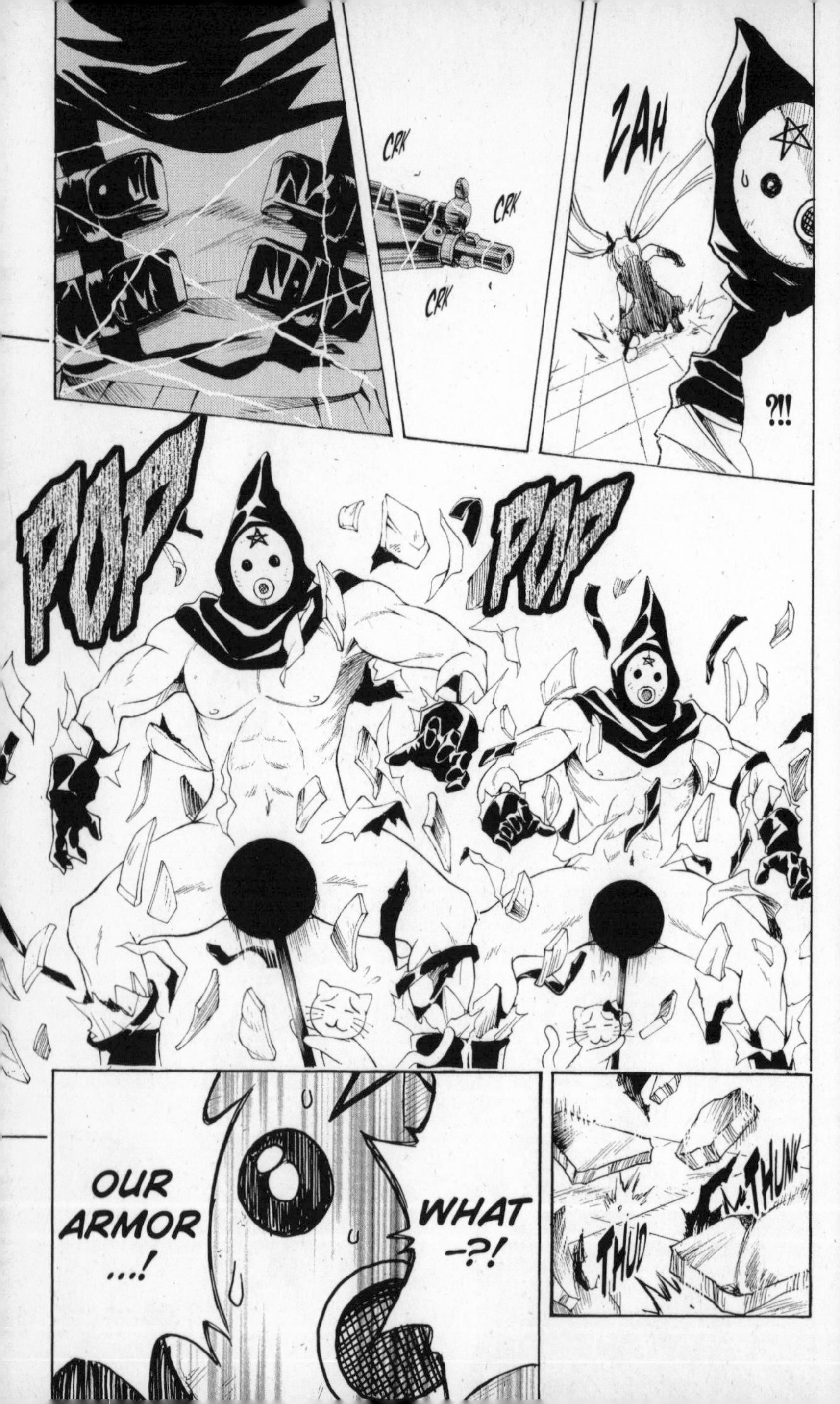
ZAH
?!!
CRK
CRK
CRK
POP
POP
THUNK
THUD
WHAT
-?!
OUR
ARMOR
...!

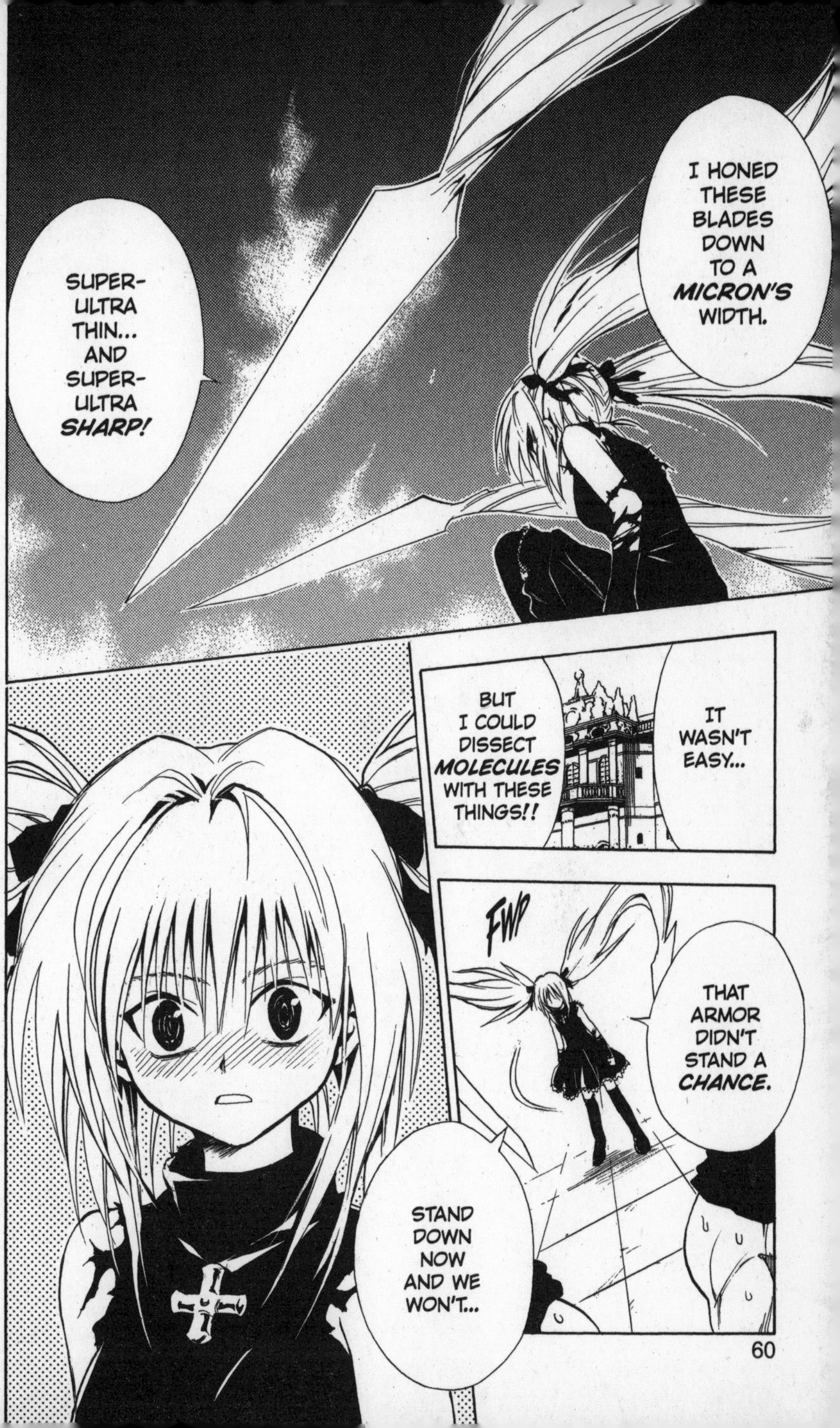
I HONED THESE BLADES DOWN TO A *MICRON'S* WIDTH.
SUPER-ULTRA THIN... AND SUPER-ULTRA *SHARP!*
IT WASN'T EASY...
BUT I COULD DISSECT *MOLECULES* WITH THESE THINGS!!
FWP
THAT ARMOR DIDN'T STAND A *CHANCE.*
STAND DOWN NOW AND WE WON'T...

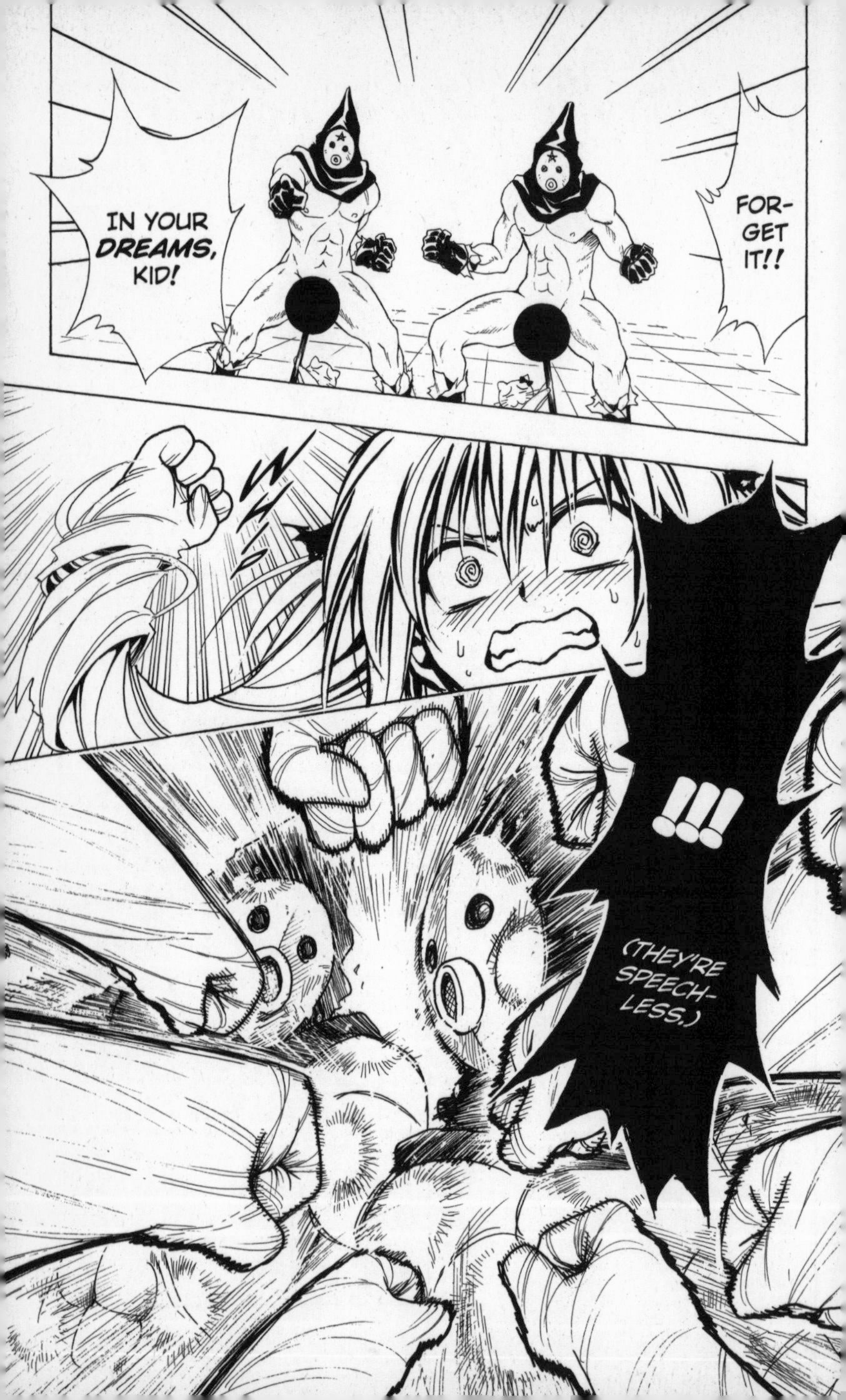
FOR-GET IT!!
IN YOUR DREAMS, KID!
!!!
(THEY'RE SPEECH-LESS.)

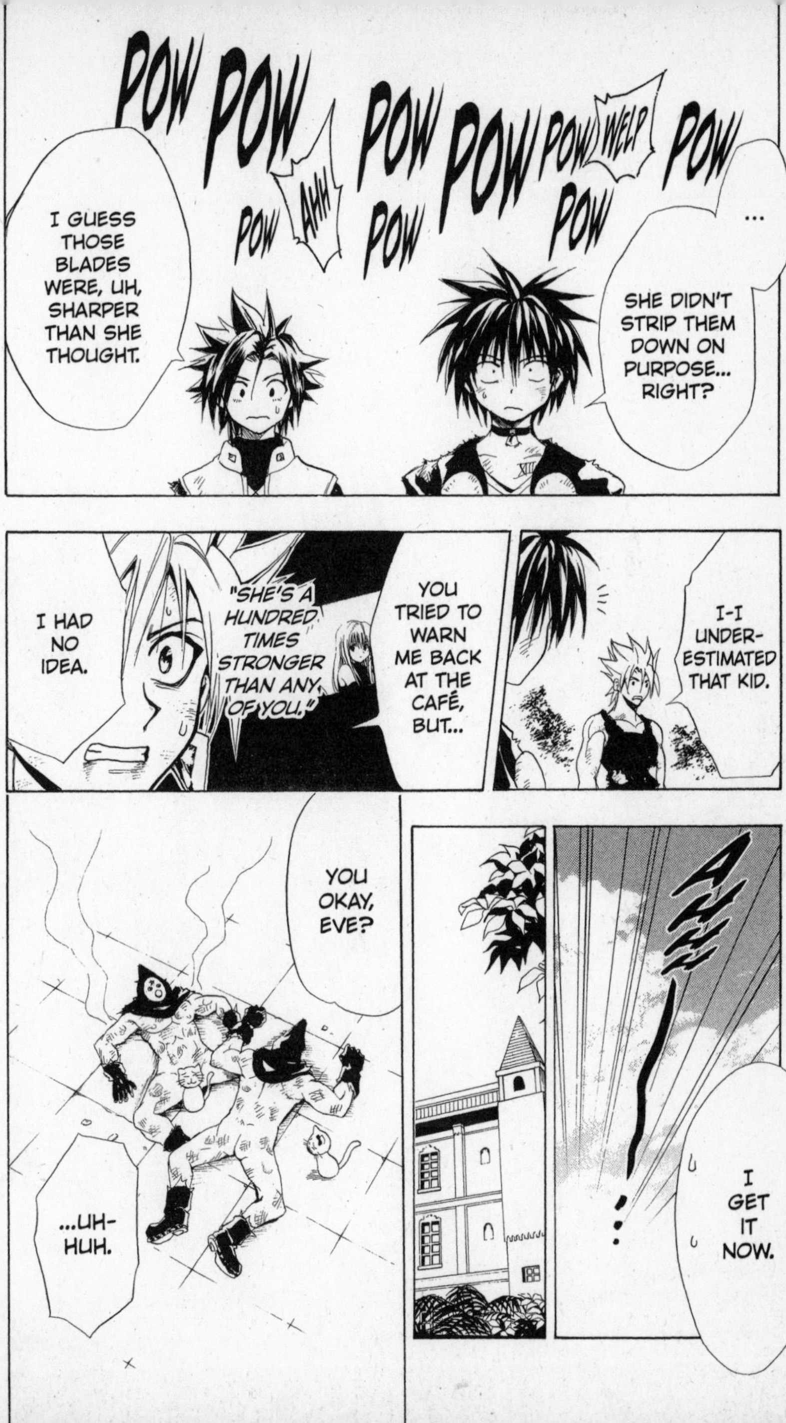
POW POW POW AHH POW POW POW POW WELP POW POW
...
SHE DIDN'T STRIP THEM DOWN ON PURPOSE... RIGHT?
I GUESS THOSE BLADES WERE, UH, SHARPER THAN SHE THOUGHT.
I-I UNDER-ESTIMATED THAT KID.
YOU TRIED TO WARN ME BACK AT THE CAFÉ, BUT...
"SHE'S A HUNDRED TIMES STRONGER THAN ANY OF YOU."
I HAD NO IDEA.
AHH—!!
I GET IT NOW.
YOU OKAY, EVE?
...UH-HUH.

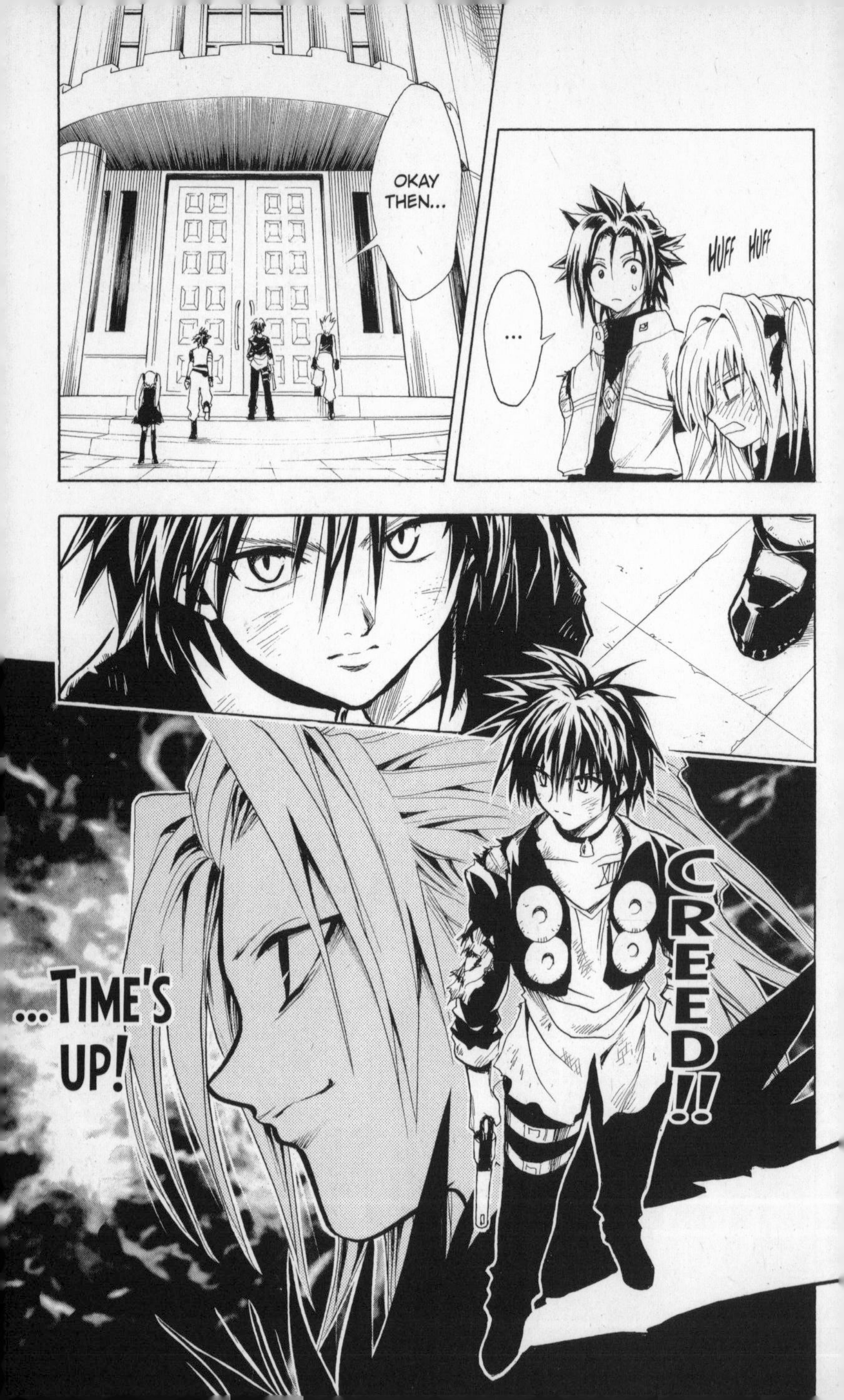
HUFF HUFF
...
OKAY THEN...
CREED!!
...TIME'S UP!

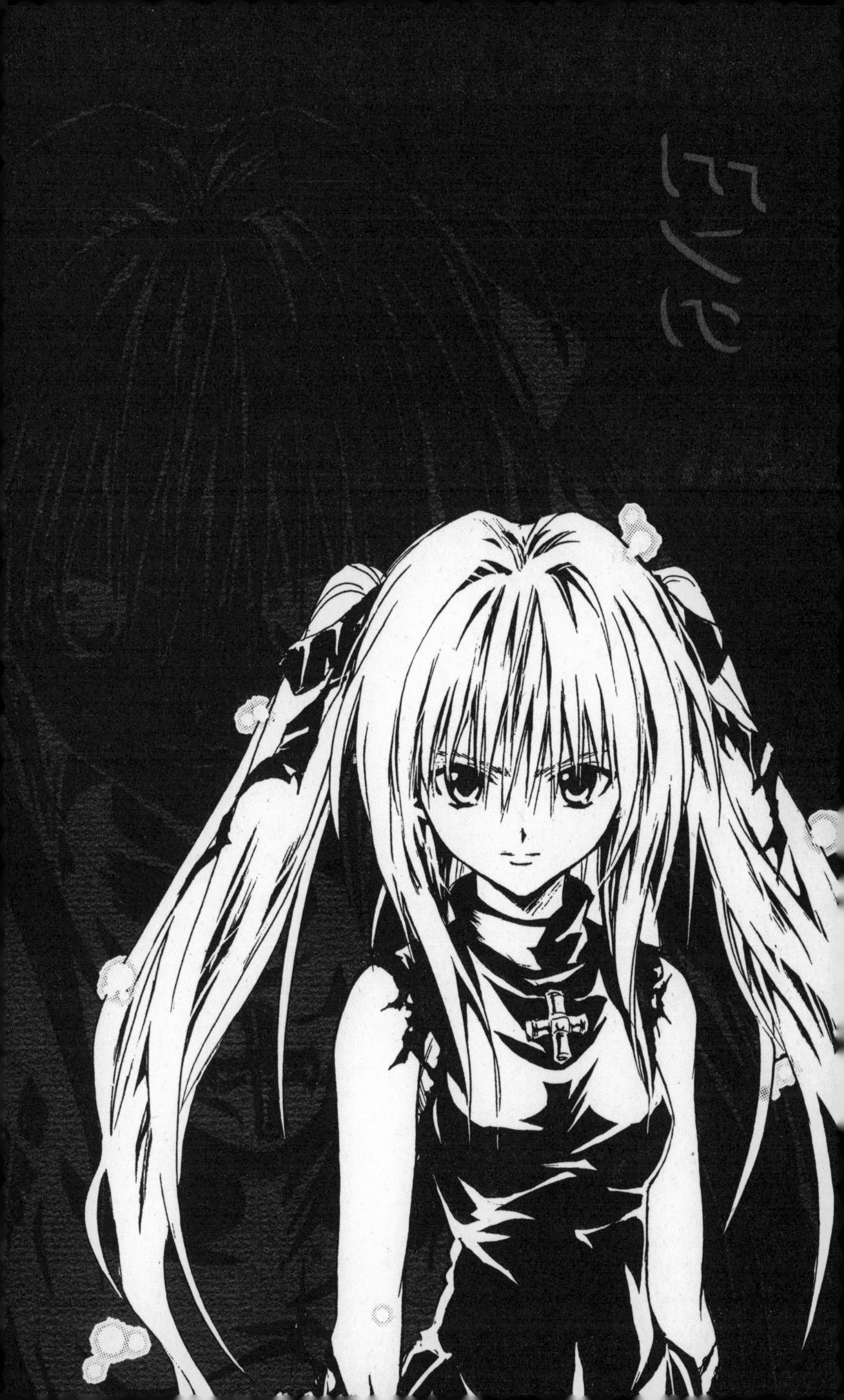

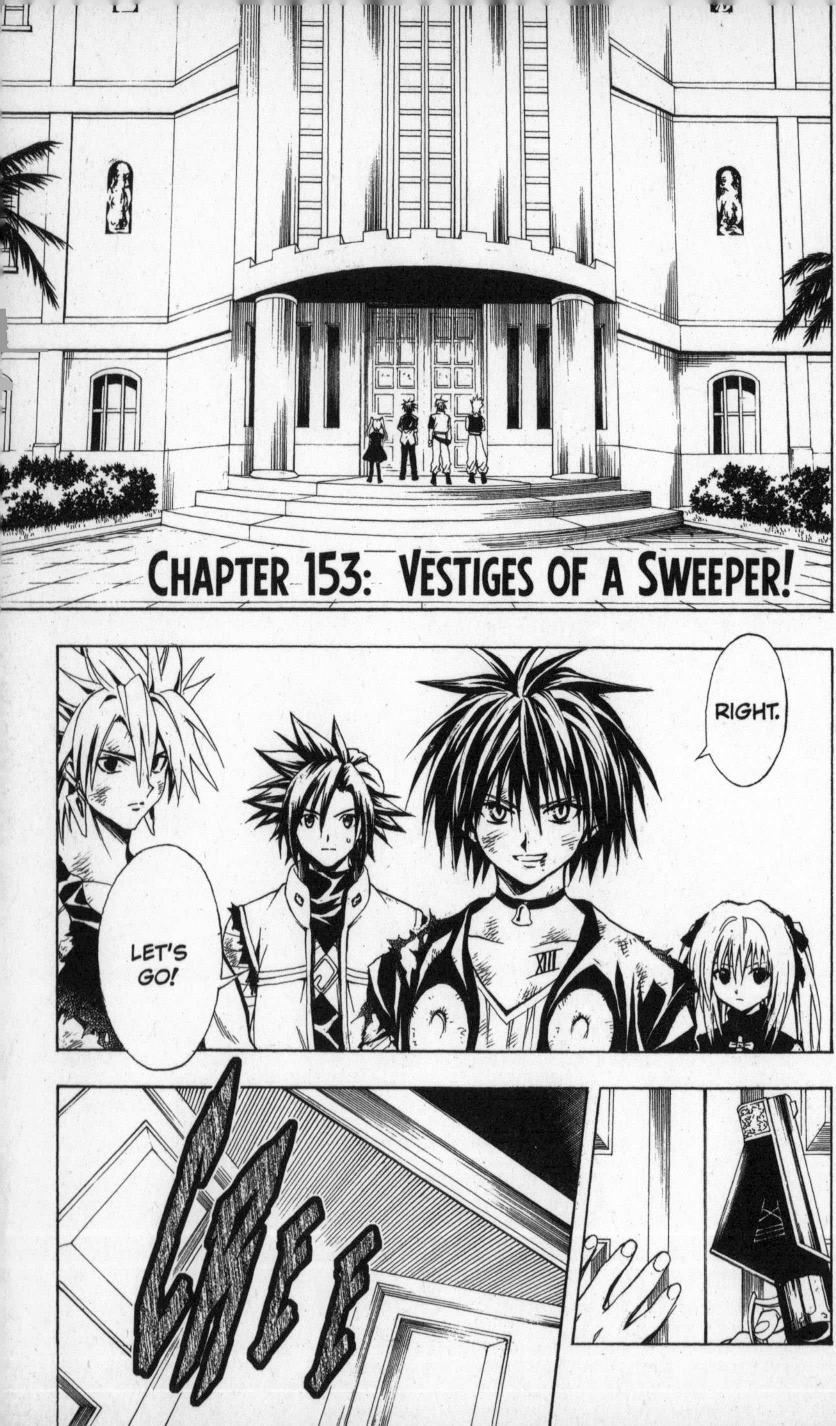
CHAPTER 153: VESTIGES OF A SWEEPER!
RIGHT.
LET'S GO!

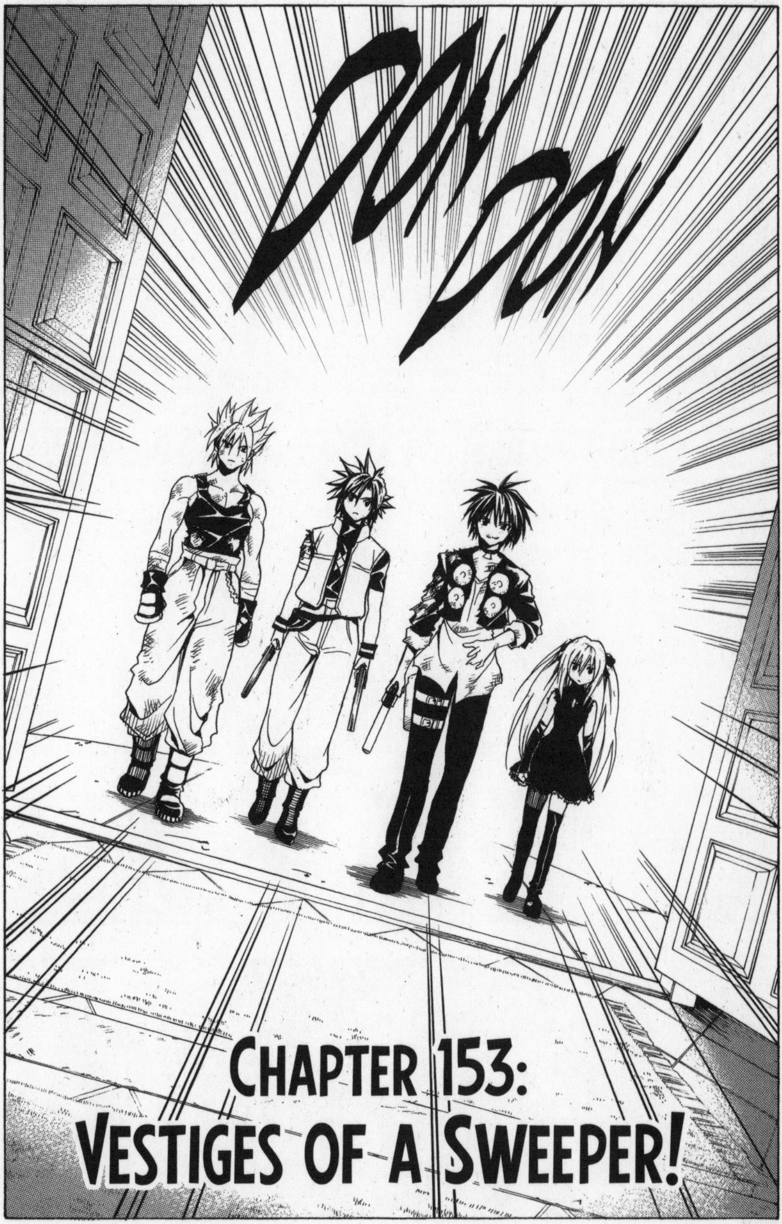
DON DON
CHAPTER 153:
VESTIGES OF A SWEEPER!

READ THIS WAY

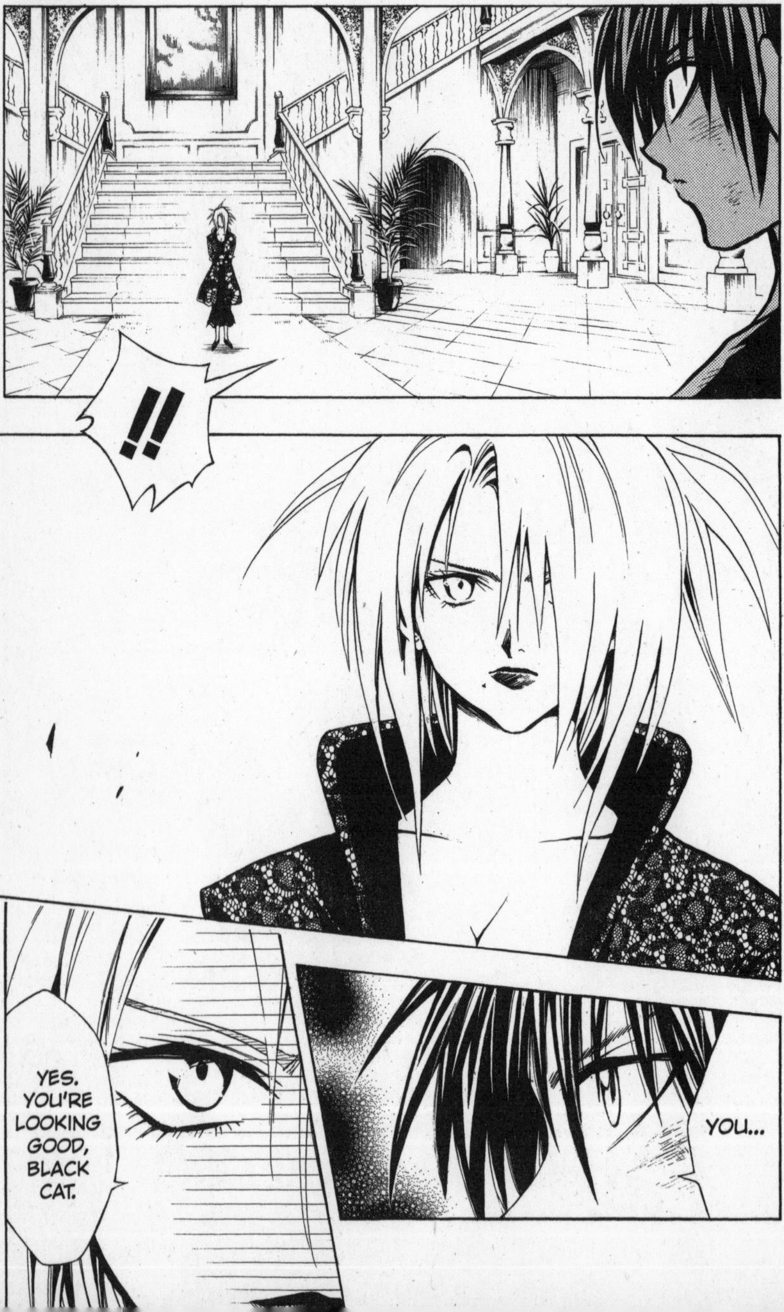
!!
YOU...
YES. YOU'RE LOOKING GOOD, BLACK CAT.

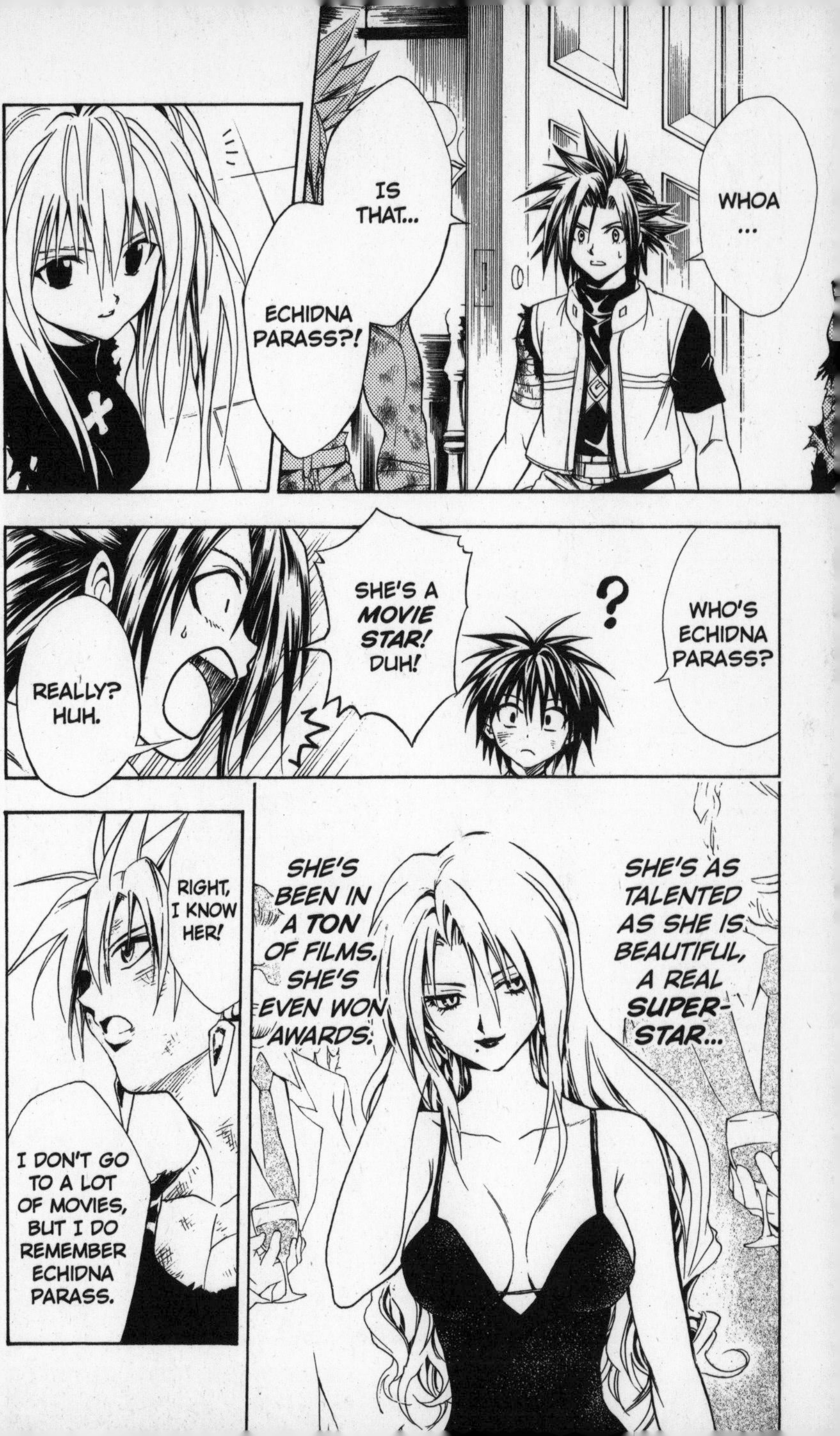
WHOA ...
IS THAT... ECHIDNA PARASS?!
WHO'S ECHIDNA PARASS?
SHE'S A *MOVIE STAR!* DUH!
REALLY? HUH.
SHE'S AS TALENTED AS SHE IS BEAUTIFUL, A REAL SUPER-STAR...
SHE'S BEEN IN A TON OF FILMS. SHE'S EVEN WON AWARDS.
RIGHT, I KNOW HER!
I DON'T GO TO A LOT OF MOVIES, BUT I DO REMEMBER ECHIDNA PARASS.

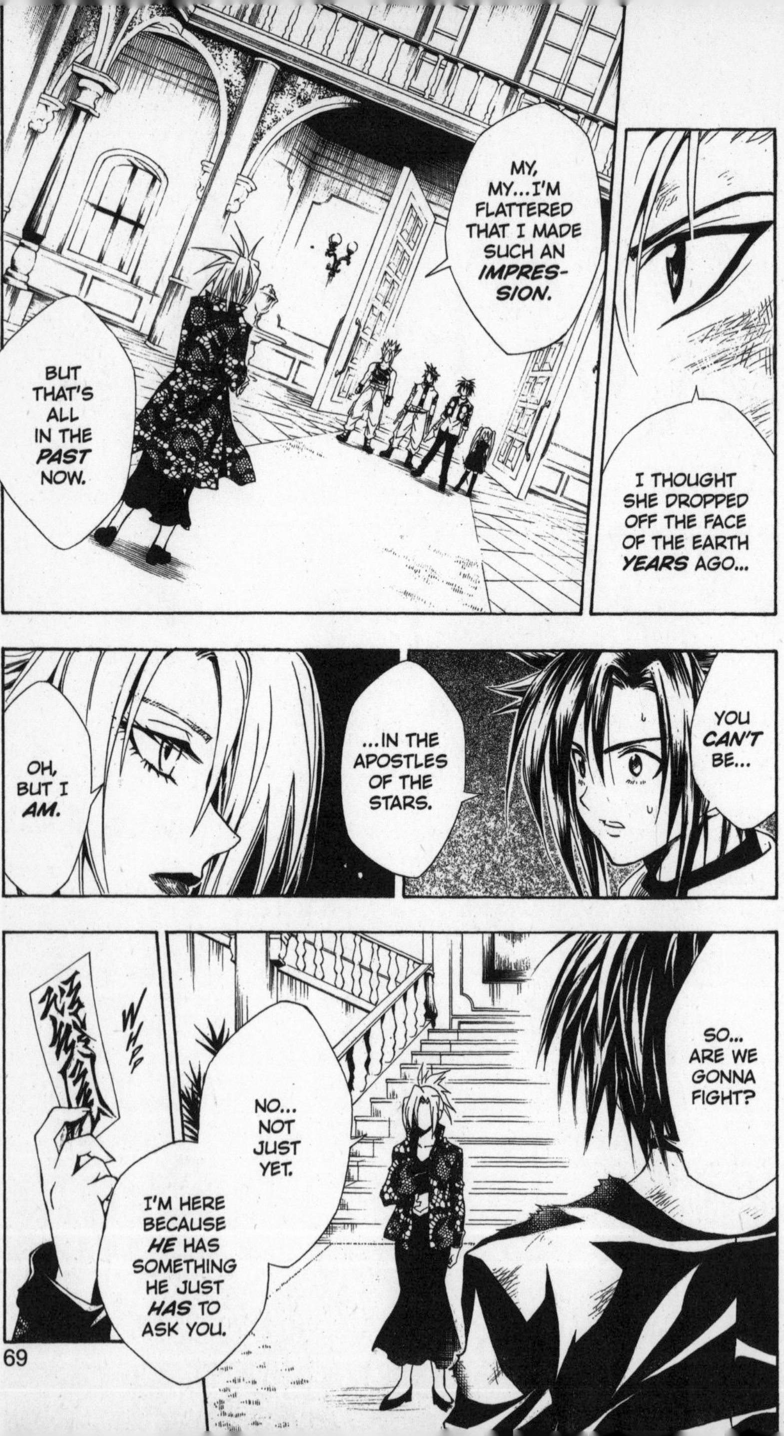
I THOUGHT SHE DROPPED OFF THE FACE OF THE EARTH YEARS AGO...
MY, MY...I'M FLATTERED THAT I MADE SUCH AN IMPRES-SION.
BUT THAT'S ALL IN THE PAST NOW.
YOU CAN'T BE...
...IN THE APOSTLES OF THE STARS.
OH, BUT I AM.
SO... ARE WE GONNA FIGHT?
NO... NOT JUST YET.
I'M HERE BECAUSE HE HAS SOMETHING HE JUST HAS TO ASK YOU.

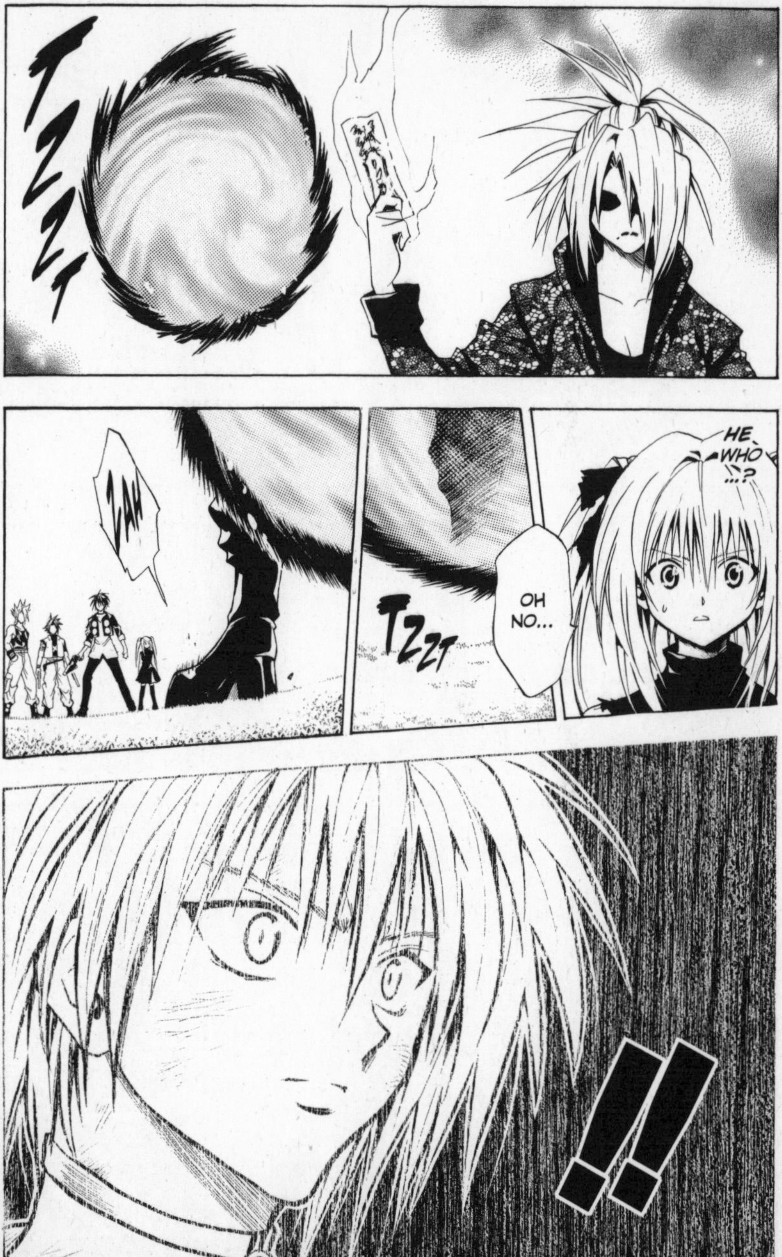
TZZZT
HE WHO ...?
OH NO...
TZZT
ZAH
!!

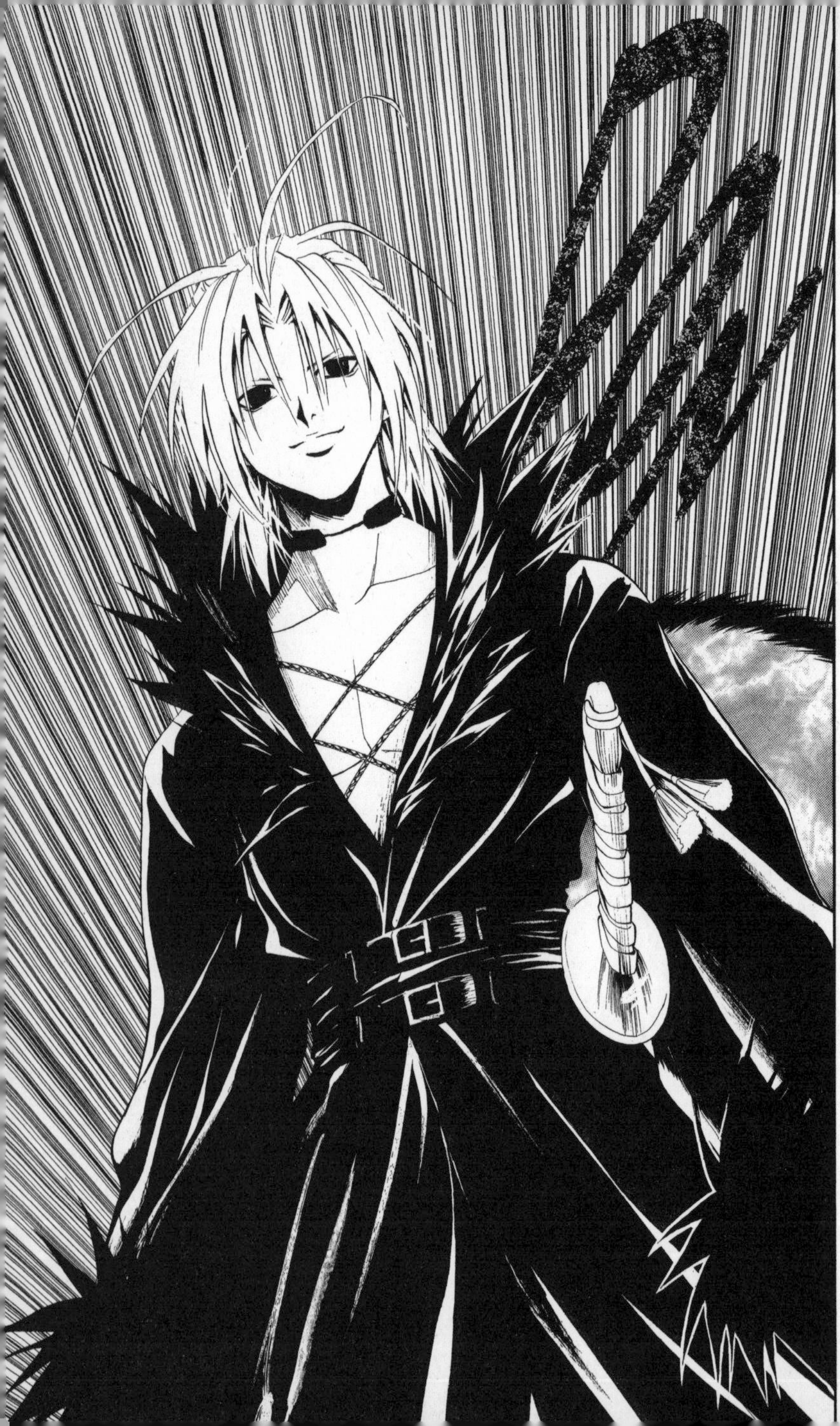

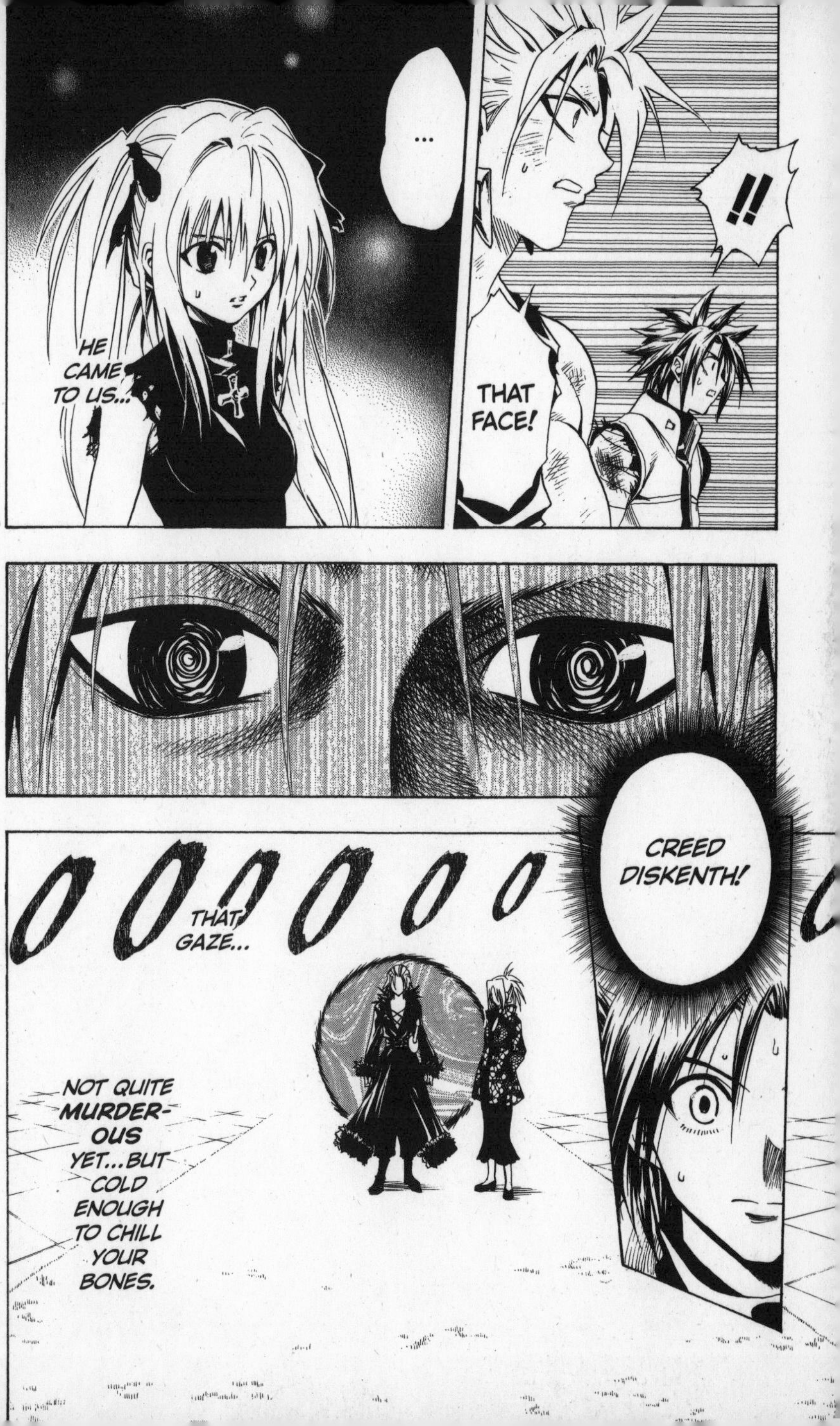
!!
THAT FACE!
...
HE CAME TO US...
CREED DISKENTH!
THAT GAZE...
NOT QUITE MURDEROUS YET...BUT COLD ENOUGH TO CHILL YOUR BONES.

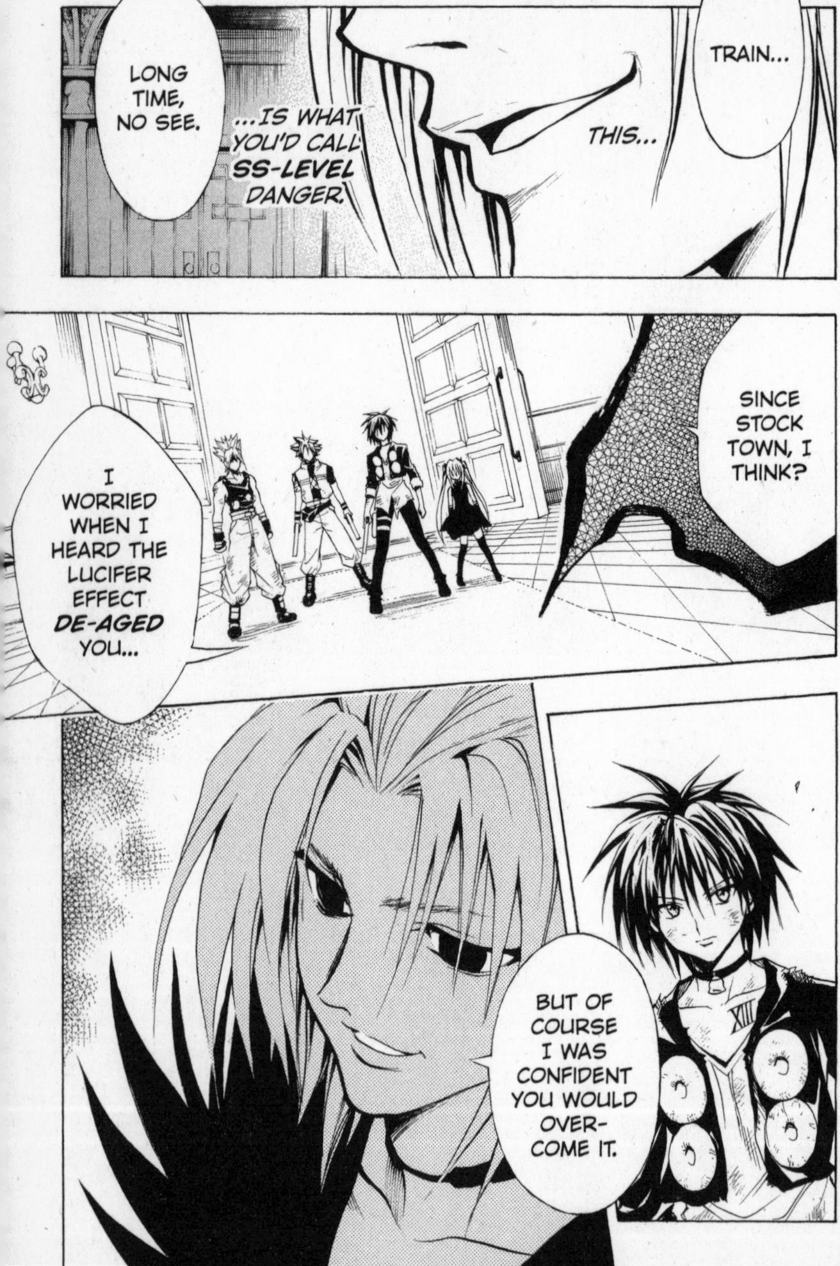
TRAIN...
THIS...
...IS WHAT YOU'D CALL SS-LEVEL DANGER.
LONG TIME, NO SEE.
SINCE STOCK TOWN, I THINK?
I WORRIED WHEN I HEARD THE LUCIFER EFFECT DE-AGED YOU...
BUT OF COURSE I WAS CONFIDENT YOU WOULD OVER-COME IT.

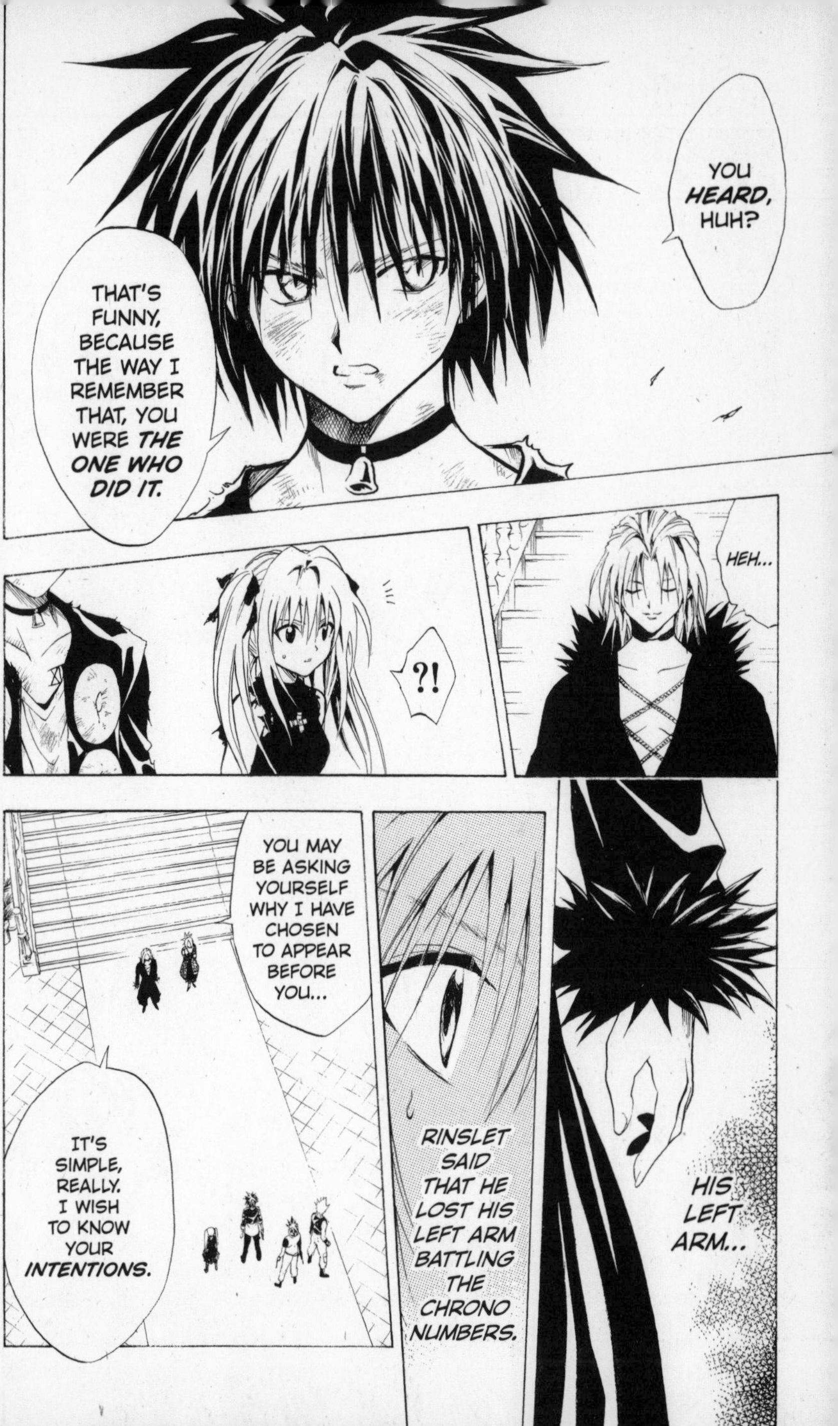
YOU HEARD, HUH?
THAT'S FUNNY, BECAUSE THE WAY I REMEMBER THAT, YOU WERE THE ONE WHO DID IT.
HEH...
?!
HIS LEFT ARM...
RINSLET SAID THAT HE LOST HIS LEFT ARM BATTLING THE CHRONO NUMBERS.
YOU MAY BE ASKING YOURSELF WHY I HAVE CHOSEN TO APPEAR BEFORE YOU...
IT'S SIMPLE, REALLY. I WISH TO KNOW YOUR INTENTIONS.

READ THIS WAY

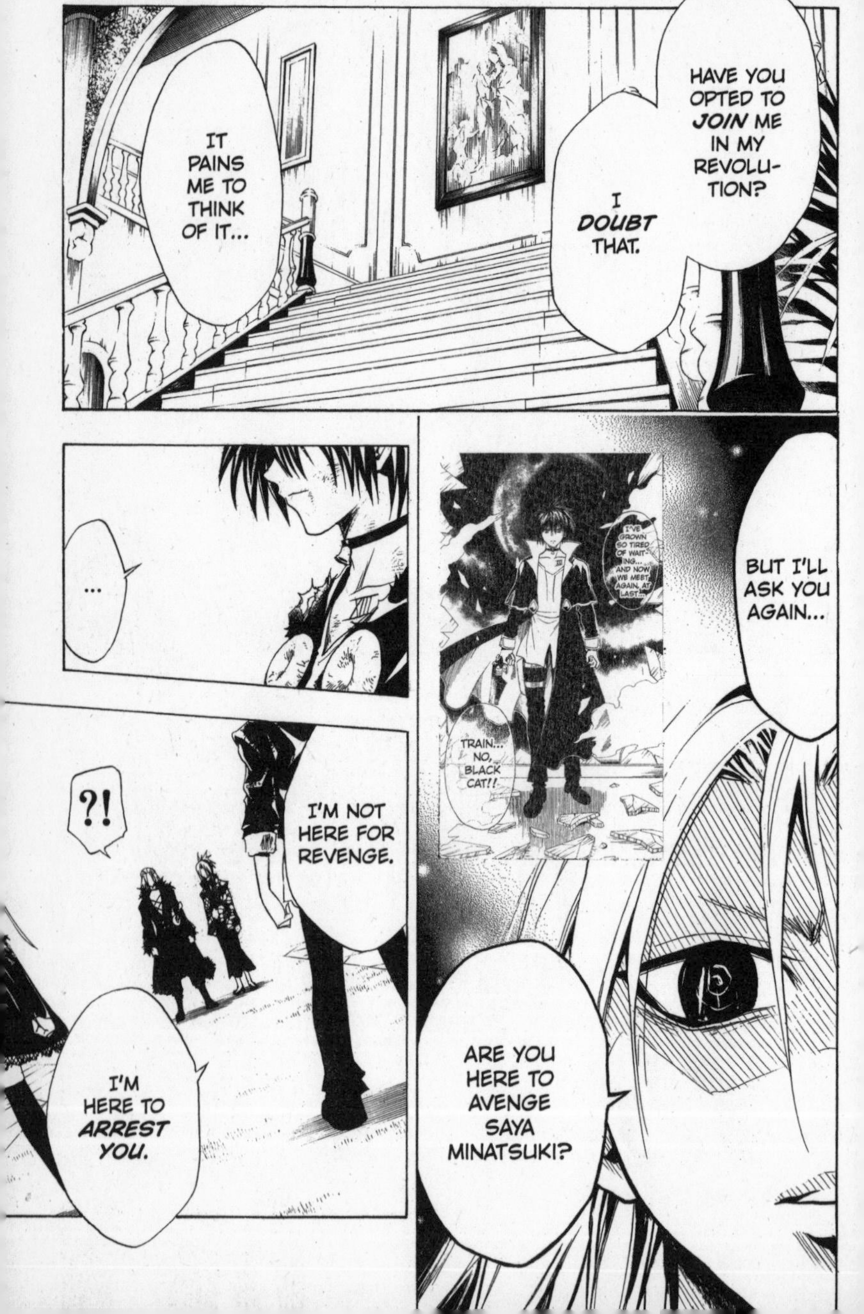
HAVE YOU OPTED TO *JOIN* ME IN MY REVOLUTION?
I *DOUBT* THAT.
IT PAINS ME TO THINK OF IT...
BUT I'LL ASK YOU AGAIN...
I'VE GROWN SO TIRED OF WAITING... AND NOW WE MEET AGAIN, AT LAST...
TRAIN... NO, BLACK CAT!!
ARE YOU HERE TO AVENGE SAYA MINATSUKI?
...
I'M NOT HERE FOR REVENGE.
?!
I'M HERE TO *ARREST YOU.*

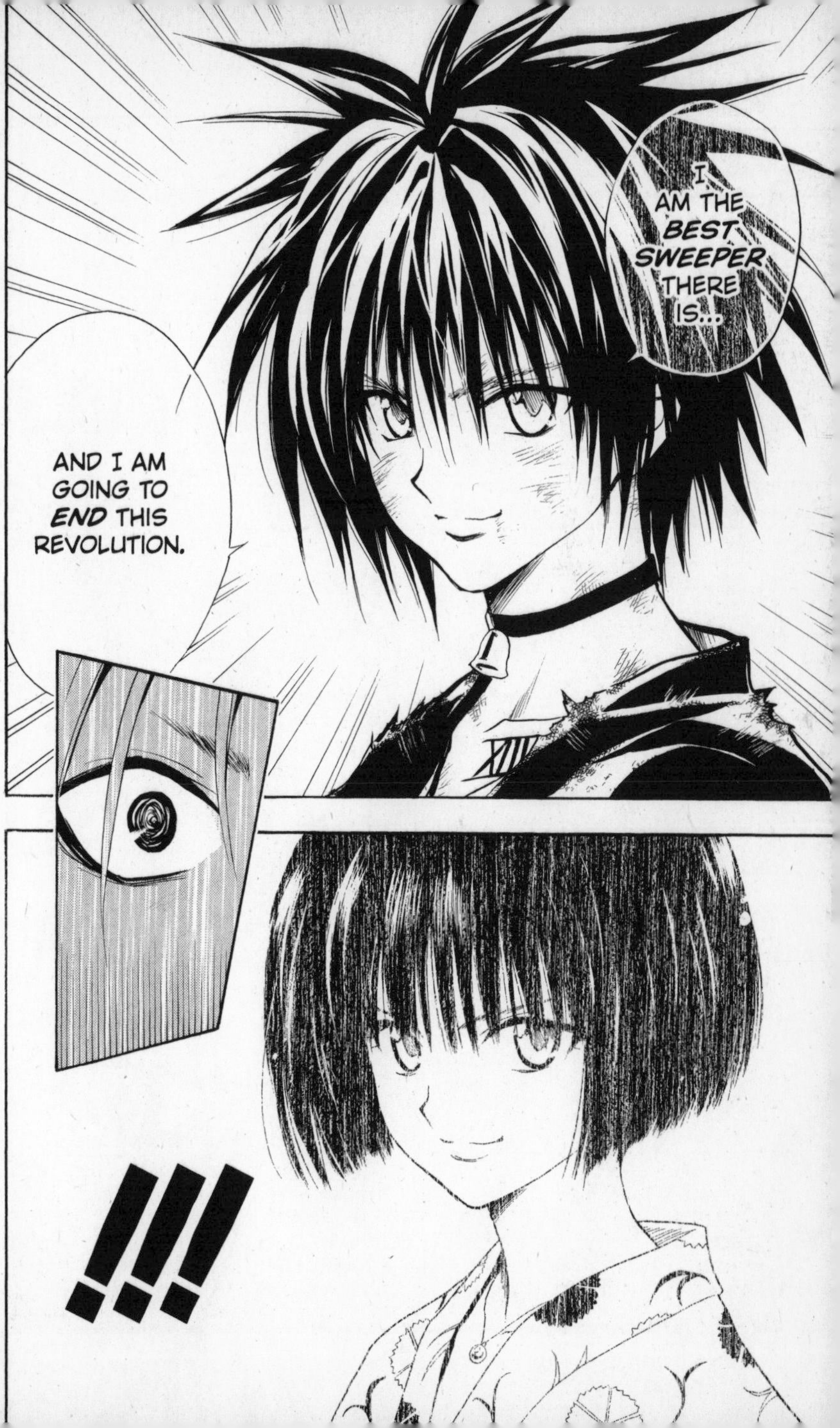
I AM THE BEST SWEEPER THERE IS...
AND I AM GOING TO END THIS REVOLUTION.
!!!

READ THIS WAY

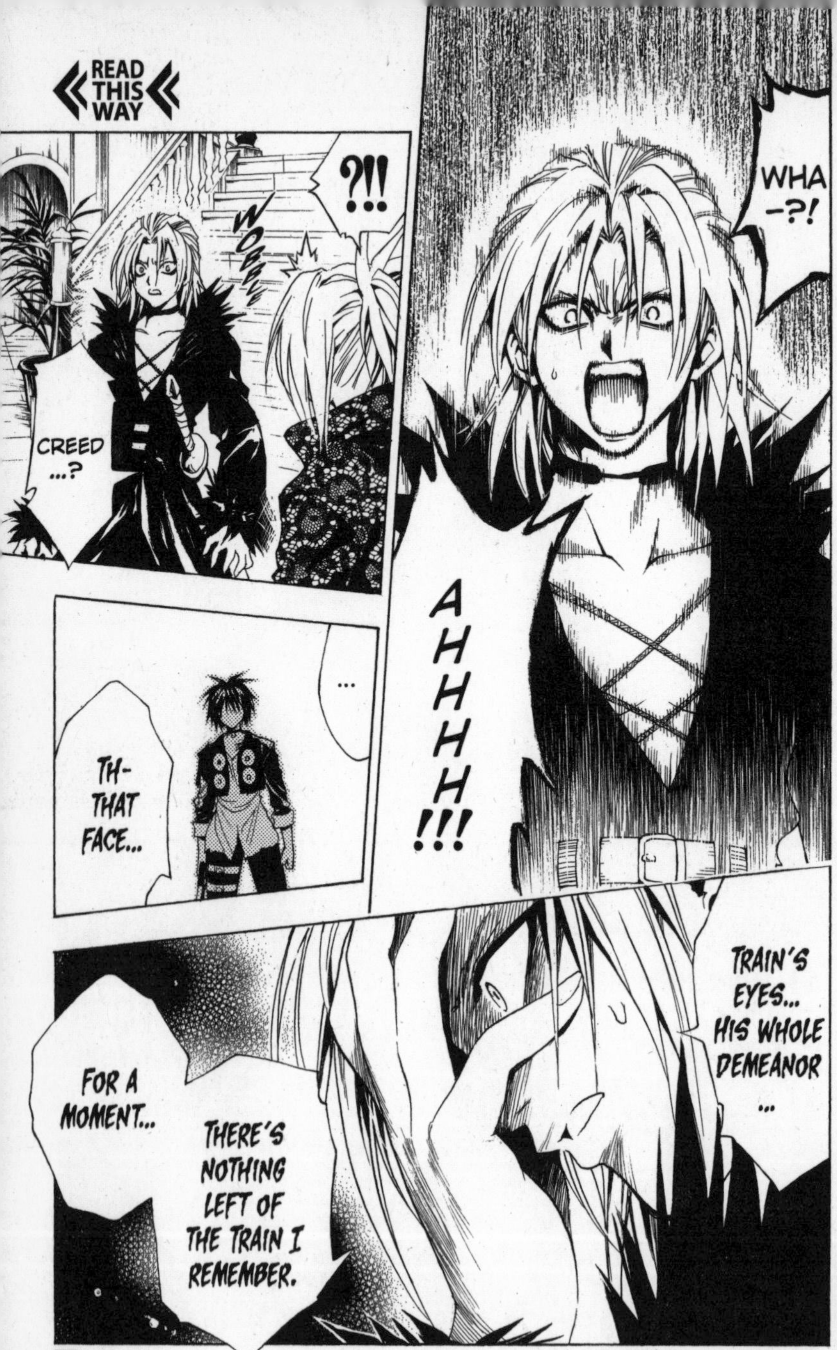

WHA-?!
AHHHH!!!
?!!
WOBBLE
CREED ...?
...
TH-THAT FACE...
TRAIN'S EYES... HIS WHOLE DEMEANOR...
FOR A MOMENT...
THERE'S NOTHING LEFT OF THE TRAIN I REMEMBER.

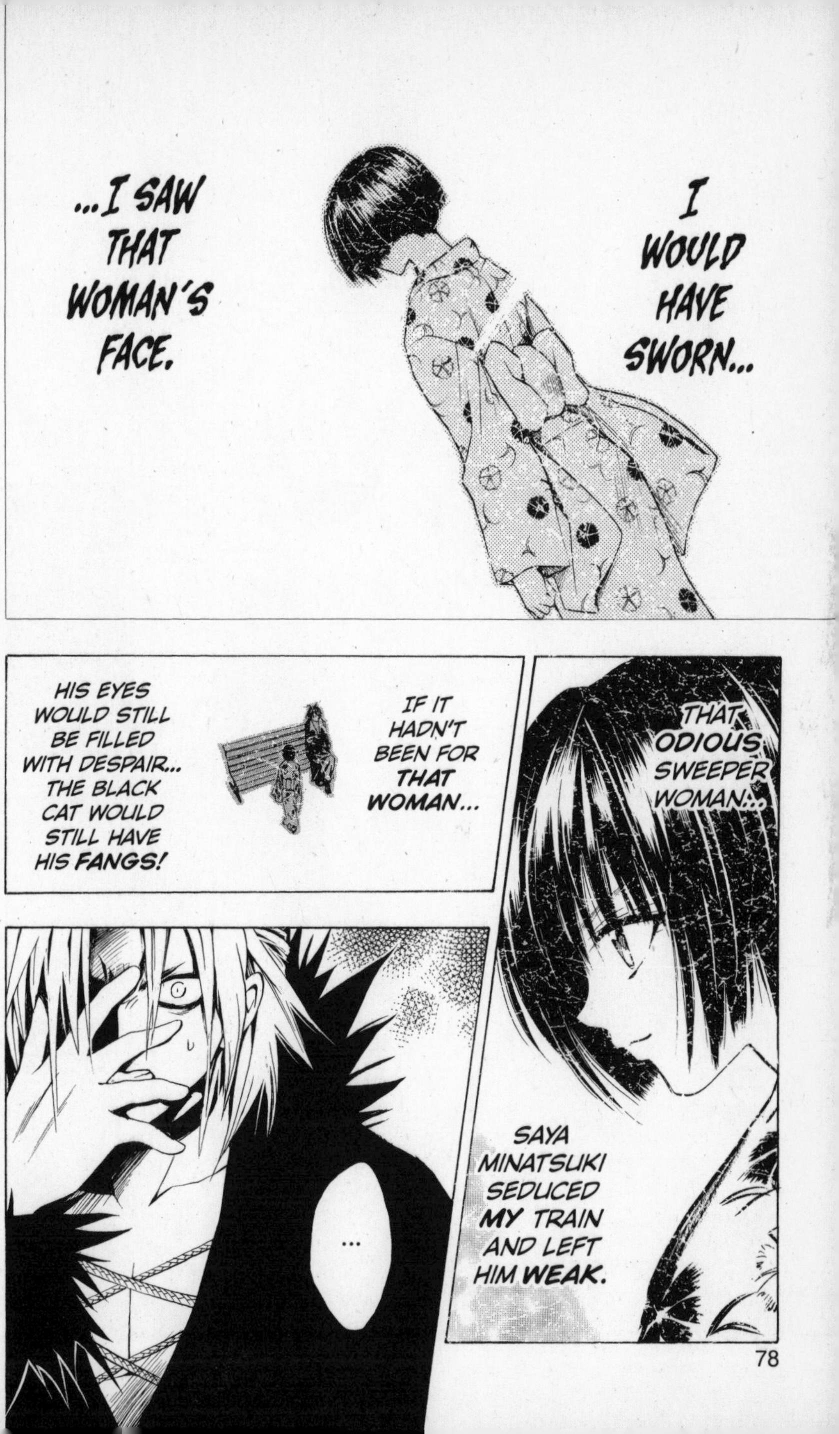
I WOULD HAVE SWORN...
...I SAW THAT WOMAN'S FACE.
THAT ODIOUS SWEEPER WOMAN...
SAYA MINATSUKI SEDUCED **MY** TRAIN AND LEFT HIM **WEAK.**
IF IT HADN'T BEEN FOR **THAT WOMAN...**
HIS EYES WOULD STILL BE FILLED WITH DESPAIR... THE BLACK CAT WOULD STILL HAVE HIS **FANGS!**
...

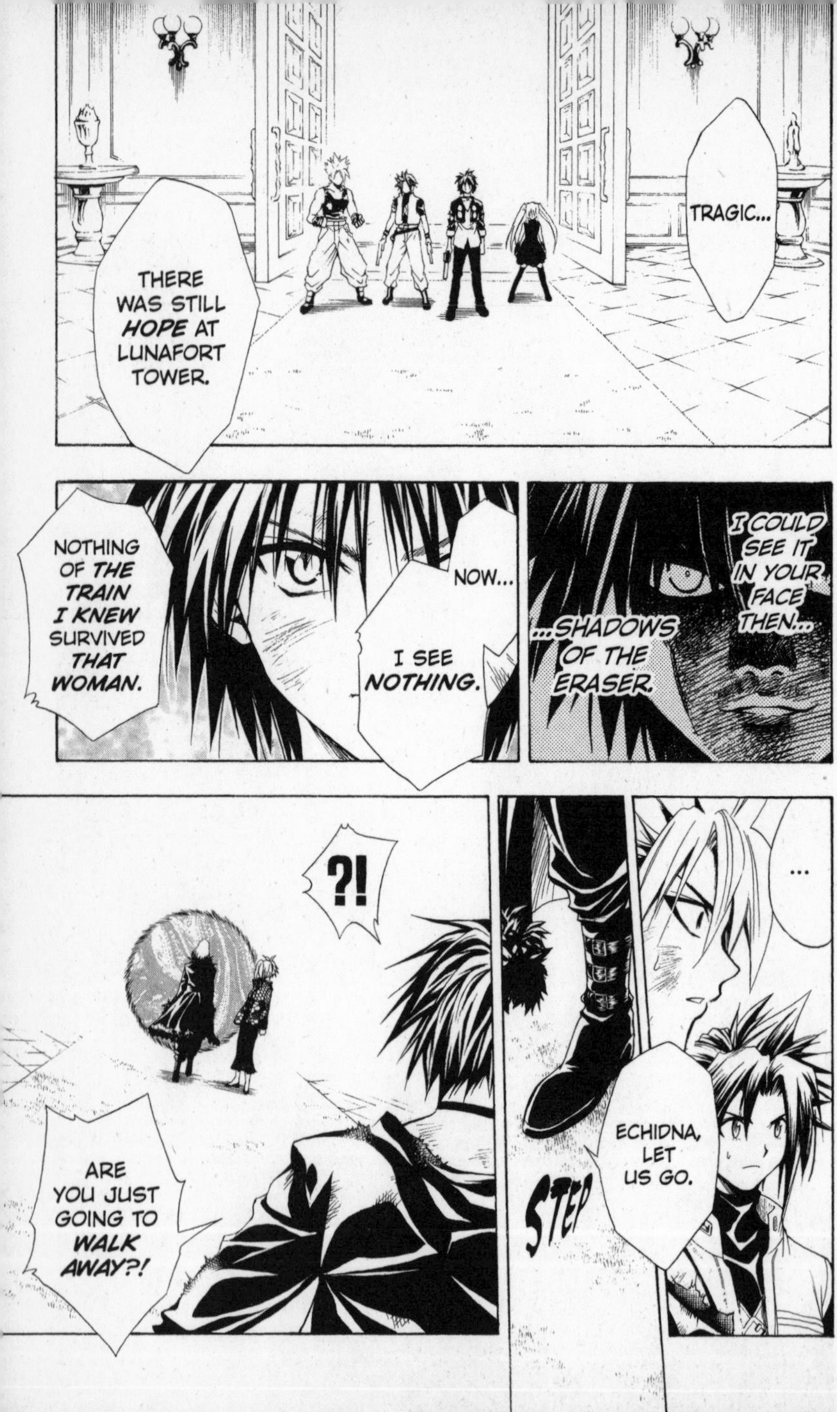
TRAGIC...
THERE WAS STILL HOPE AT LUNAFORT TOWER.
I COULD SEE IT IN YOUR FACE THEN...
...SHADOWS OF THE ERASER.
NOW...
I SEE NOTHING.
NOTHING OF THE TRAIN I KNEW SURVIVED THAT WOMAN.
...
ECHIDNA, LET US GO.
STEP
?!
ARE YOU JUST GOING TO WALK AWAY?!

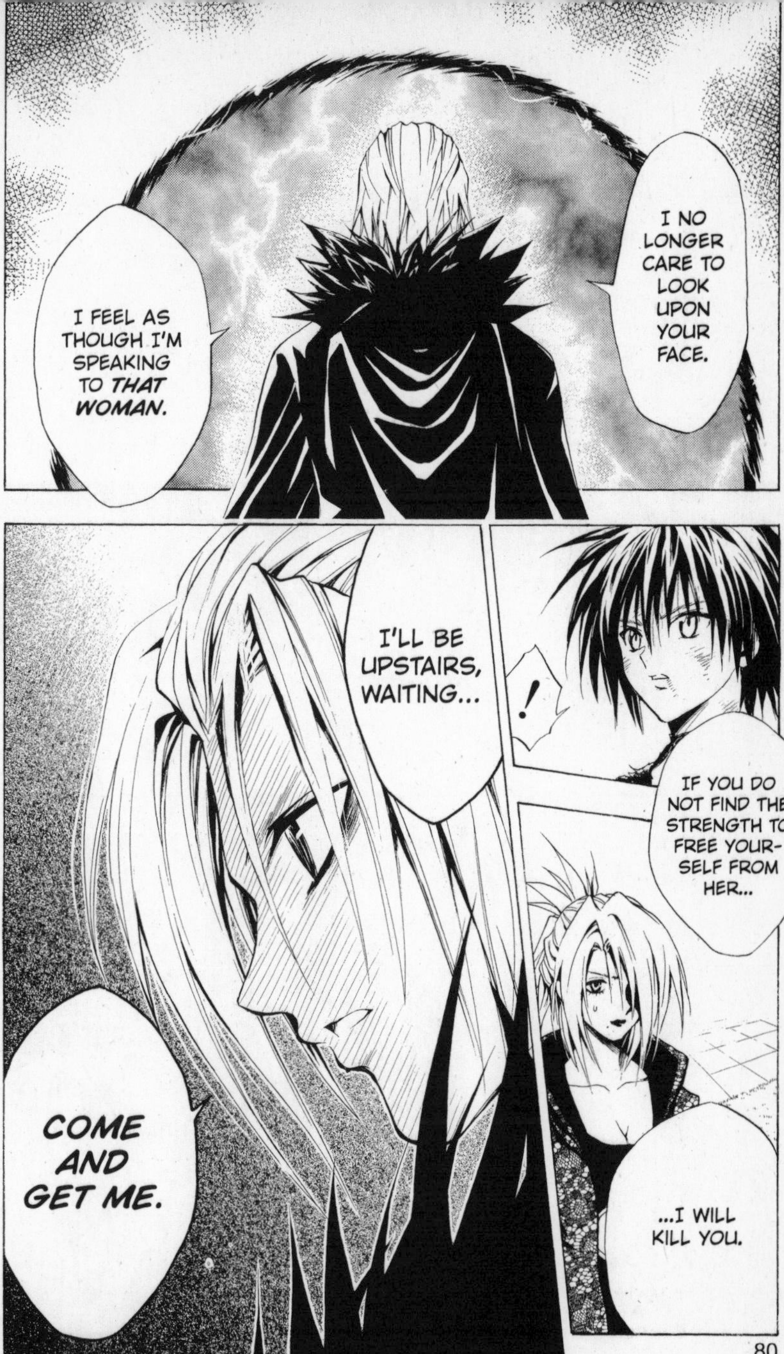
I NO LONGER CARE TO LOOK UPON YOUR FACE.
I FEEL AS THOUGH I'M SPEAKING TO *THAT WOMAN.*
!
IF YOU DO NOT FIND THE STRENGTH TO FREE YOUR-SELF FROM HER...
...I WILL KILL YOU.
I'LL BE UPSTAIRS, WAITING...
COME AND GET ME.

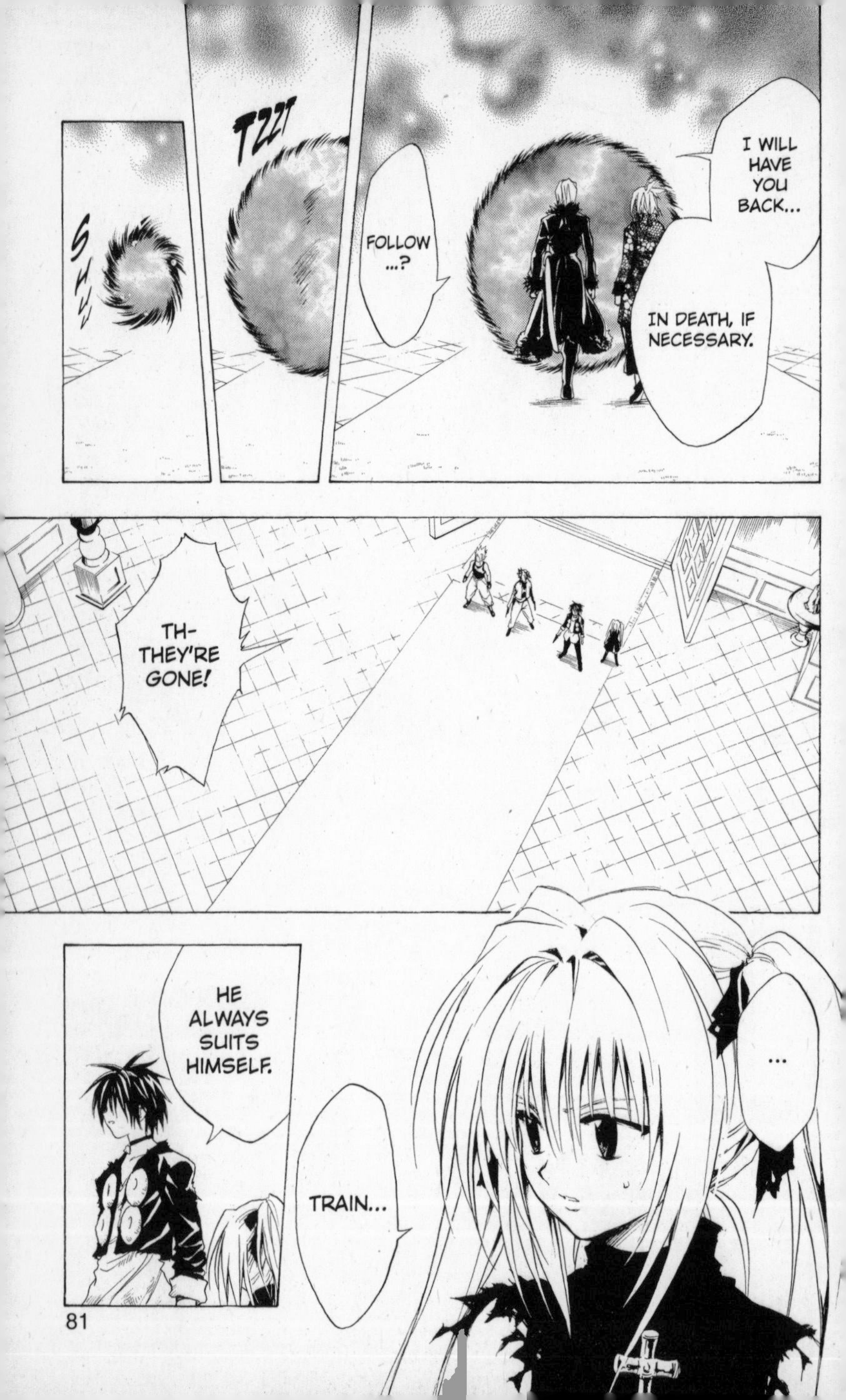
I WILL HAVE YOU BACK...
IN DEATH, IF NECESSARY.
FOLLOW ...?
TZZT
SHUU
TH- THEY'RE GONE!
...
TRAIN...
HE ALWAYS SUITS HIMSELF.

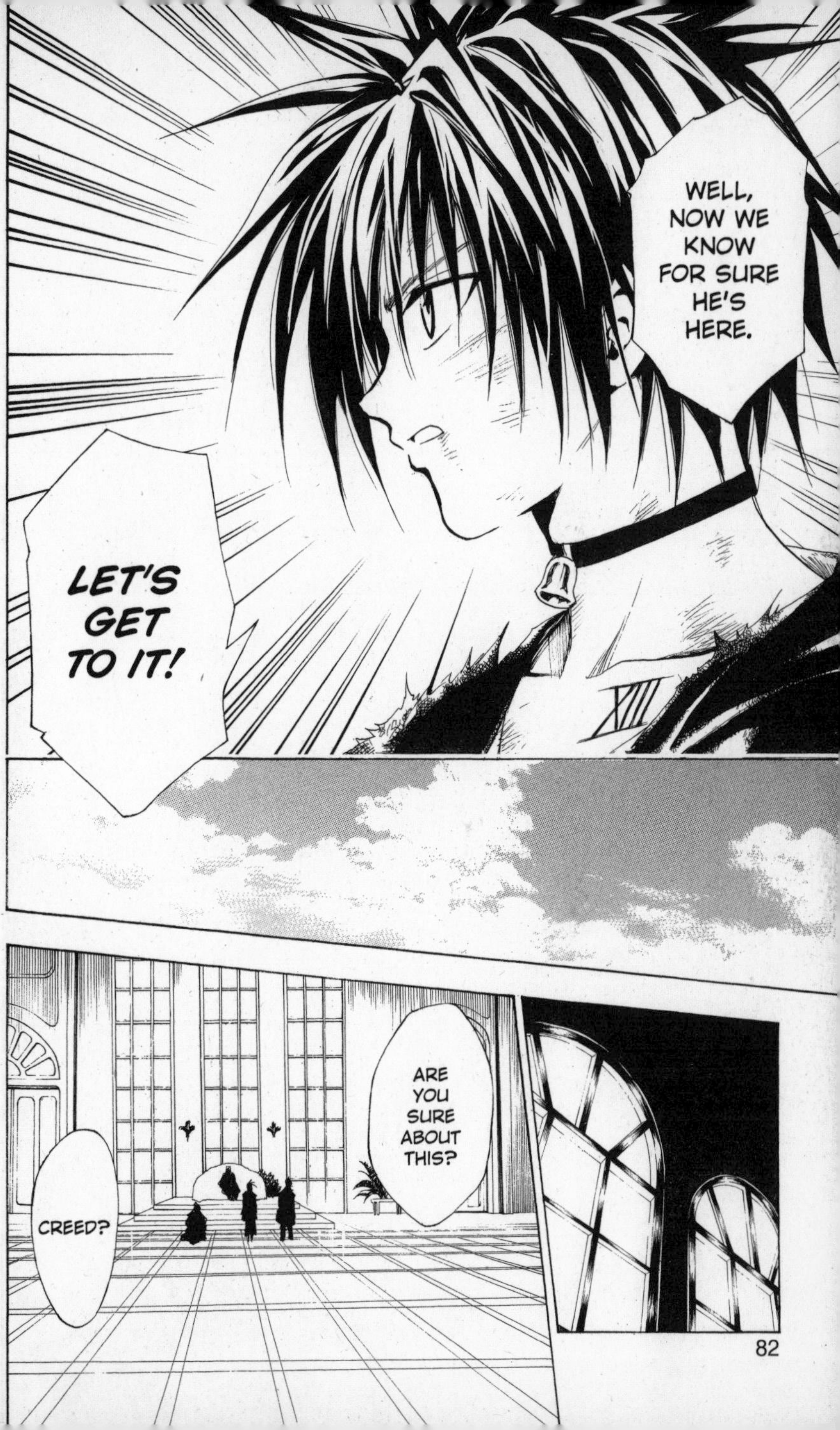

WELL, NOW WE KNOW FOR SURE HE'S HERE.
LET'S GET TO IT!
ARE YOU SURE ABOUT THIS?
CREED?

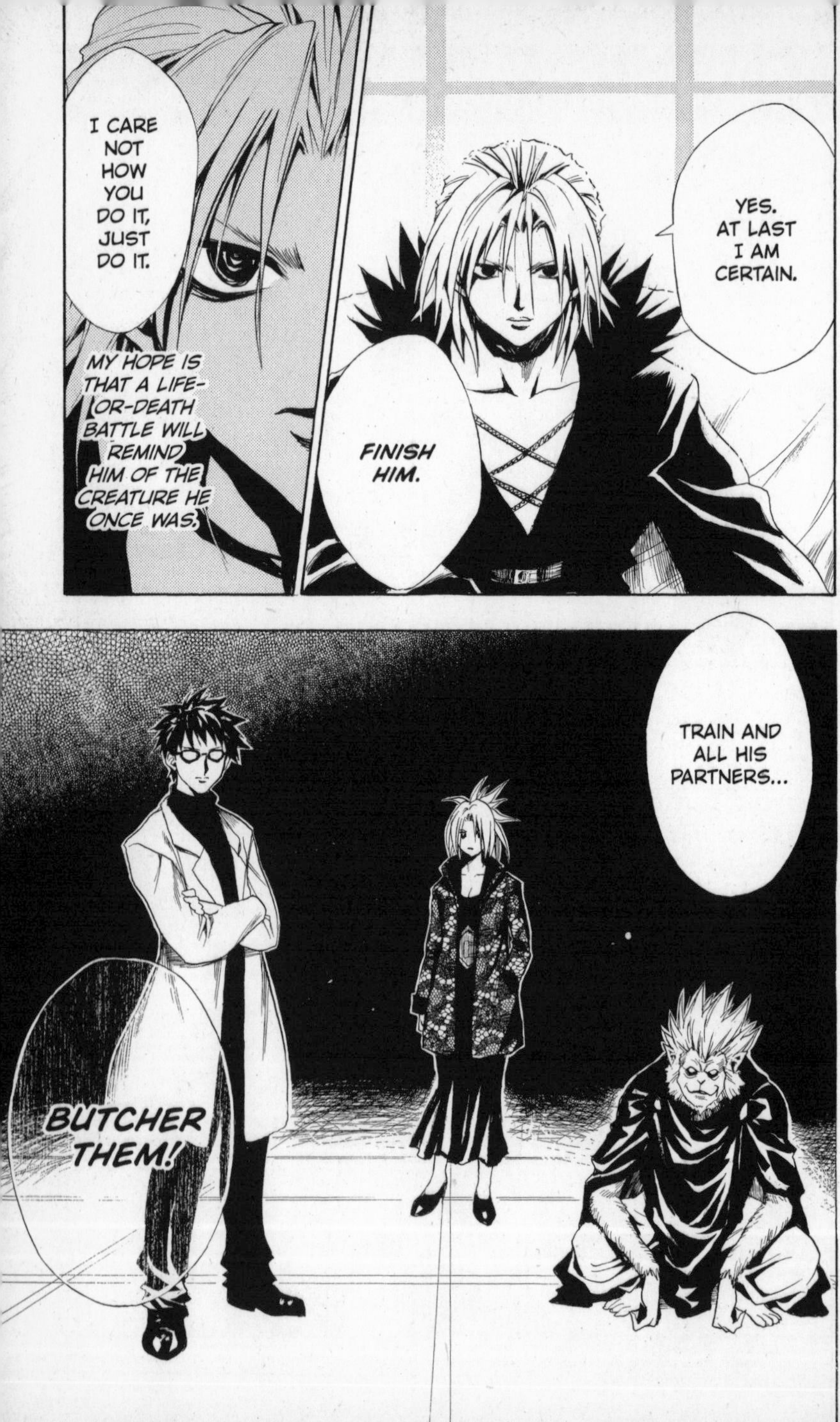
YES. AT LAST I AM CERTAIN.
FINISH HIM.
I CARE NOT HOW YOU DO IT, JUST DO IT.
MY HOPE IS THAT A LIFE-OR-DEATH BATTLE WILL REMIND HIM OF THE CREATURE HE ONCE WAS.
TRAIN AND ALL HIS PARTNERS...
BUTCHER THEM!

DANGER AT THE WORKPLACE! BY KATSUNORI HIDA

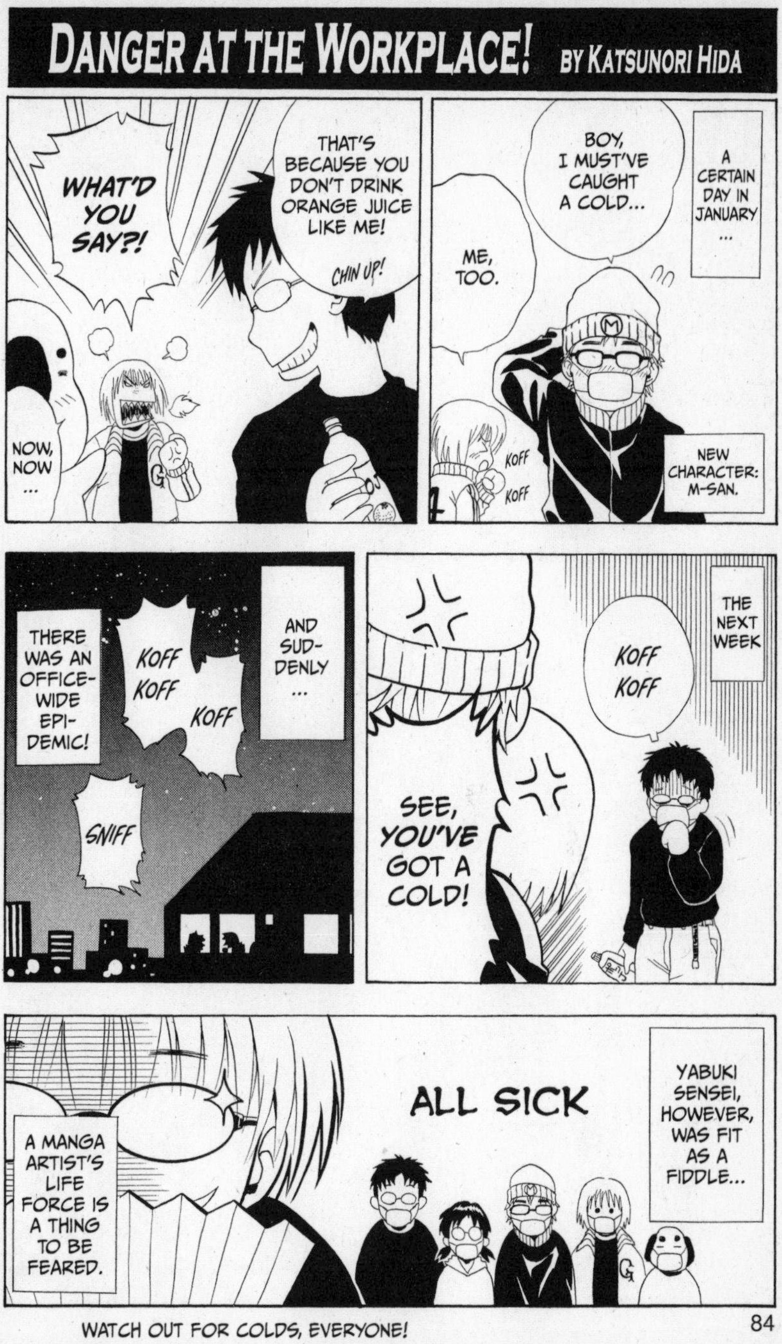
A CERTAIN DAY IN JANUARY ...
BOY, I MUST'VE CAUGHT A COLD...
ME, TOO.
NEW CHARACTER: M-SAN.
KOFF KOFF
THAT'S BECAUSE YOU DON'T DRINK ORANGE JUICE LIKE ME!
CHIN UP!
WHAT'D YOU SAY?!
NOW, NOW ...
THE NEXT WEEK
KOFF KOFF
SEE, YOU'VE GOT A COLD!
AND SUDDENLY ...
KOFF KOFF KOFF
THERE WAS AN OFFICE-WIDE EPIDEMIC!
SNIFF
YABUKI SENSEI, HOWEVER, WAS FIT AS A FIDDLE...
ALL SICK
A MANGA ARTIST'S LIFE FORCE IS A THING TO BE FEARED.

WATCH OUT FOR COLDS, EVERYONE!

Chapter 154: Coming Through!

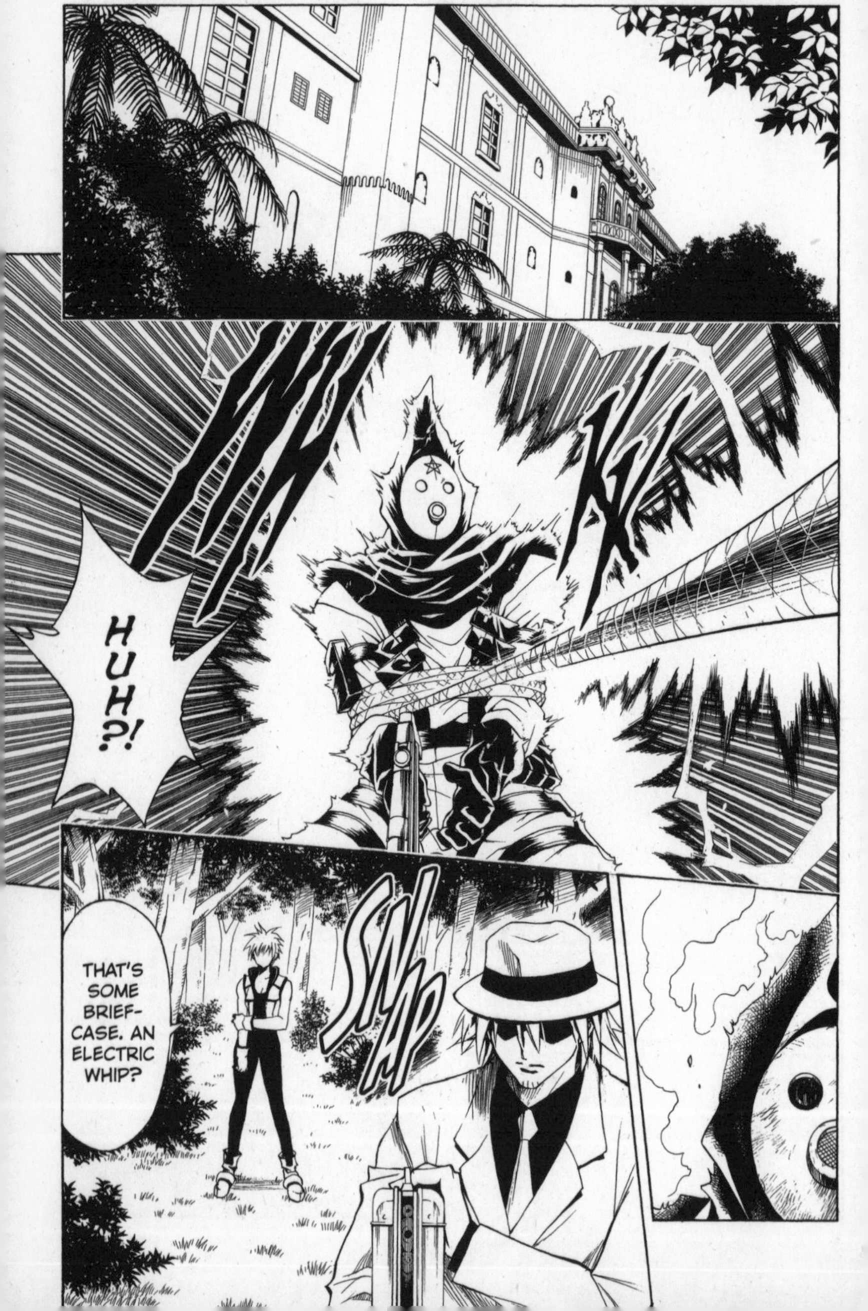
HUH?!
SNAP
THAT'S SOME BRIEF-CASE. AN ELECTRIC WHIP?

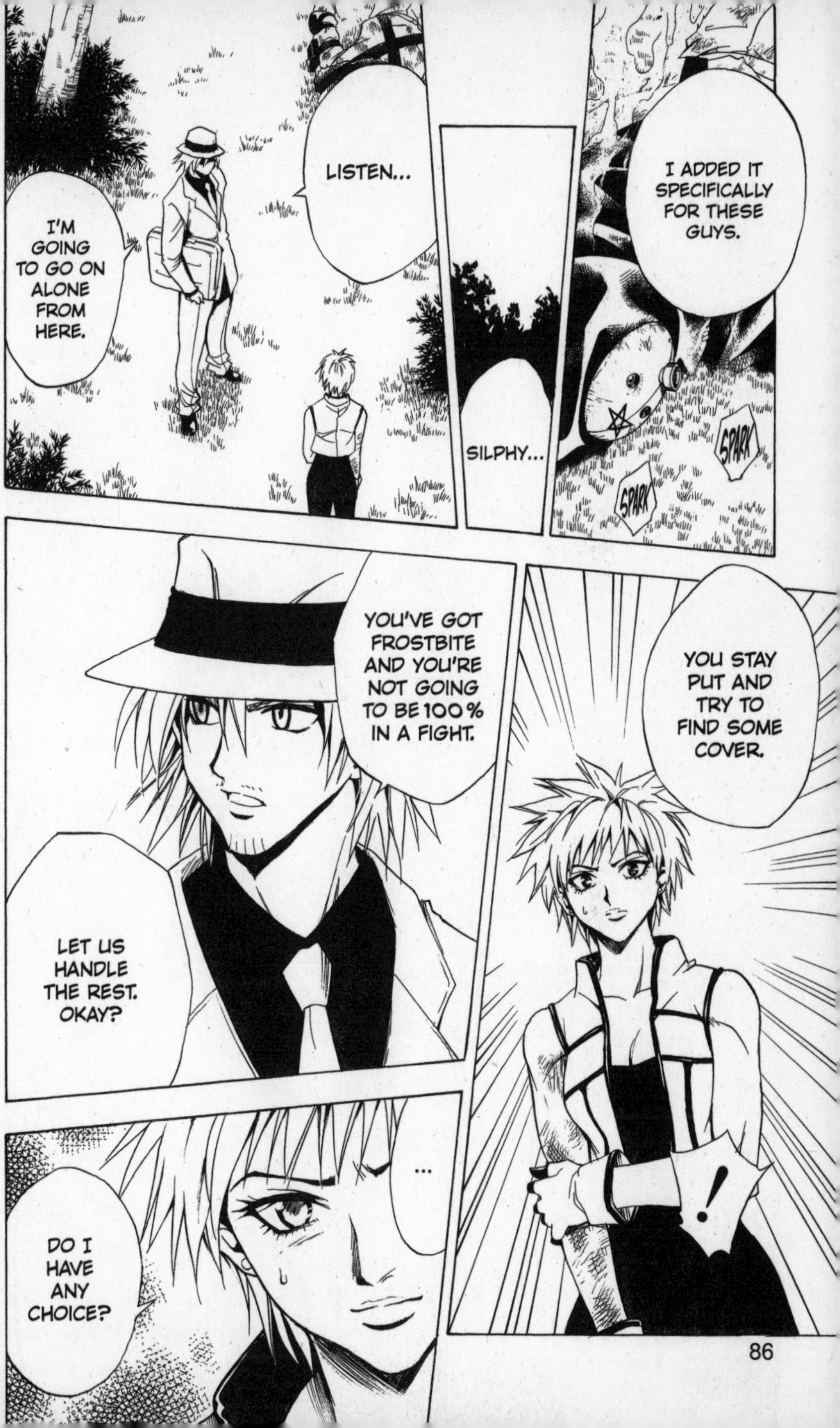
I ADDED IT SPECIFICALLY FOR THESE GUYS.
SPARK
SPARK
SILPHY...
LISTEN...
I'M GOING TO GO ON ALONE FROM HERE.
YOU STAY PUT AND TRY TO FIND SOME COVER.
!
YOU'VE GOT FROSTBITE AND YOU'RE NOT GOING TO BE 100% IN A FIGHT.
LET US HANDLE THE REST. OKAY?
...
DO I HAVE ANY CHOICE?

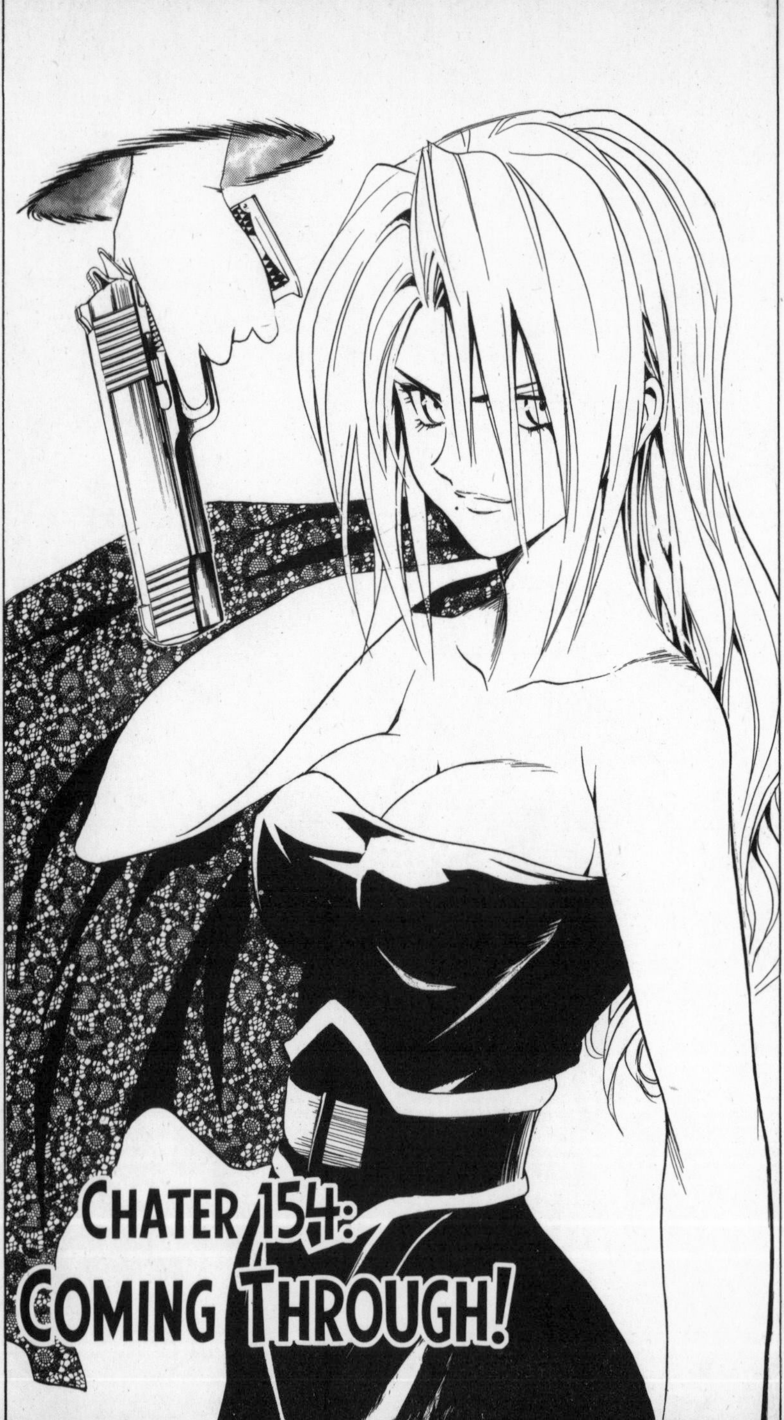
CHATER 154:
COMING THROUGH!

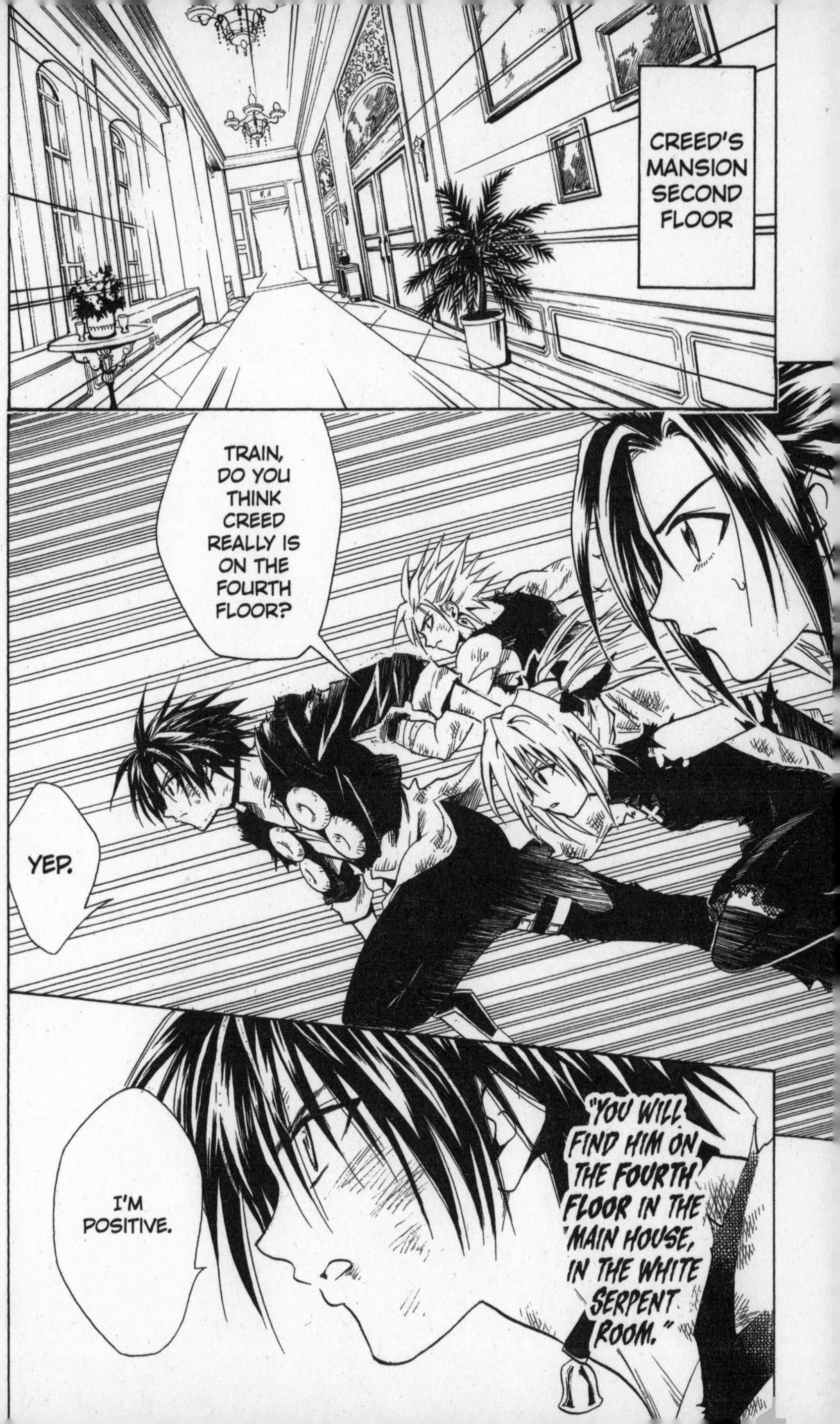
CREED'S MANSION SECOND FLOOR
TRAIN, DO YOU THINK CREED REALLY IS ON THE FOURTH FLOOR?
YEP.
"YOU WILL FIND HIM ON THE FOURTH FLOOR IN THE MAIN HOUSE, IN THE WHITE SERPENT ROOM."
I'M POSITIVE.

READ THIS WAY

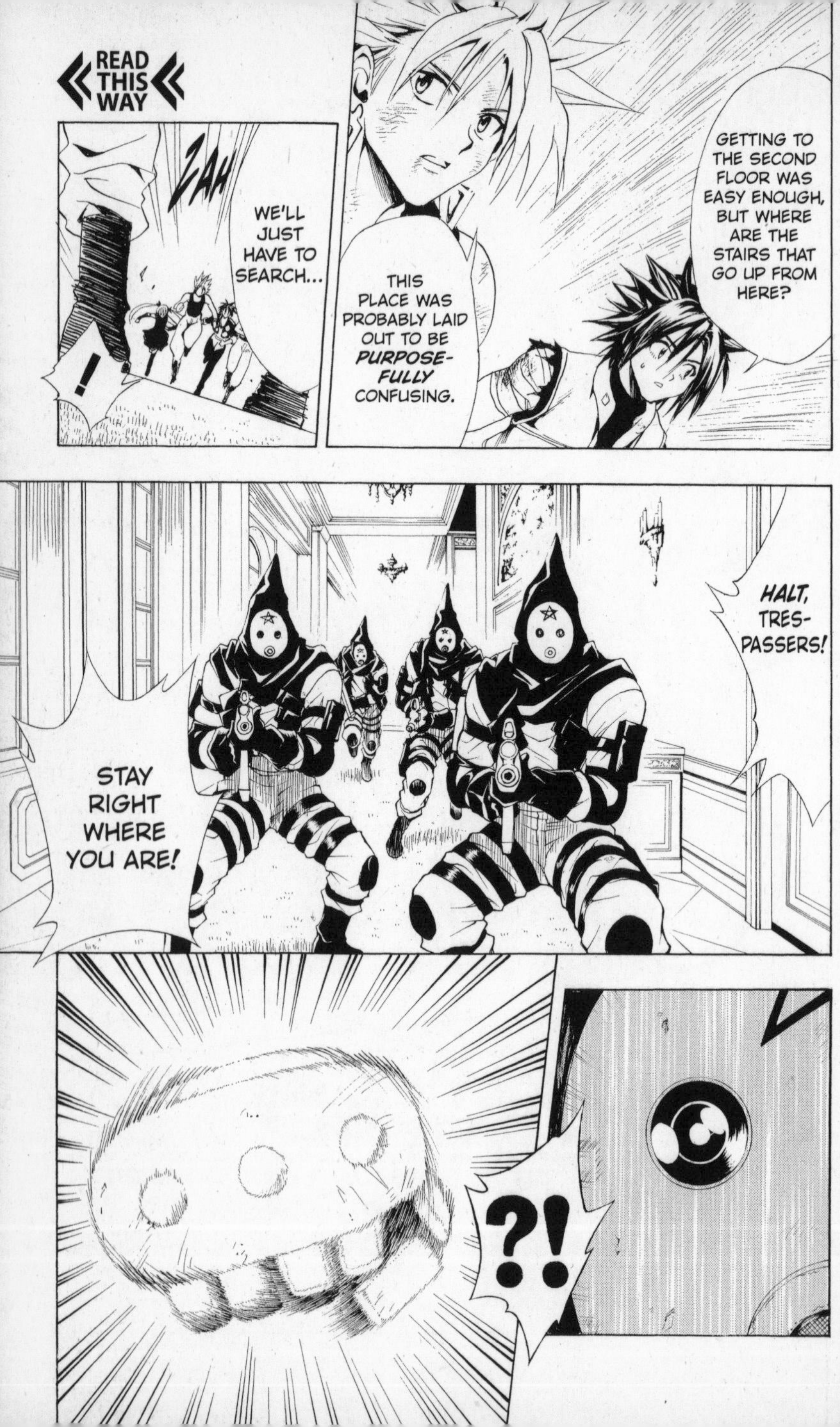

GETTING TO THE SECOND FLOOR WAS EASY ENOUGH, BUT WHERE ARE THE STAIRS THAT GO UP FROM HERE?
THIS PLACE WAS PROBABLY LAID OUT TO BE *PURPOSE-FULLY* CONFUSING.
WE'LL JUST HAVE TO SEARCH...
ZAH
!
HALT, TRES-PASSERS!
STAY RIGHT WHERE YOU ARE!
?!

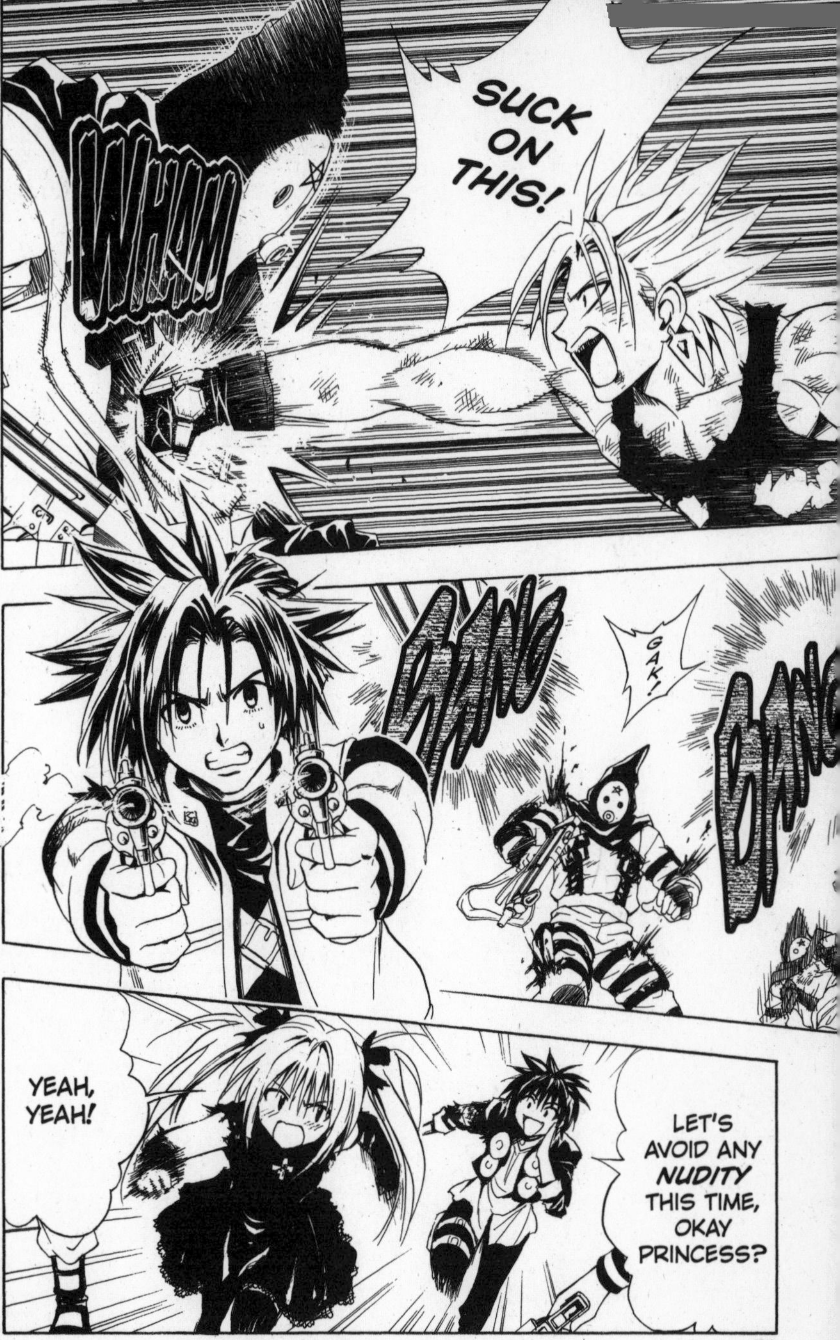
SUCK ON THIS!
WHAM
BANG
GAK!
BANG
LET'S AVOID ANY *NUDITY* THIS TIME, OKAY PRINCESS?
YEAH, YEAH!

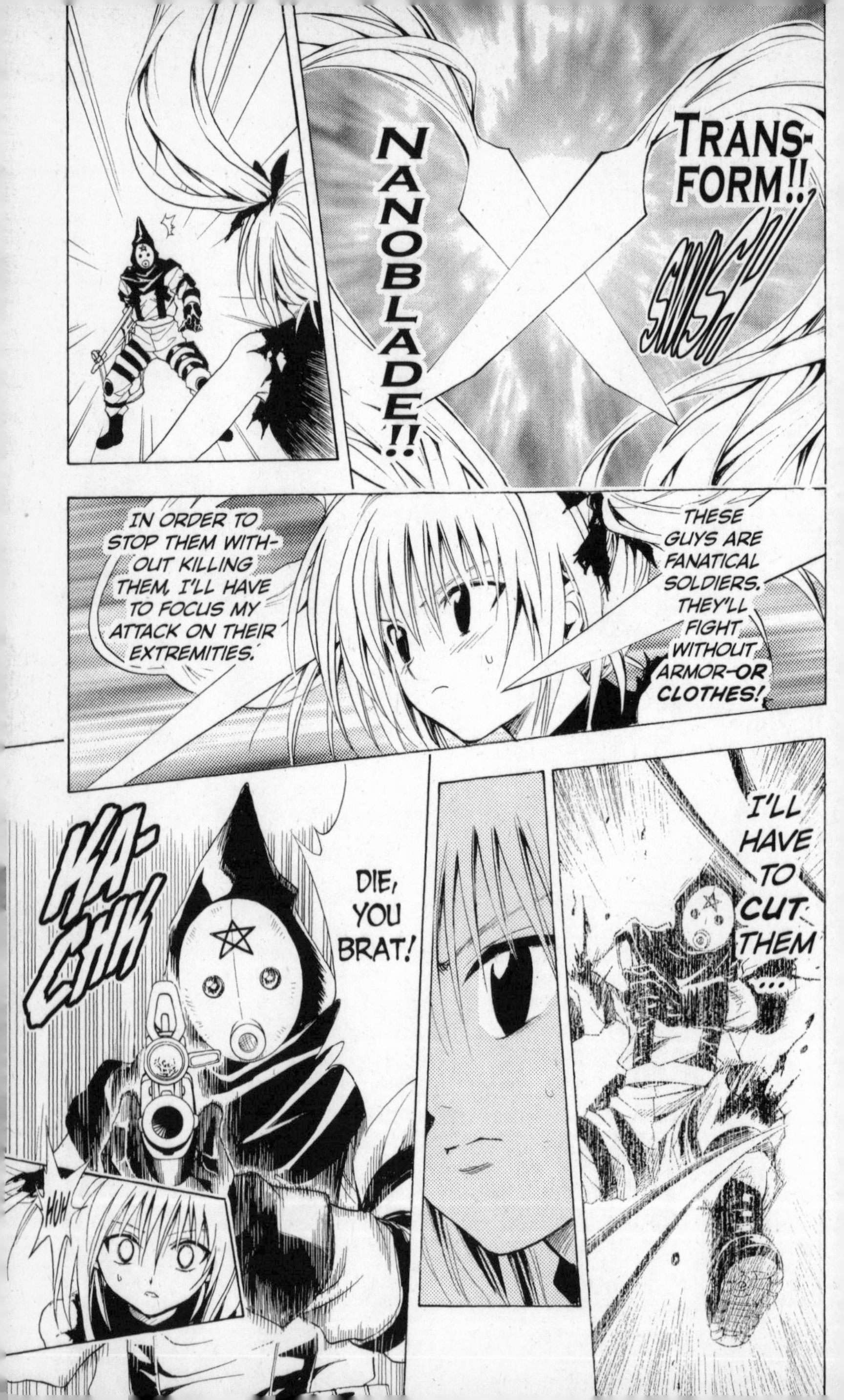
TRANS-FORM!!
SWISH
NANOBLADE!!
THESE GUYS ARE FANATICAL SOLDIERS. THEY'LL FIGHT WITHOUT ARMOR—OR CLOTHES!
IN ORDER TO STOP THEM WITH-OUT KILLING THEM, I'LL HAVE TO FOCUS MY ATTACK ON THEIR EXTREMITIES.
I'LL HAVE TO CUT THEM...
DIE, YOU BRAT!
KA-CHK
HUH

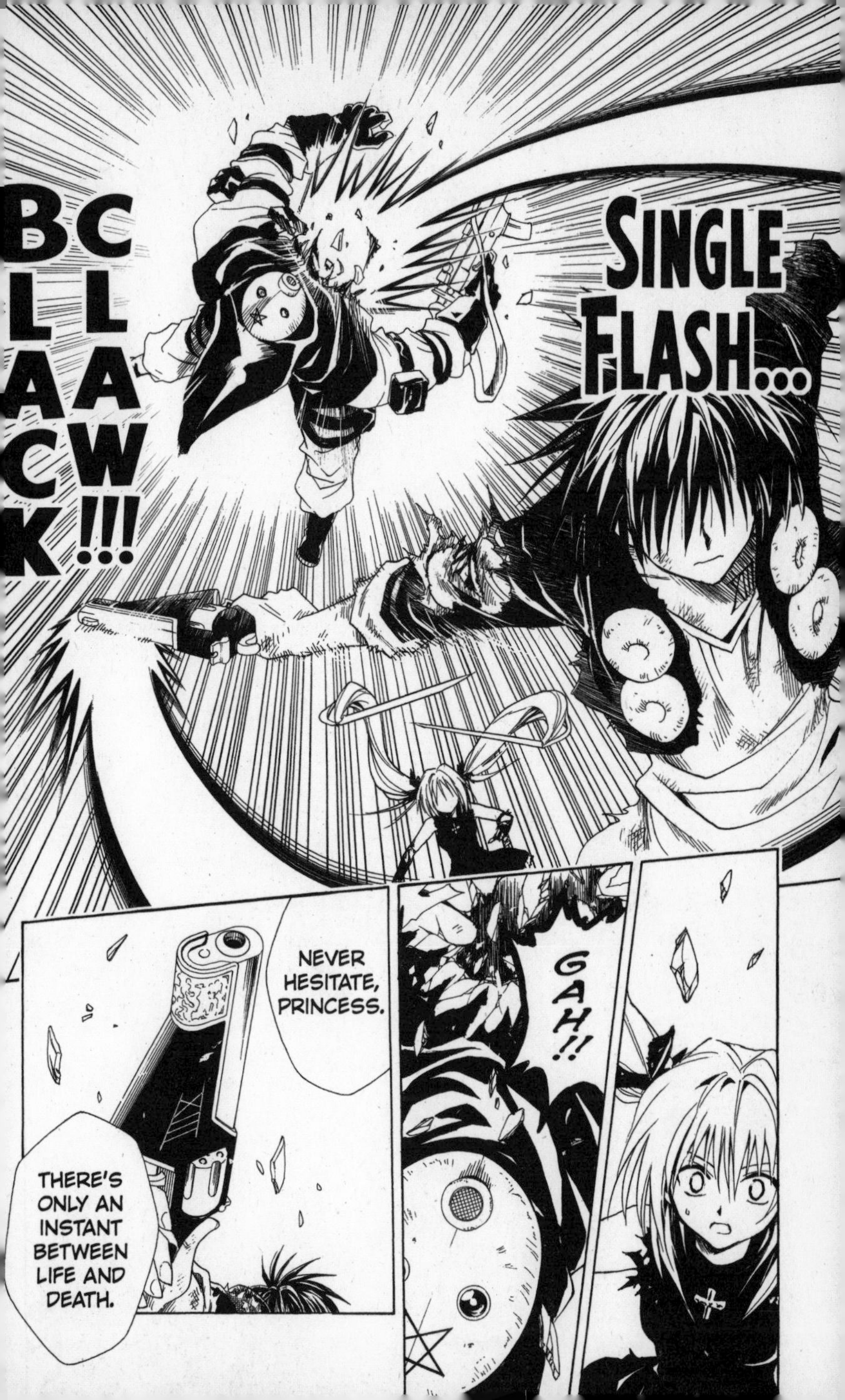

SINGLE FLASH...
BLACK CLAW!!!
GAH!!
NEVER HESITATE, PRINCESS.
THERE'S ONLY AN INSTANT BETWEEN LIFE AND DEATH.

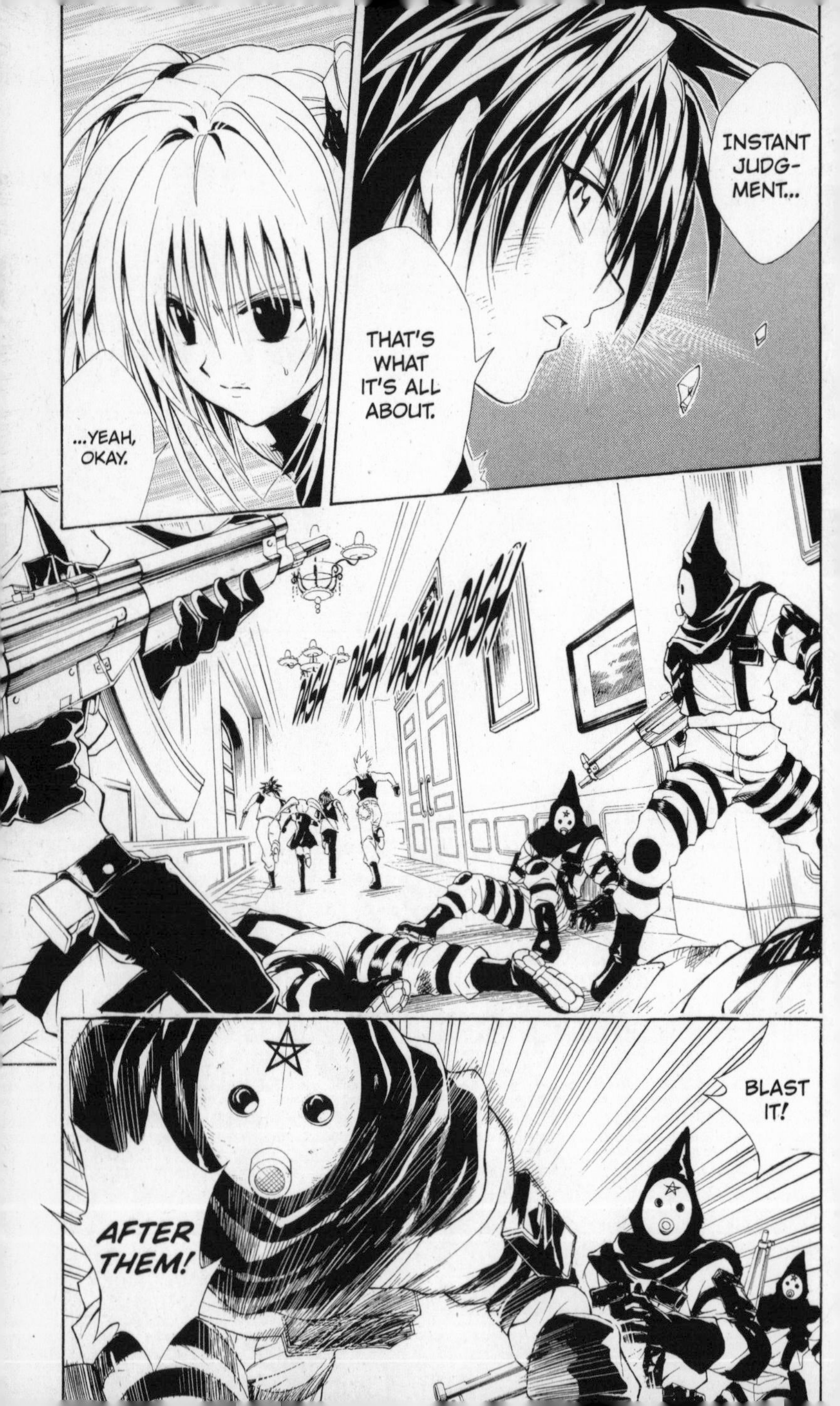
INSTANT JUDG-MENT...
THAT'S WHAT IT'S ALL ABOUT.
...YEAH, OKAY.
DASH DASH DASH DASH
BLAST IT!
AFTER THEM!

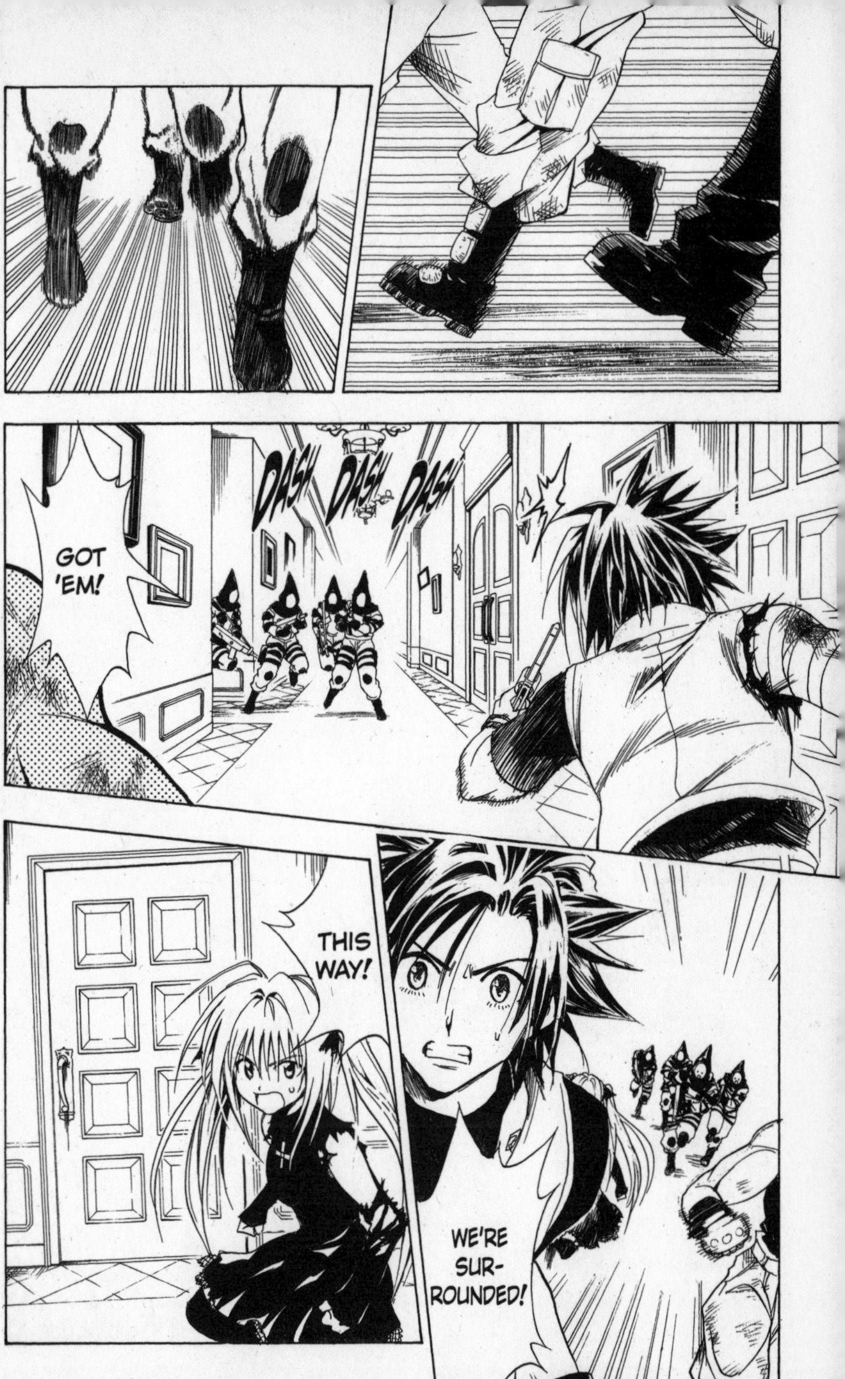
DASH
DASH
DASH
GOT 'EM!
WE'RE SUR-ROUNDED!
THIS WAY!

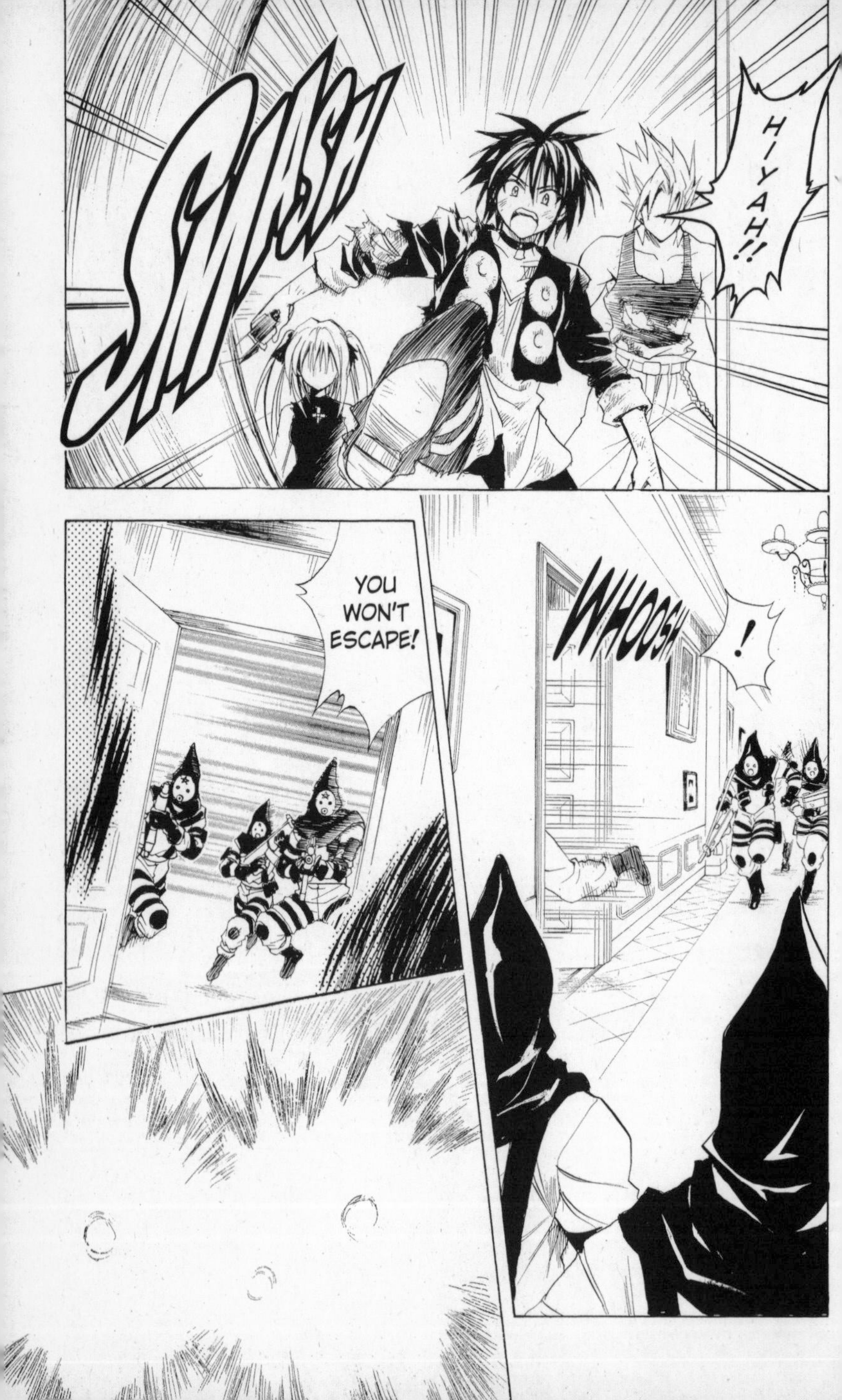
HIYAH!!
SLASH
WHOOSH
!
YOU WON'T ESCAPE!

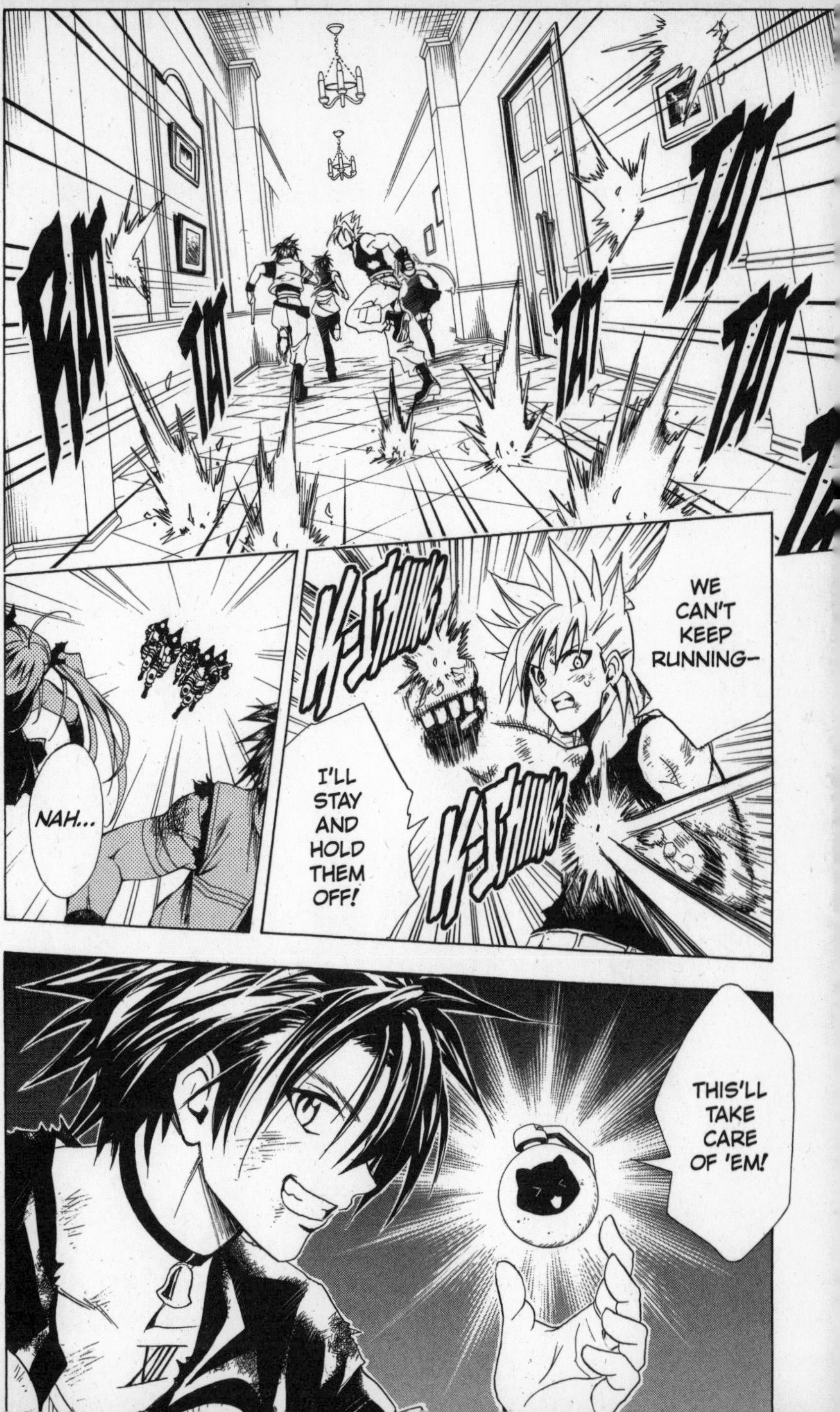

TA TA TA
RA TA
KA-CHINK
WE CAN'T KEEP RUNNING–
I'LL STAY AND HOLD THEM OFF!
KA-CHINK
NAH...
THIS'LL TAKE CARE OF 'EM!

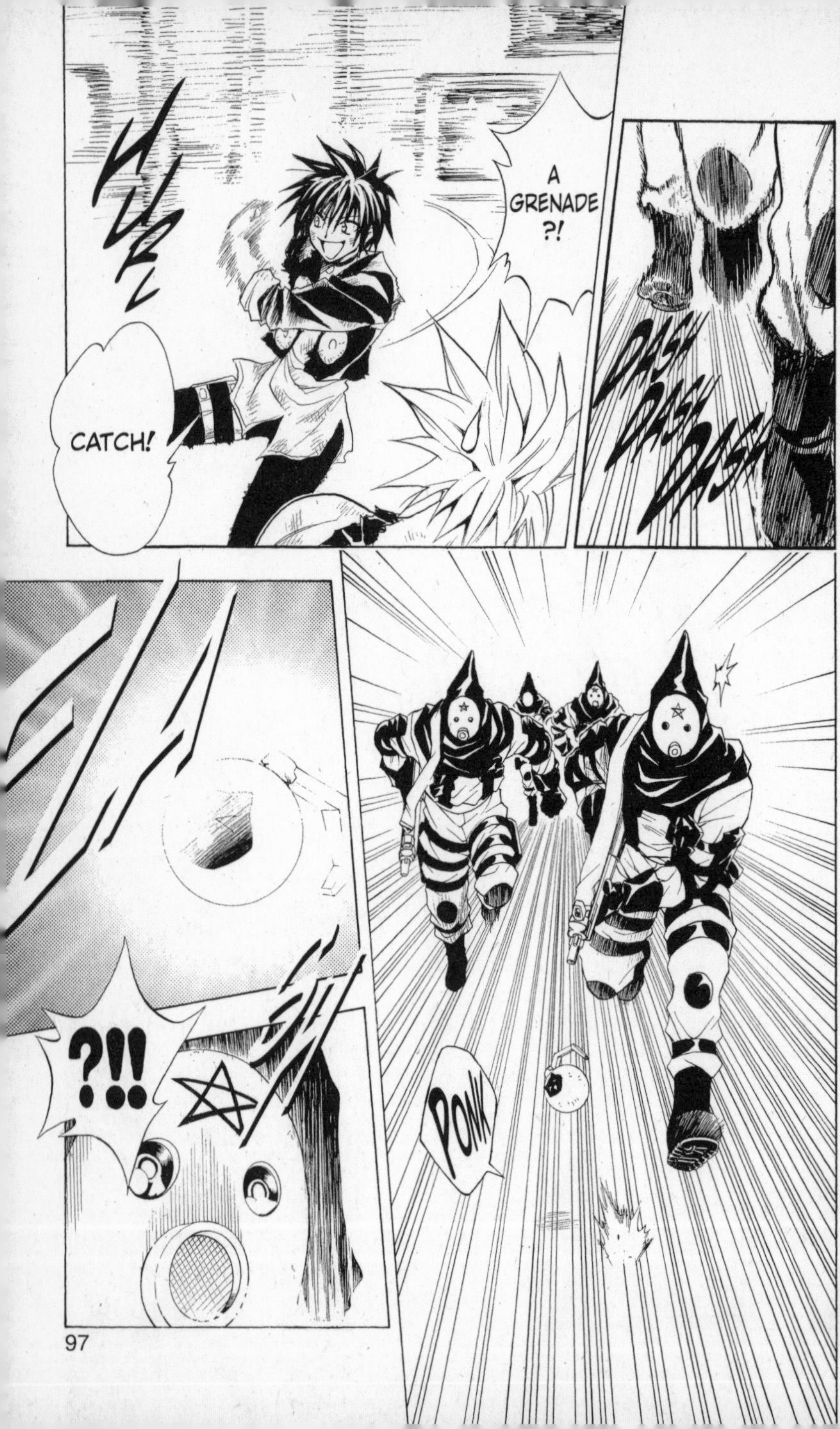
DASH DASH DASH
A GRENADE ?!
CATCH!
PONK
?!!

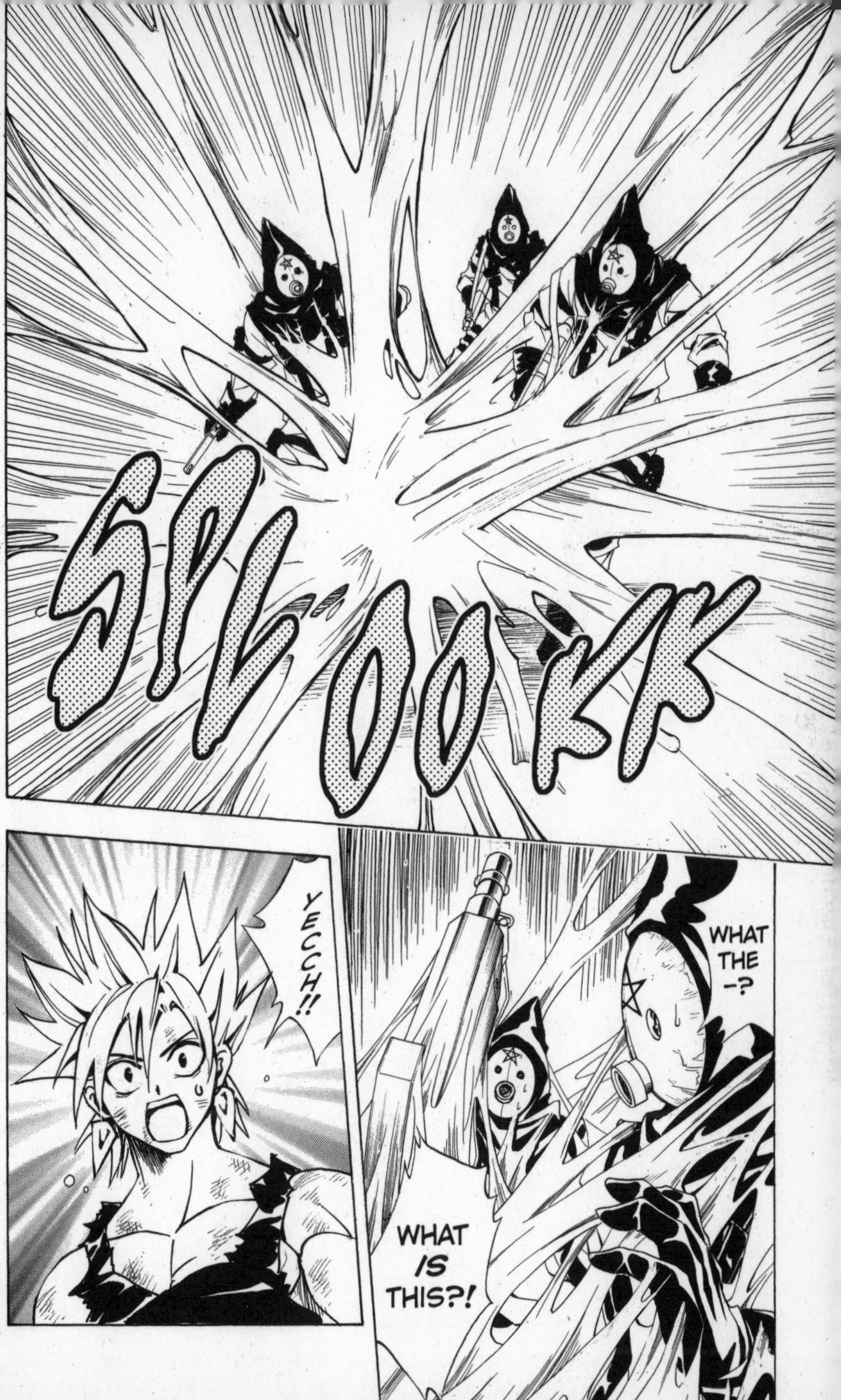
SPLOOKK
WHAT THE --?
WHAT IS THIS?!
YECCH!!

READ THIS WAY

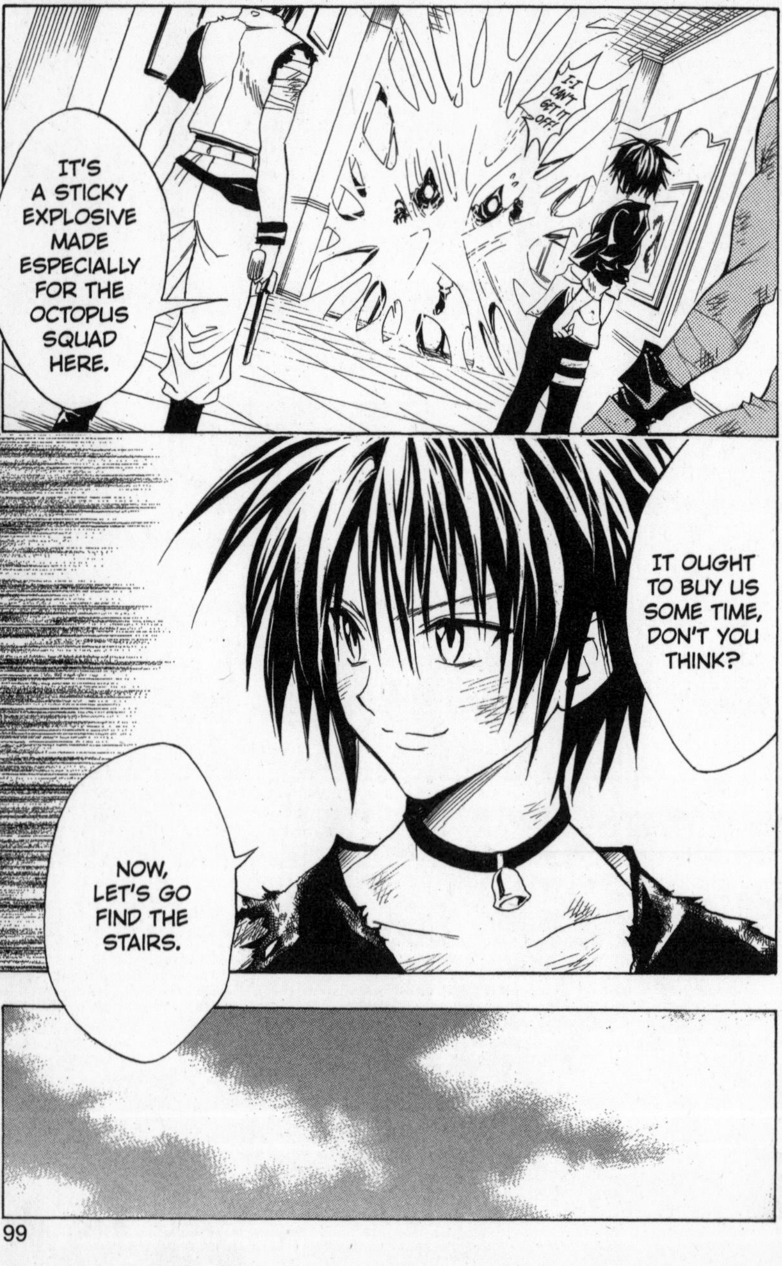

I-I CAN'T GET IT OFF!
IT'S A STICKY EXPLOSIVE MADE ESPECIALLY FOR THE OCTOPUS SQUAD HERE.
IT OUGHT TO BUY US SOME TIME, DON'T YOU THINK?
NOW, LET'S GO FIND THE STAIRS.

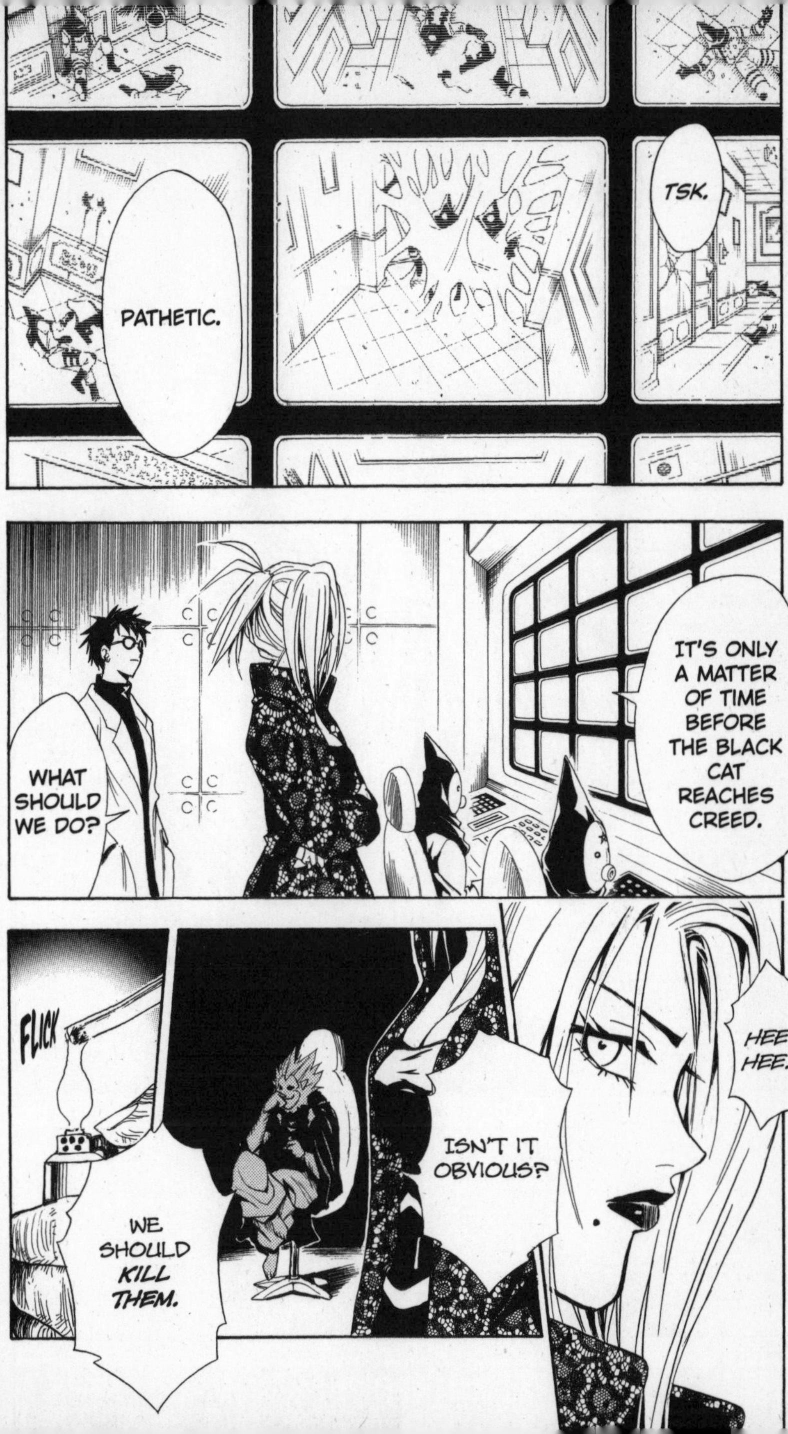
TSK.
PATHETIC.
IT'S ONLY A MATTER OF TIME BEFORE THE BLACK CAT REACHES CREED.
WHAT SHOULD WE DO?
HEE HEE.
ISN'T IT OBVIOUS?
FLICK
WE SHOULD *KILL* THEM.

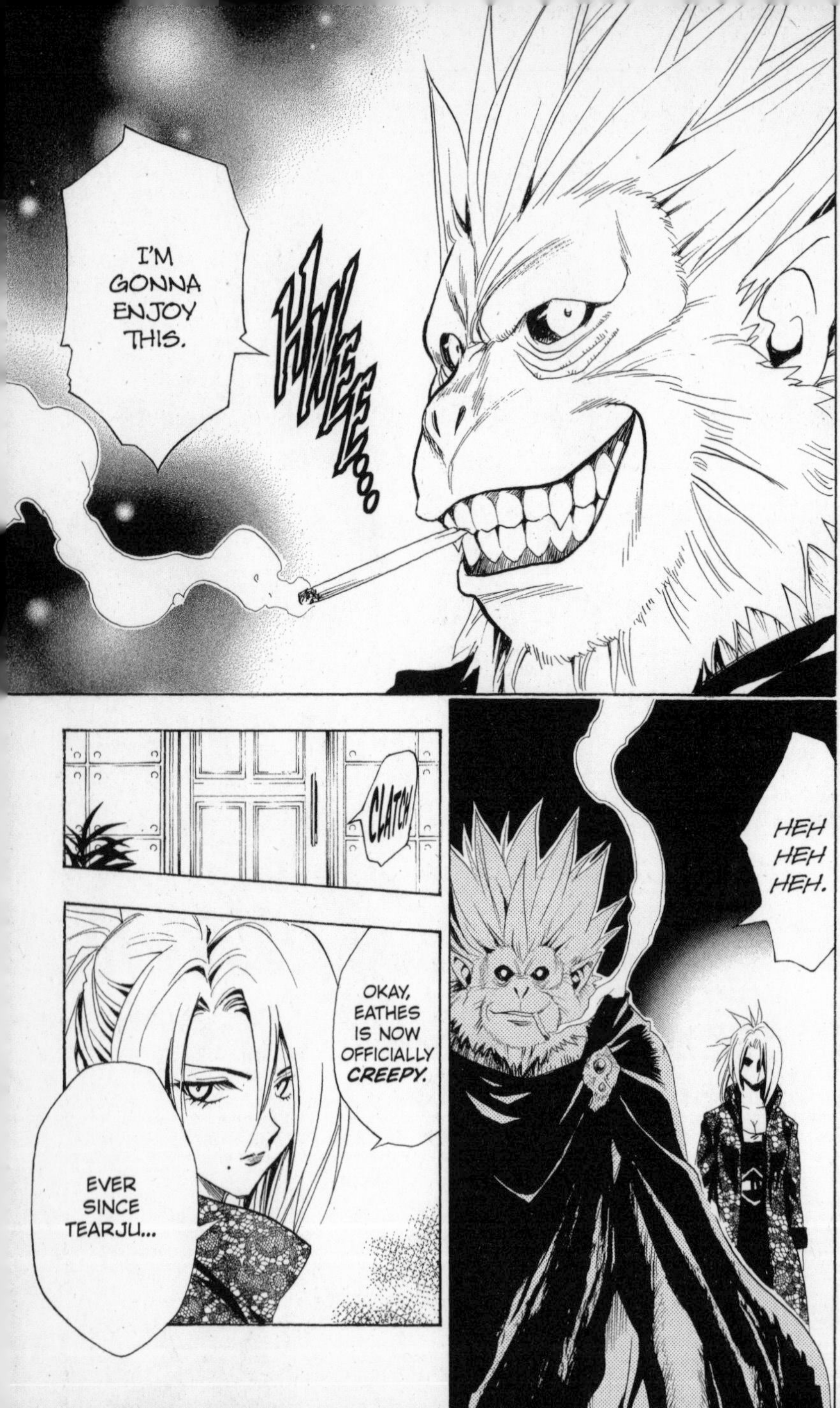
I'M GONNA ENJOY THIS.
HWEEE...
HEH HEH HEH.
CLATCH
OKAY, EATHES IS NOW OFFICIALLY *CREEPY.*
EVER SINCE TEARJU...

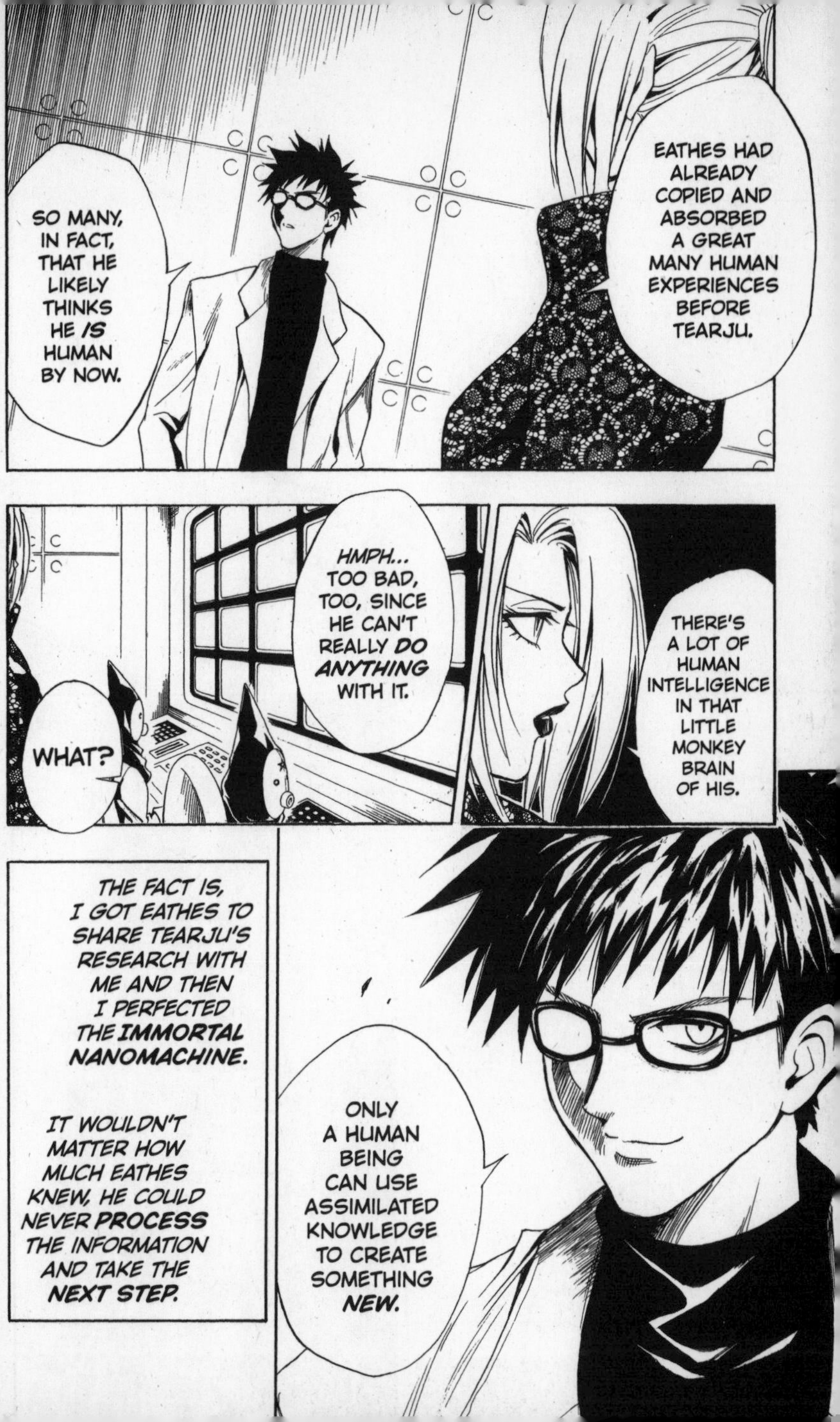
EATHES HAD ALREADY COPIED AND ABSORBED A GREAT MANY HUMAN EXPERIENCES BEFORE TEARJU.
SO MANY, IN FACT, THAT HE LIKELY THINKS HE *IS* HUMAN BY NOW.
THERE'S A LOT OF HUMAN INTELLIGENCE IN THAT LITTLE MONKEY BRAIN OF HIS.
HMPH... TOO BAD, TOO, SINCE HE CAN'T REALLY ***DO ANYTHING*** WITH IT.
WHAT?
ONLY A HUMAN BEING CAN USE ASSIMILATED KNOWLEDGE TO CREATE SOMETHING ***NEW***.
THE FACT IS, I GOT EATHES TO SHARE TEARJU'S RESEARCH WITH ME AND THEN I PERFECTED THE ***IMMORTAL NANOMACHINE***.
IT WOULDN'T MATTER HOW MUCH EATHES KNEW, HE COULD NEVER ***PROCESS*** *THE INFORMATION AND TAKE THE* ***NEXT STEP***.

READ THIS WAY

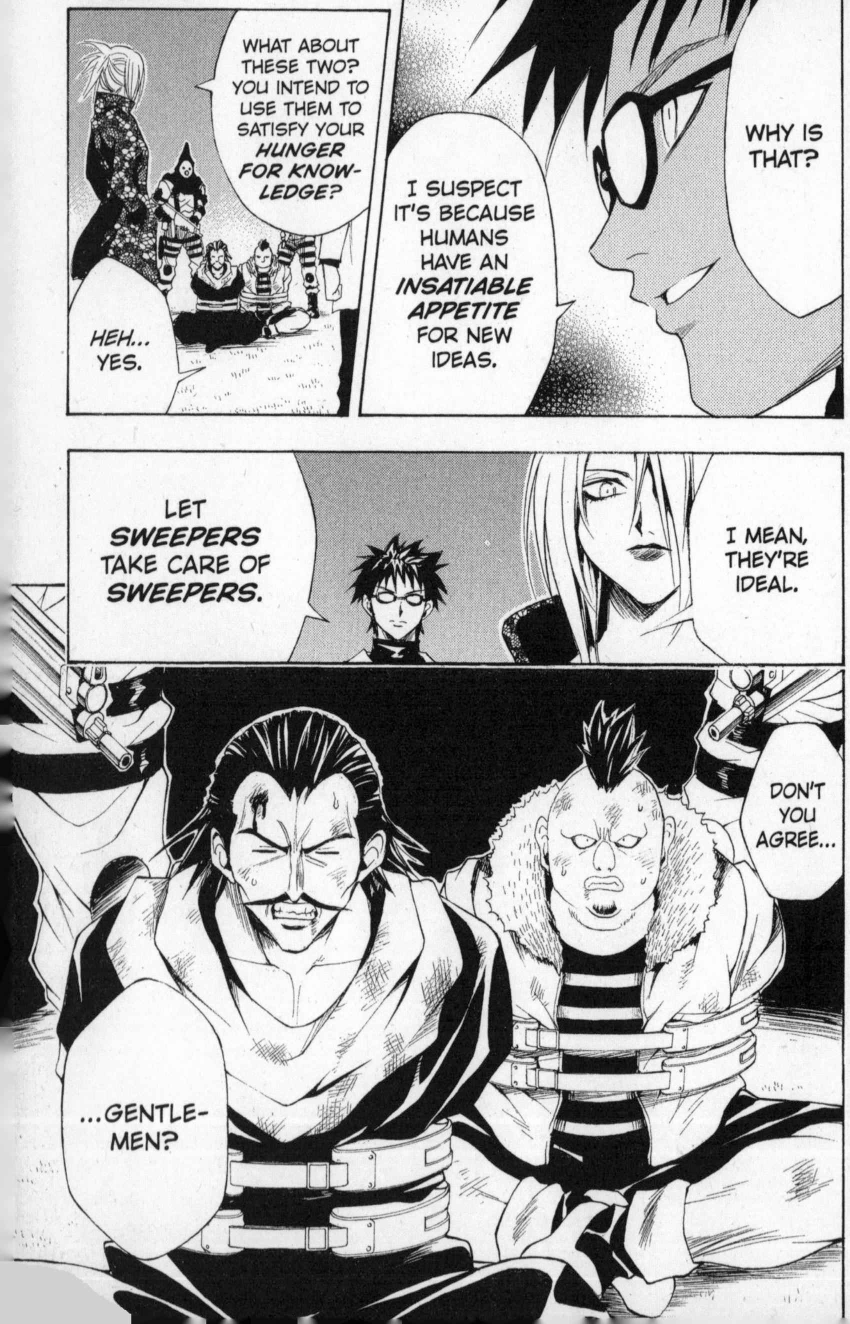
WHY IS THAT?
I SUSPECT IT'S BECAUSE HUMANS HAVE AN INSATIABLE APPETITE FOR NEW IDEAS.
WHAT ABOUT THESE TWO? YOU INTEND TO USE THEM TO SATISFY YOUR HUNGER FOR KNOW-LEDGE?
HEH... YES.
I MEAN, THEY'RE IDEAL.
LET SWEEPERS TAKE CARE OF SWEEPERS.
DON'T YOU AGREE...
...GENTLE-MEN?

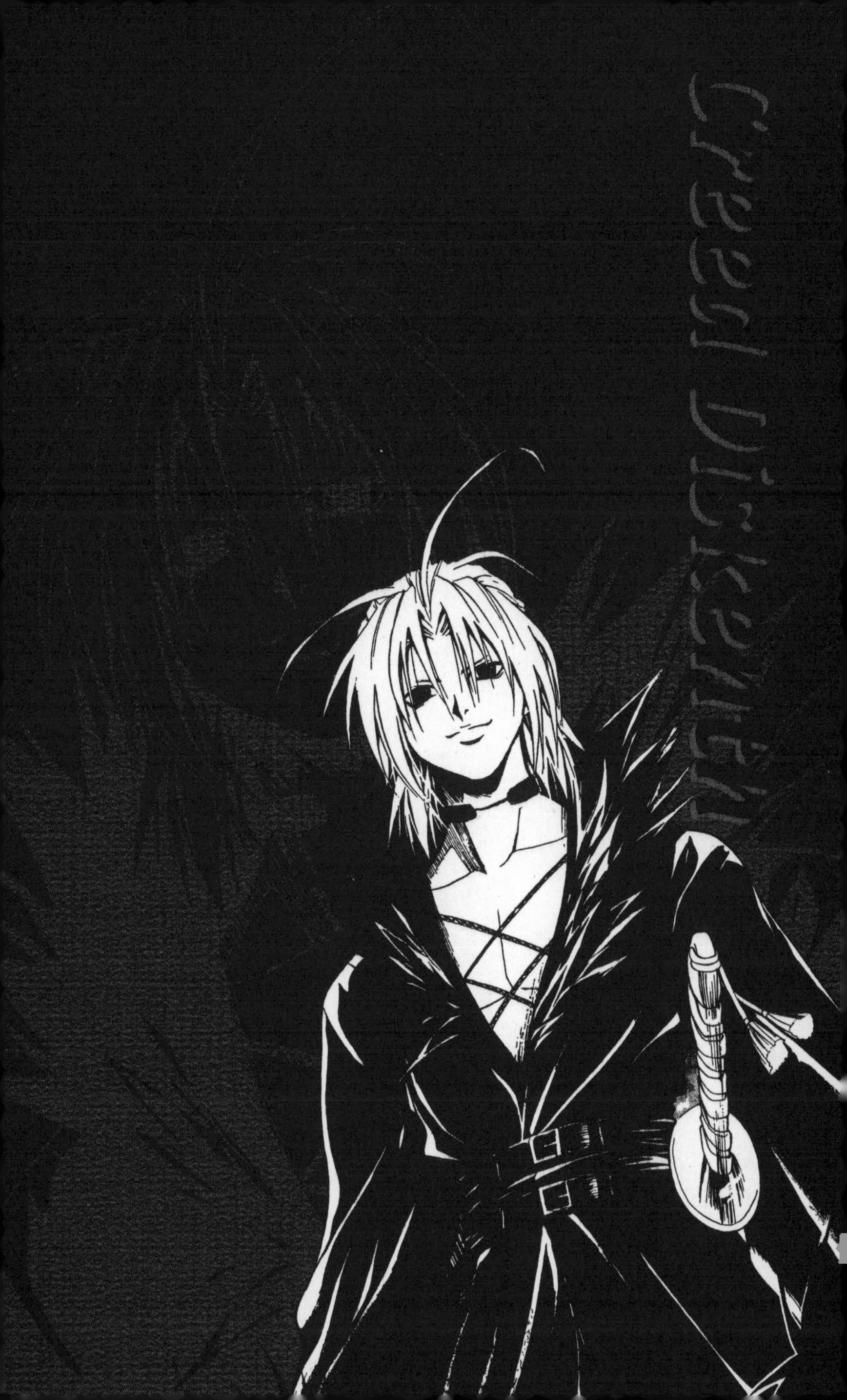

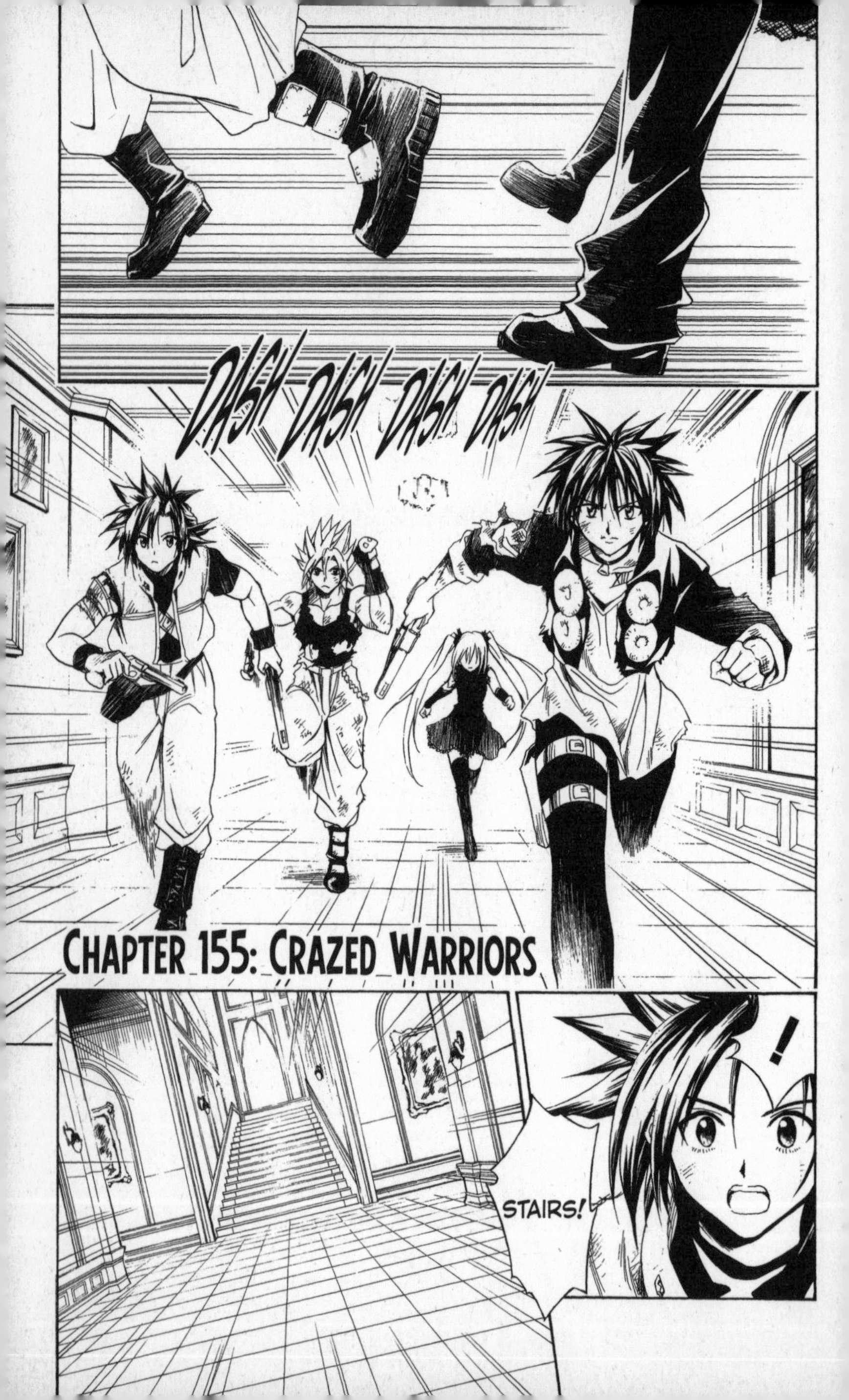
DASH DASH DASH DASH
CHAPTER 155: CRAZED WARRIORS
!
STAIRS!

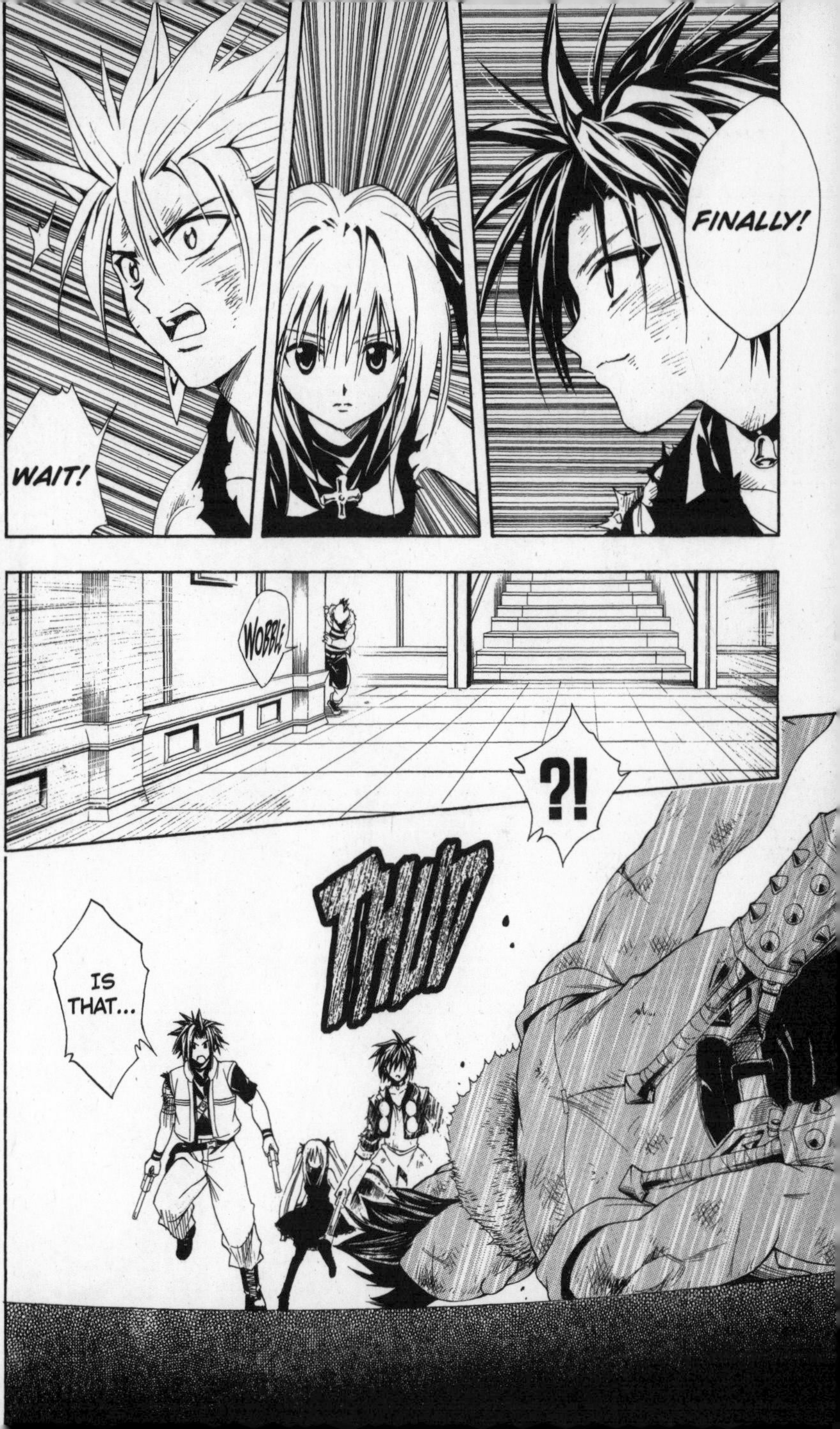
FINALLY!
WAIT!
WOBBLE
?!
THUD
IS THAT...

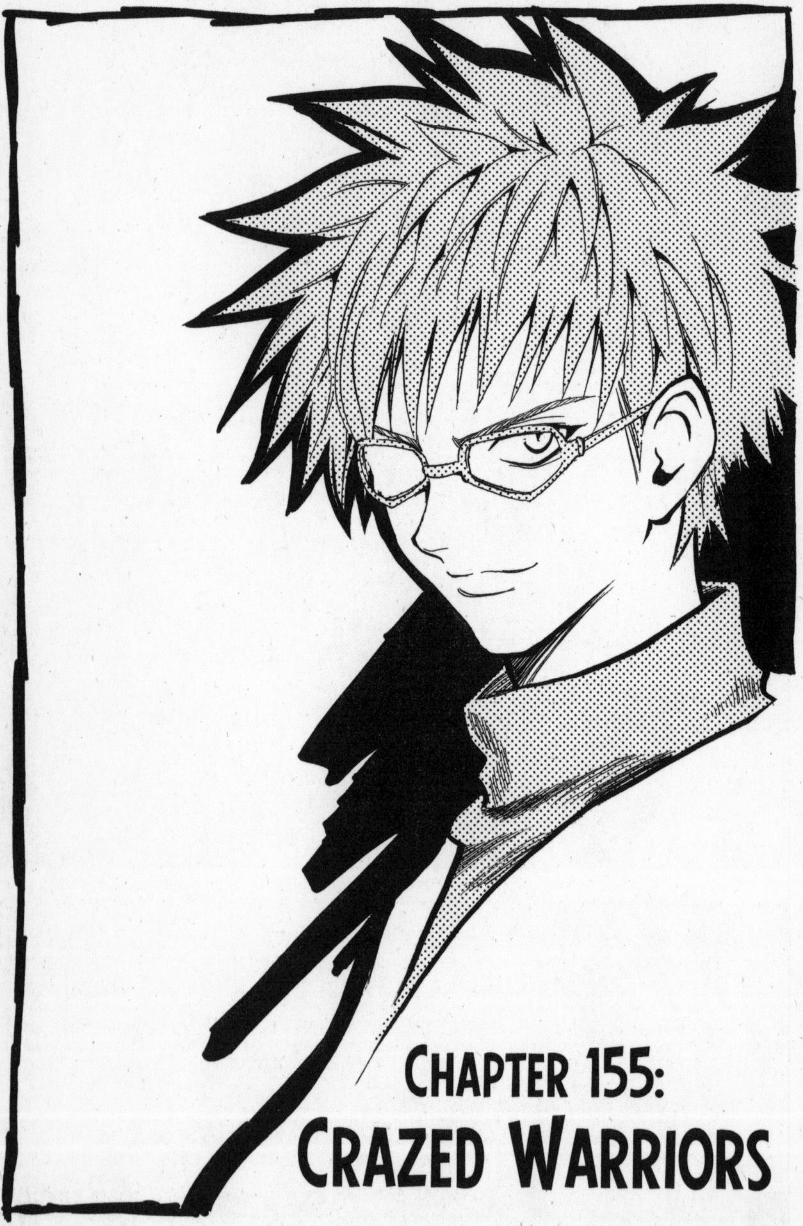

Chapter 155: Crazed Warriors

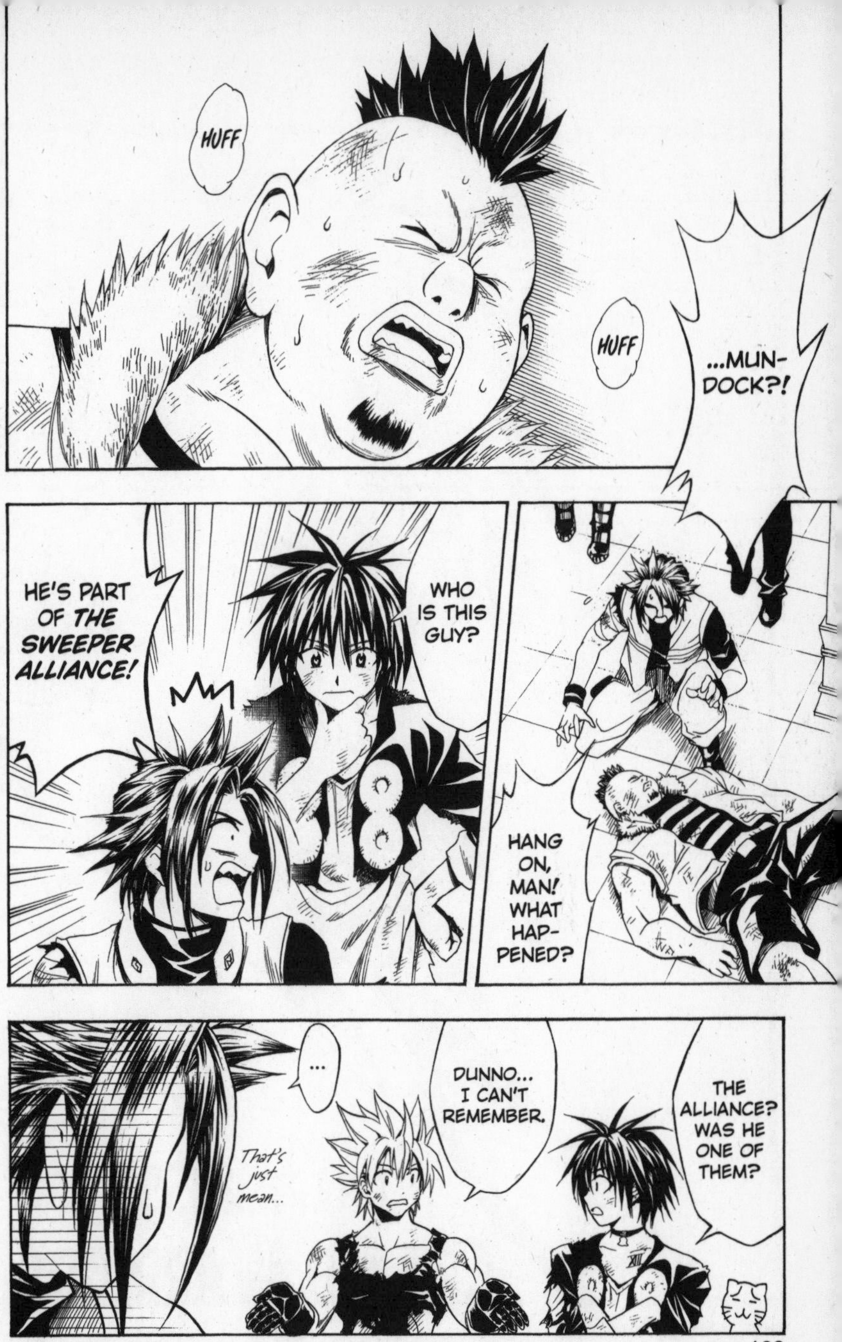
HUFF
HUFF
...MUN-DOCK?!
HANG ON, MAN! WHAT HAPPENED?
WHO IS THIS GUY?
HE'S PART OF THE SWEEPER ALLIANCE!
THE ALLIANCE? WAS HE ONE OF THEM?
DUNNO... I CAN'T REMEMBER.
...
That's just mean...

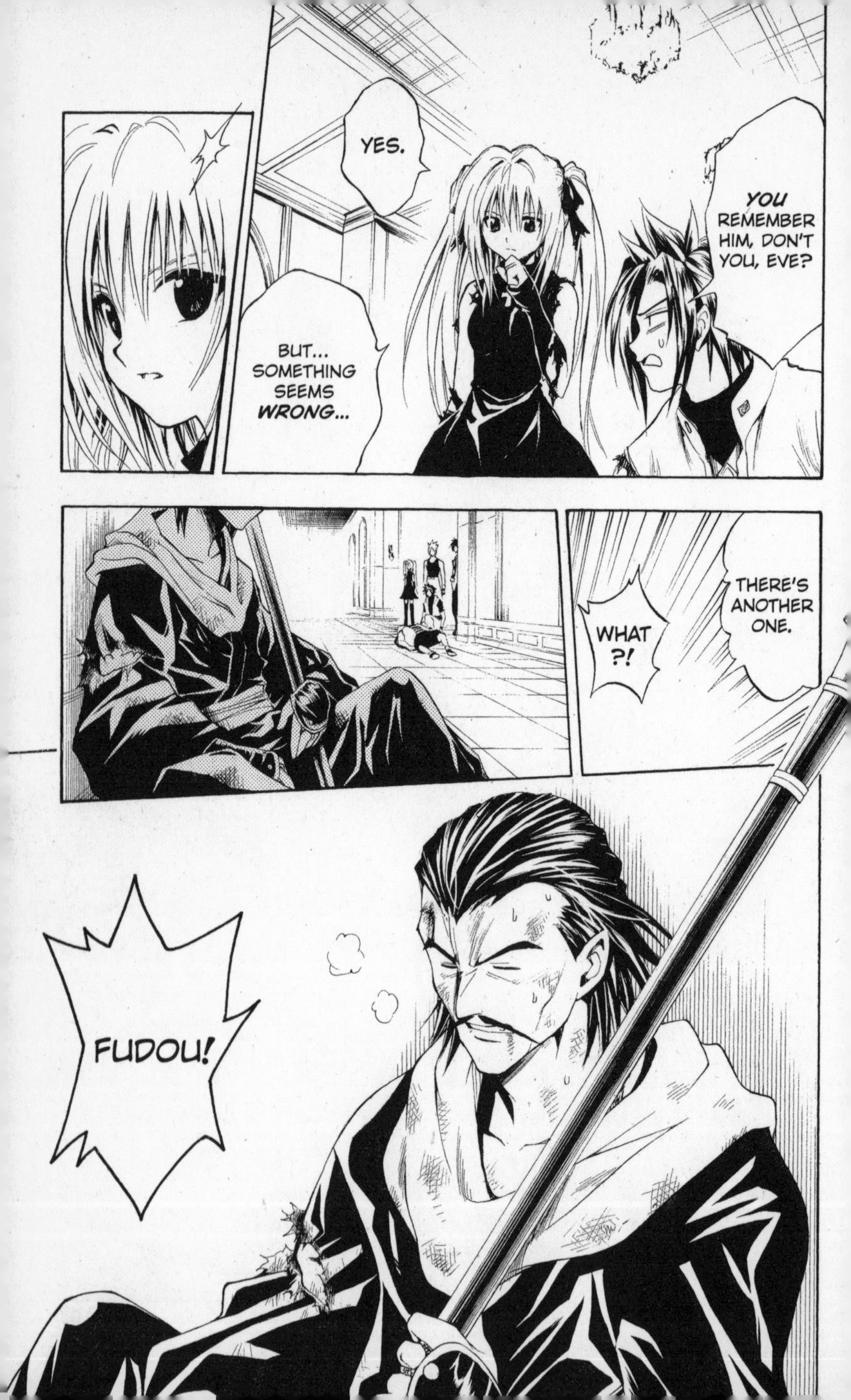
YOU REMEMBER HIM, DON'T YOU, EVE?
YES.
BUT... SOMETHING SEEMS WRONG...
THERE'S ANOTHER ONE.
WHAT ?!
FUDOU!

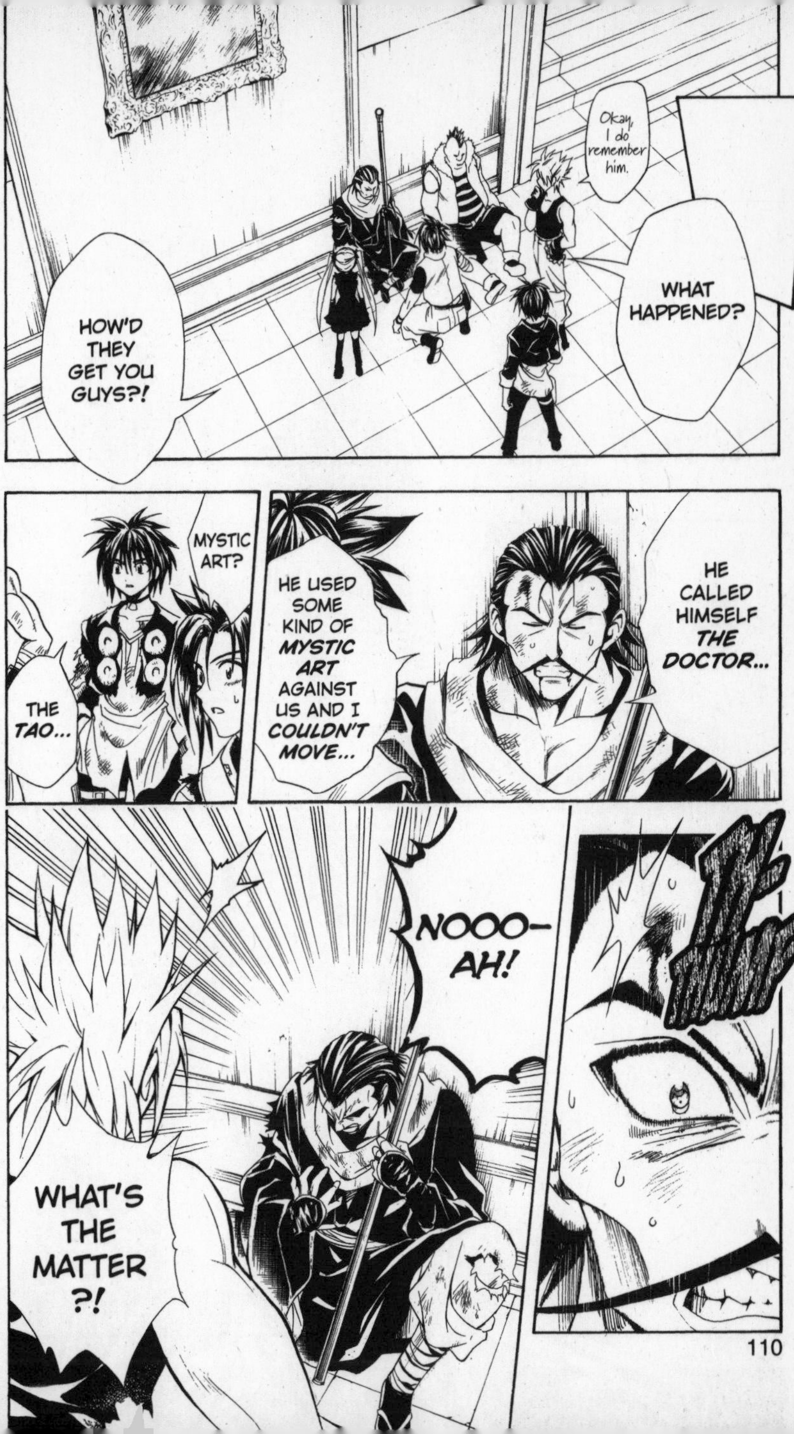
Okay, I do remember him.
WHAT HAPPENED?
HOW'D THEY GET YOU GUYS?!
HE CALLED HIMSELF THE DOCTOR...
HE USED SOME KIND OF MYSTIC ART AGAINST US AND I COULDN'T MOVE...
MYSTIC ART?
THE TAO...
NOOO-AH!
WHAT'S THE MATTER?!

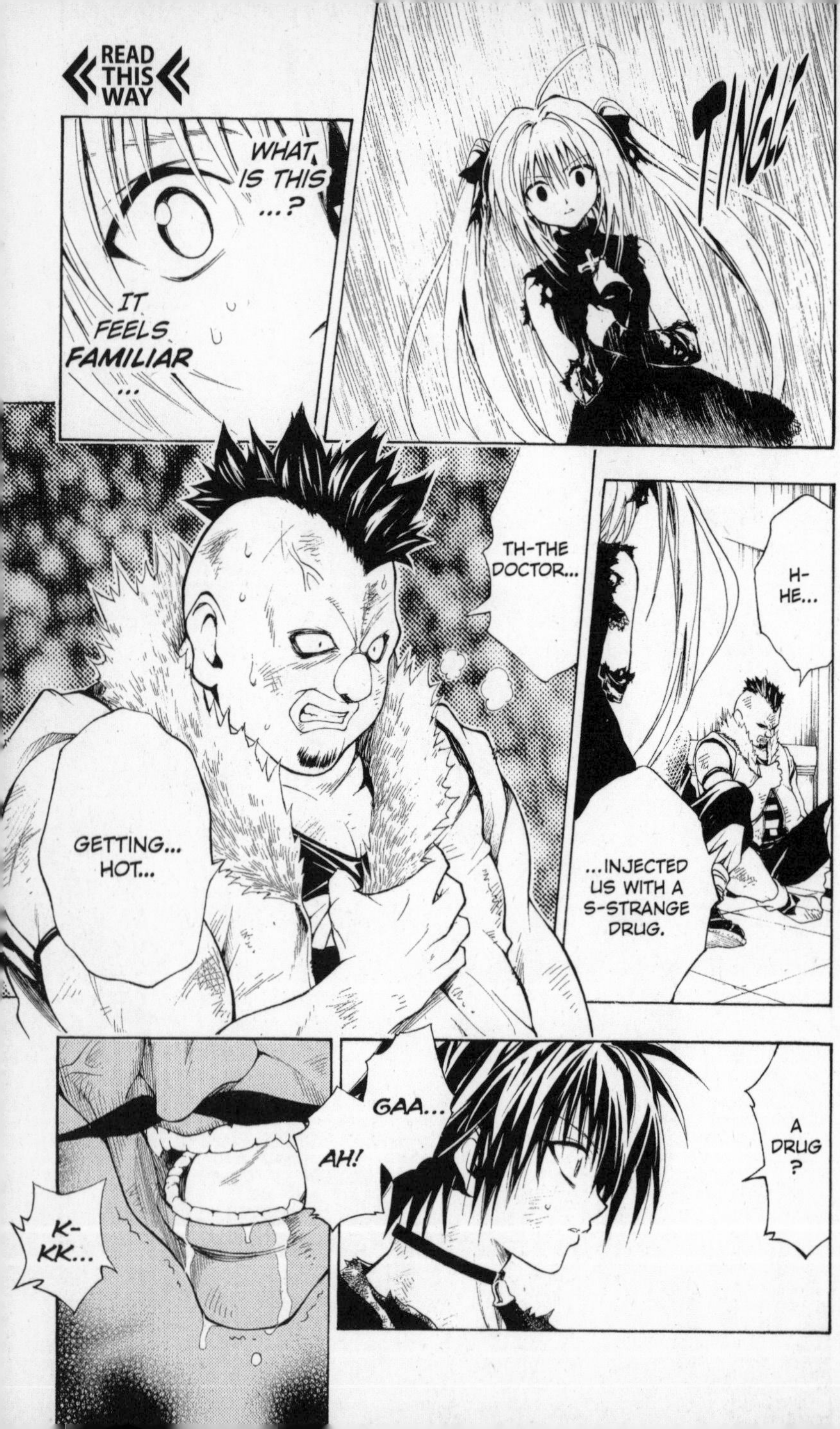
READ THIS WAY
TINGLE
WHAT IS THIS ...?
IT FEELS FAMILIAR ...
H- HE...
...INJECTED US WITH A S-STRANGE DRUG.
TH-THE DOCTOR...
GETTING... HOT...
A DRUG?
GAA...
AH!
K- KK...

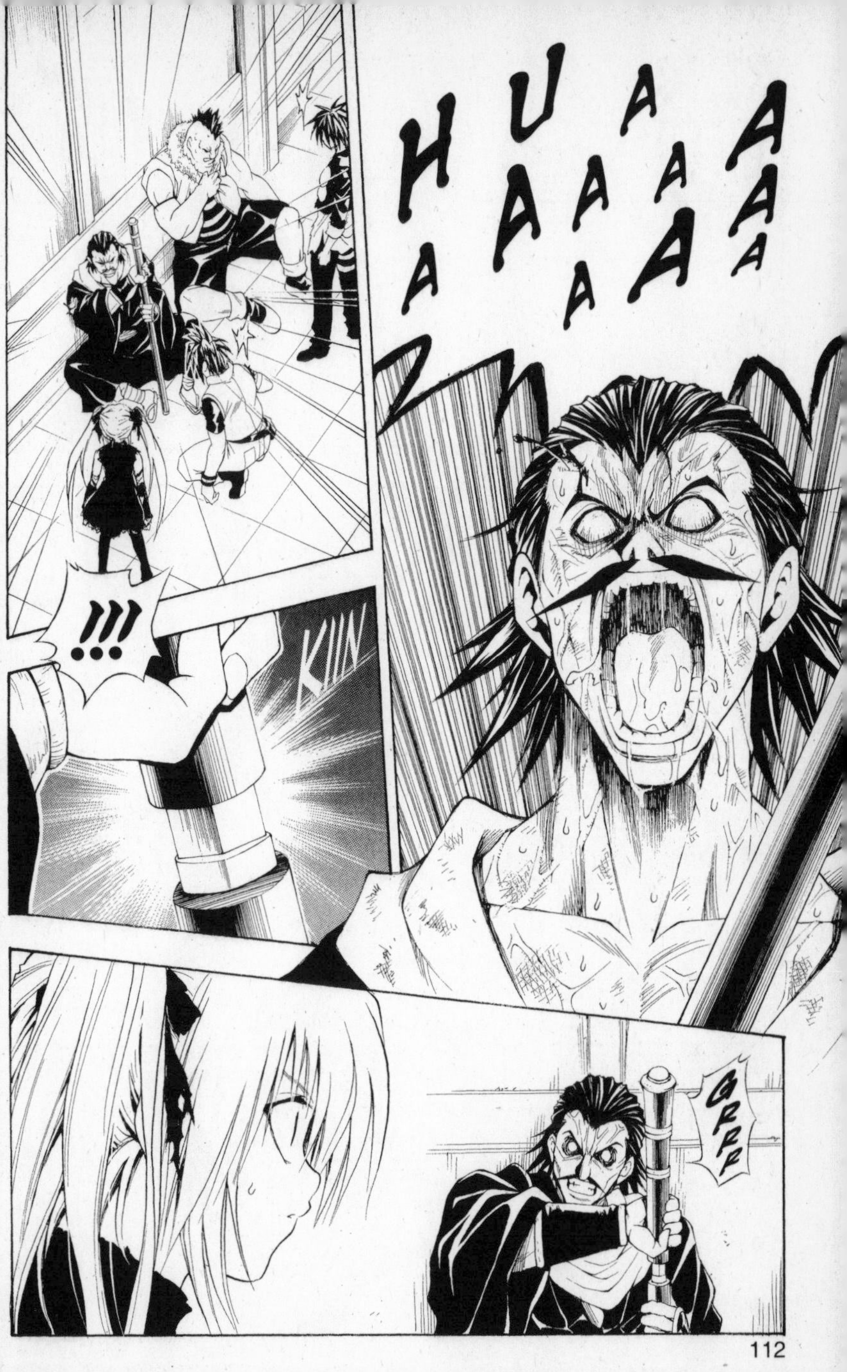
HUAAAAAAAAAAAAA
!!!
KIIN
GRRR

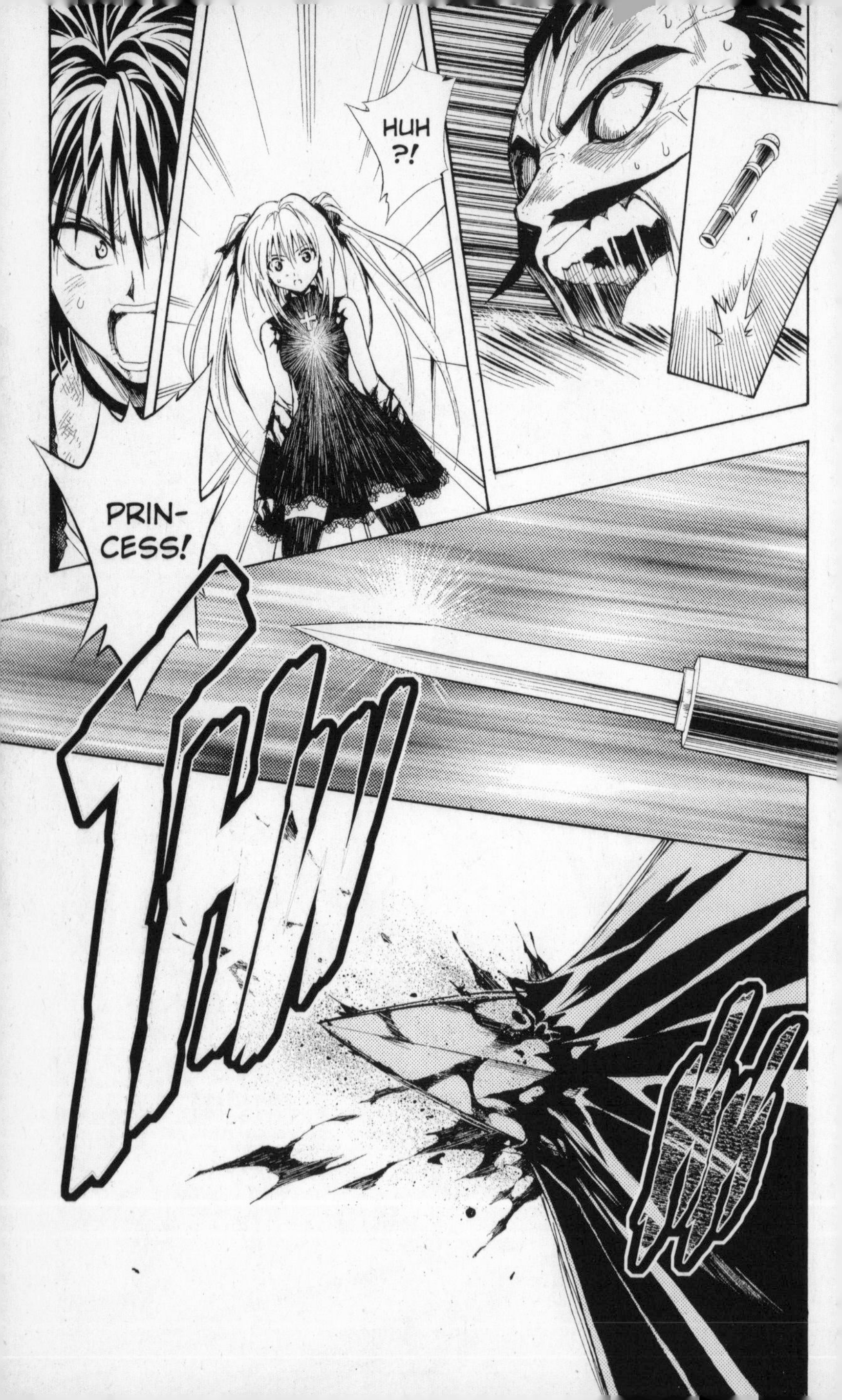
HUH ?!
PRIN- CESS!

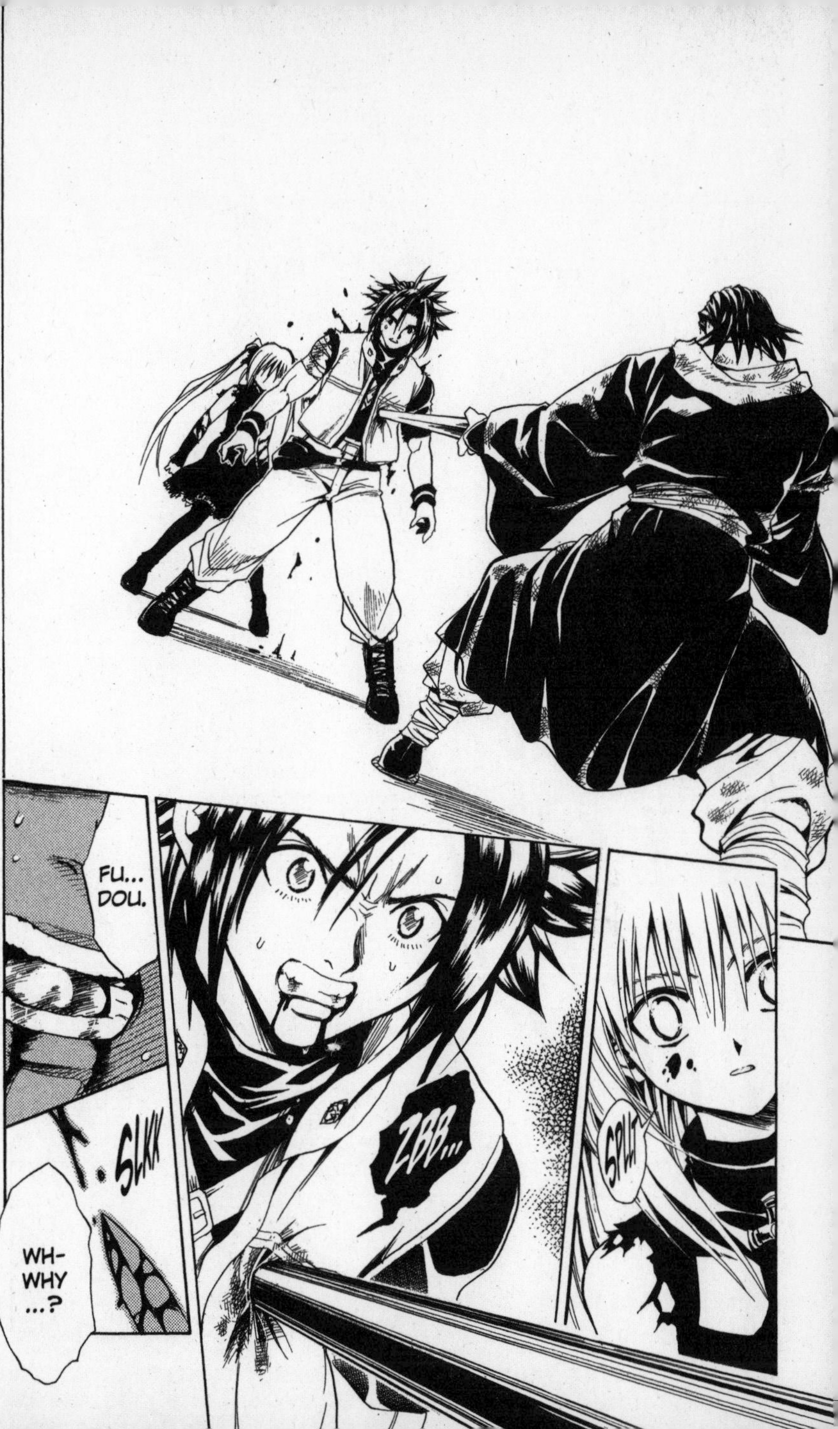
SPLT
ZBB...
FU... DOU.
SLKK
WH- WHY ...?

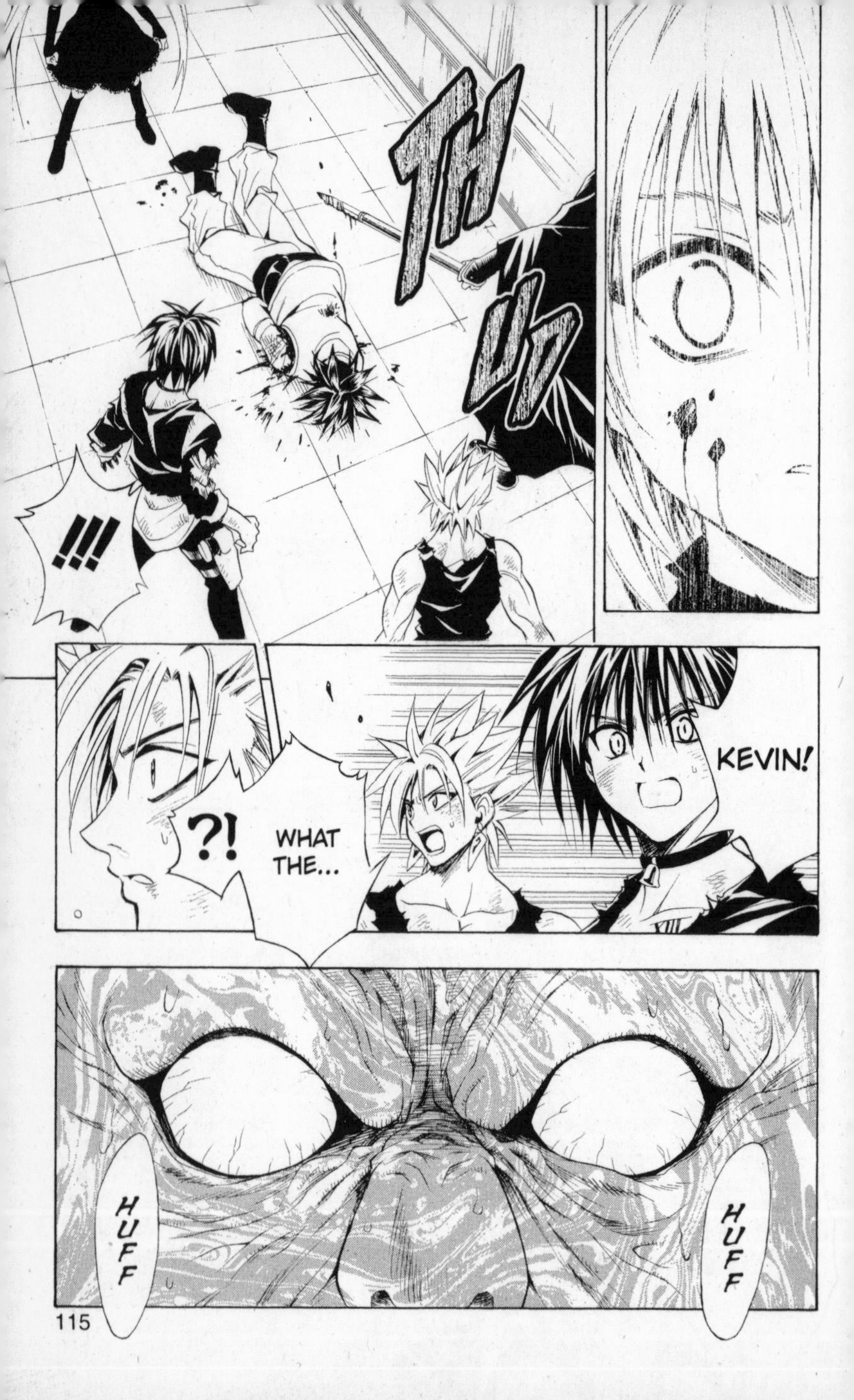
THUD
!!!!
KEVIN!
WHAT THE...
?!
HUFF
HUFF

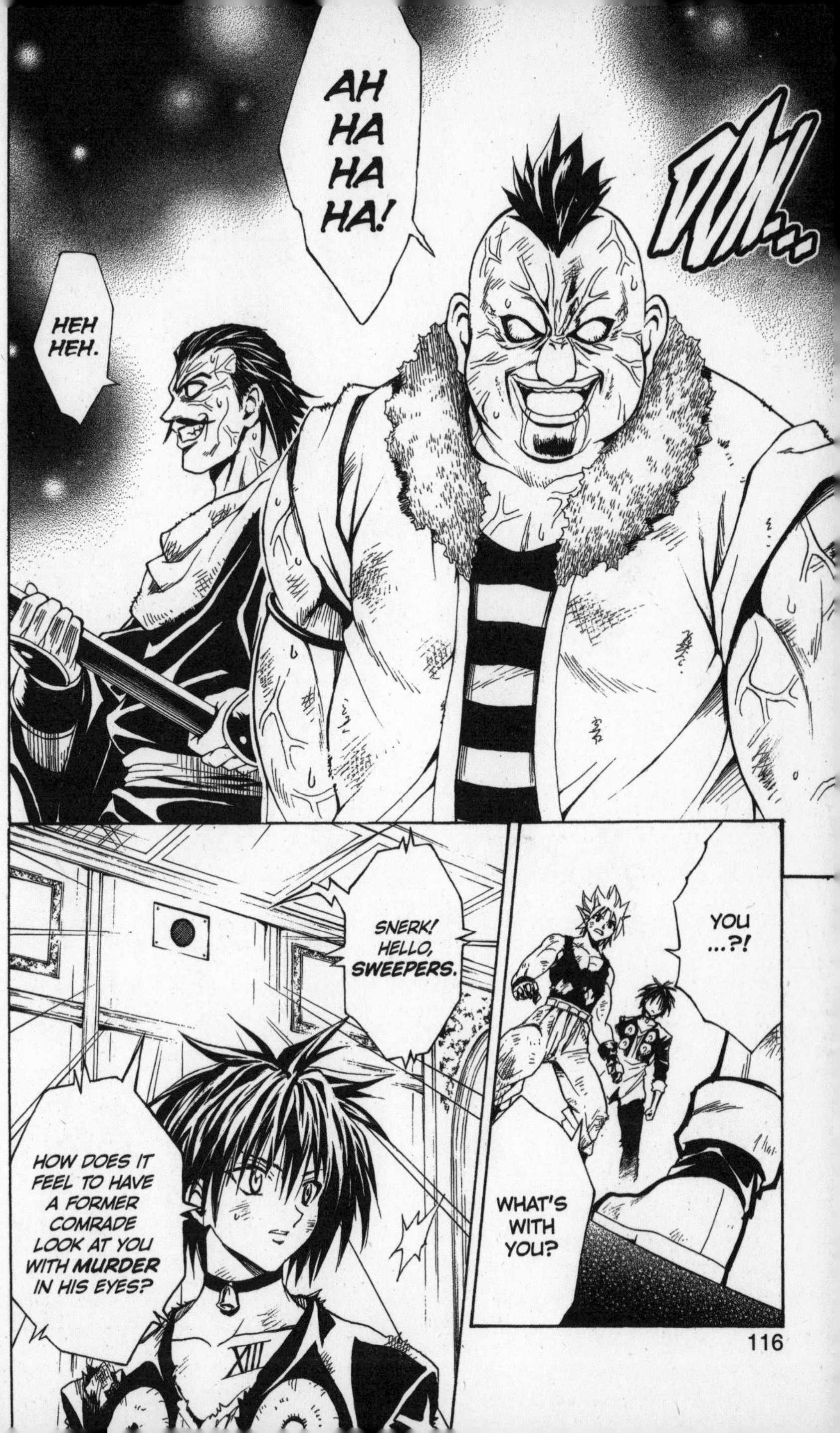
AH HA HA HA!
HEH HEH.
YOU ...?!
WHAT'S WITH YOU?
SNERK! HELLO, SWEEPERS.
HOW DOES IT FEEL TO HAVE A FORMER COMRADE LOOK AT YOU WITH MURDER IN HIS EYES?

READ THIS WAY

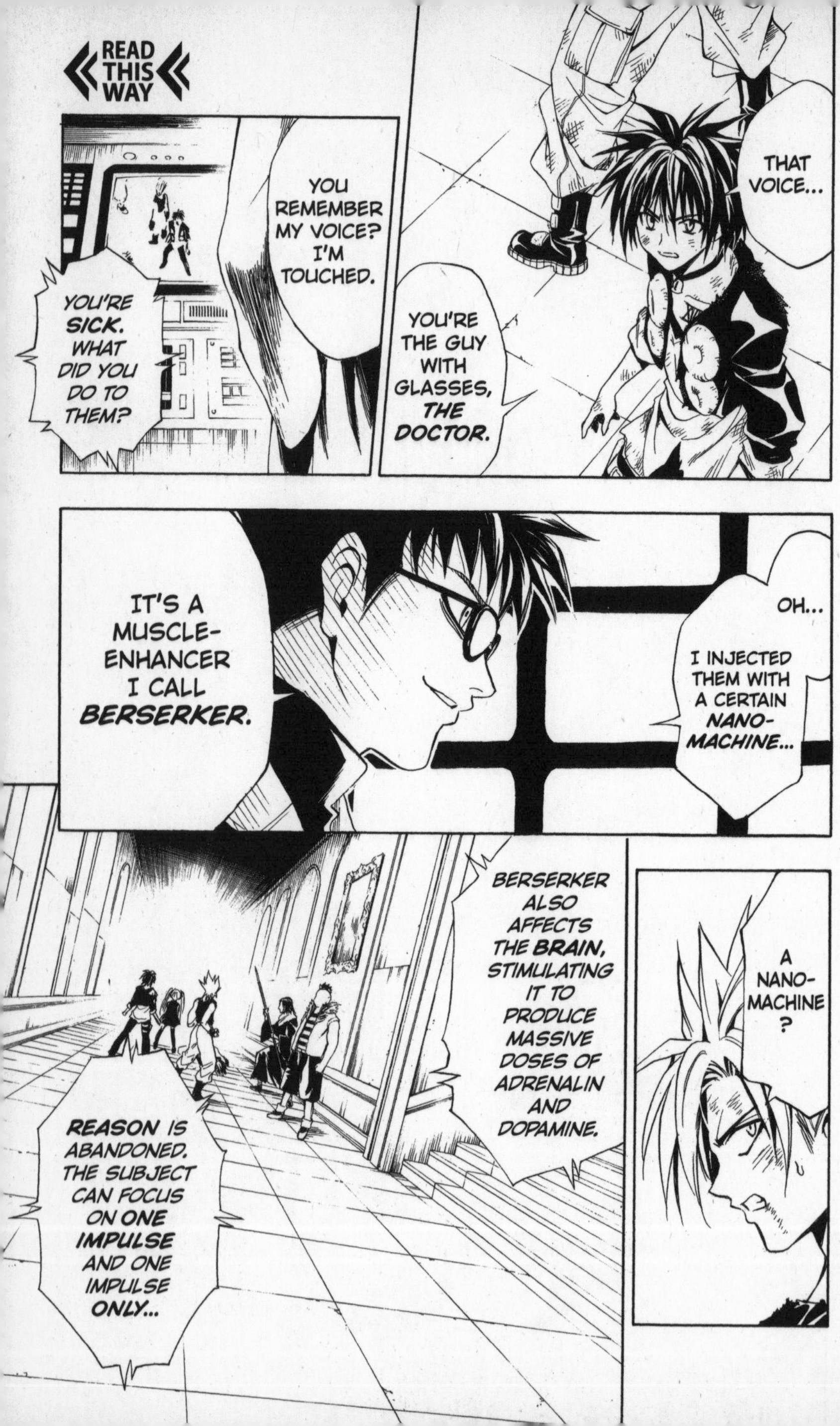
THAT VOICE...
YOU'RE THE GUY WITH GLASSES, THE DOCTOR.
YOU REMEMBER MY VOICE? I'M TOUCHED.
YOU'RE SICK. WHAT DID YOU DO TO THEM?
OH...
I INJECTED THEM WITH A CERTAIN NANO-MACHINE...
IT'S A MUSCLE-ENHANCER I CALL BERSERKER.
A NANO-MACHINE?
BERSERKER ALSO AFFECTS THE BRAIN, STIMULATING IT TO PRODUCE MASSIVE DOSES OF ADRENALIN AND DOPAMINE.
REASON IS ABANDONED. THE SUBJECT CAN FOCUS ON ONE IMPULSE AND ONE IMPULSE ONLY...

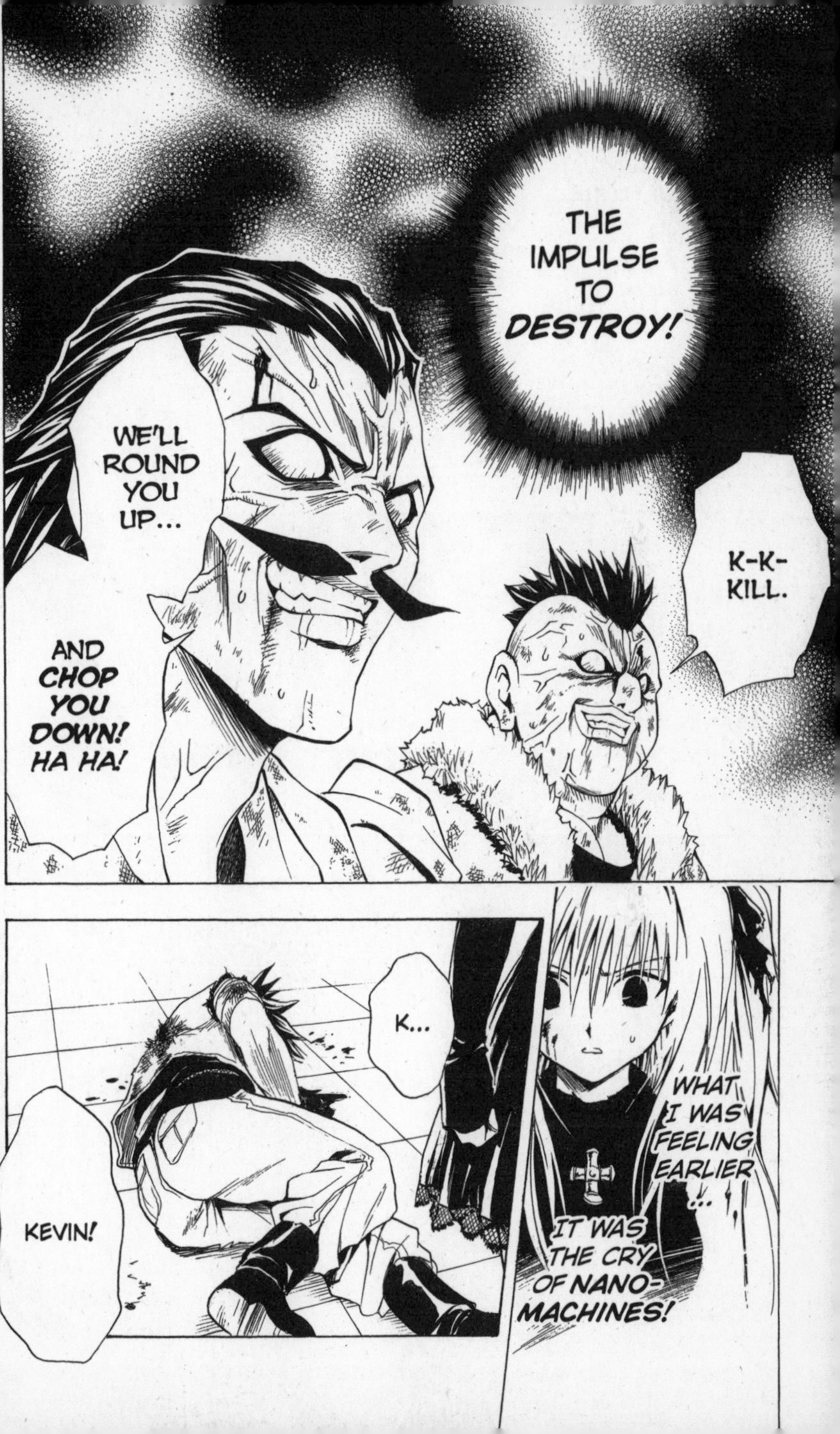
THE IMPULSE TO DESTROY!
K-K-KILL.
WE'LL ROUND YOU UP...
AND CHOP YOU DOWN! HA HA!
WHAT I WAS FEELING EARLIER...
IT WAS THE CRY OF NANO-MACHINES!
K...
KEVIN!

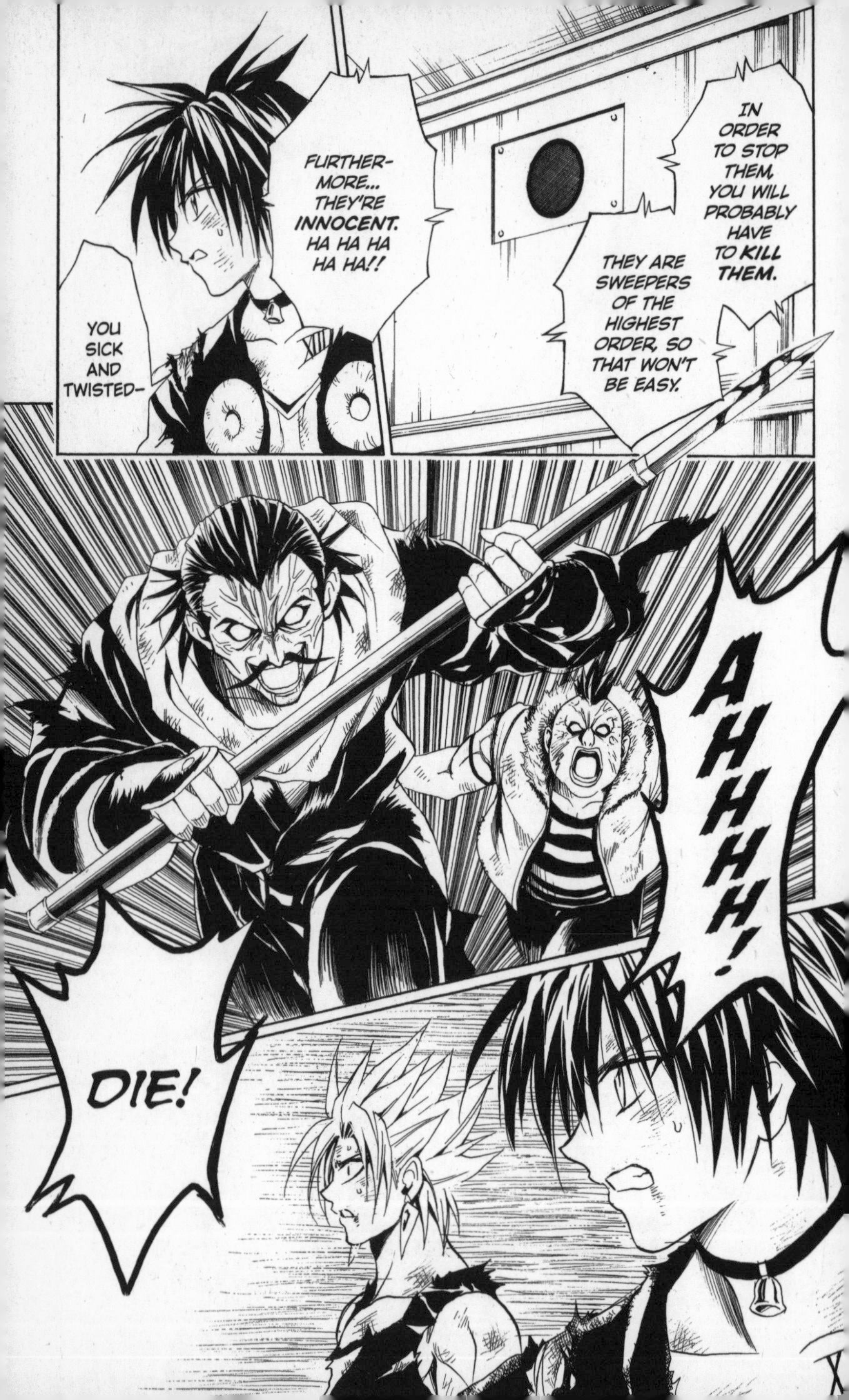

IN ORDER TO STOP THEM, YOU WILL PROBABLY HAVE TO KILL THEM.
THEY ARE SWEEPERS OF THE HIGHEST ORDER, SO THAT WON'T BE EASY.
FURTHERMORE... THEY'RE INNOCENT. HA HA HA HA HA!!
YOU SICK AND TWISTED-
AHHHHH!
DIE!

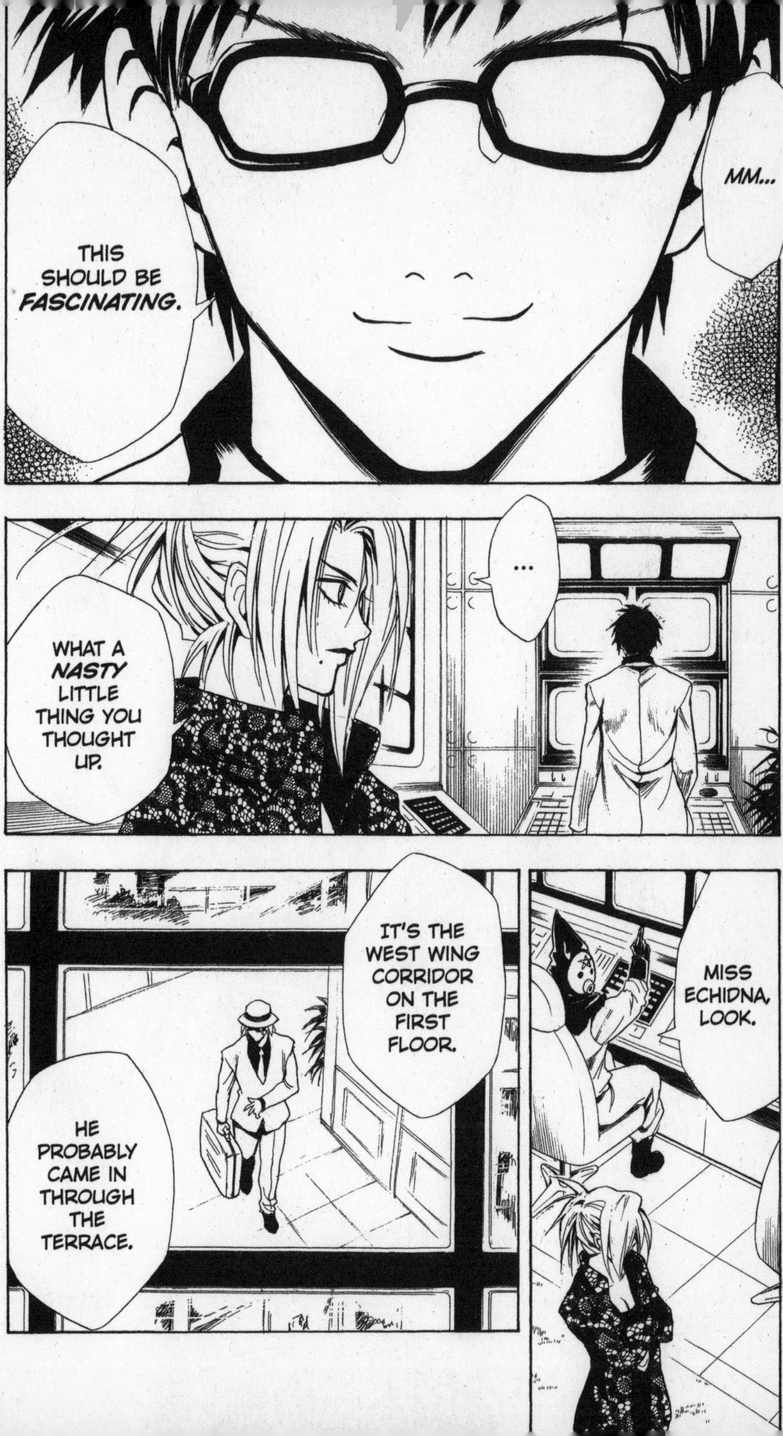
MM...
THIS SHOULD BE FASCINATING.
...
WHAT A NASTY LITTLE THING YOU THOUGHT UP.
MISS ECHIDNA, LOOK.
IT'S THE WEST WING CORRIDOR ON THE FIRST FLOOR.
HE PROBABLY CAME IN THROUGH THE TERRACE.

READ THIS WAY

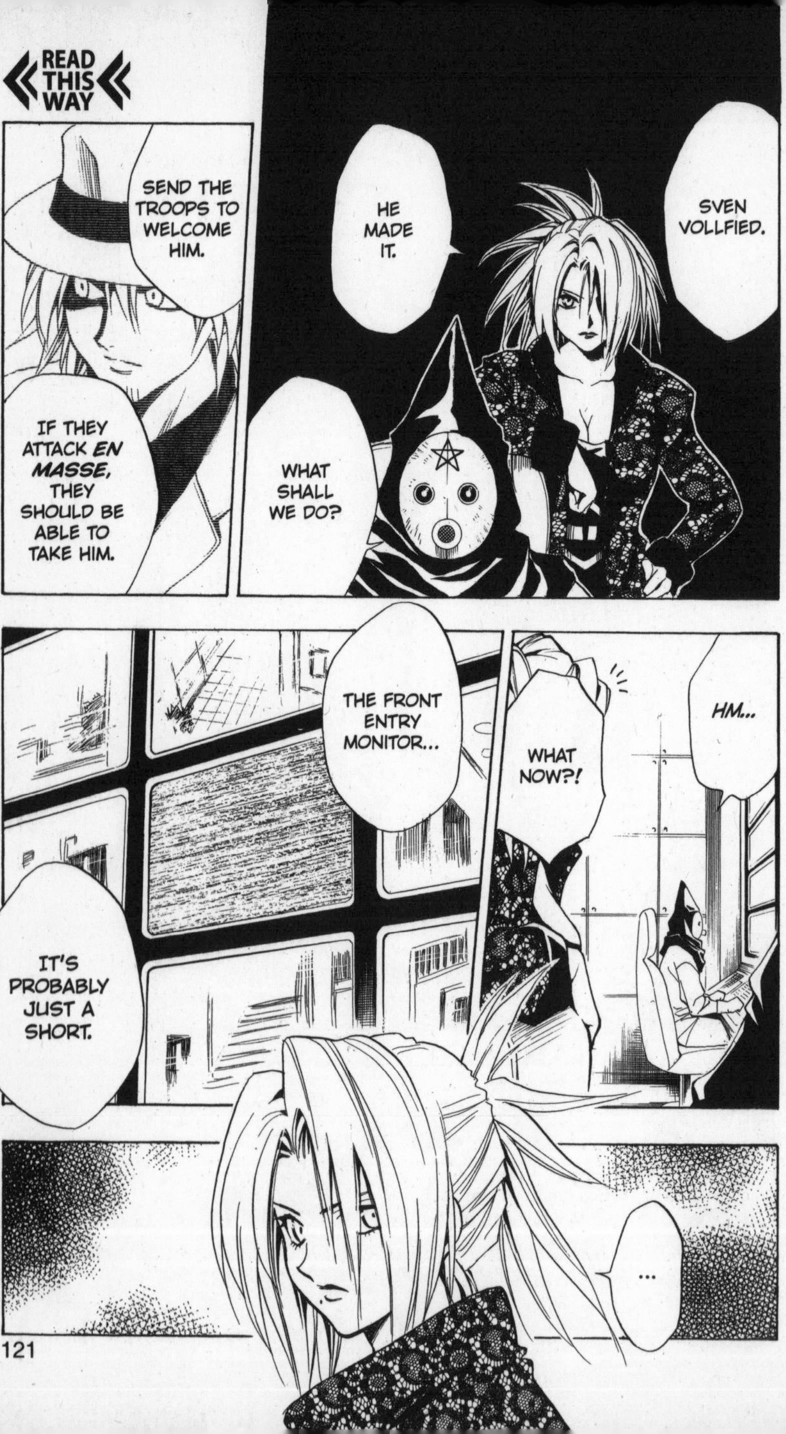
SVEN VOLLFIED.
HE MADE IT.
WHAT SHALL WE DO?
SEND THE TROOPS TO WELCOME HIM.
IF THEY ATTACK *EN MASSE,* THEY SHOULD BE ABLE TO TAKE HIM.
HM...
WHAT NOW?!
THE FRONT ENTRY MONITOR...
IT'S PROBABLY JUST A SHORT.
...

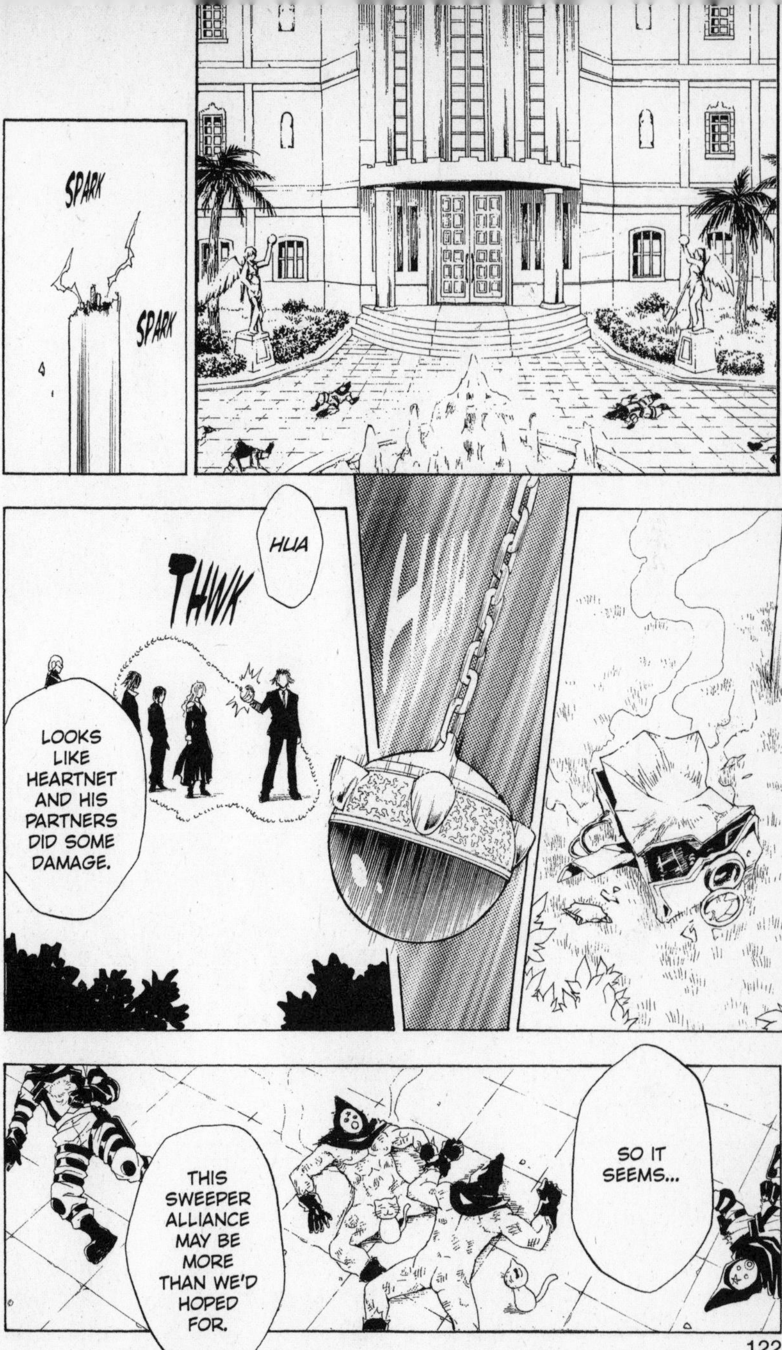
SPARK
SPARK
HUA
THWK
LOOKS LIKE HEARTNET AND HIS PARTNERS DID SOME DAMAGE.
SO IT SEEMS...
THIS SWEEPER ALLIANCE MAY BE MORE THAN WE'D HOPED FOR.

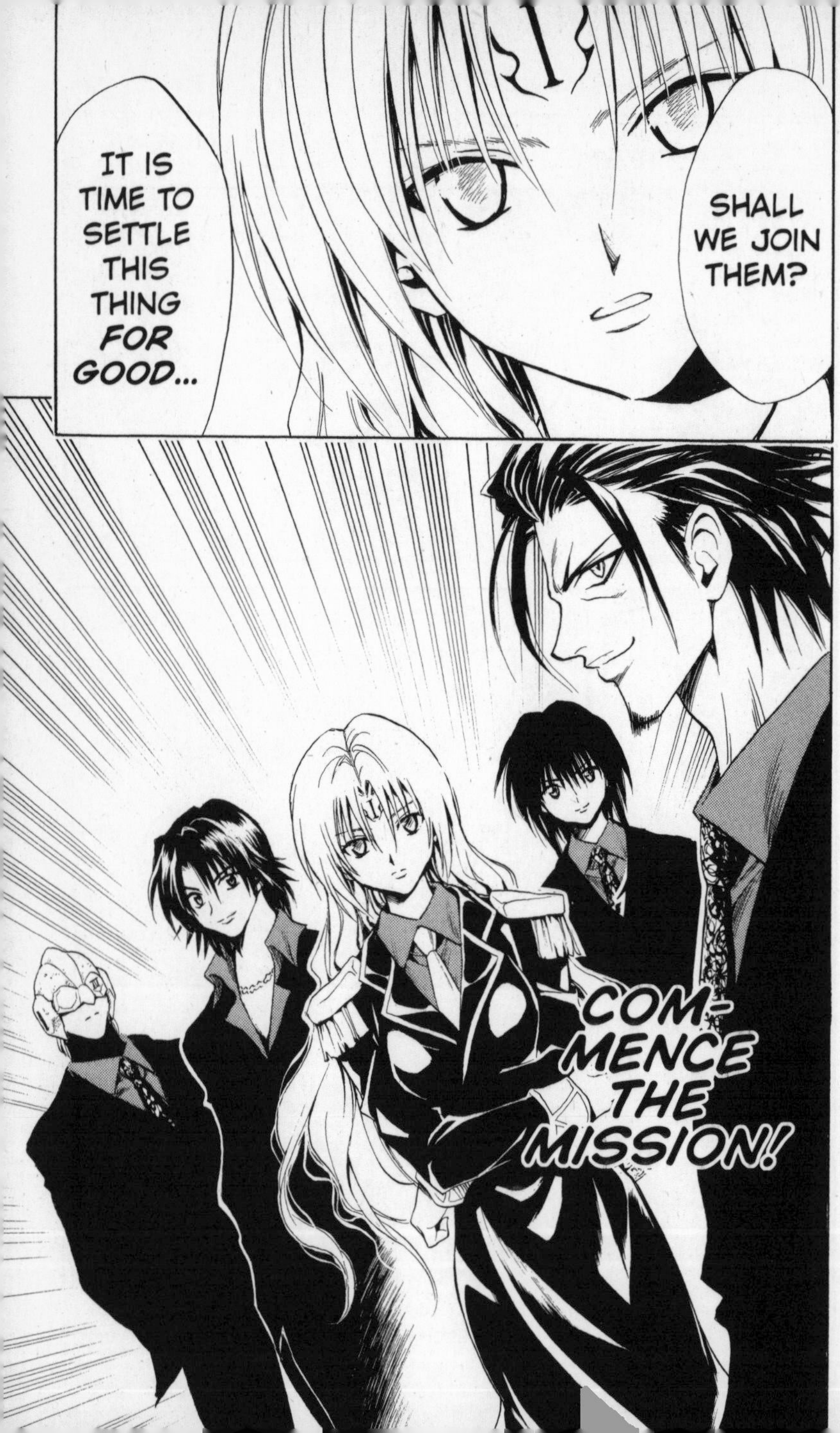
SHALL WE JOIN THEM?
IT IS TIME TO SETTLE THIS THING FOR GOOD...
COM-MENCE THE MISSION!

HE WENT OUT TO BUY LUNCH AND NEVER RETURNED.

BY AKIRA MIYAZAKI

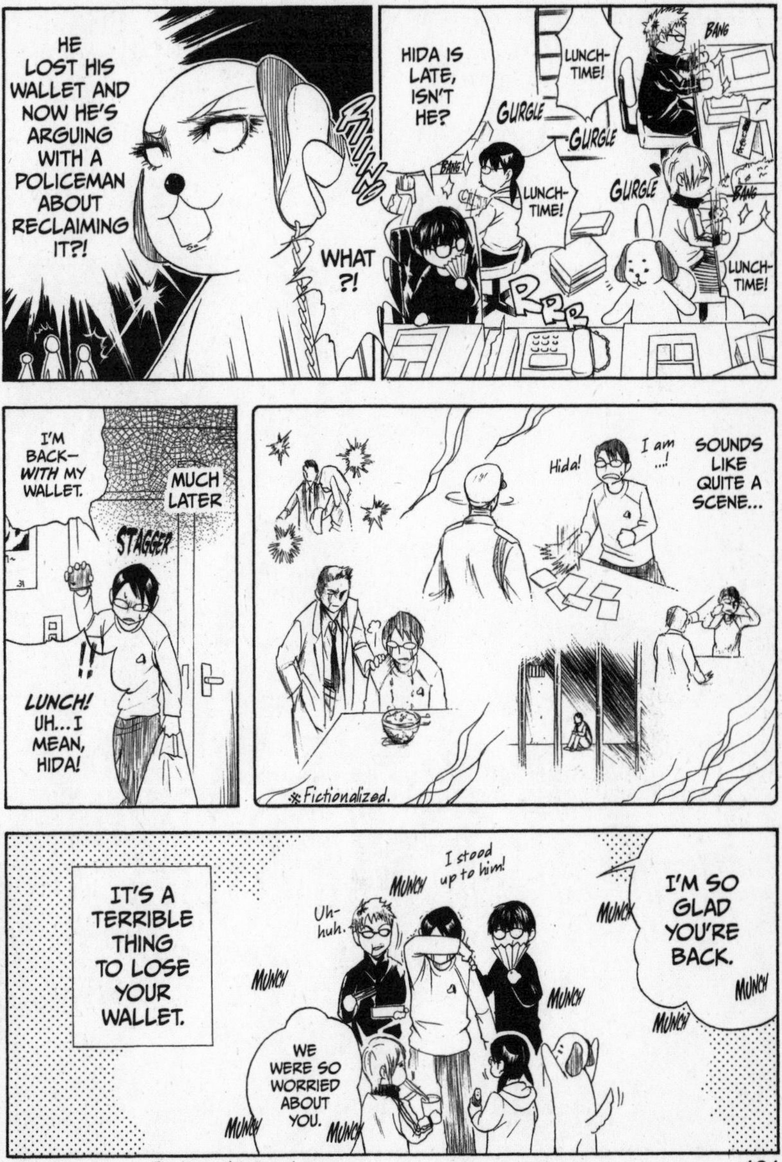
BANG
LUNCH-TIME!
HIDA IS LATE, ISN'T HE?
GURGLE
GURGLE
LUNCH-TIME!
BANG
GURGLE
BANG
LUNCH-TIME!
WHAT ?!
RRR
HE LOST HIS WALLET AND NOW HE'S ARGUING WITH A POLICEMAN ABOUT RECLAIMING IT?!
SOUNDS LIKE QUITE A SCENE...
I am ...!
Hida!
※Fictionalized.
MUCH LATER
I'M BACK—WITH MY WALLET.
STAGGER
!!
LUNCH! UH...I MEAN, HIDA!
I'M SO GLAD YOU'RE BACK.
MUNCH
I stood up to him!
MUNCH
Uh-huh.
MUNCH
MUNCH
MUNCH
MUNCH
WE WERE SO WORRIED ABOUT YOU.
MUNCH
MUNCH
IT'S A TERRIBLE THING TO LOSE YOUR WALLET.

Thank you for your time.

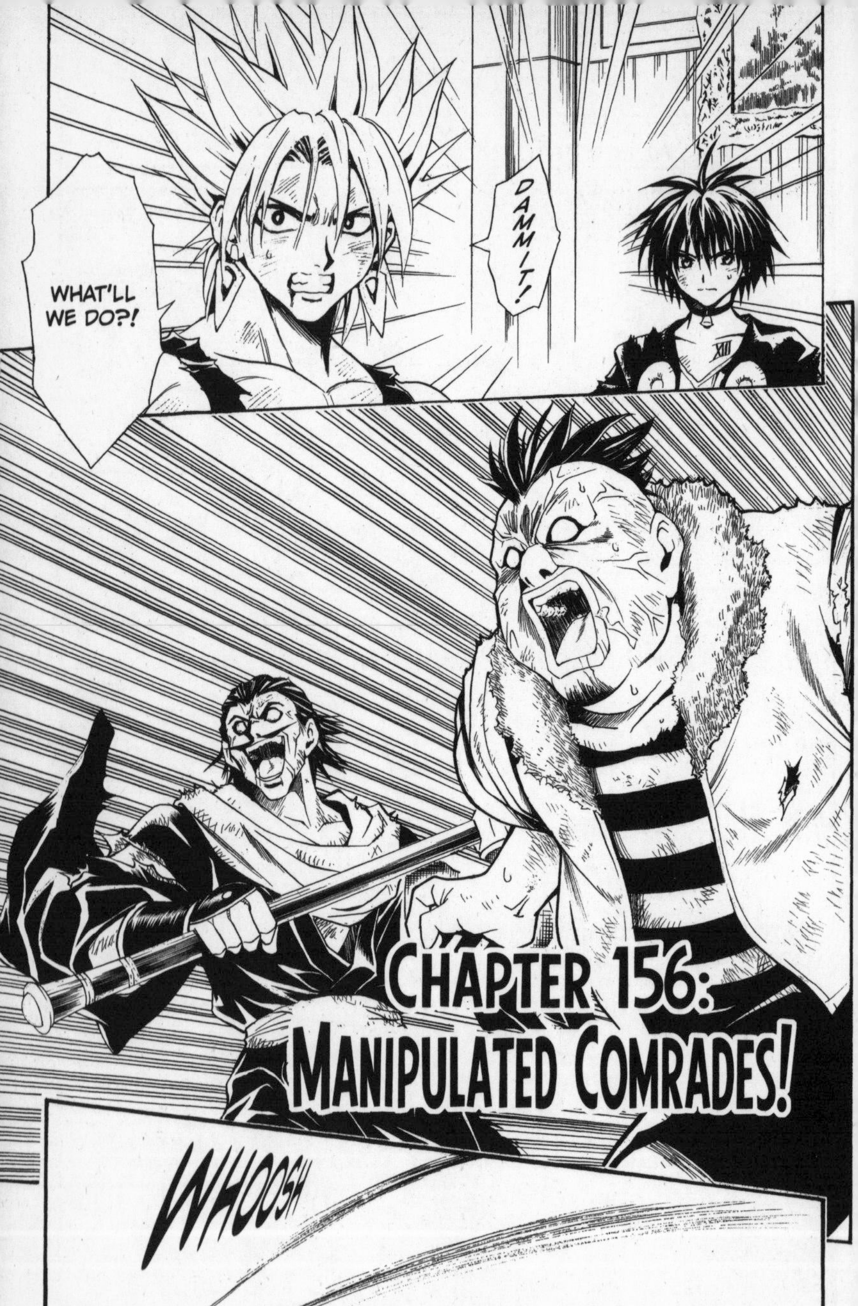
DAMMIT!
WHAT'LL WE DO?!
CHAPTER 156: MANIPULATED COMRADES!
WHOOSH

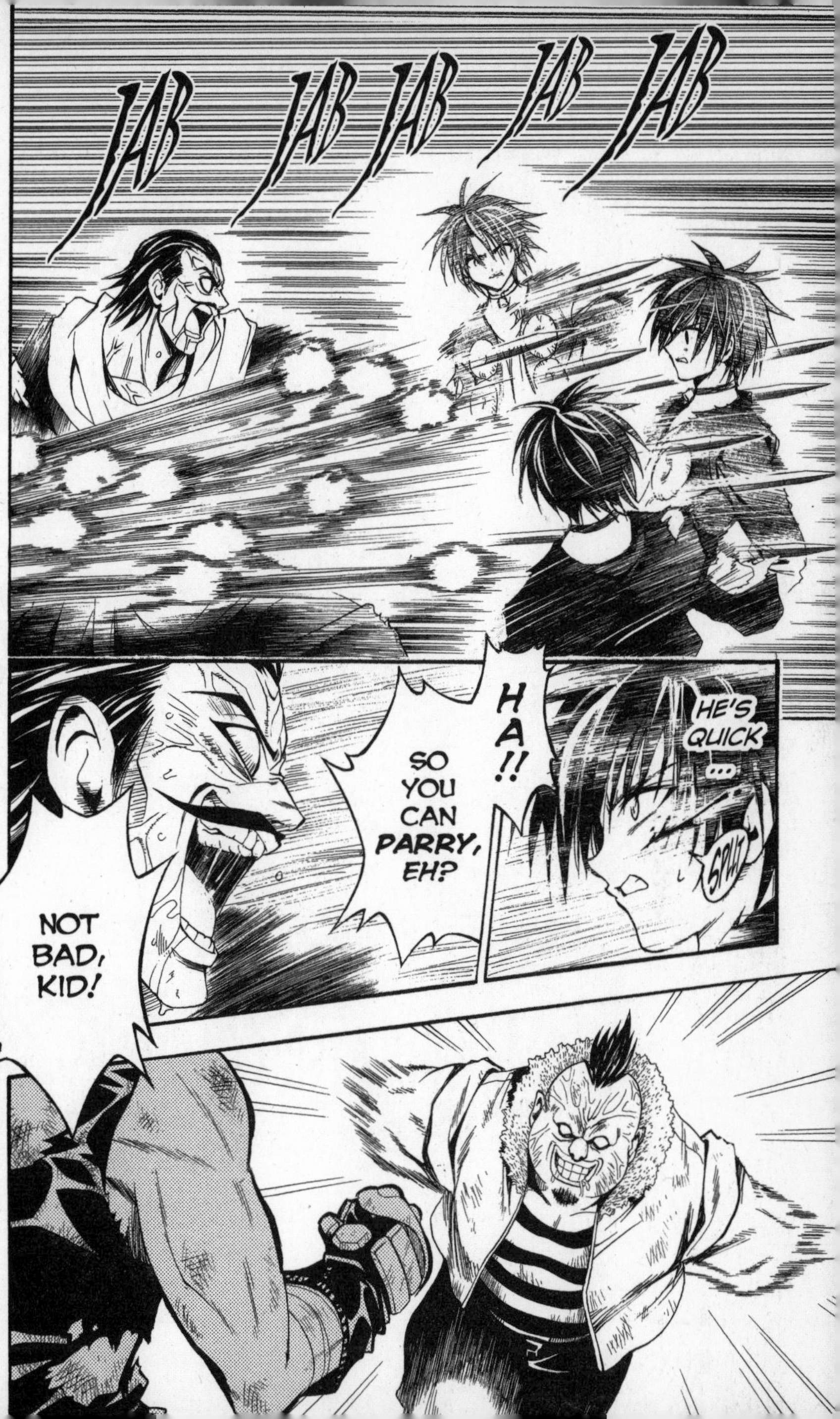
JAB JAB JAB JAB JAB
HE'S QUICK...
SPLIT
HA!!
SO YOU CAN PARRY, EH?
NOT BAD, KID!

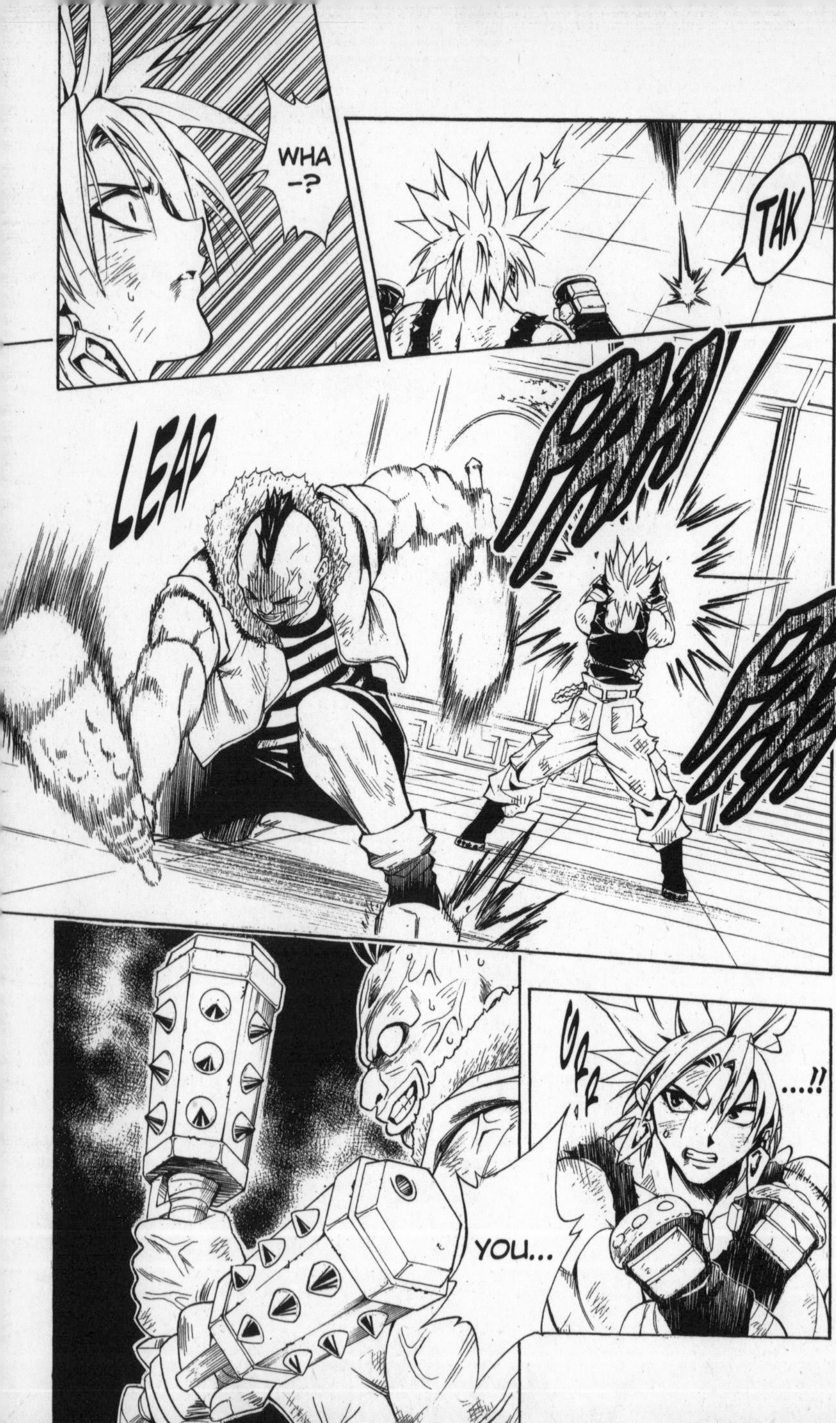
TAK
WHA–?
PAH
PAH
LEAP
...!!
GRR
YOU...

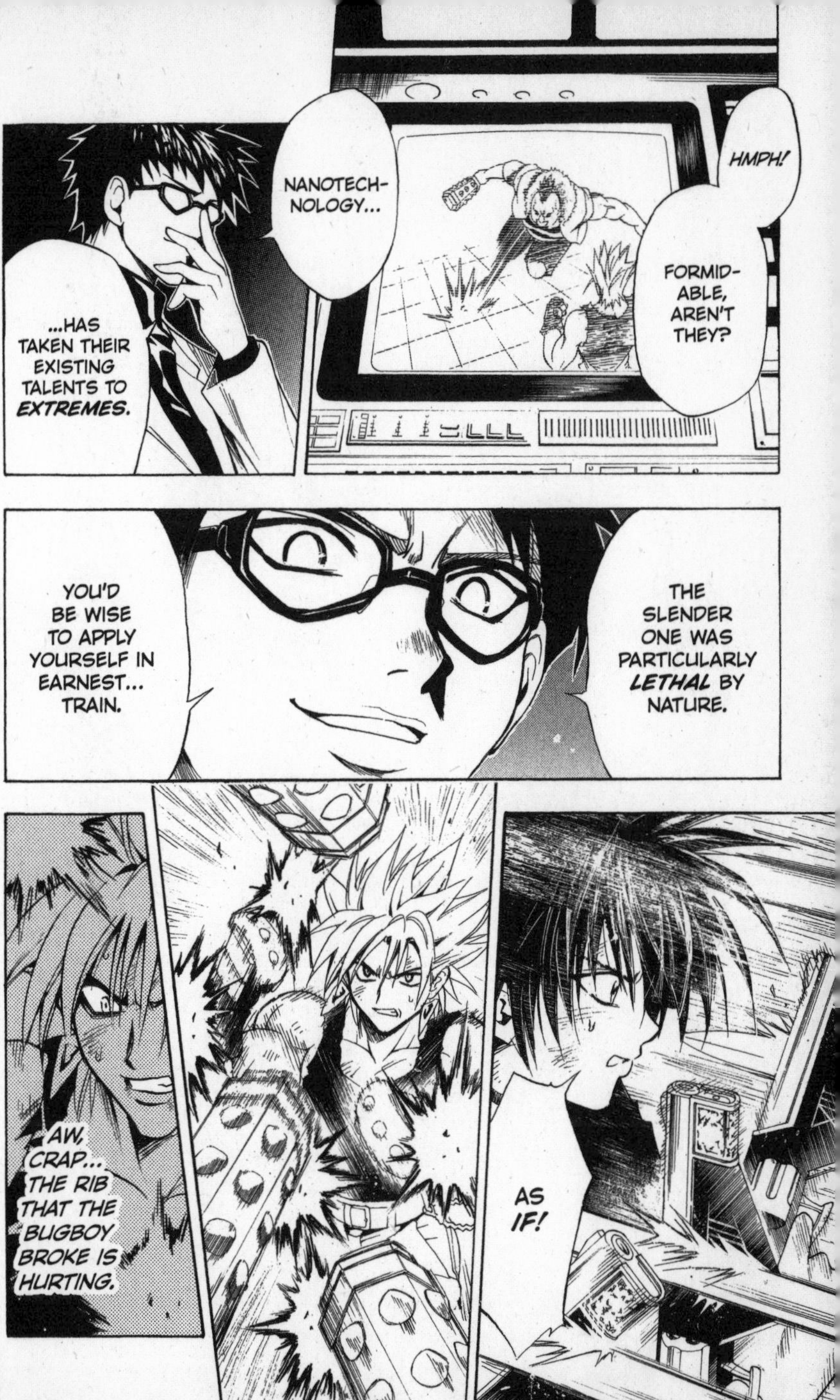
HMPH!
FORMID-ABLE, AREN'T THEY?
NANOTECH-NOLOGY...
...HAS TAKEN THEIR EXISTING TALENTS TO *EXTREMES.*
THE SLENDER ONE WAS PARTICULARLY *LETHAL* BY NATURE.
YOU'D BE WISE TO APPLY YOURSELF IN EARNEST... TRAIN.
AS *IF!*
AW, CRAP... THE RIB THAT THE BUGBOY BROKE IS HURTING.

READ THIS WAY

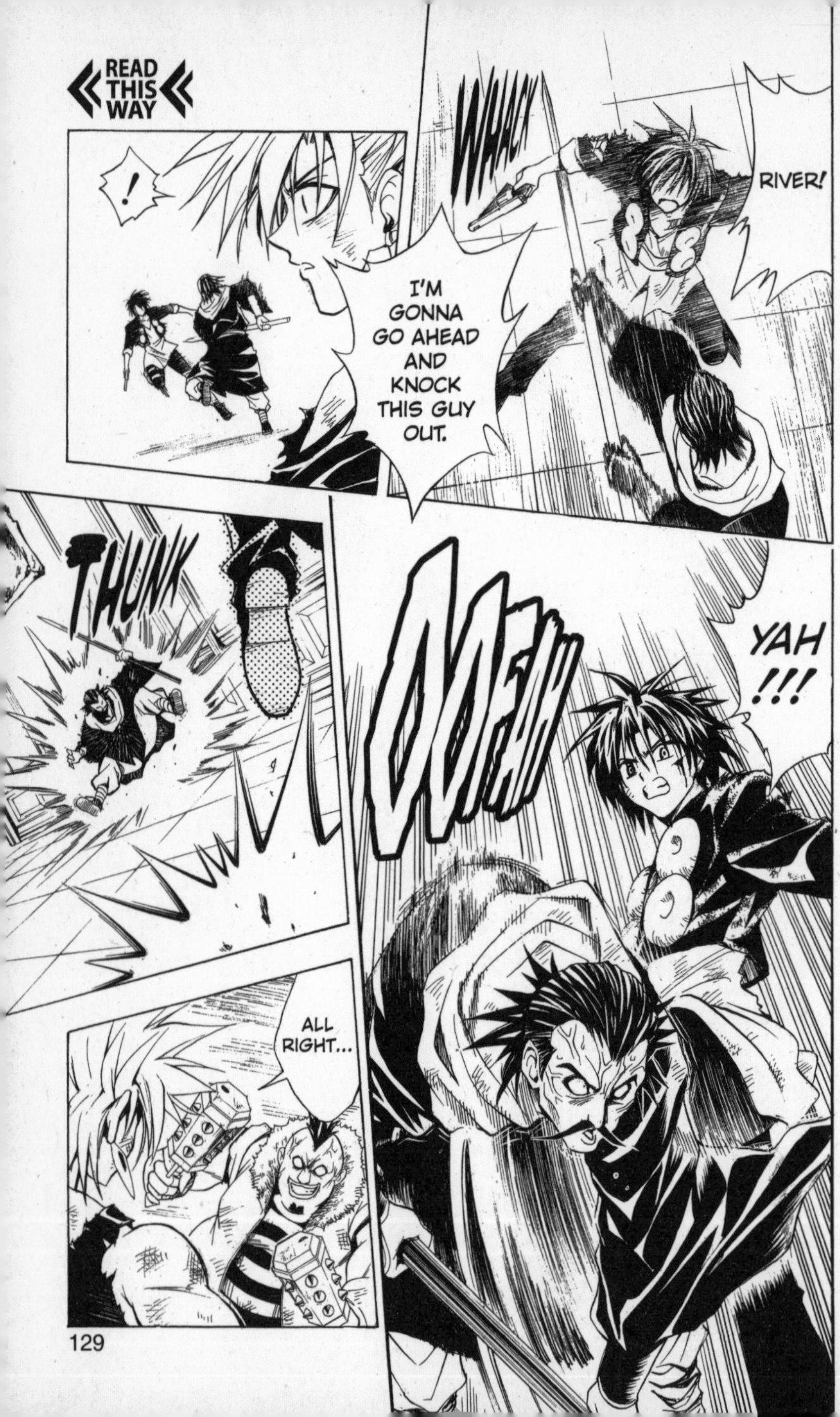
WHACK
RIVER!
!
I'M GONNA GO AHEAD AND KNOCK THIS GUY OUT.
YAH !!!
THUNK
ALL RIGHT...

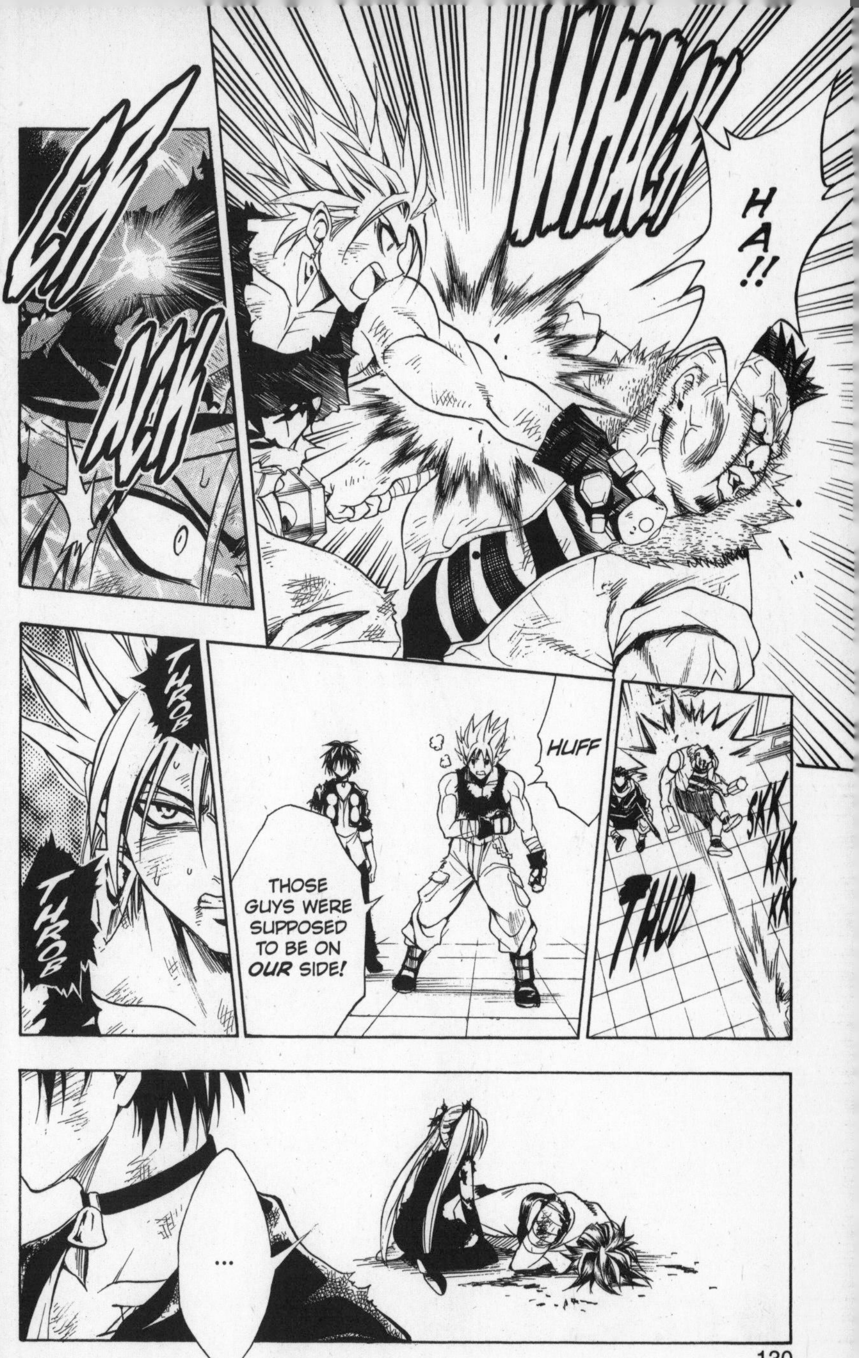

HA!!
WHACK
THUD
HUFF
THOSE GUYS WERE SUPPOSED TO BE ON *OUR* SIDE!
THROB
THROB
...

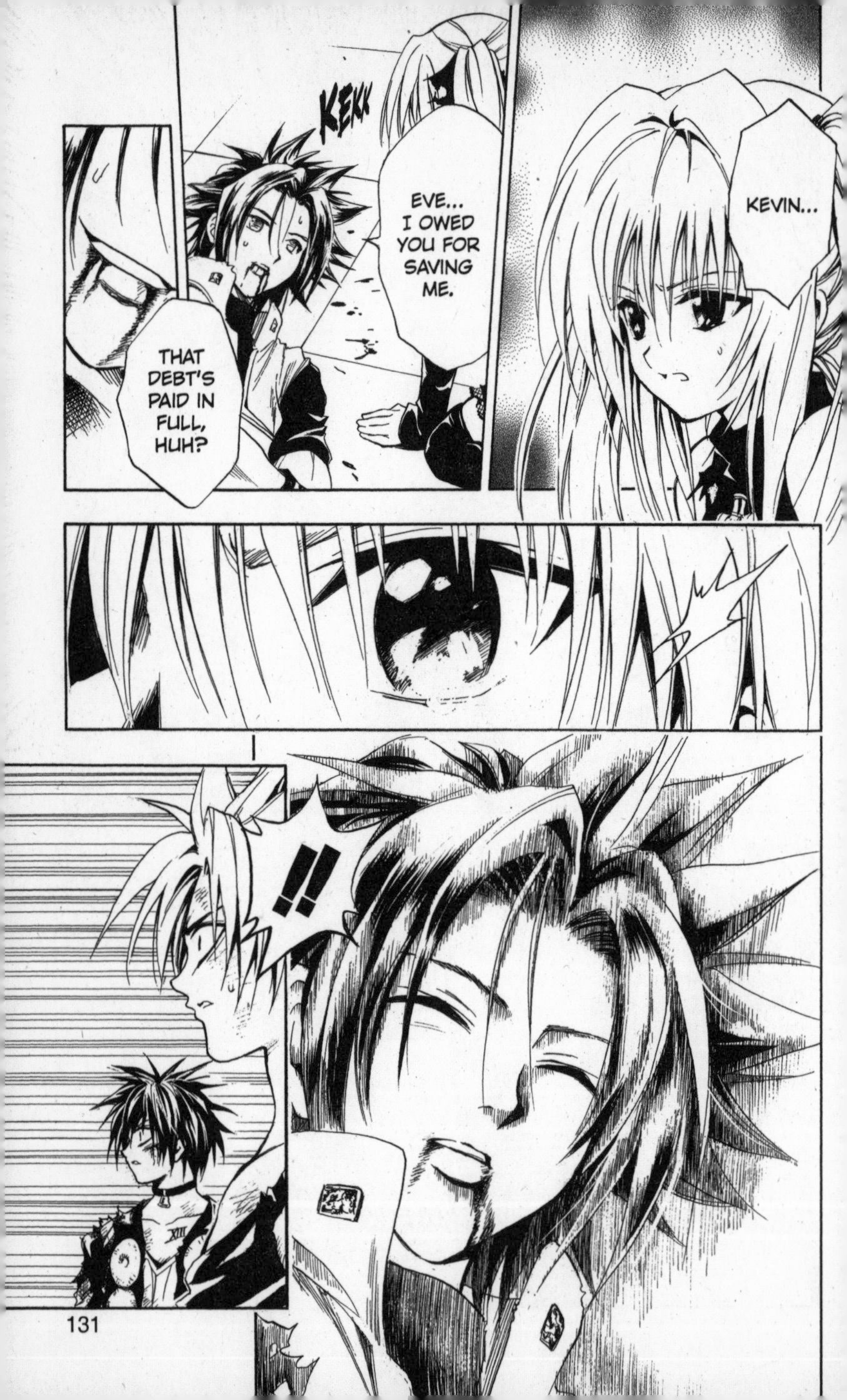
KEVIN...
KEKK
EVE... I OWED YOU FOR SAVING ME.
THAT DEBT'S PAID IN FULL, HUH?
!!

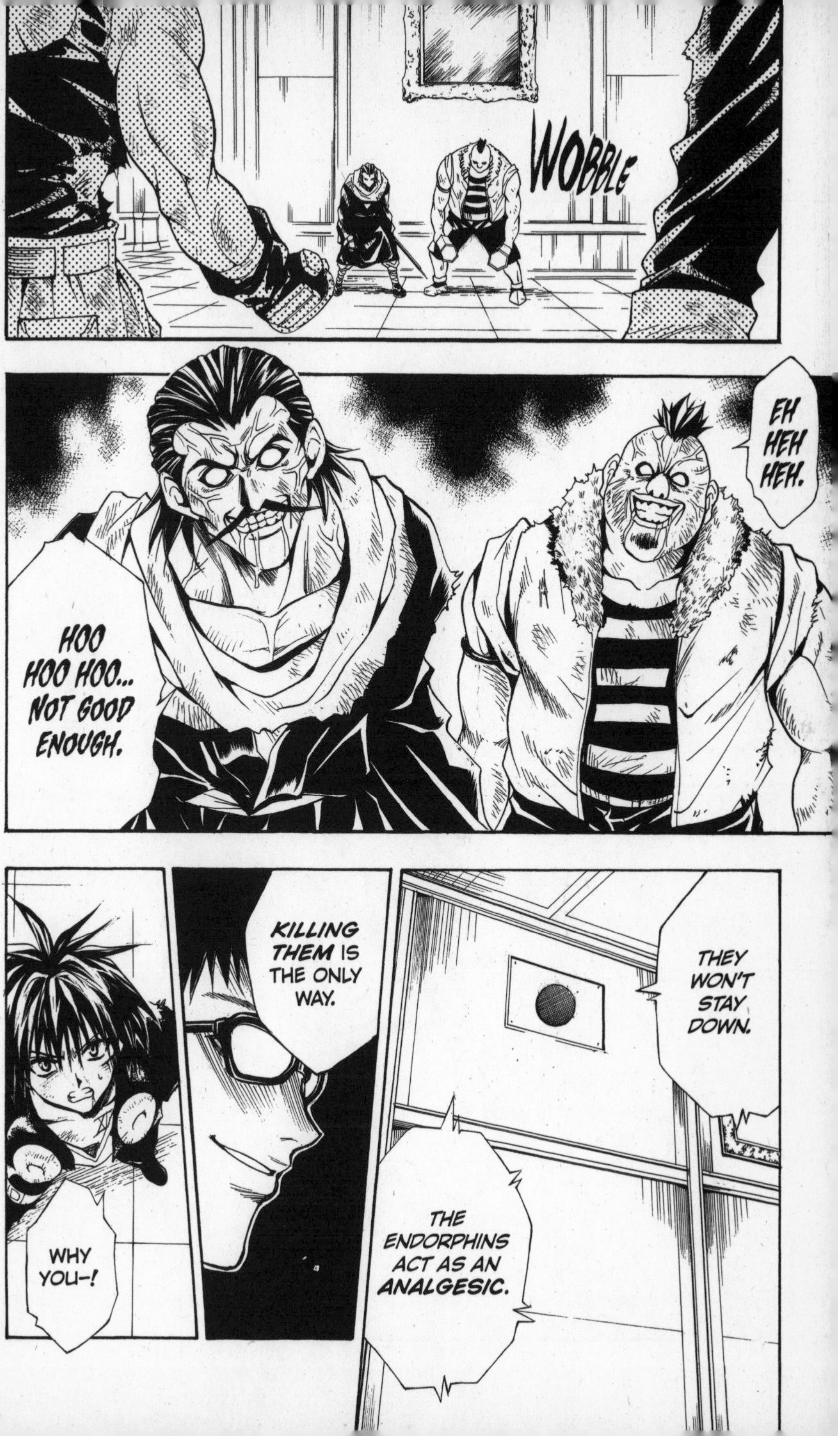
WOBBLE
EH HEH HEH.
HOO HOO HOO... NOT GOOD ENOUGH.
THEY WON'T STAY DOWN.
THE ENDORPHINS ACT AS AN *ANALGESIC.*
KILLING THEM IS THE ONLY WAY.
WHY YOU-!

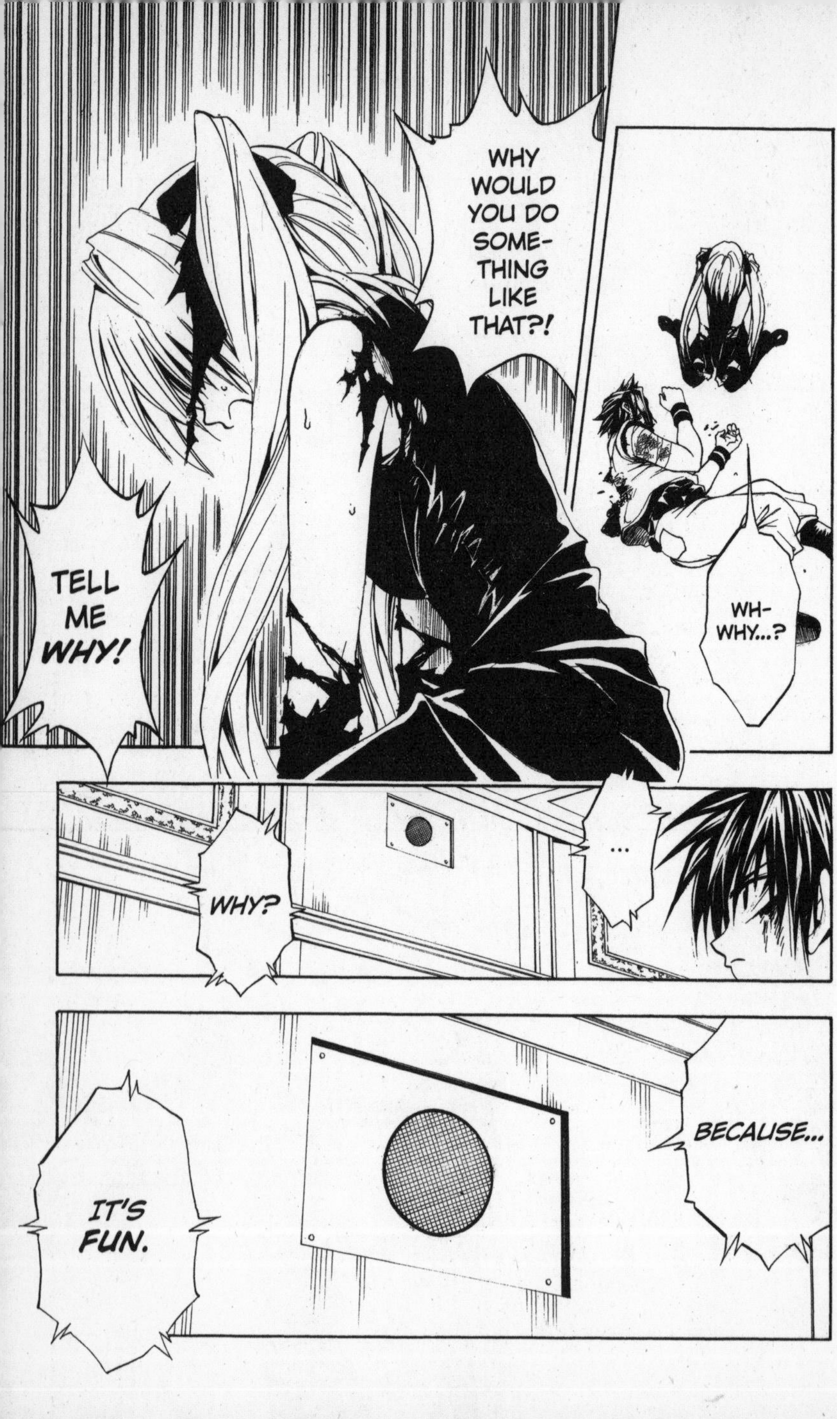
WH-WHY...?
WHY WOULD YOU DO SOME-THING LIKE THAT?!
TELL ME WHY!
...
WHY?
BECAUSE...
IT'S FUN.

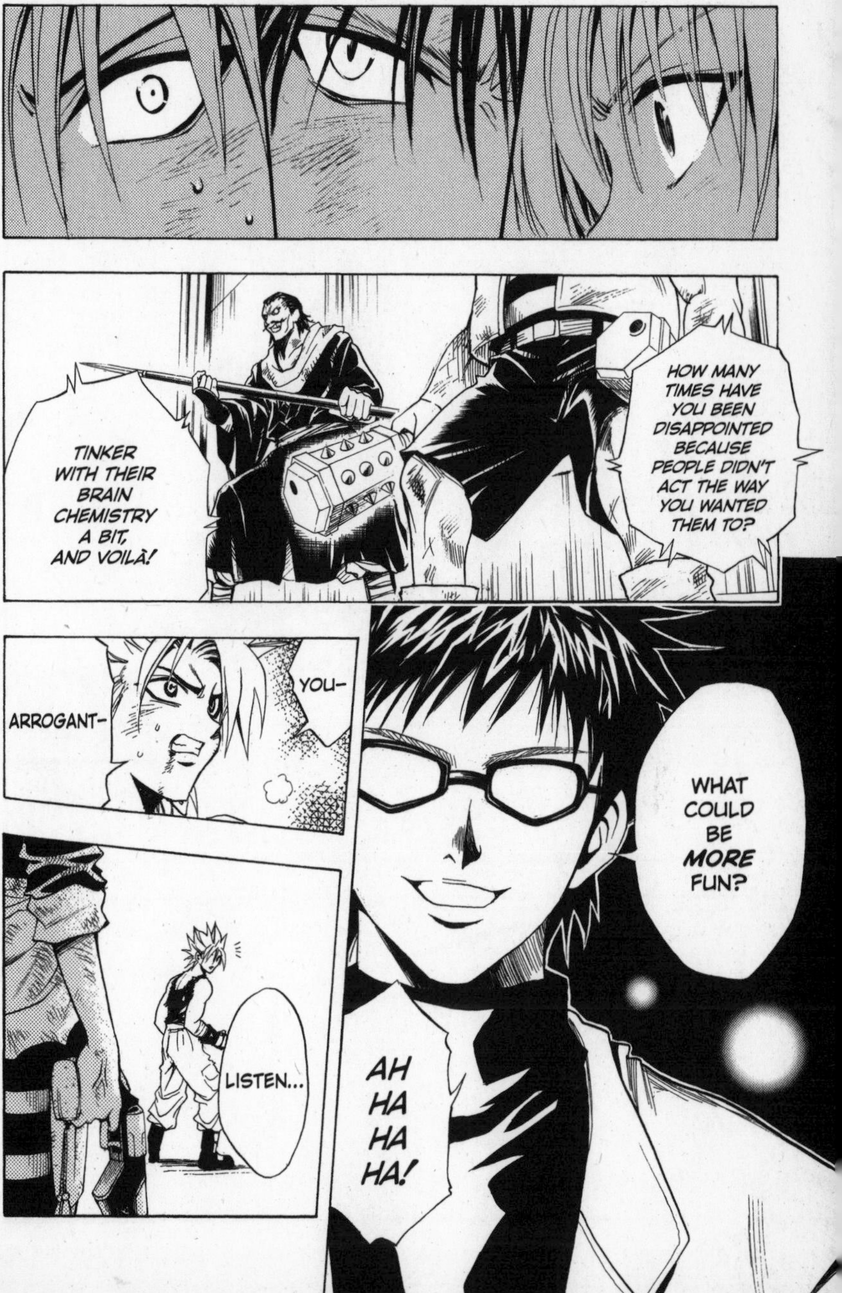
HOW MANY TIMES HAVE YOU BEEN DISAPPOINTED BECAUSE PEOPLE DIDN'T ACT THE WAY YOU WANTED THEM TO?
TINKER WITH THEIR BRAIN CHEMISTRY A BIT, AND VOILÀ!
WHAT COULD BE *MORE* FUN?
AH HA HA HA!
YOU-
ARROGANT-
LISTEN...

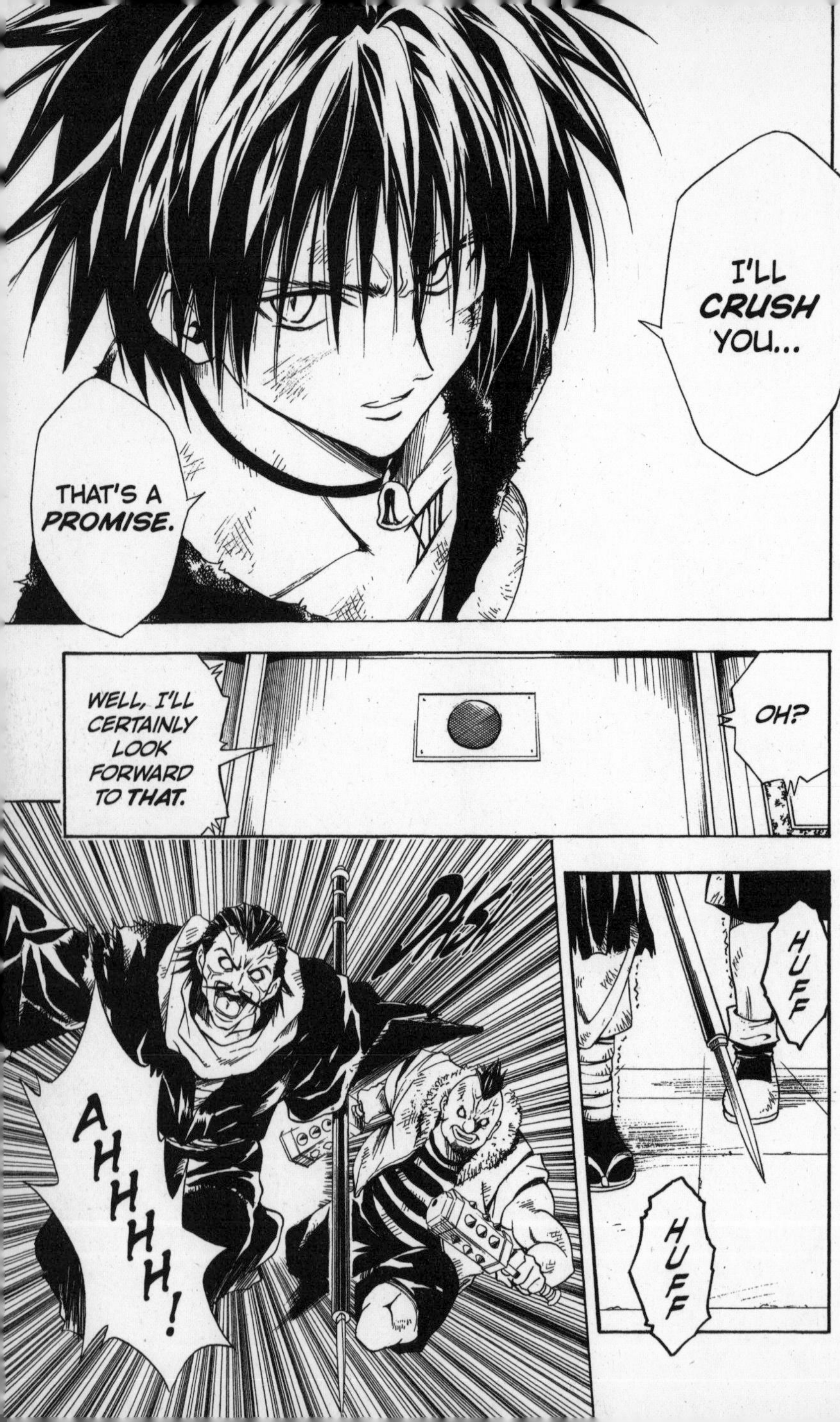
I'LL CRUSH YOU...
THAT'S A PROMISE.
OH?
WELL, I'LL CERTAINLY LOOK FORWARD TO THAT.
HUFF
HUFF
AHHHH!

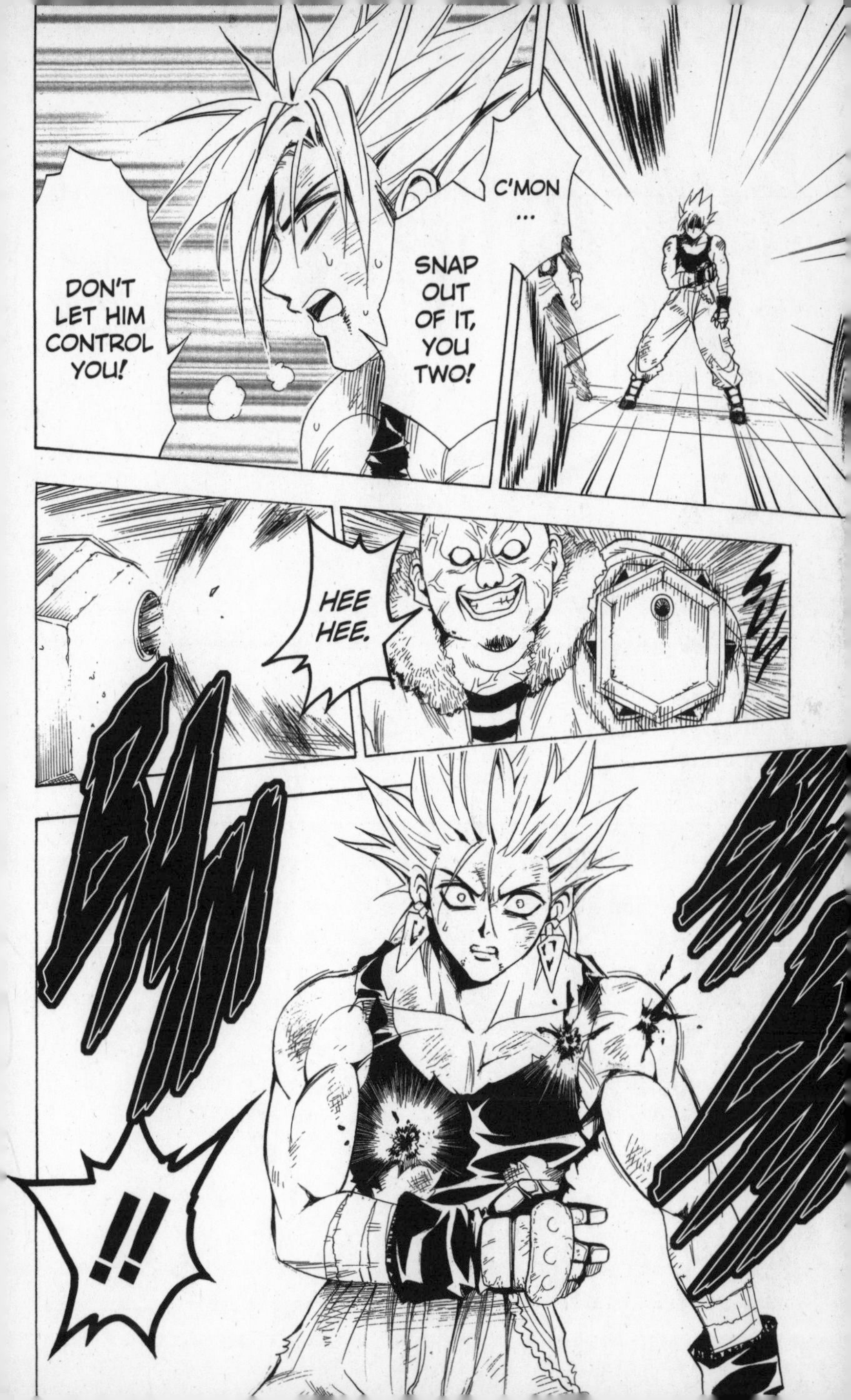
C'MON ...
SNAP OUT OF IT, YOU TWO!
DON'T LET HIM CONTROL YOU!
HEE HEE.
!!

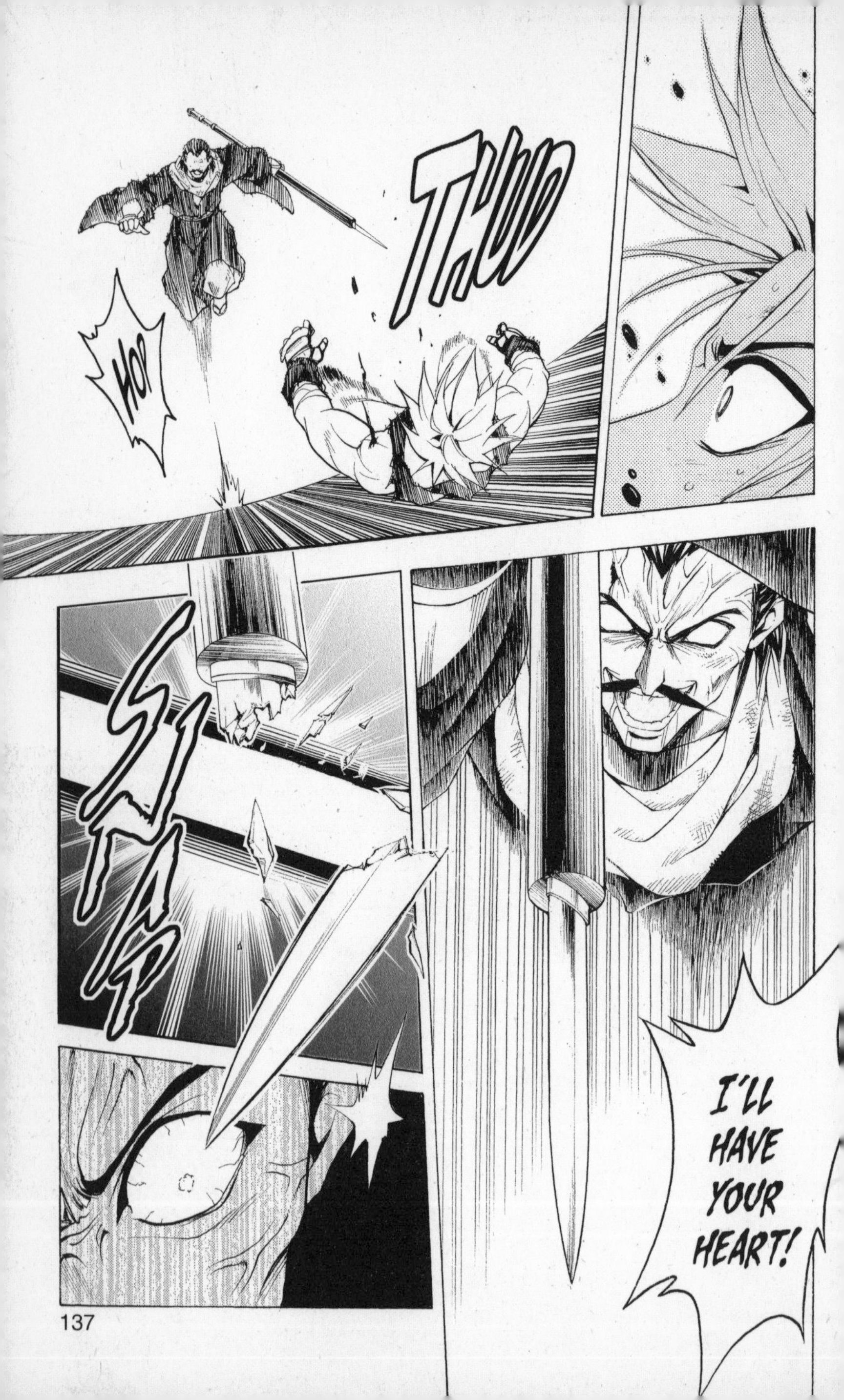
TUD
HOP
I'LL HAVE YOUR HEART!
SHING

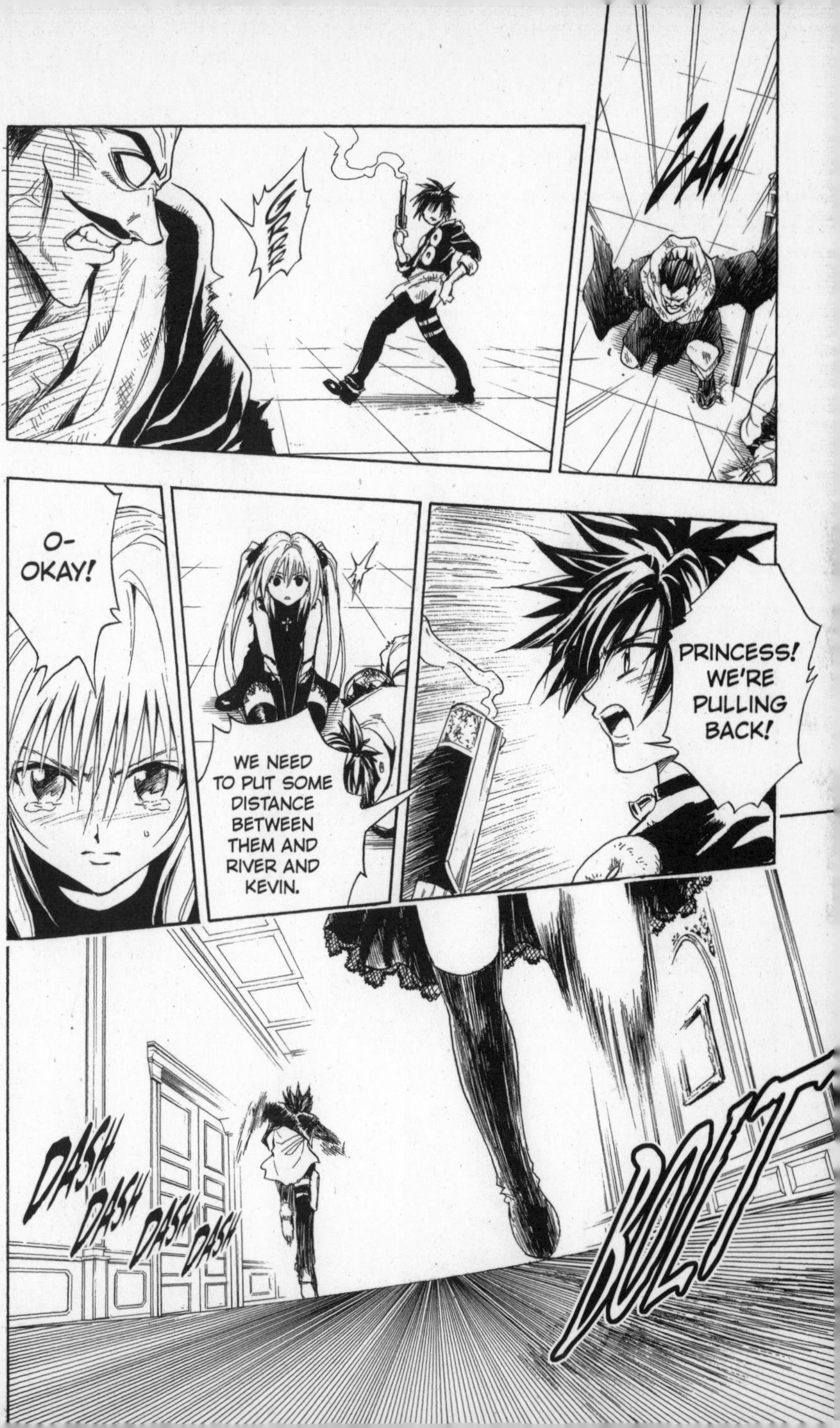
ZAH
GRRRR
PRINCESS! WE'RE PULLING BACK!
WE NEED TO PUT SOME DISTANCE BETWEEN THEM AND RIVER AND KEVIN.
O- OKAY!
BOLT
DASH DASH DASH DASH

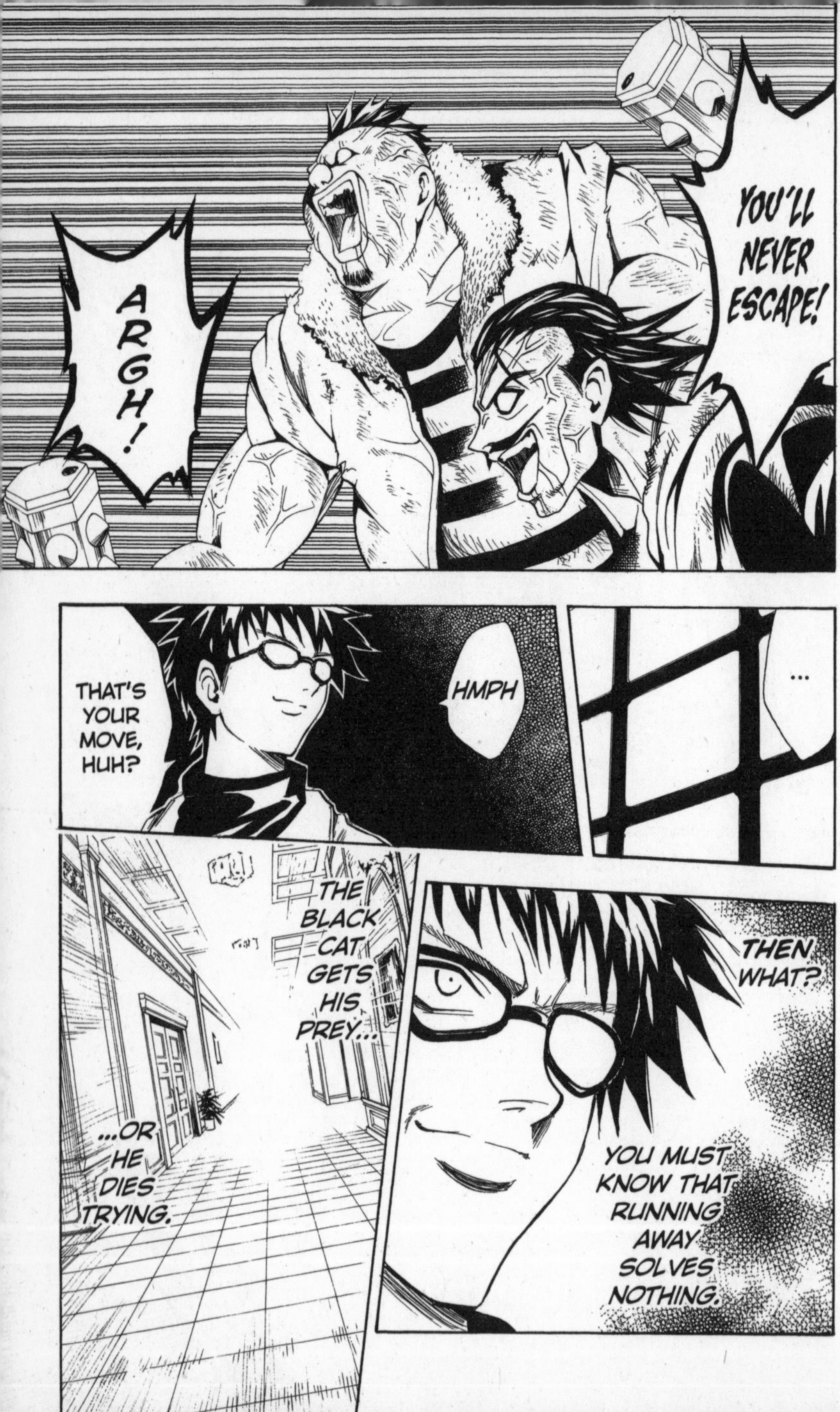
YOU'LL NEVER ESCAPE!
ARGH!
...
HMPH
THAT'S YOUR MOVE, HUH?
THEN WHAT?
YOU MUST KNOW THAT RUNNING AWAY SOLVES NOTHING.
THE BLACK CAT GETS HIS PREY...
...OR HE DIES TRYING.

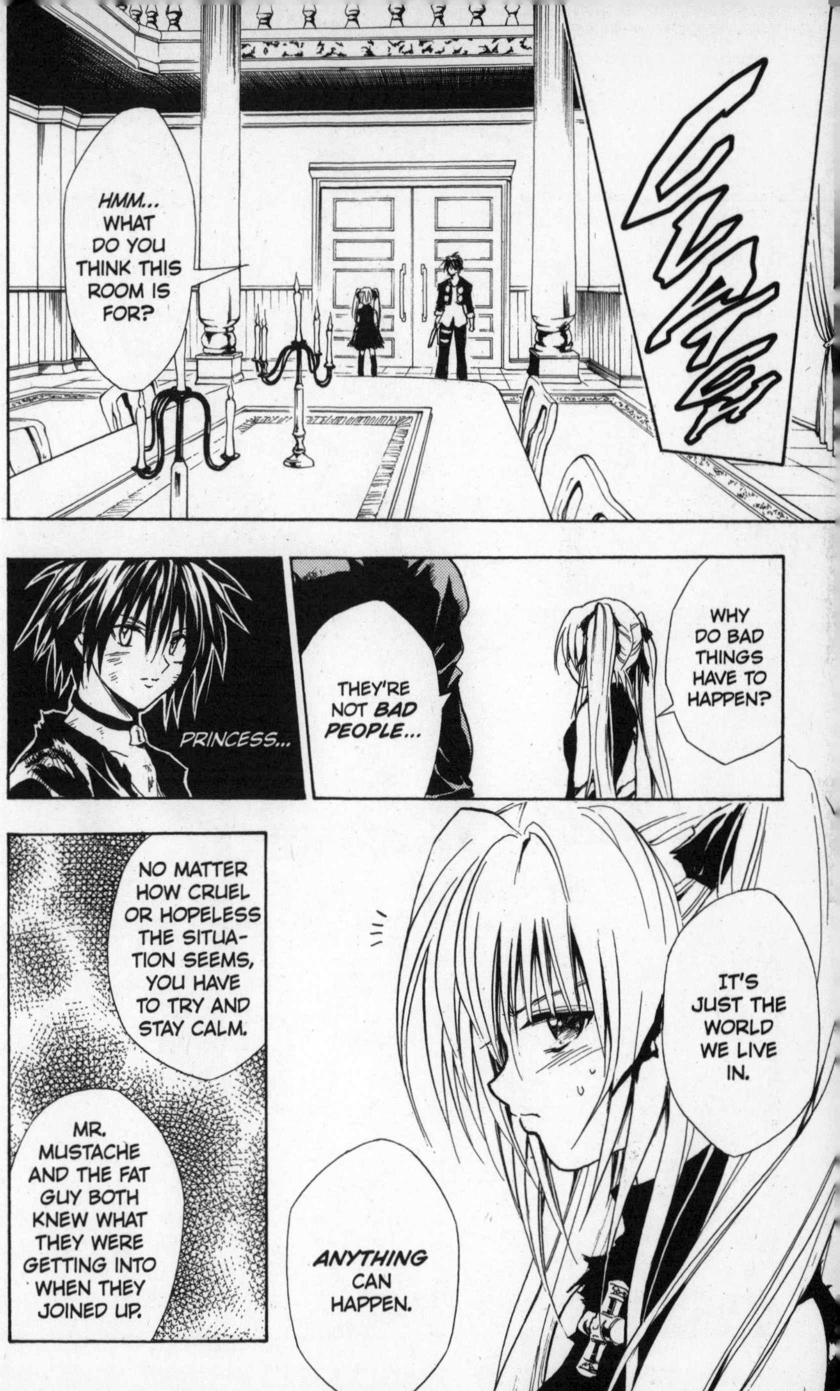
HMM... WHAT DO YOU THINK THIS ROOM IS FOR?
WHY DO BAD THINGS HAVE TO HAPPEN?
THEY'RE NOT BAD PEOPLE...
PRINCESS...
IT'S JUST THE WORLD WE LIVE IN.
ANYTHING CAN HAPPEN.
NO MATTER HOW CRUEL OR HOPELESS THE SITUATION SEEMS, YOU HAVE TO TRY AND STAY CALM.
MR. MUSTACHE AND THE FAT GUY BOTH KNEW WHAT THEY WERE GETTING INTO WHEN THEY JOINED UP.

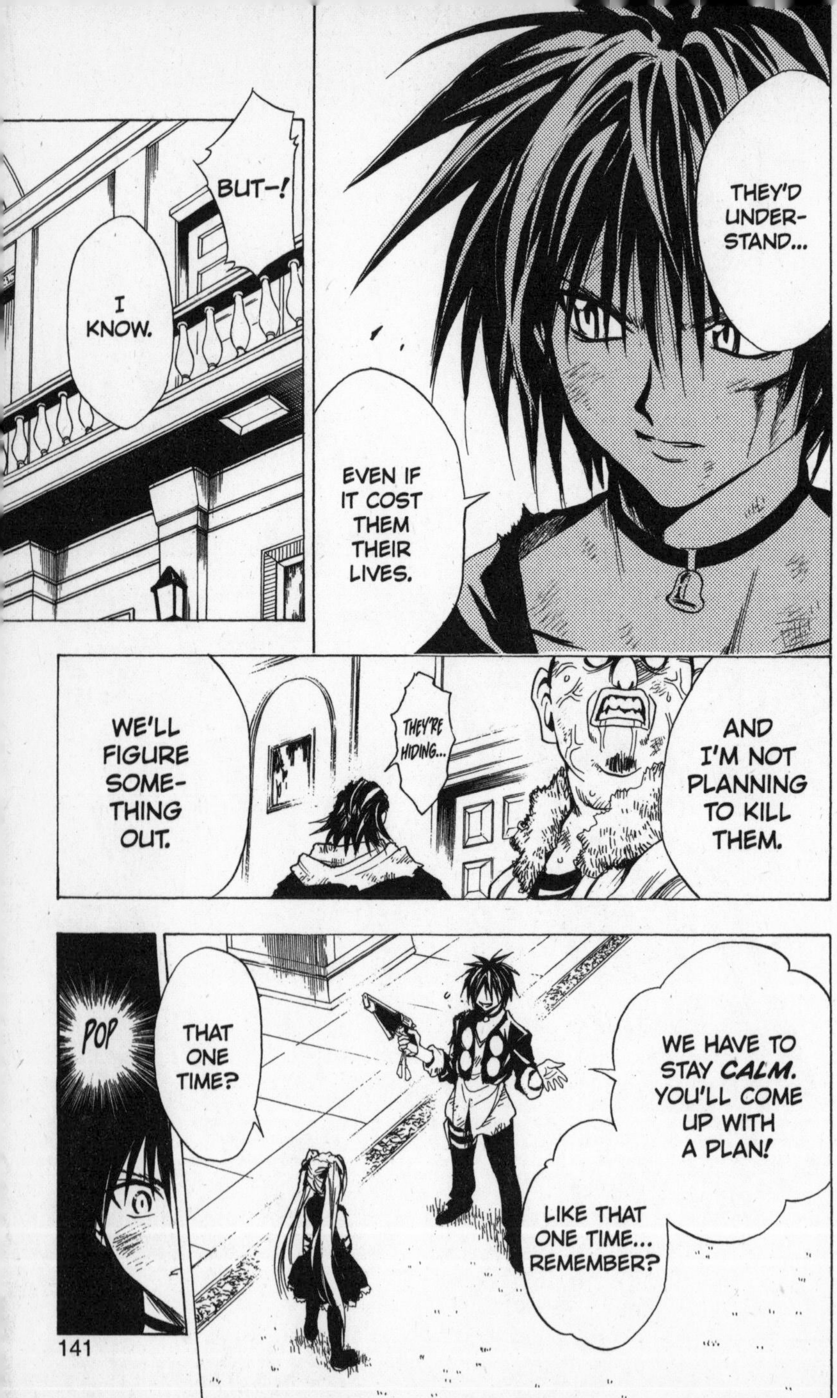
THEY'D UNDER-STAND...
EVEN IF IT COST THEM THEIR LIVES.
BUT-!
I KNOW.
AND I'M NOT PLANNING TO KILL THEM.
THEY'RE HIDING...
WE'LL FIGURE SOME-THING OUT.
WE HAVE TO STAY CALM. YOU'LL COME UP WITH A PLAN!
LIKE THAT ONE TIME... REMEMBER?
THAT ONE TIME?
POP

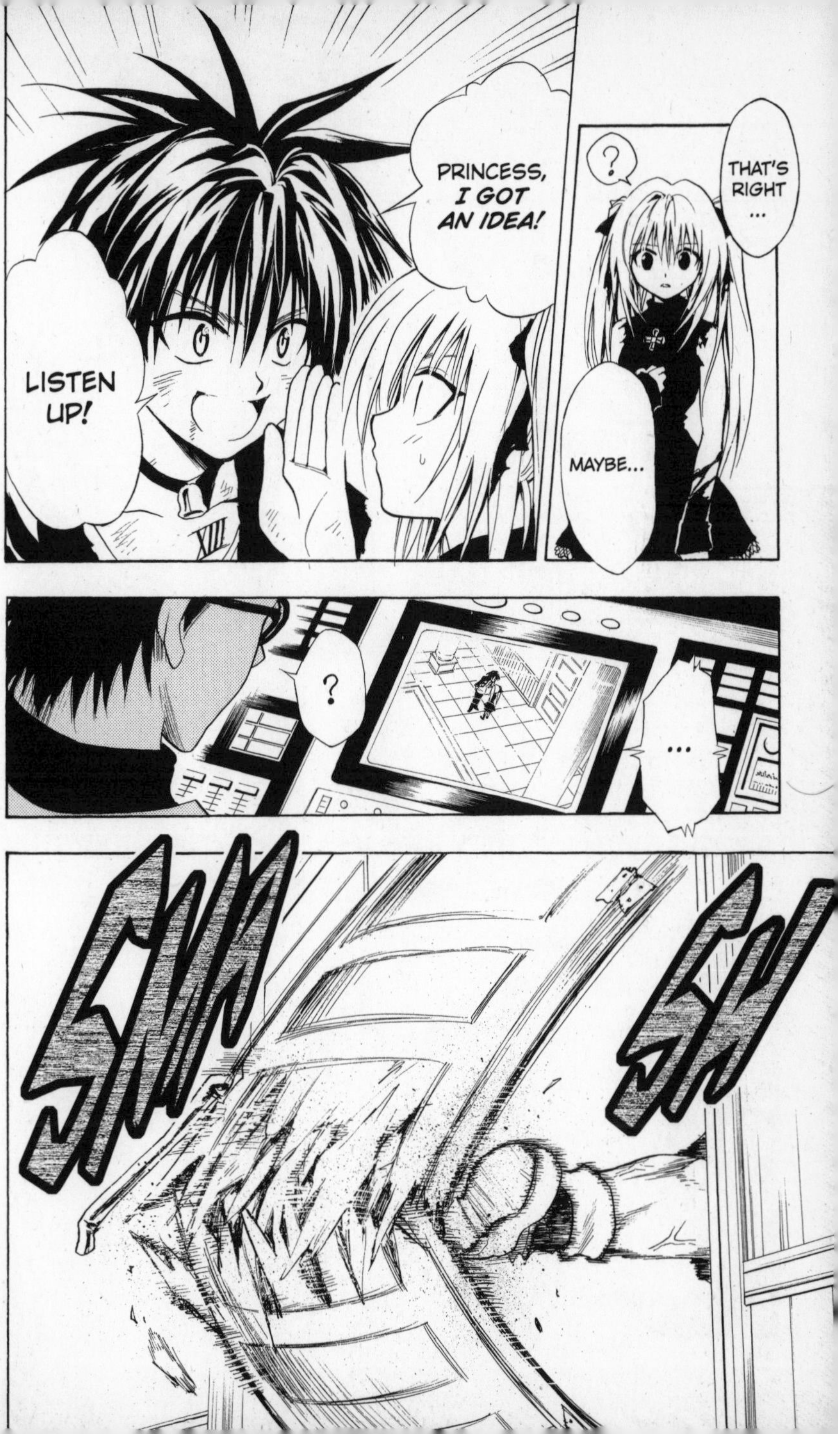
THAT'S RIGHT ...
?
MAYBE...
PRINCESS, I GOT AN IDEA!
LISTEN UP!
...
?

READ THIS WAY

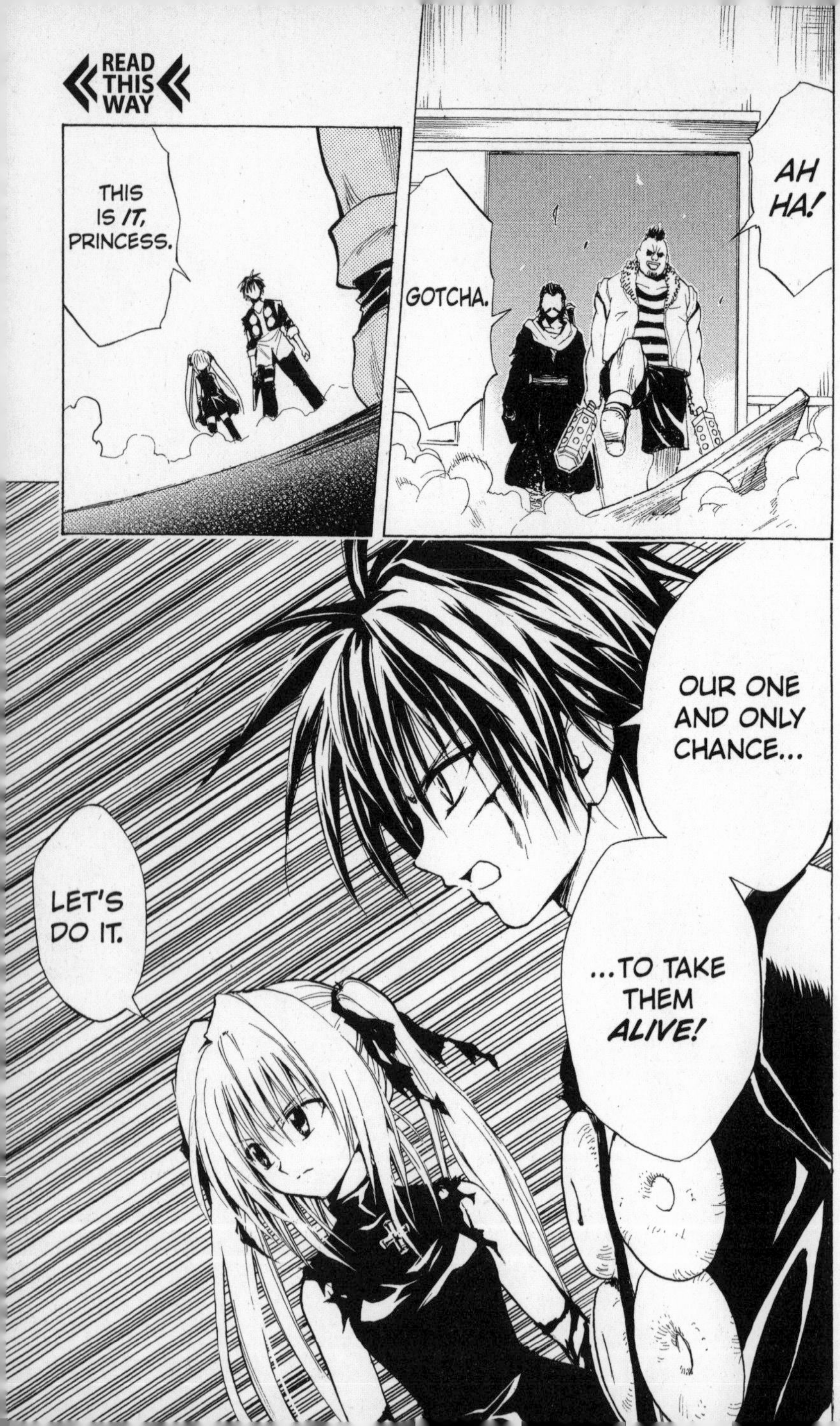
AH HA!
GOTCHA.
THIS IS IT, PRINCESS.
OUR ONE AND ONLY CHANCE...
...TO TAKE THEM ALIVE!
LET'S DO IT.

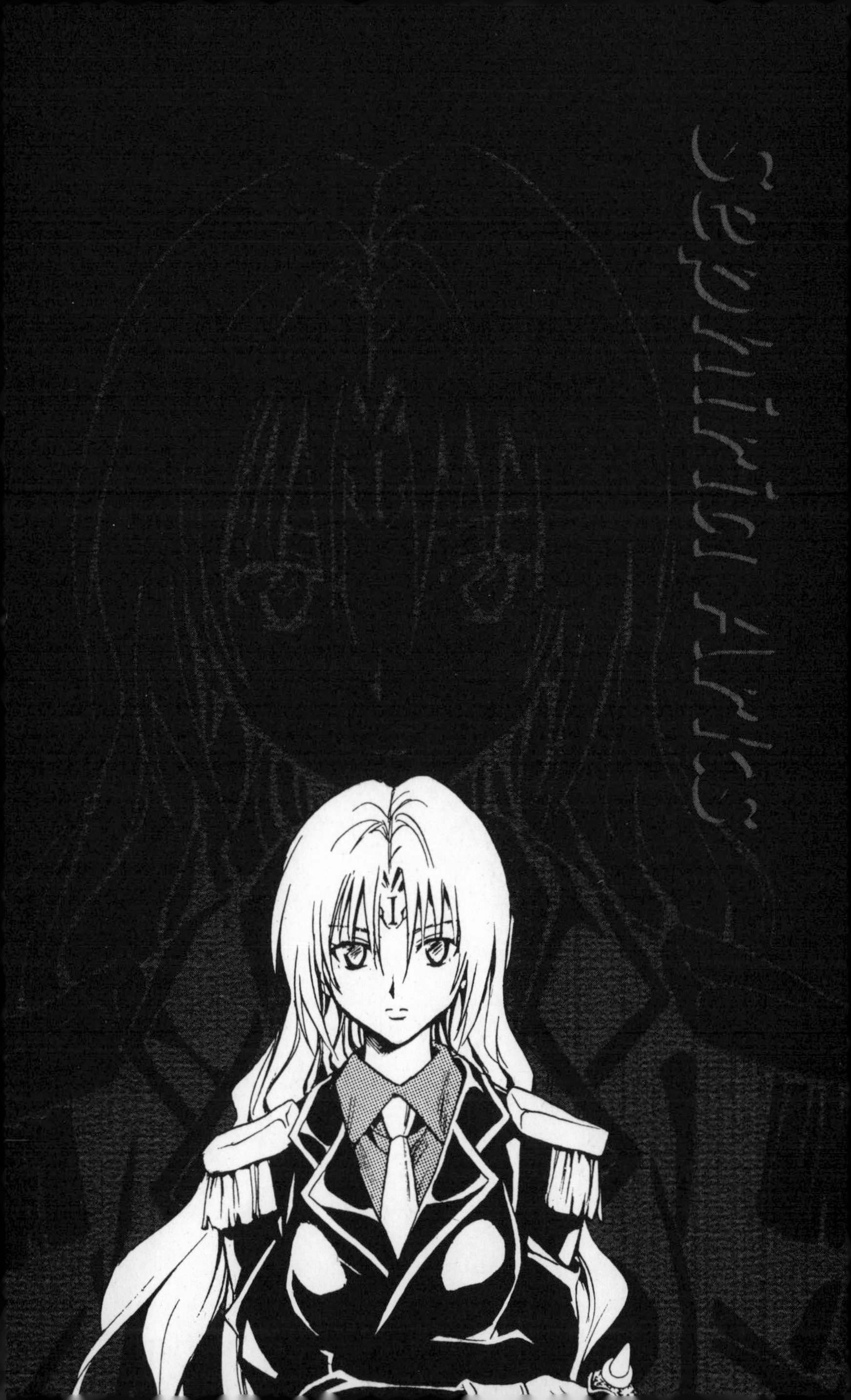
Sephiria Arks

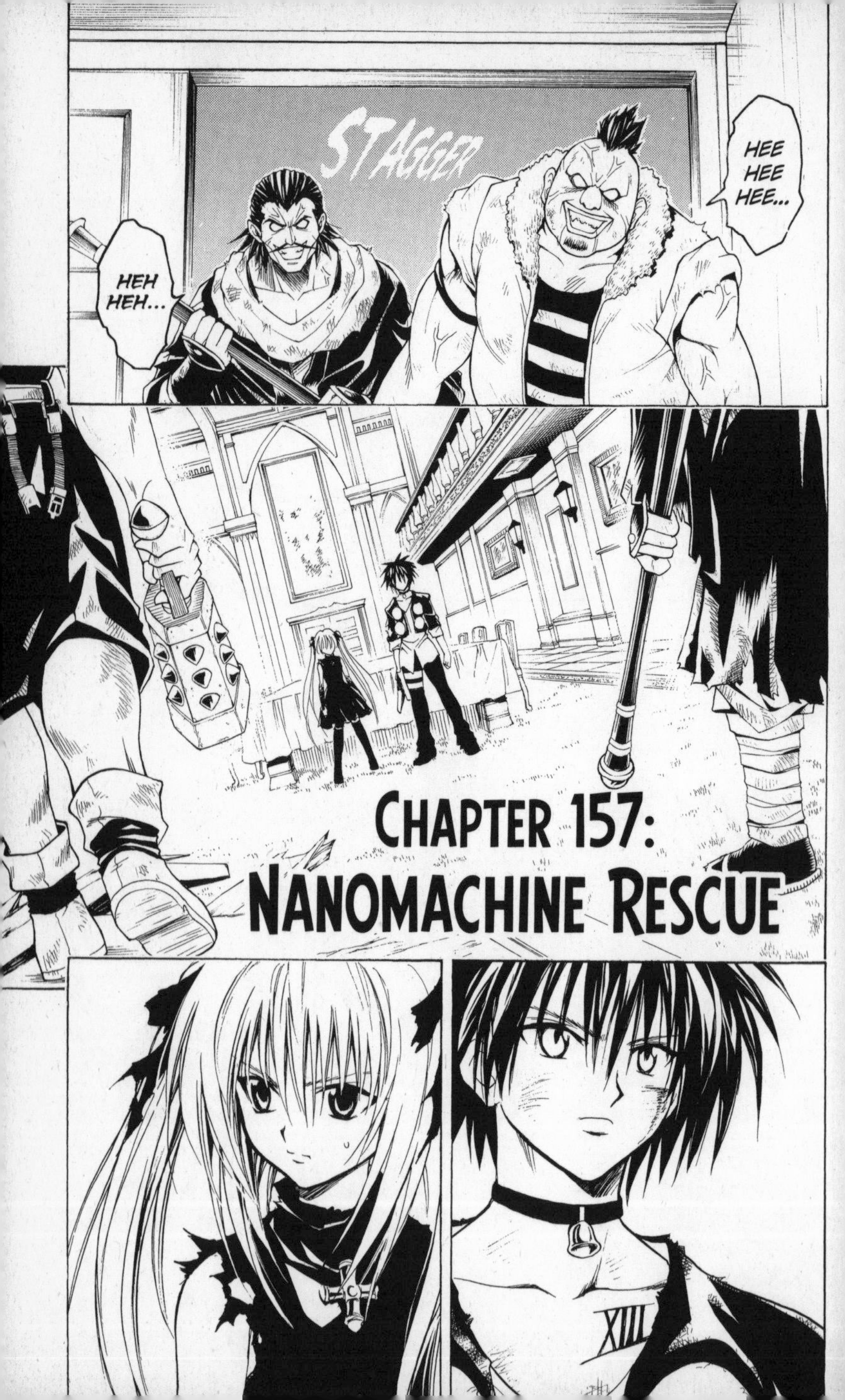
HEE HEE HEE...
STAGGER
HEH HEH...
CHAPTER 157:
NANOMACHINE RESCUE
XIII

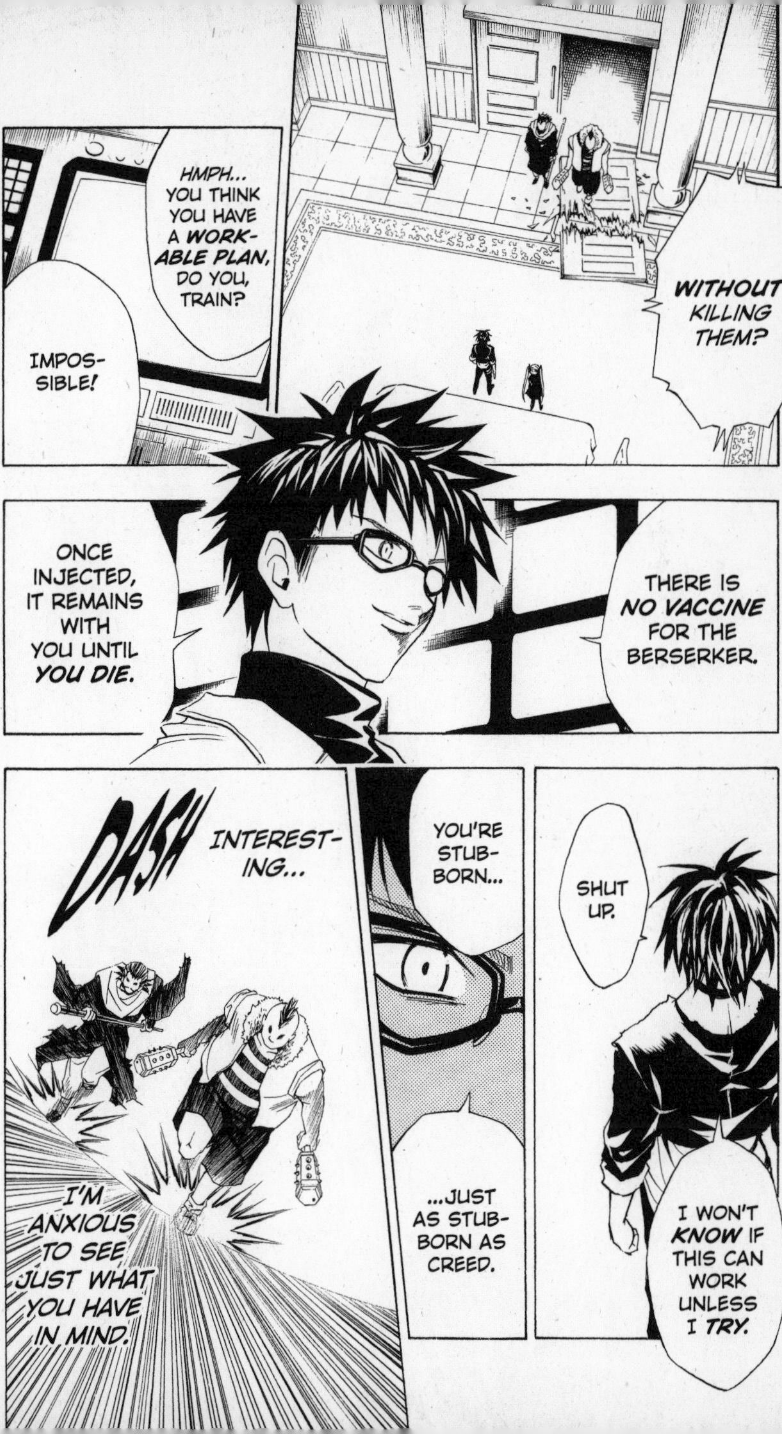
WITHOUT KILLING THEM?
HMPH... YOU THINK YOU HAVE A WORKABLE PLAN, DO YOU, TRAIN?
IMPOSSIBLE!
THERE IS NO VACCINE FOR THE BERSERKER.
ONCE INJECTED, IT REMAINS WITH YOU UNTIL YOU DIE.
SHUT UP.
I WON'T KNOW IF THIS CAN WORK UNLESS I TRY.
YOU'RE STUBBORN...
...JUST AS STUBBORN AS CREED.
DASH
INTERESTING...
I'M ANXIOUS TO SEE JUST WHAT YOU HAVE IN MIND.

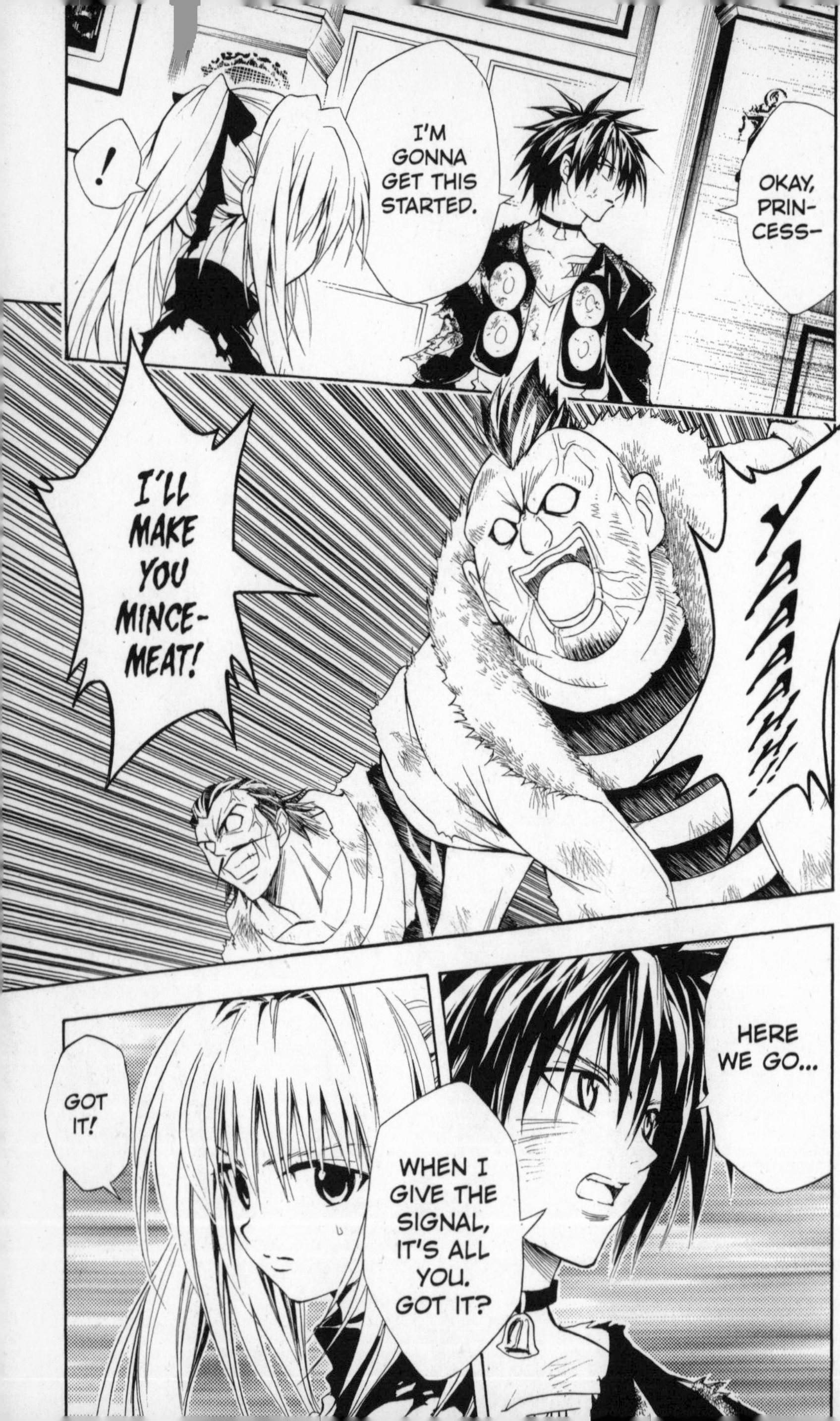
OKAY, PRINCESS-
I'M GONNA GET THIS STARTED.
!
YAAAAHH!!
I'LL MAKE YOU MINCE-MEAT!
HERE WE GO...
WHEN I GIVE THE SIGNAL, IT'S ALL YOU. GOT IT?
GOT IT!

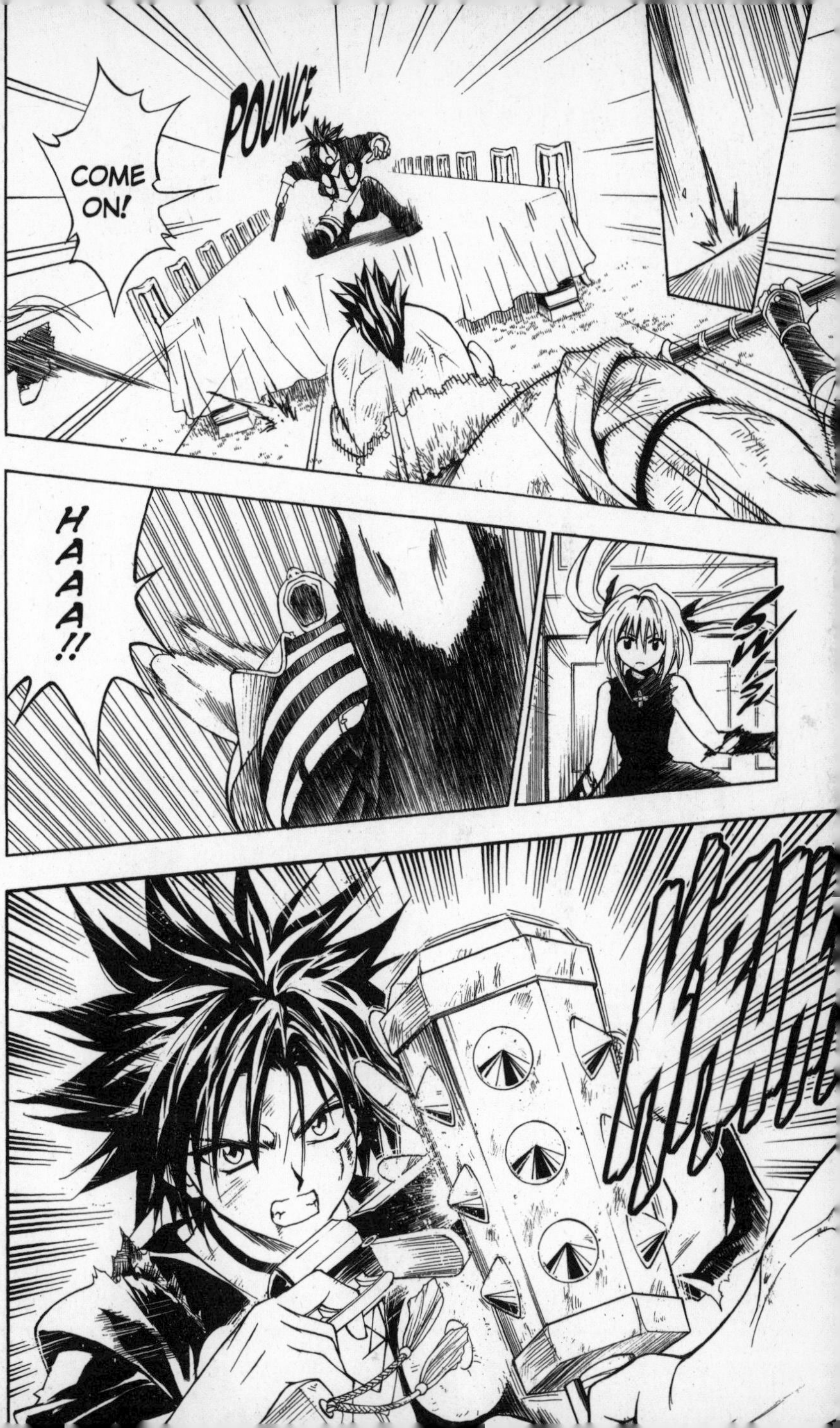
POUNCE
COME ON!
SWISH
HAAAA!!

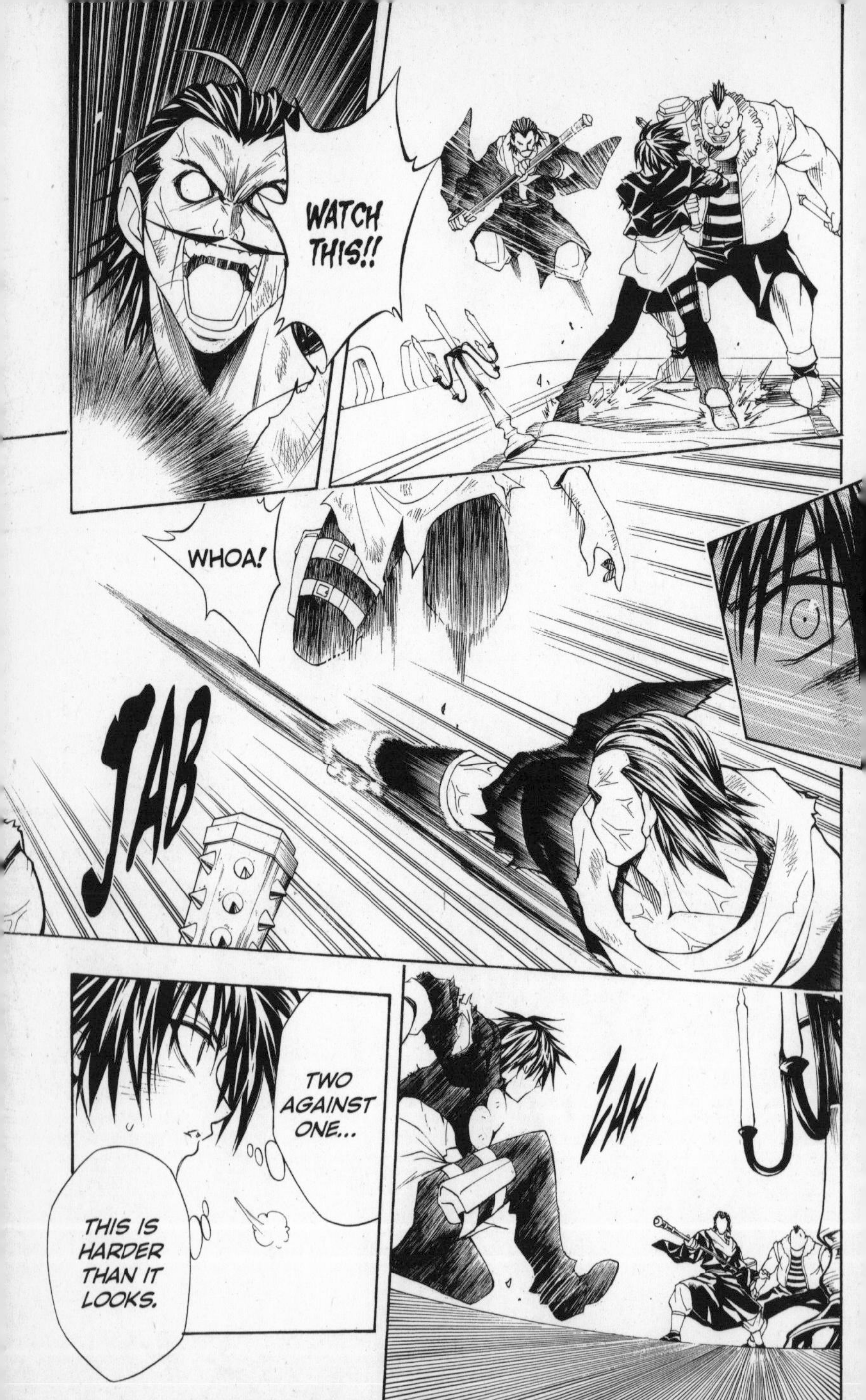
WATCH THIS!!
WHOA!
JAB
ZAH
TWO AGAINST ONE...
THIS IS HARDER THAN IT LOOKS.

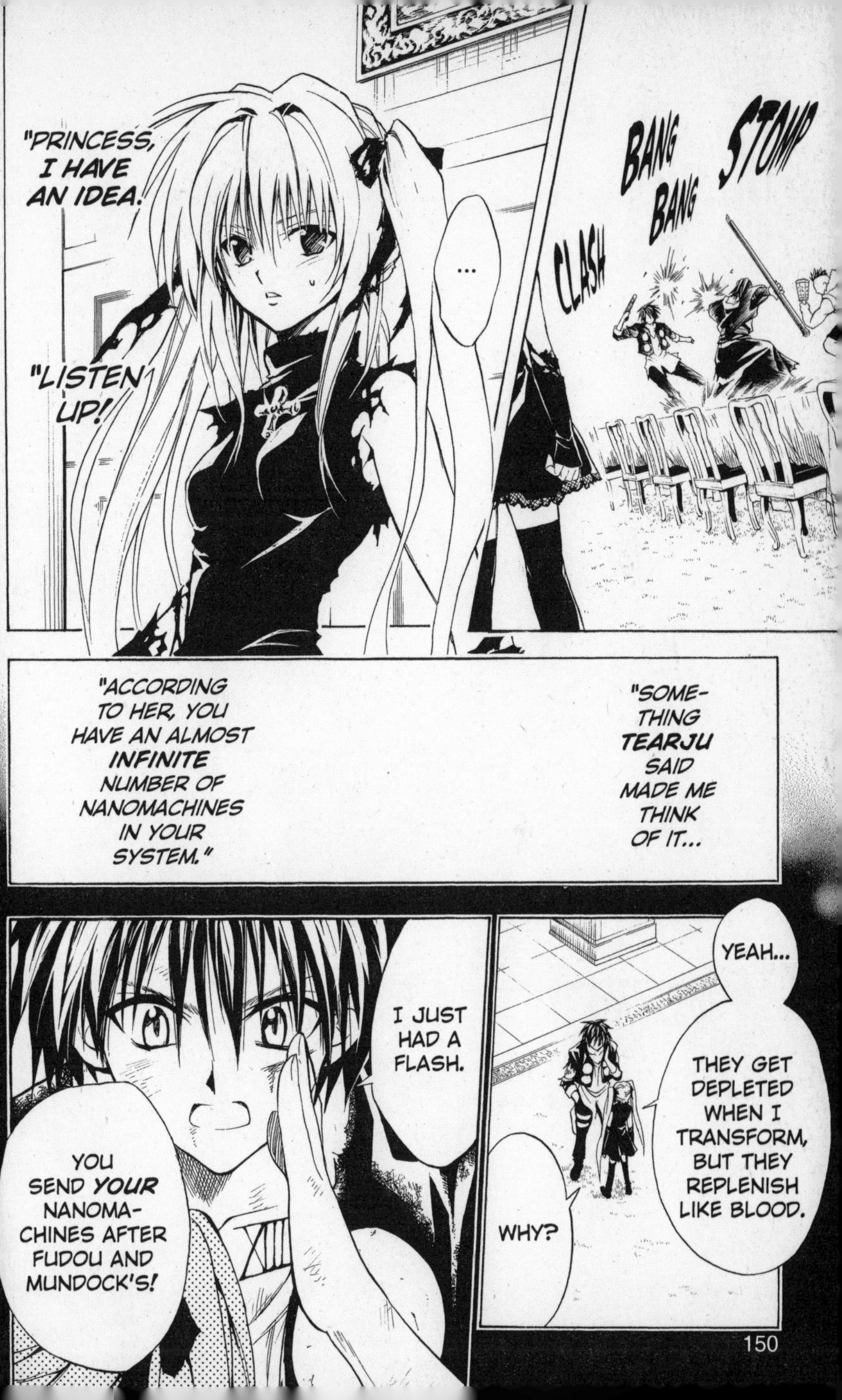
STOMP
BANG BANG
CLASH
...
"PRINCESS, I HAVE AN IDEA.
"LISTEN UP!
"SOMETHING TEARJU SAID MADE ME THINK OF IT...
"ACCORDING TO HER, YOU HAVE AN ALMOST INFINITE NUMBER OF NANOMACHINES IN YOUR SYSTEM."
YEAH...
THEY GET DEPLETED WHEN I TRANSFORM, BUT THEY REPLENISH LIKE BLOOD.
WHY?
I JUST HAD A FLASH.
YOU SEND YOUR NANOMACHINES AFTER FUDOU AND MUNDOCK'S!

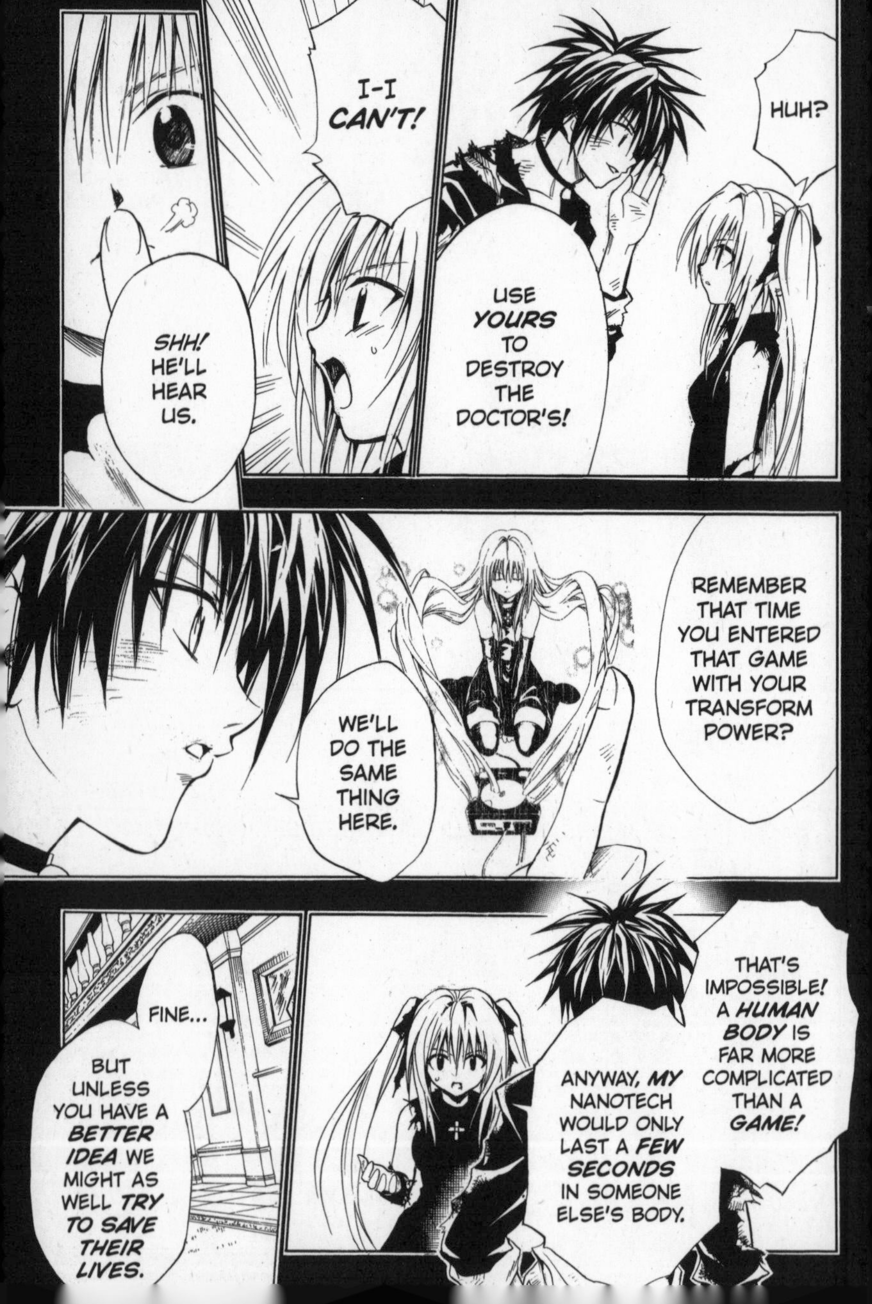
HUH?
USE YOURS TO DESTROY THE DOCTOR'S!
I-I CAN'T!
SHH! HE'LL HEAR US.
REMEMBER THAT TIME YOU ENTERED THAT GAME WITH YOUR TRANSFORM POWER?
WE'LL DO THE SAME THING HERE.
THAT'S IMPOSSIBLE! A HUMAN BODY IS FAR MORE COMPLICATED THAN A GAME!
ANYWAY, MY NANOTECH WOULD ONLY LAST A FEW SECONDS IN SOMEONE ELSE'S BODY.
FINE...
BUT UNLESS YOU HAVE A BETTER IDEA WE MIGHT AS WELL TRY TO SAVE THEIR LIVES.

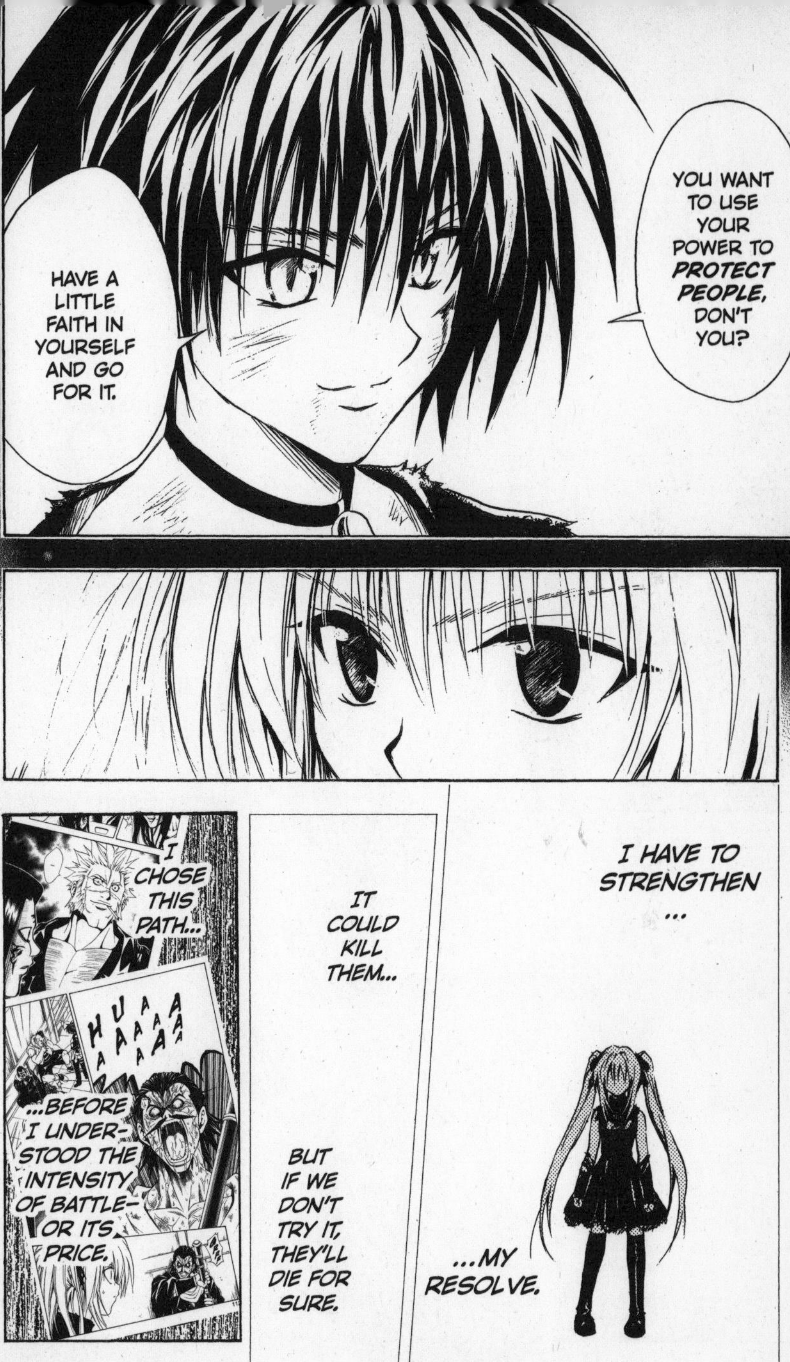
YOU WANT TO USE YOUR POWER TO PROTECT PEOPLE, DON'T YOU?
HAVE A LITTLE FAITH IN YOURSELF AND GO FOR IT.
I HAVE TO STRENGTHEN ...
...MY RESOLVE.
IT COULD KILL THEM...
BUT IF WE DON'T TRY IT, THEY'LL DIE FOR SURE.
I CHOSE THIS PATH...
HUAAAAAAAAAA
...BEFORE I UNDER-STOOD THE INTENSITY OF BATTLE—OR ITS PRICE.

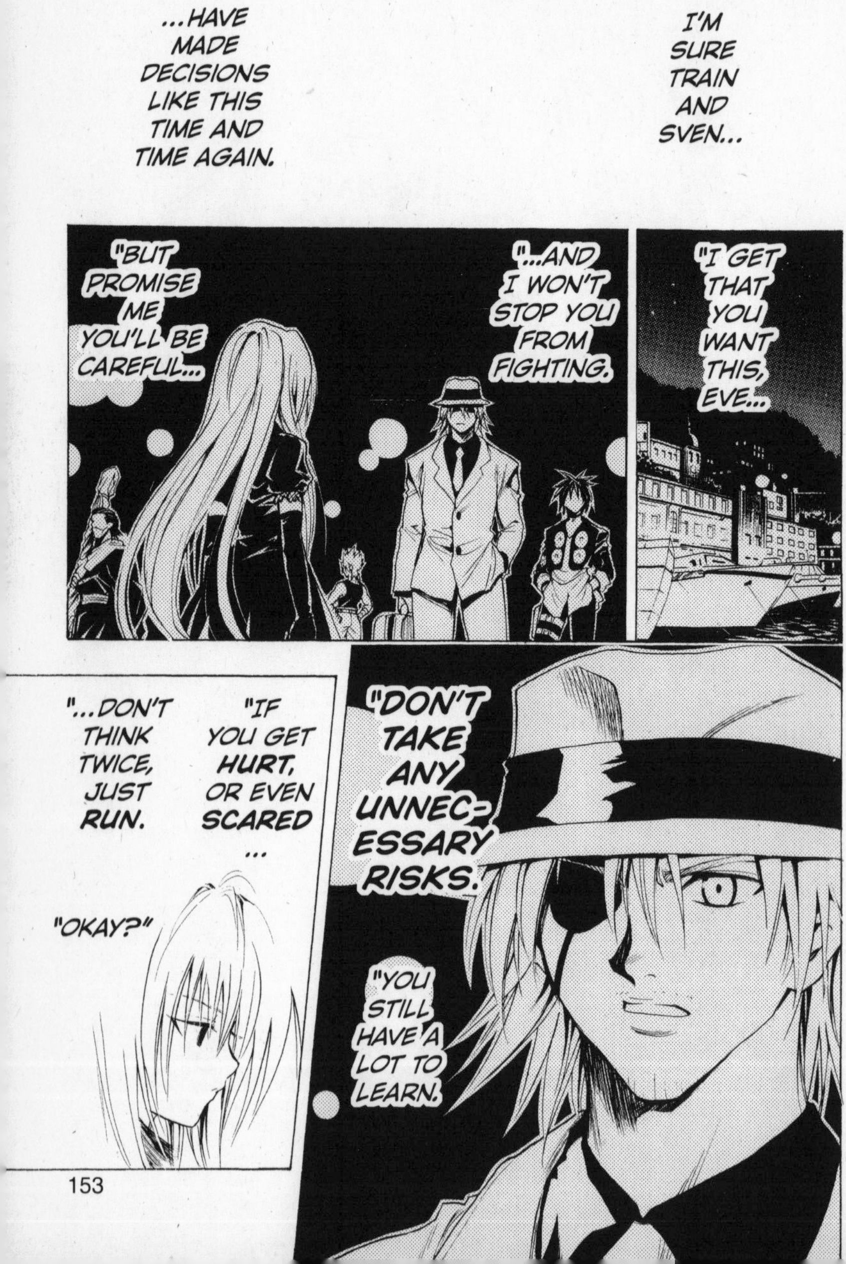
I'M SURE TRAIN AND SVEN...
...HAVE MADE DECISIONS LIKE THIS TIME AND TIME AGAIN.
"I GET THAT YOU WANT THIS, EVE...
"...AND I WON'T STOP YOU FROM FIGHTING.
"BUT PROMISE ME YOU'LL BE CAREFUL...
"DON'T TAKE ANY UNNEC-ESSARY RISKS.
"YOU STILL HAVE A LOT TO LEARN.
"IF YOU GET HURT, OR EVEN SCARED ...
"...DON'T THINK TWICE, JUST RUN.
"OKAY?"

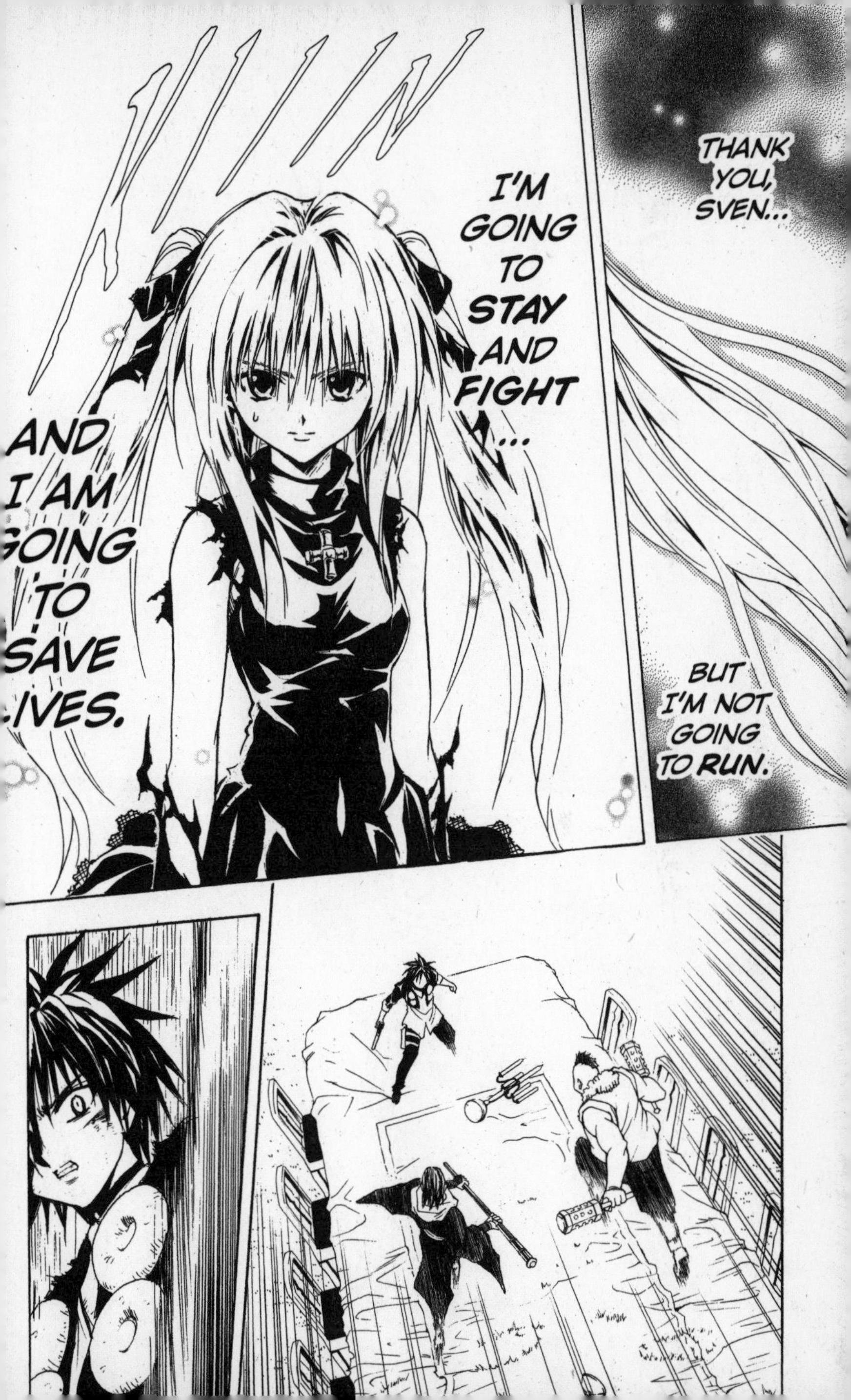
THANK YOU, SVEN...
BUT I'M NOT GOING TO RUN.
KIIIN
I'M GOING TO STAY AND FIGHT...
AND I AM GOING TO SAVE LIVES.

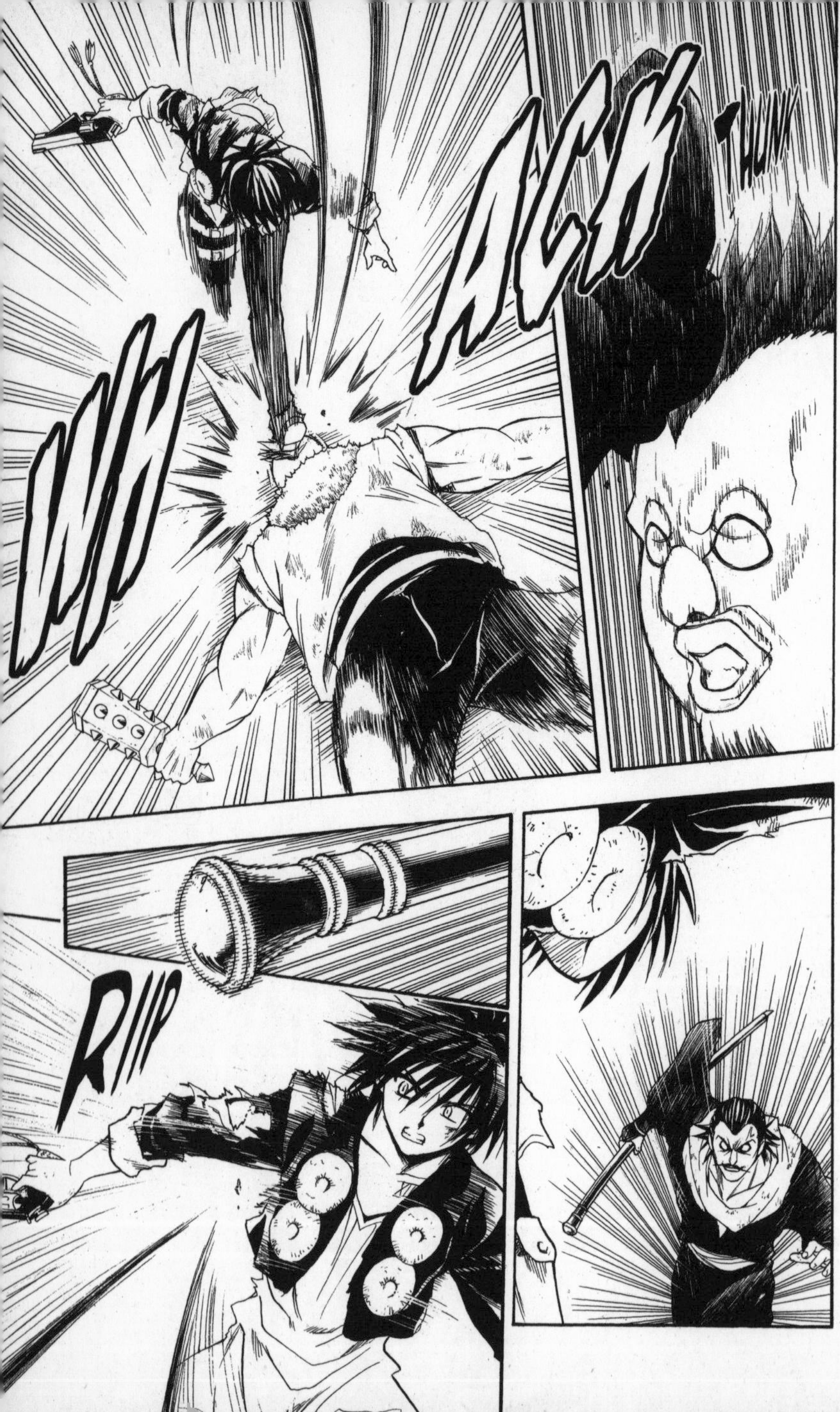
THUNK
WHACK
RIIP

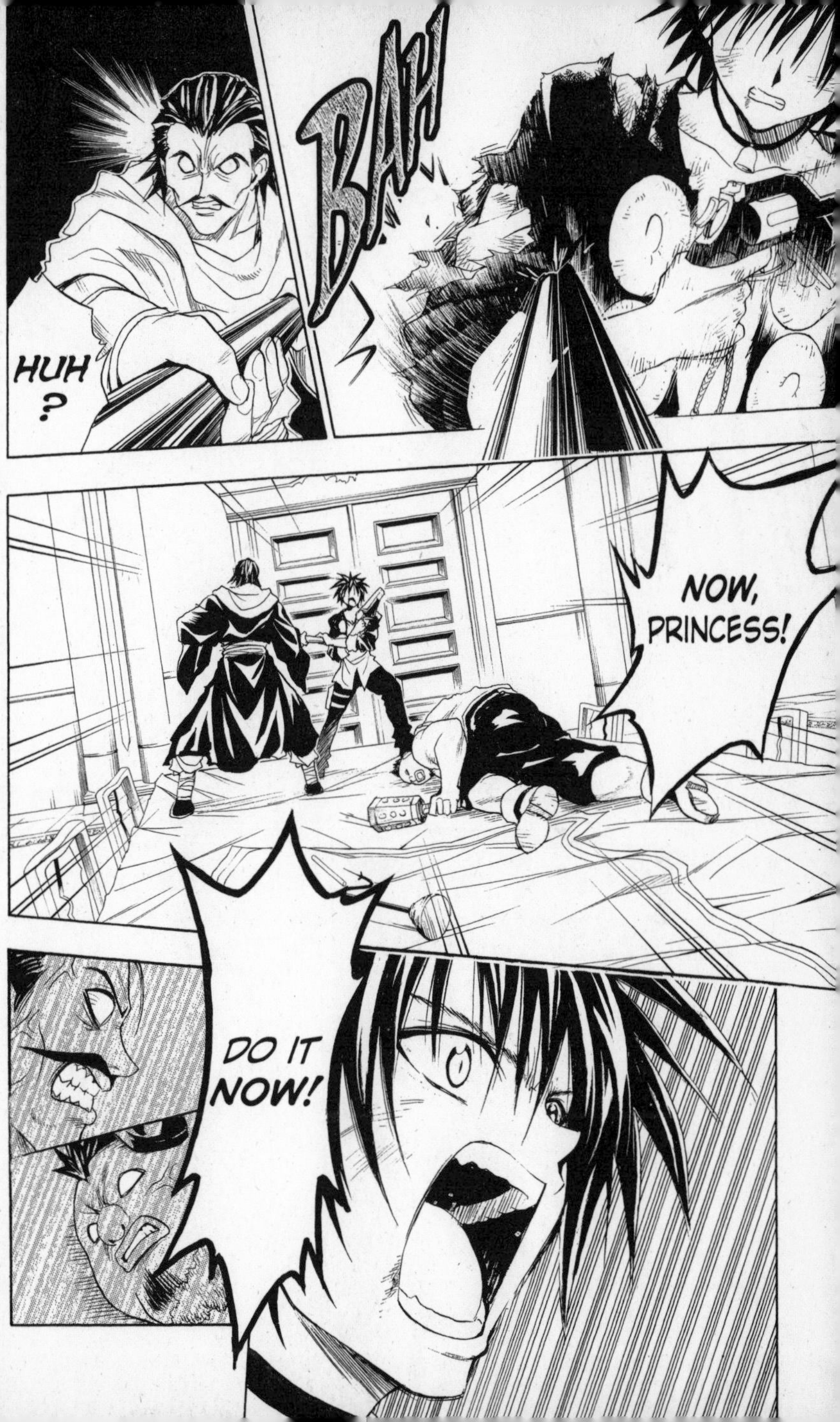
BAH
HUH ?
NOW, PRINCESS!
DO IT NOW!

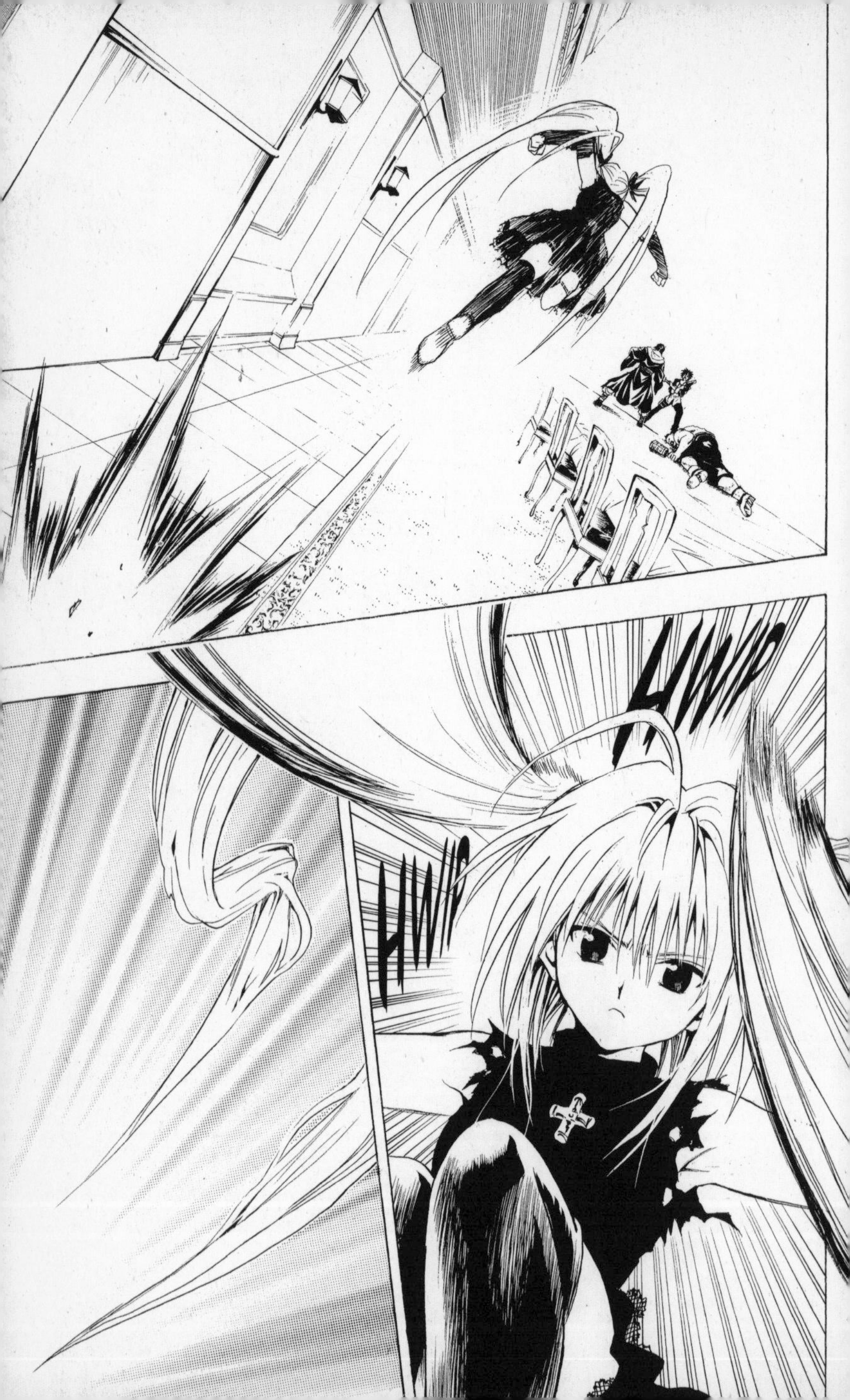
HWIP
HWIP

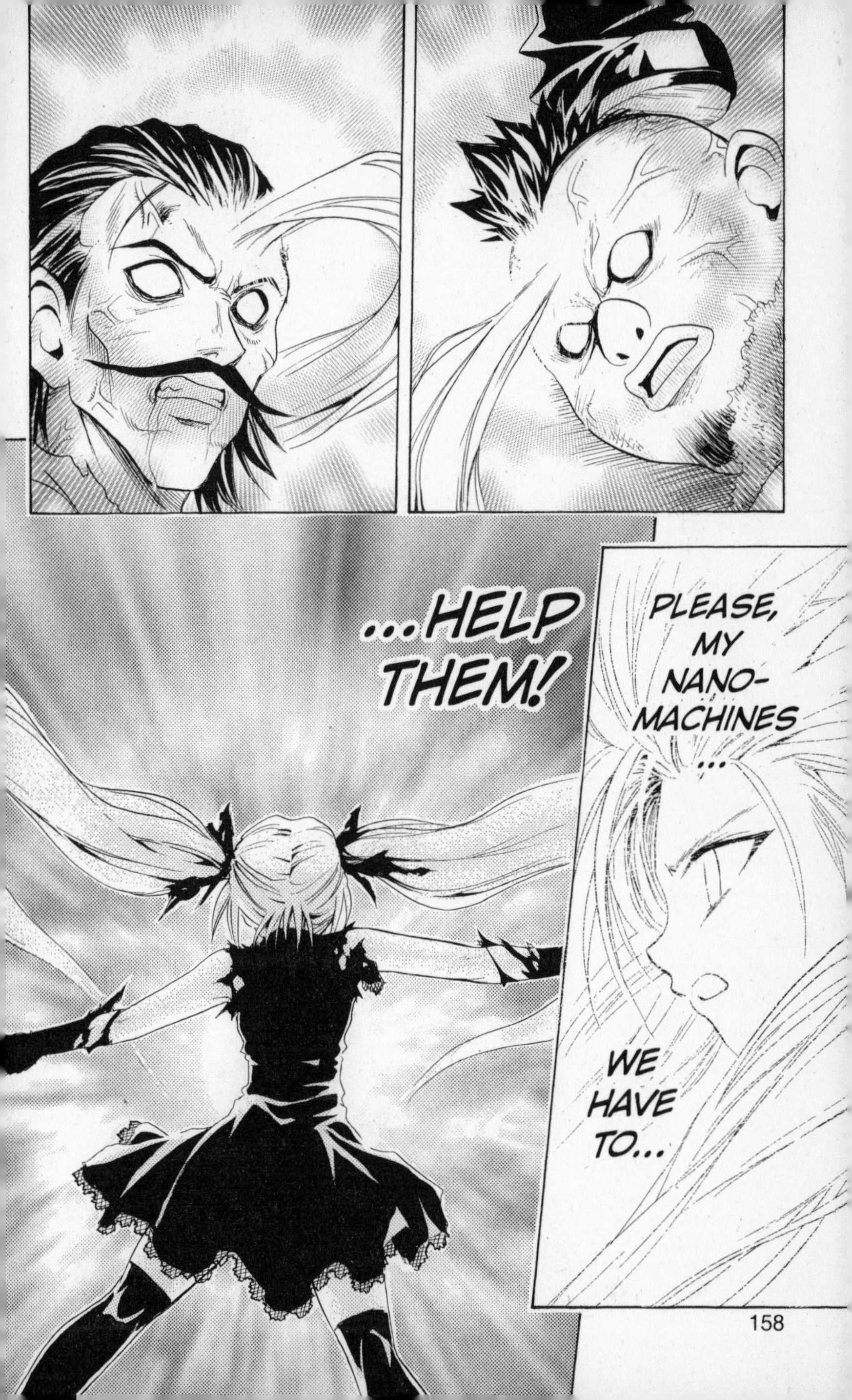
PLEASE, MY NANO-MACHINES...
WE HAVE TO...
...HELP THEM!

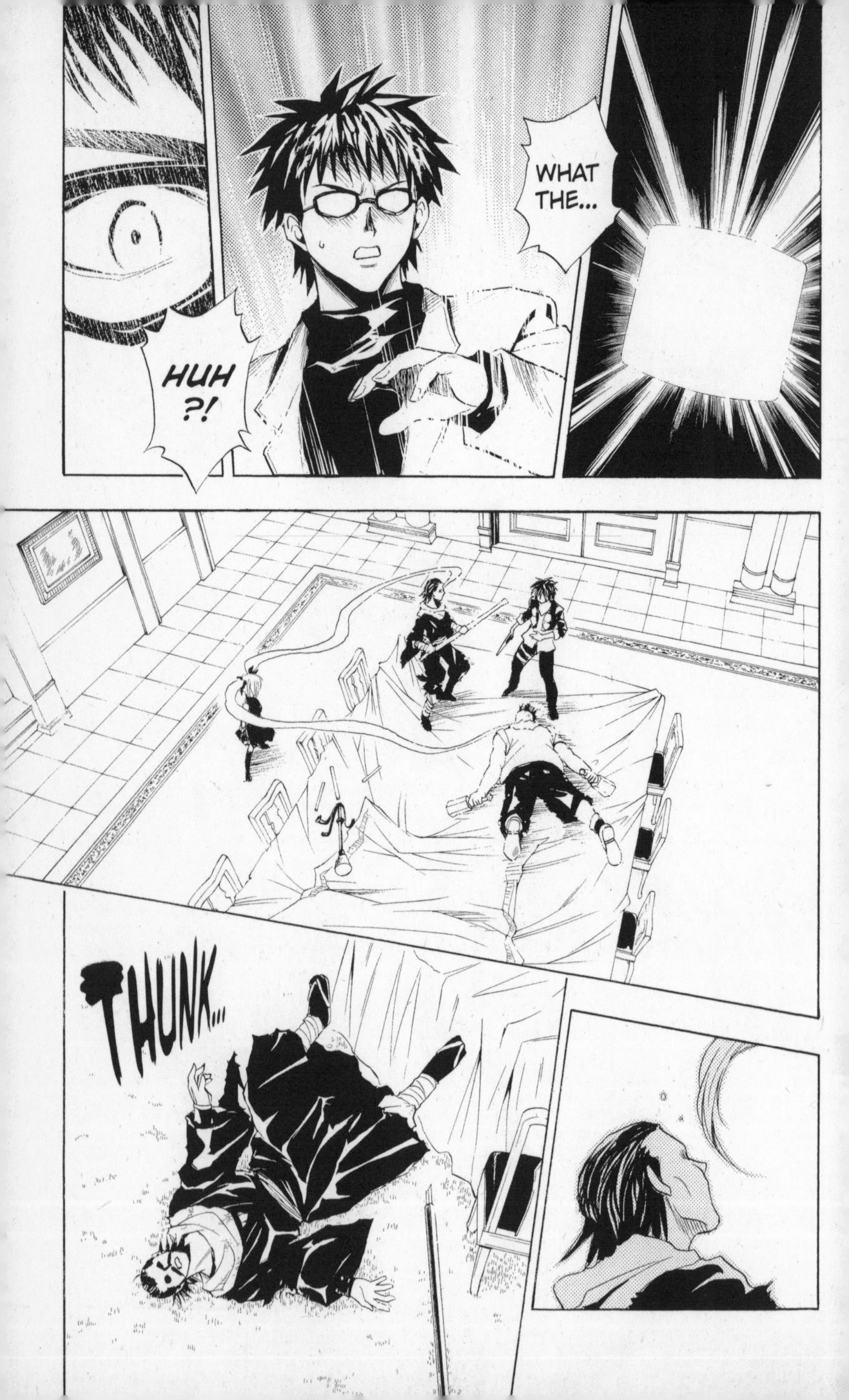
WHAT THE...
HUH ?!
THUNK...

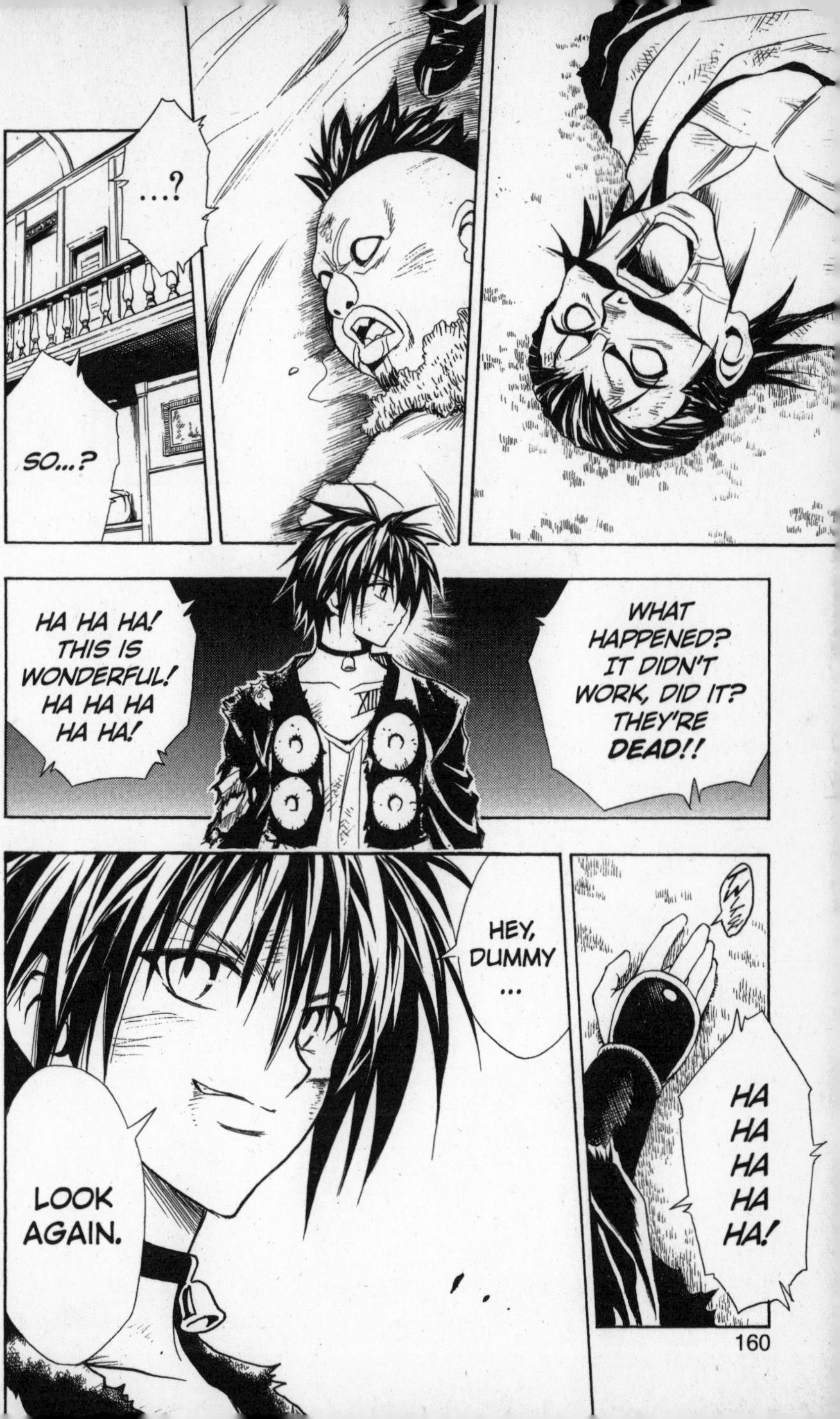
...?
SO...?
WHAT HAPPENED? IT DIDN'T WORK, DID IT? THEY'RE DEAD!!
HA HA HA! THIS IS WONDERFUL! HA HA HA HA HA!
HA HA HA HA HA HA!
HEY, DUMMY ...
LOOK AGAIN.

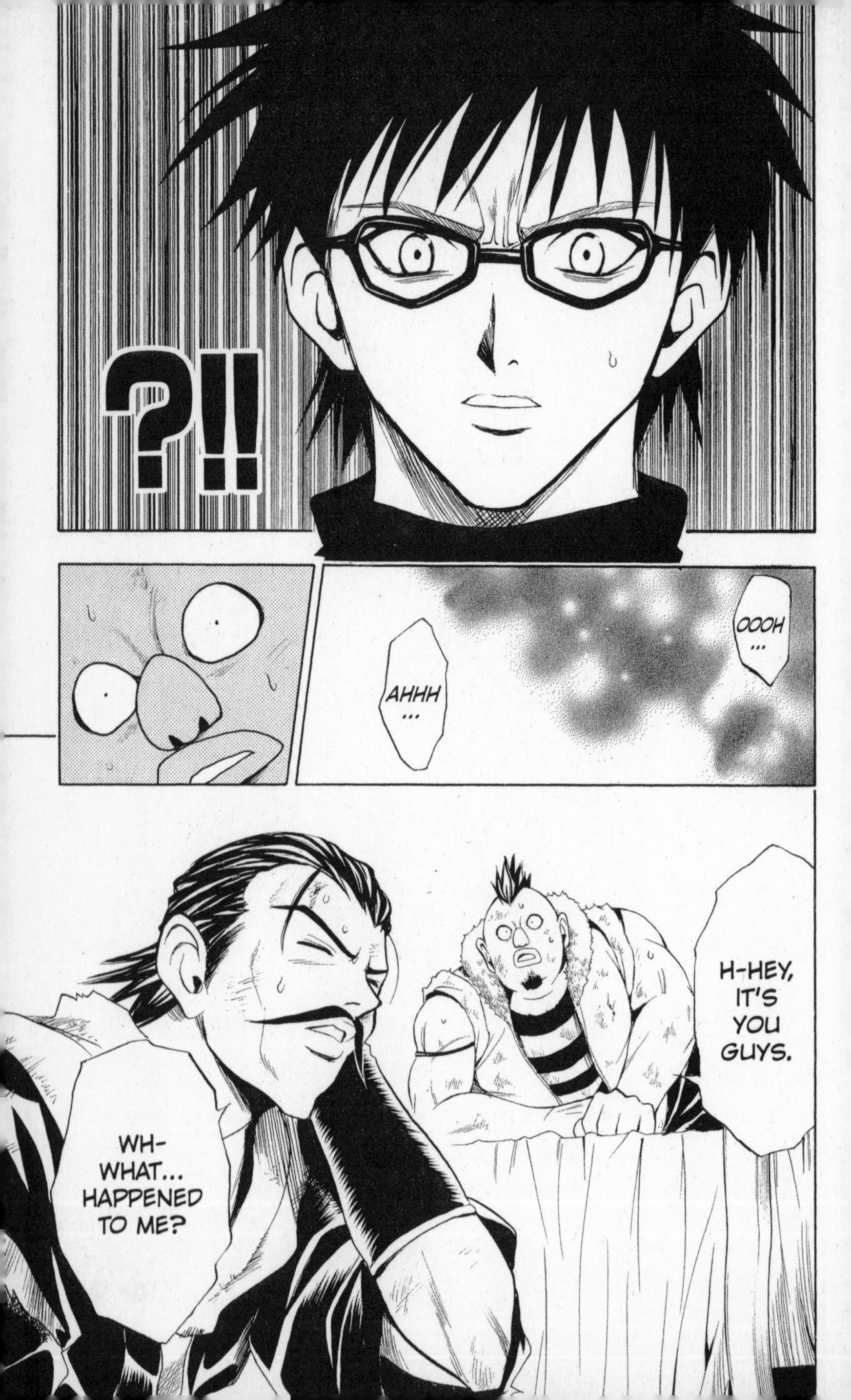
?!!
OOOH ...
AHHH ...
H-HEY, IT'S YOU GUYS.
WH- WHAT... HAPPENED TO ME?

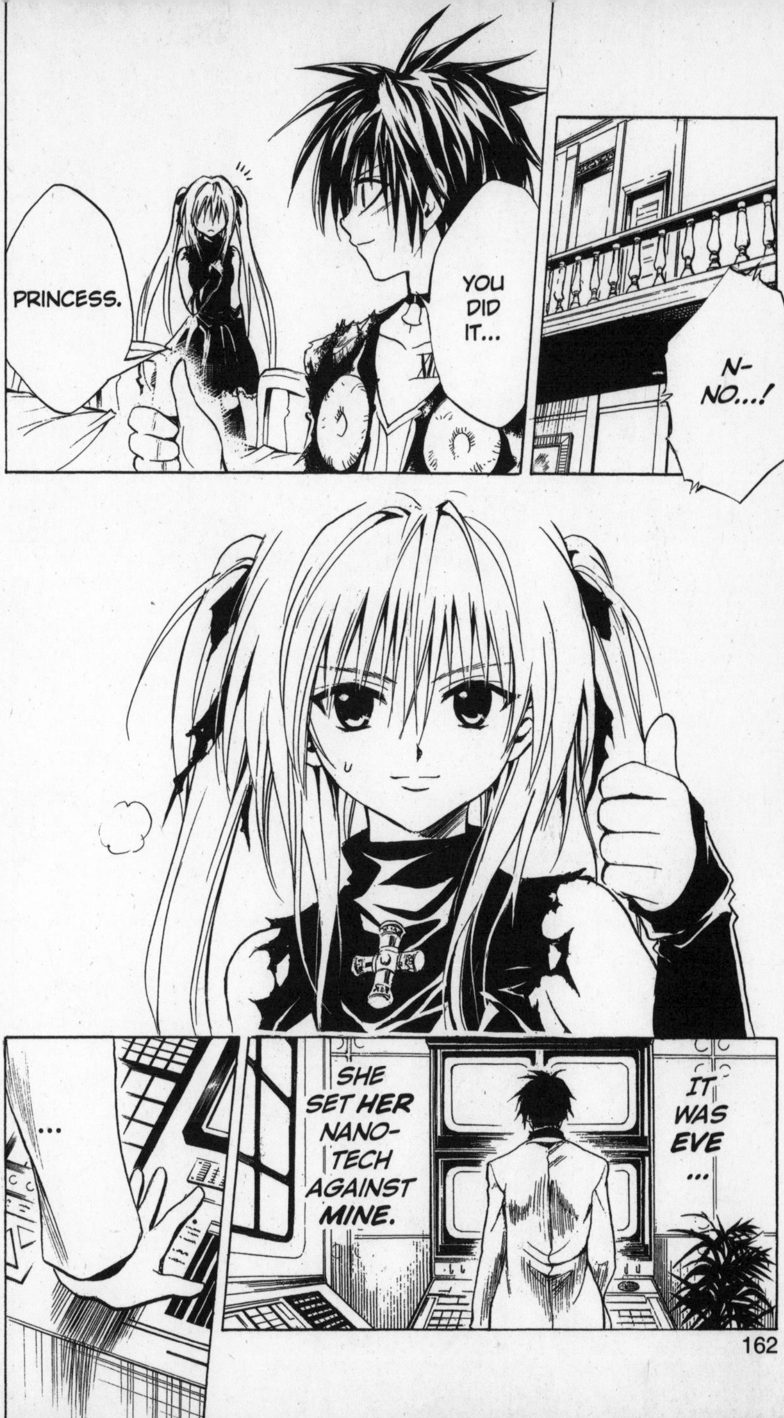
N-NO...!
YOU DID IT...
PRINCESS.
IT WAS EVE...
SHE SET HER NANO-TECH AGAINST MINE.
...

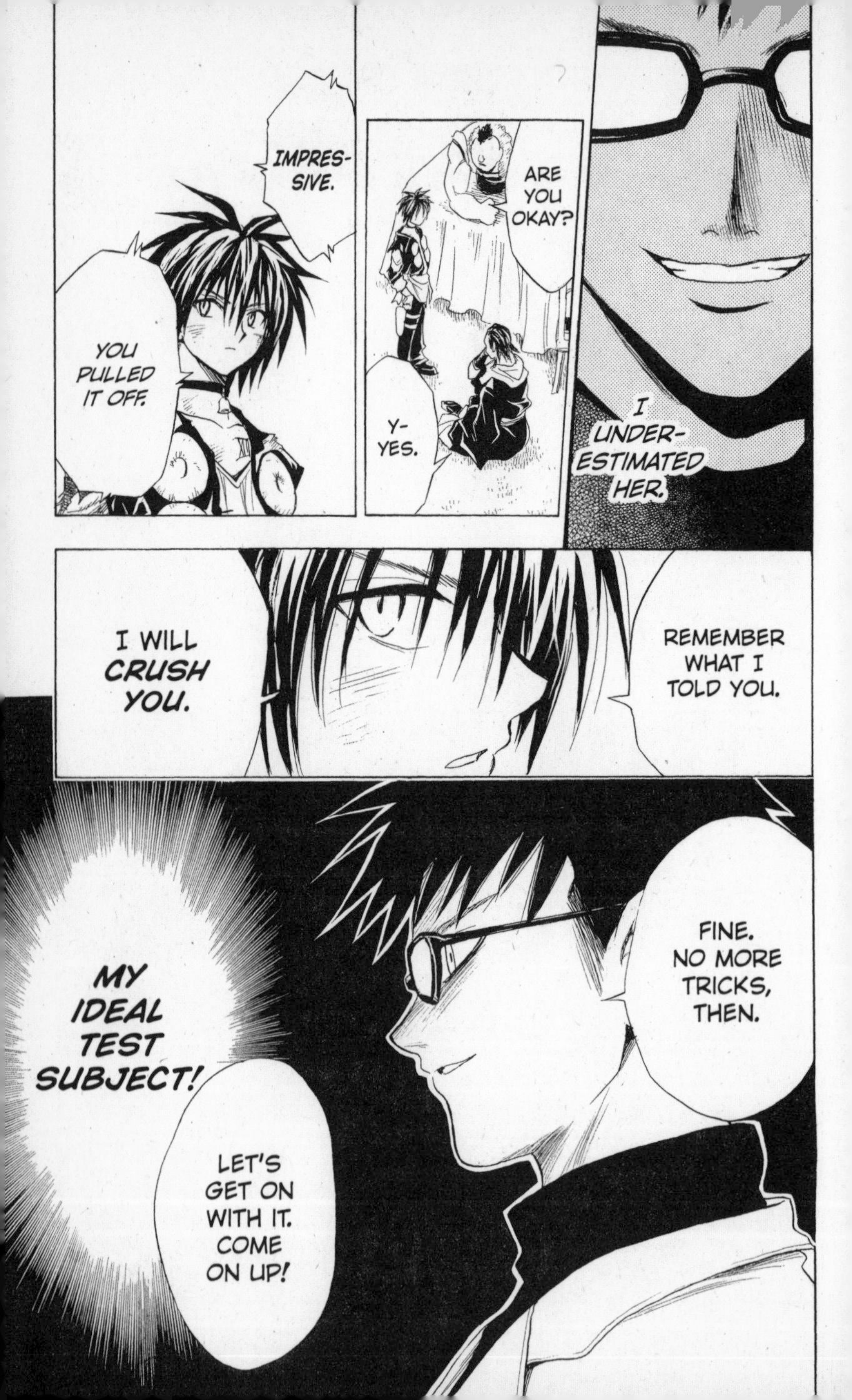
I UNDER-ESTIMATED HER.
ARE YOU OKAY?
Y-YES.
IMPRES-SIVE.
YOU PULLED IT OFF.
REMEMBER WHAT I TOLD YOU.
I WILL CRUSH YOU.
FINE. NO MORE TRICKS, THEN.
MY IDEAL TEST SUBJECT!
LET'S GET ON WITH IT. COME ON UP!

BEWARE! THERE'S A GUY WITH A STRANGE HEAD NEAR YABUKI SENSEI! BY TAKASHI MORI

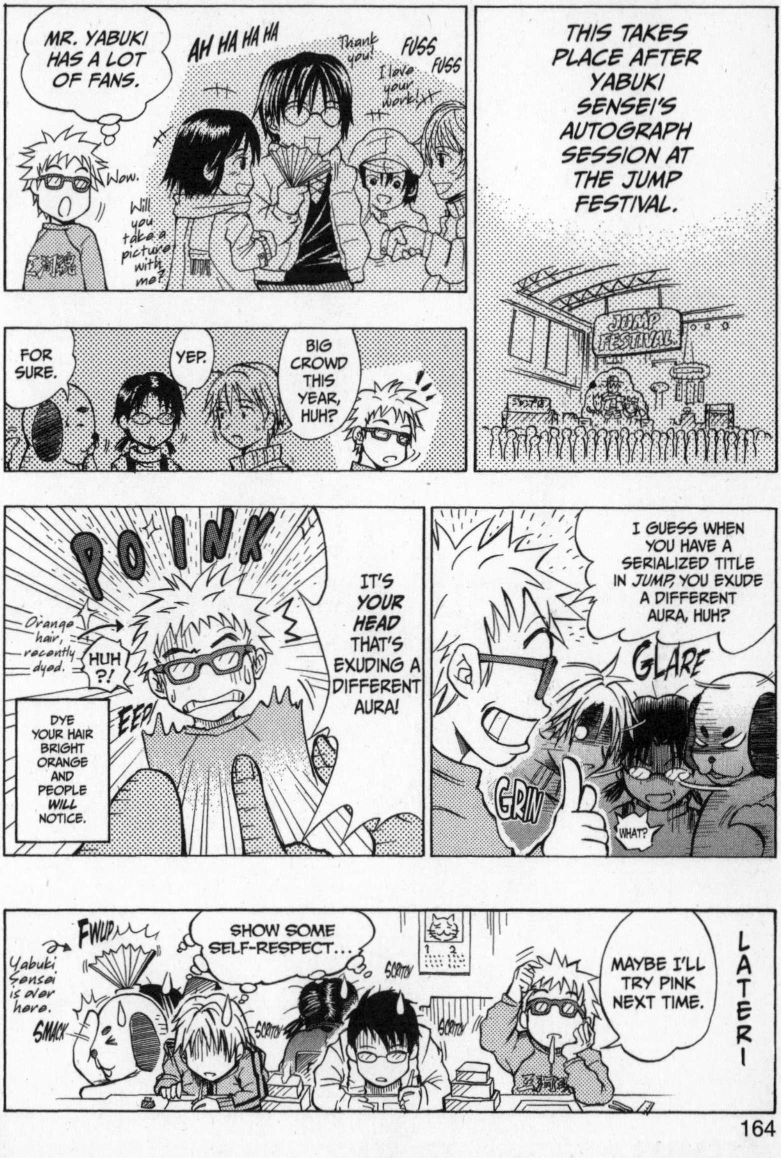
THIS TAKES PLACE AFTER YABUKI SENSEI'S AUTOGRAPH SESSION AT THE JUMP FESTIVAL.
JUMP FESTIVAL
FUSS FUSS
I love your work!
Thank you!
AH HA HA HA
Will you take a picture with me?
MR. YABUKI HAS A LOT OF FANS.
Wow.
BIG CROWD THIS YEAR, HUH?
YEP.
FOR SURE.
I GUESS WHEN YOU HAVE A SERIALIZED TITLE IN JUMP, YOU EXUDE A DIFFERENT AURA, HUH?
GLARE
WHAT?
GRIN
IT'S YOUR HEAD THAT'S EXUDING A DIFFERENT AURA!
POINK
HUH ?!
Orange hair, recently dyed.
EEP!
DYE YOUR HAIR BRIGHT ORANGE AND PEOPLE WILL NOTICE.
LATER
MAYBE I'LL TRY PINK NEXT TIME.
SCRITCH
SCRITCH
SHOW SOME SELF-RESPECT...
SCRITCH
FWUP
Yabuki Sensei is over here.
SMACK

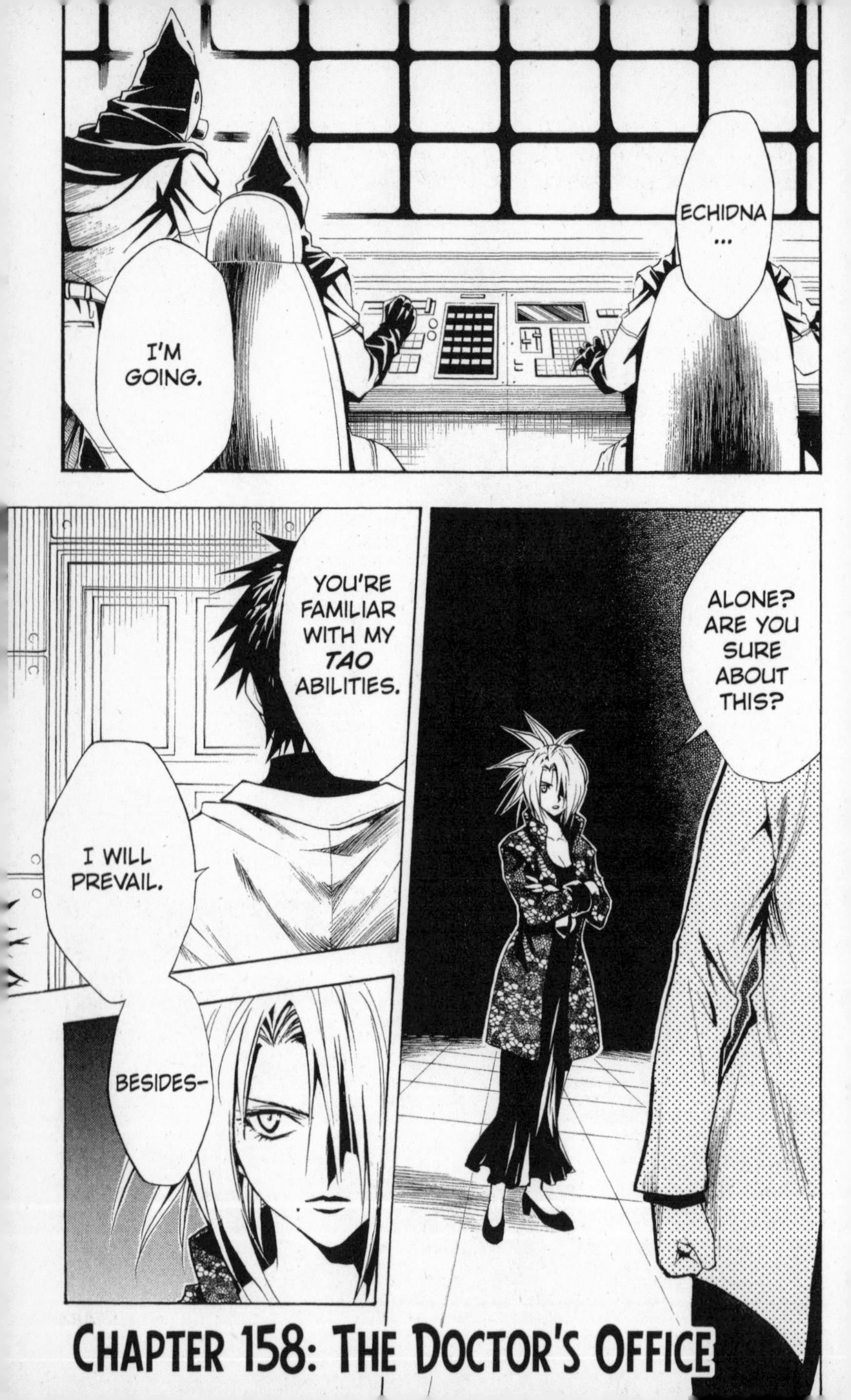
ECHIDNA ...
I'M GOING.
ALONE? ARE YOU SURE ABOUT THIS?
YOU'RE FAMILIAR WITH MY *TAO* ABILITIES.
I WILL PREVAIL.
BESIDES-

CHAPTER 158: THE DOCTOR'S OFFICE

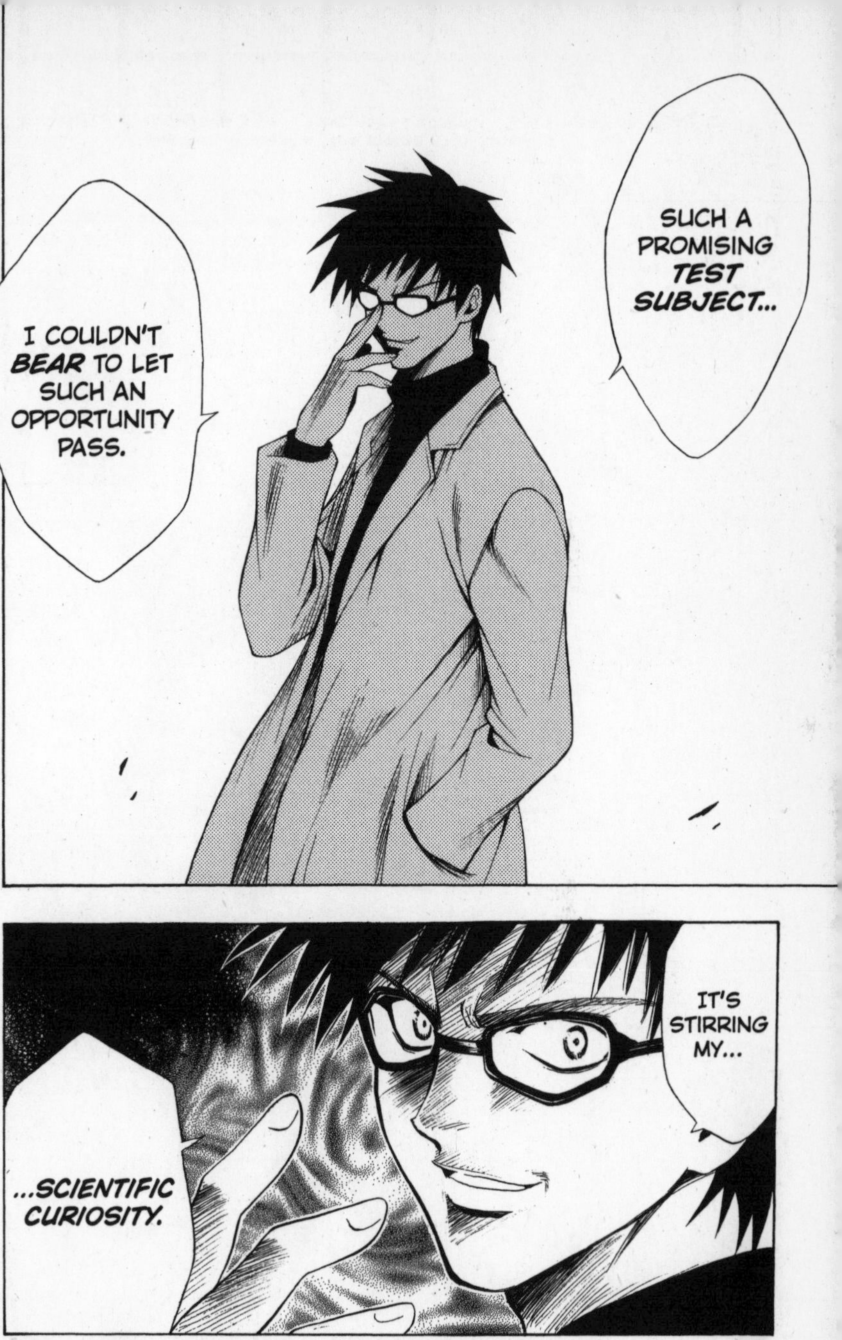
SUCH A PROMISING *TEST SUBJECT*...
I COULDN'T *BEAR* TO LET SUCH AN OPPORTUNITY PASS.
IT'S STIRRING MY...
...SCIENTIFIC CURIOSITY.

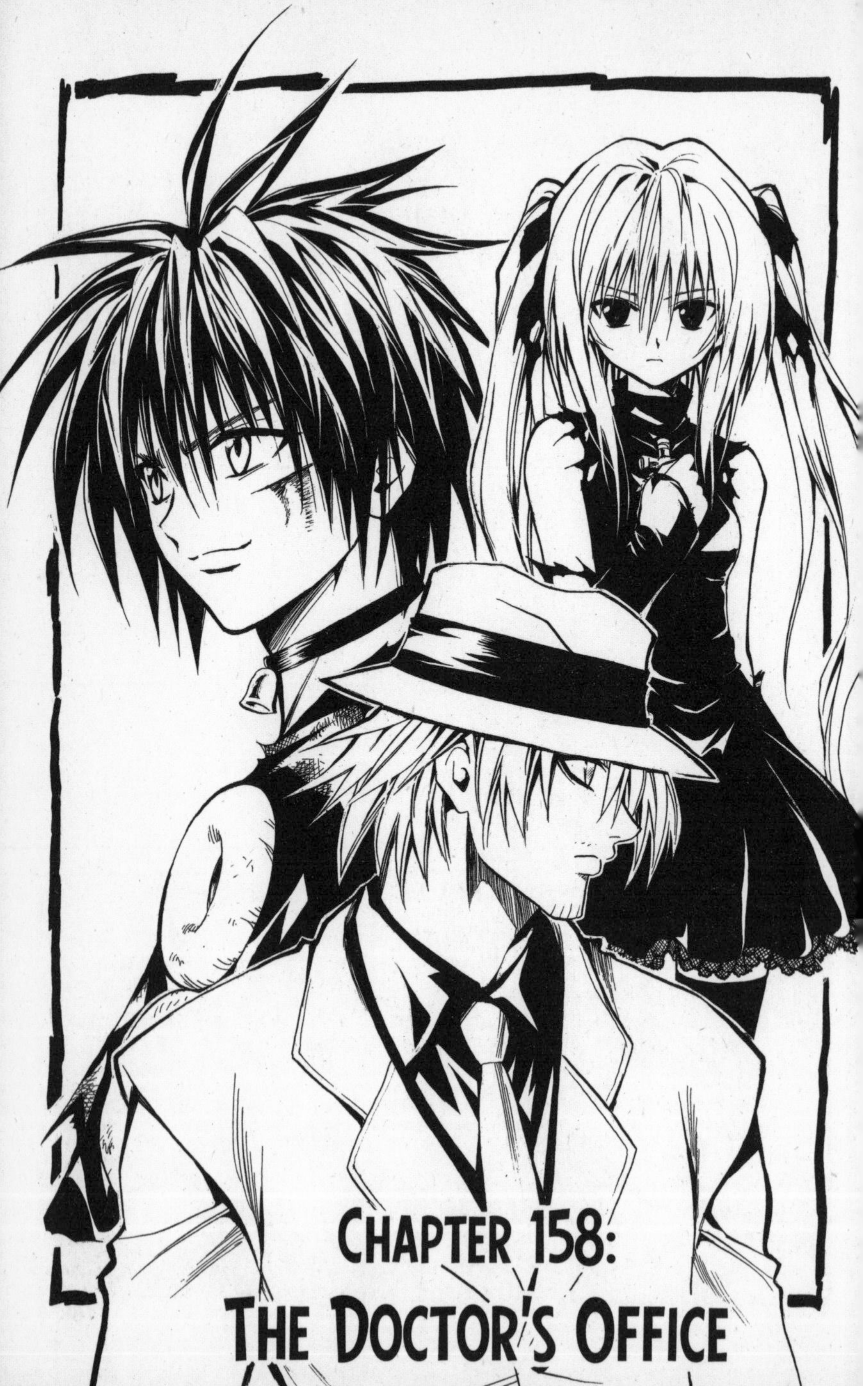

Chapter 158: The Doctor's Office

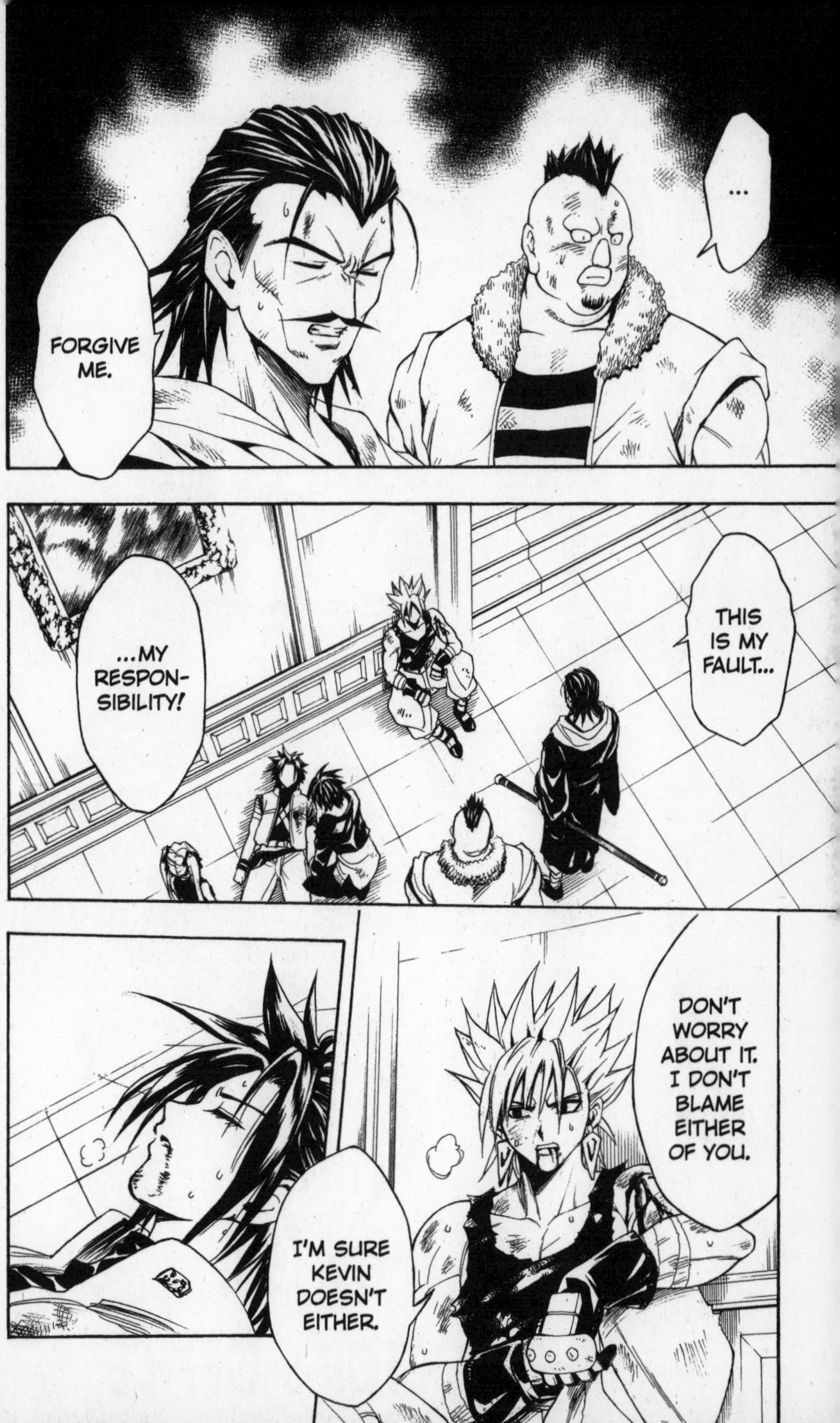
...
FORGIVE ME.
THIS IS MY FAULT...
...MY RESPONSIBILITY!
DON'T WORRY ABOUT IT. I DON'T BLAME EITHER OF YOU.
I'M SURE KEVIN DOESN'T EITHER.

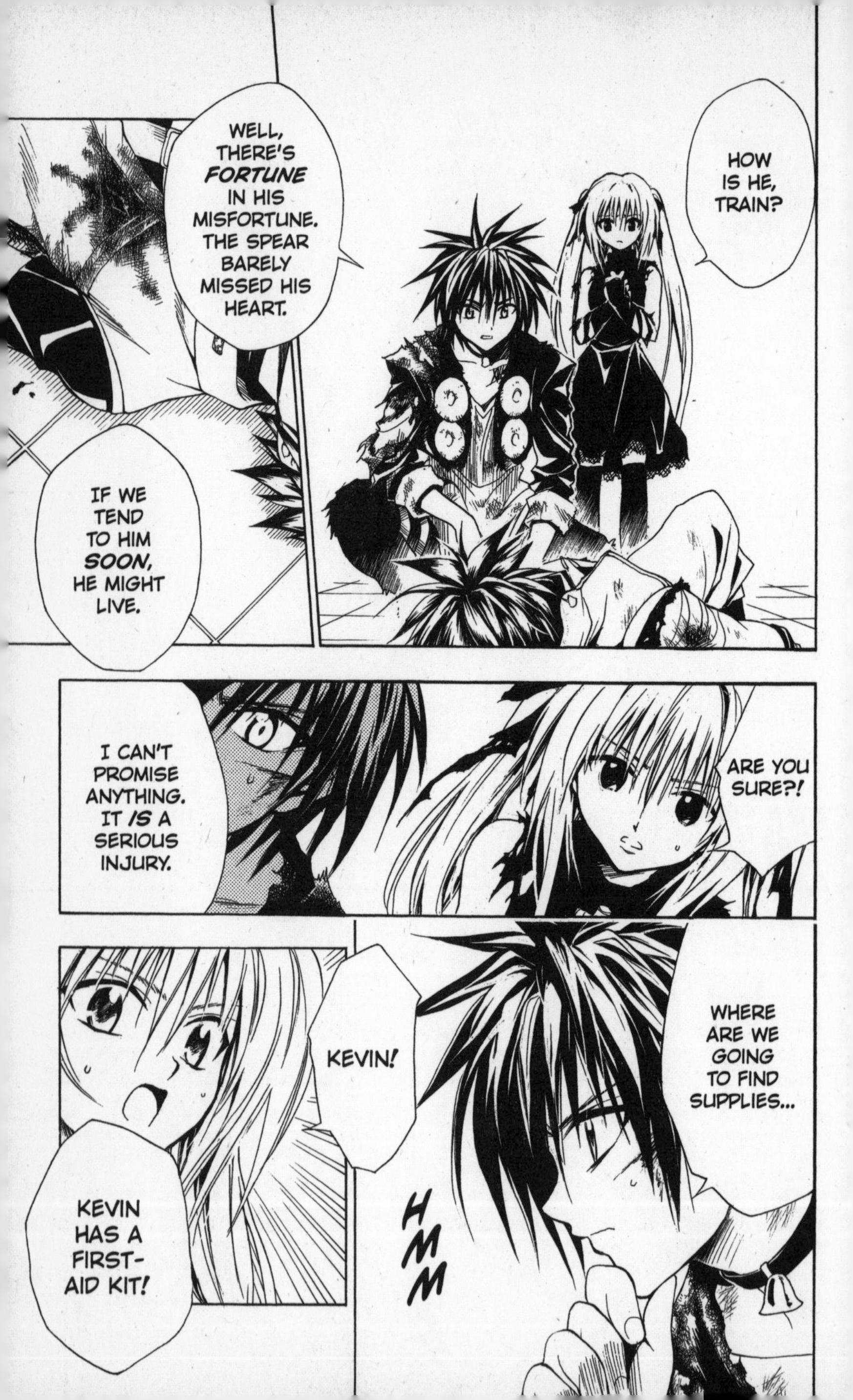
HOW IS HE, TRAIN?
WELL, THERE'S *FORTUNE* IN HIS MISFORTUNE. THE SPEAR BARELY MISSED HIS HEART.
IF WE TEND TO HIM *SOON,* HE MIGHT LIVE.
ARE YOU SURE?!
I CAN'T PROMISE ANYTHING. IT *IS* A SERIOUS INJURY.
WHERE ARE WE GOING TO FIND SUPPLIES...
HMM
KEVIN!
KEVIN HAS A FIRST-AID KIT!

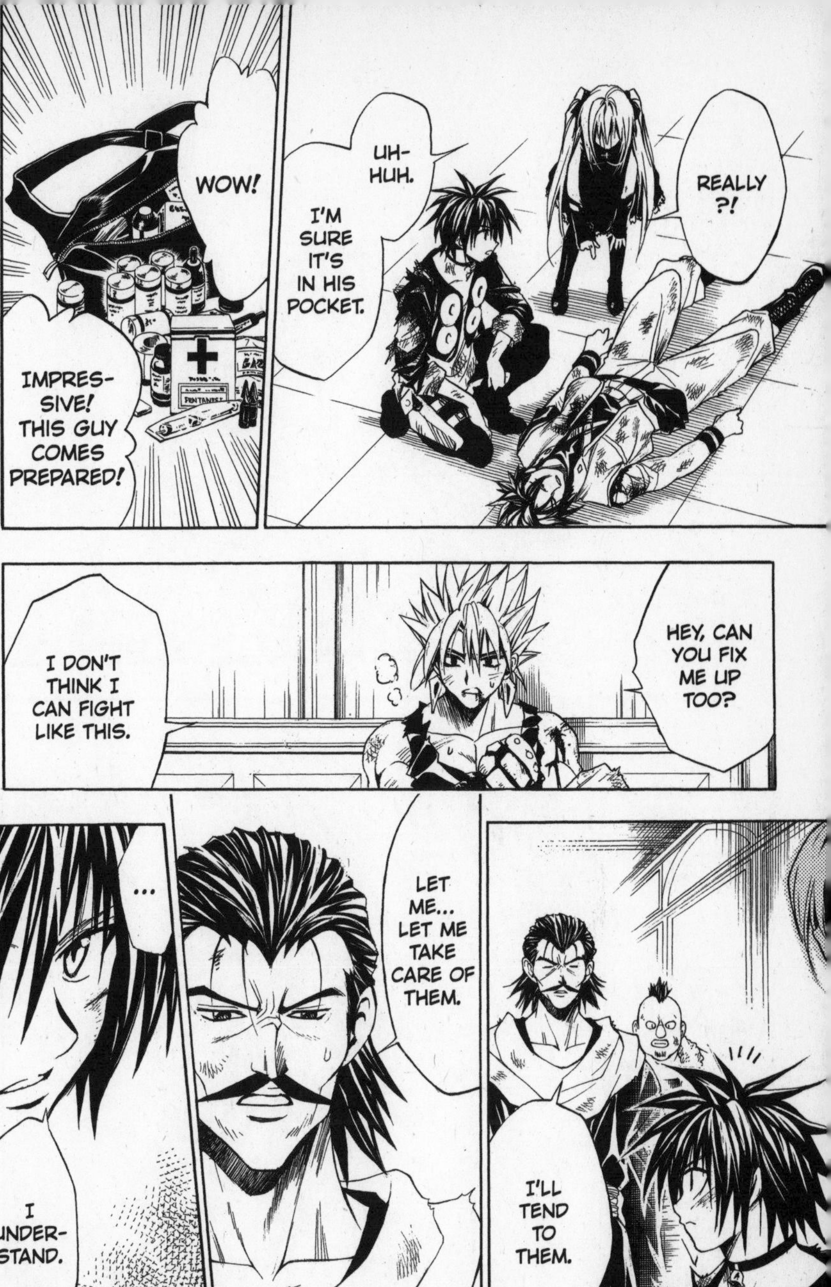
REALLY ?!
UH-HUH.
I'M SURE IT'S IN HIS POCKET.
WOW!
IMPRES-SIVE! THIS GUY COMES PREPARED!
HEY, CAN YOU FIX ME UP TOO?
I DON'T THINK I CAN FIGHT LIKE THIS.
I'LL TEND TO THEM.
LET ME... LET ME TAKE CARE OF THEM.
...
I UNDER-STAND.

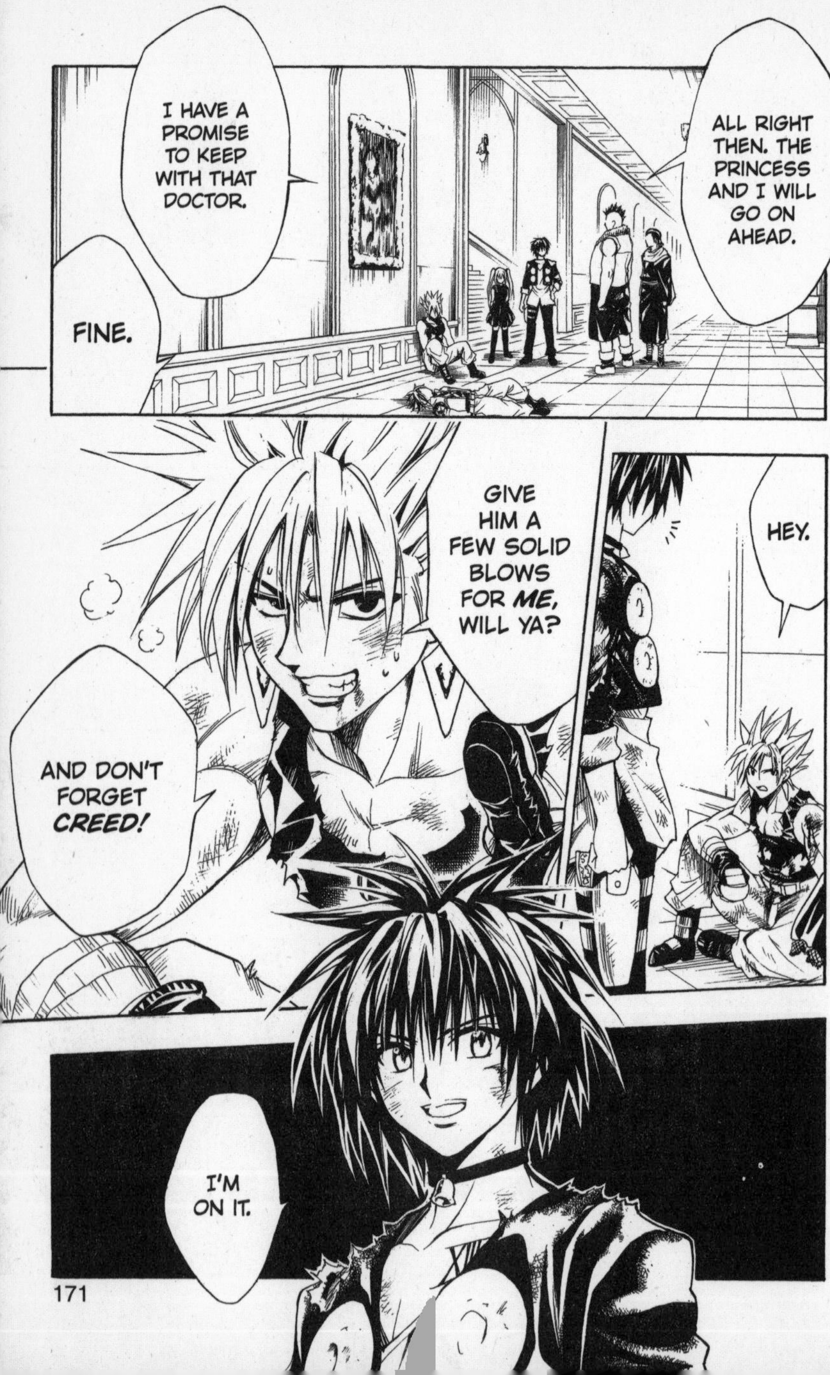
ALL RIGHT THEN. THE PRINCESS AND I WILL GO ON AHEAD.
I HAVE A PROMISE TO KEEP WITH THAT DOCTOR.
FINE.
HEY.
GIVE HIM A FEW SOLID BLOWS FOR *ME*, WILL YA?
AND DON'T FORGET *CREED!*
I'M ON IT.

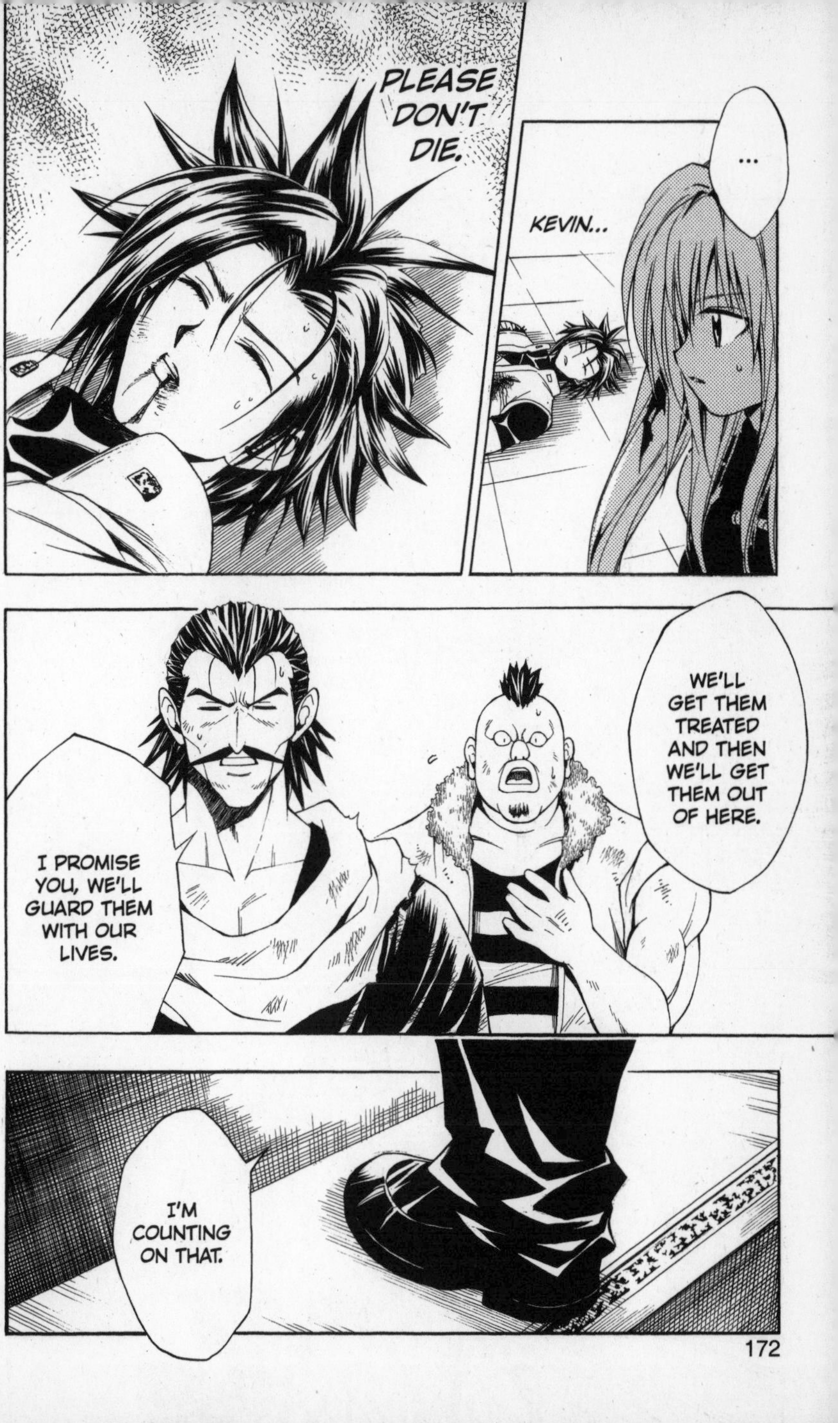
...
KEVIN...
PLEASE DON'T DIE.
WE'LL GET THEM TREATED AND THEN WE'LL GET THEM OUT OF HERE.
I PROMISE YOU, WE'LL GUARD THEM WITH OUR LIVES.
I'M COUNTING ON THAT.

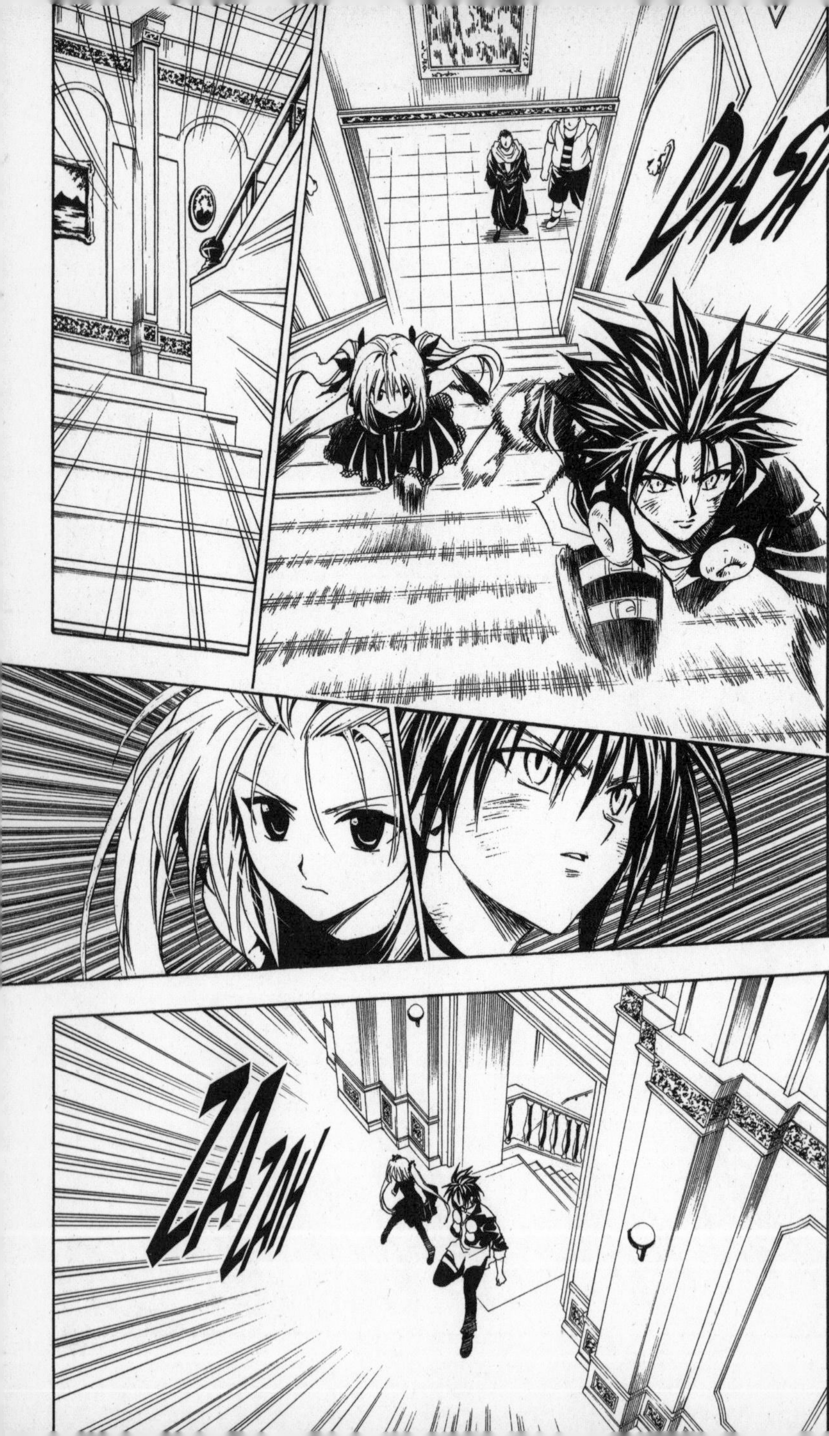
DASH
ZA ZAH

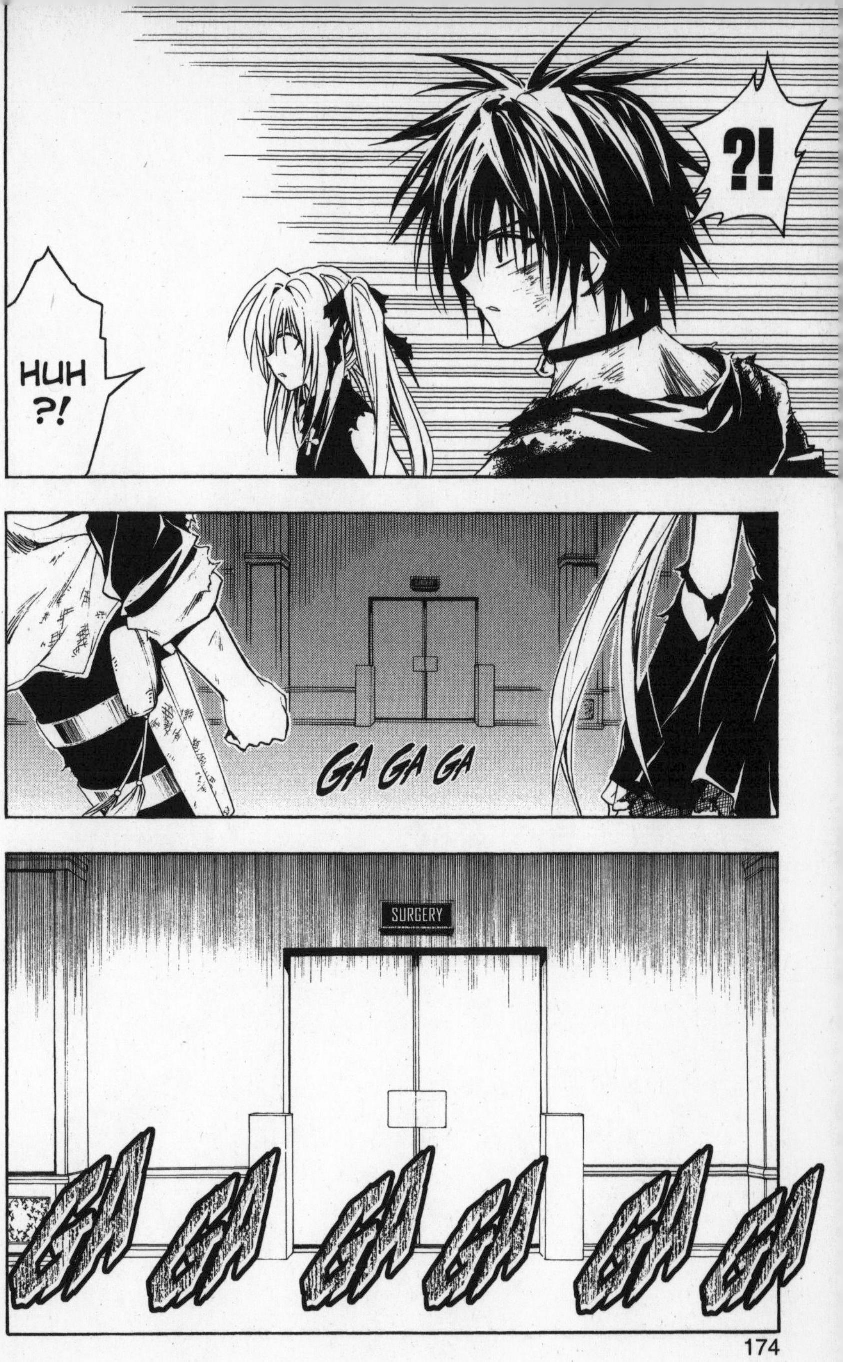
?!
HUH ?!
GA GA GA
SURGERY
GA GA GA GA GA GA

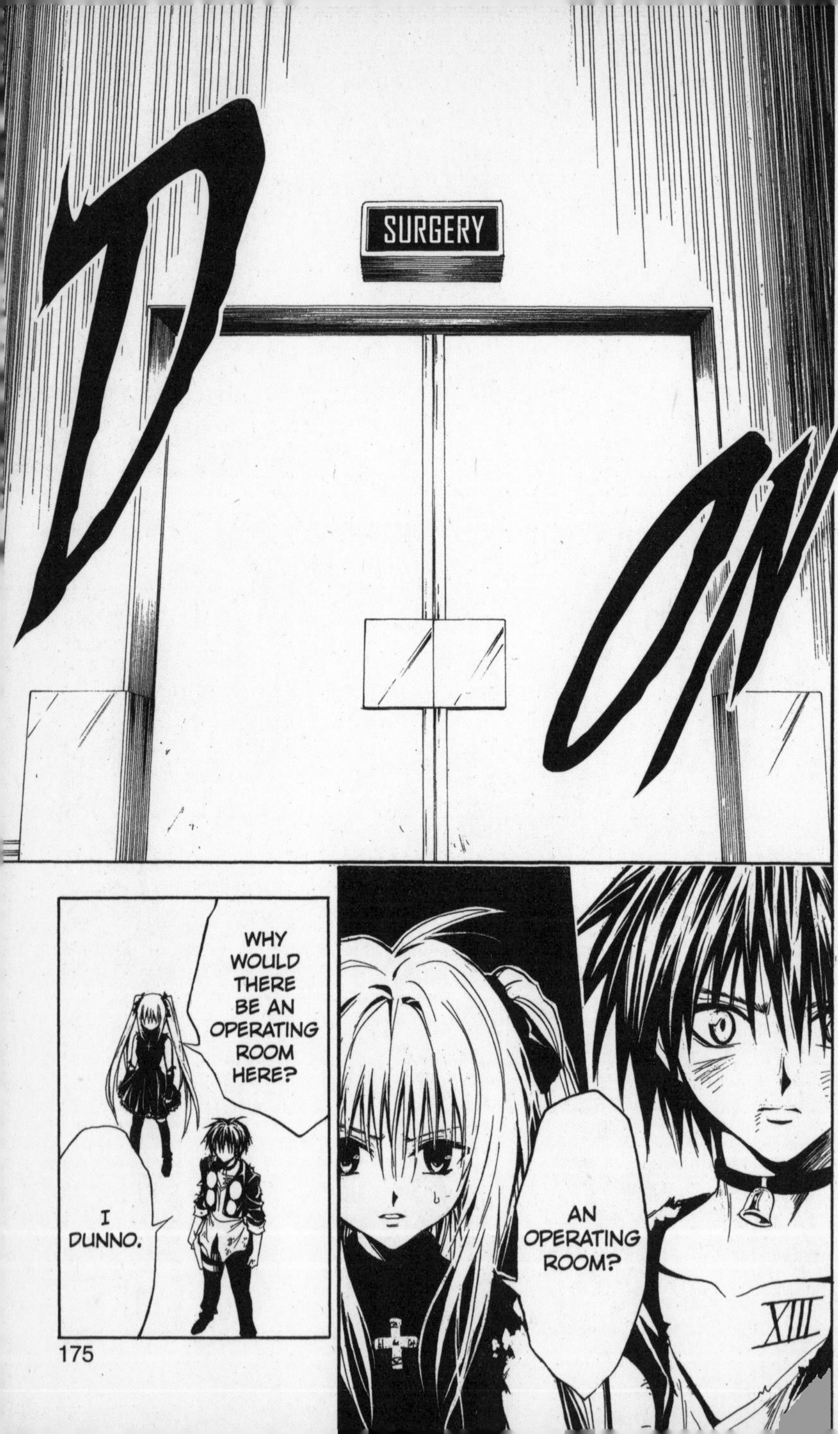
SURGERY
AN OPERATING ROOM?
WHY WOULD THERE BE AN OPERATING ROOM HERE?
I DUNNO.

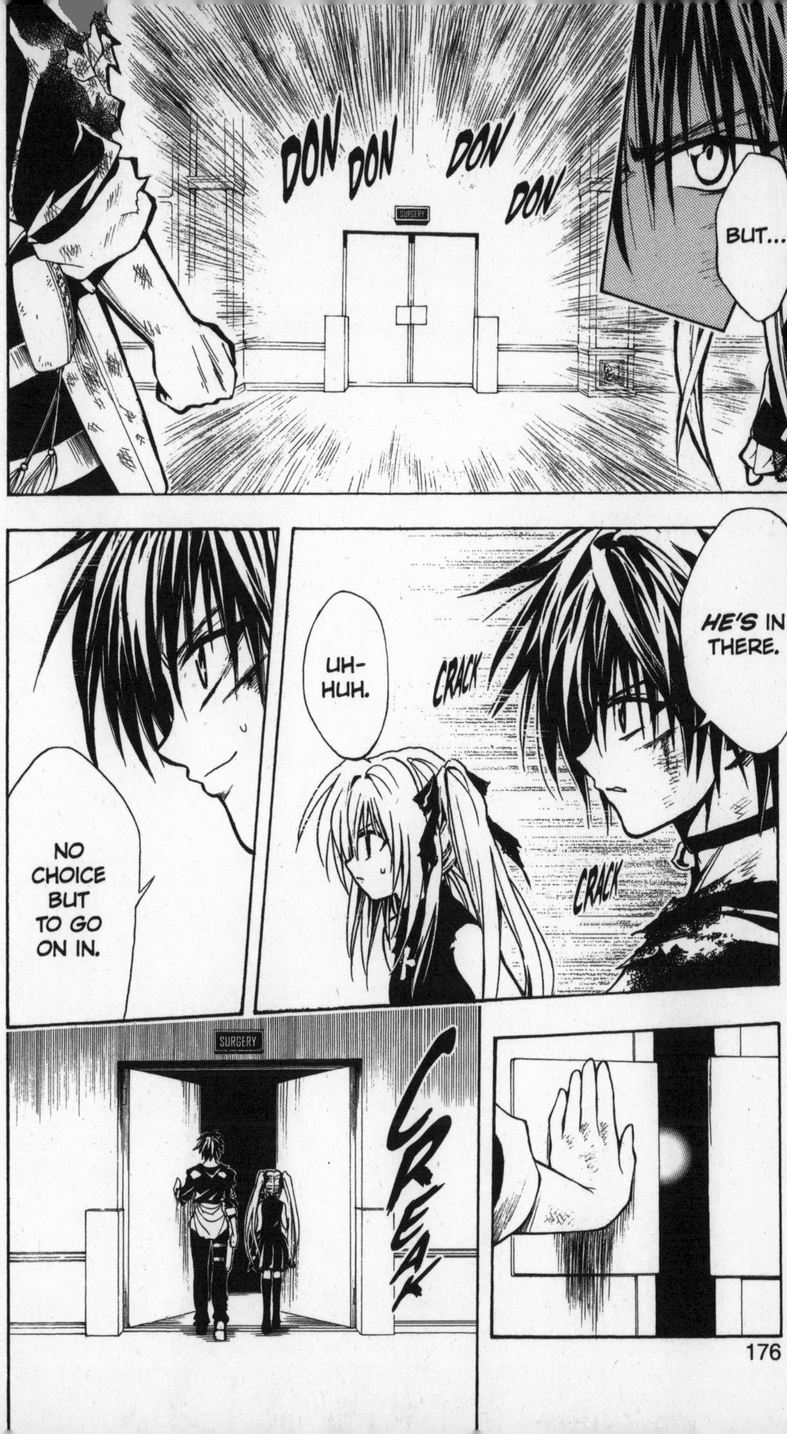

DON DON DON DON
BUT...
HE'S IN THERE.
UH-HUH.
CRACK
CRACK
NO CHOICE BUT TO GO ON IN.
CREAK

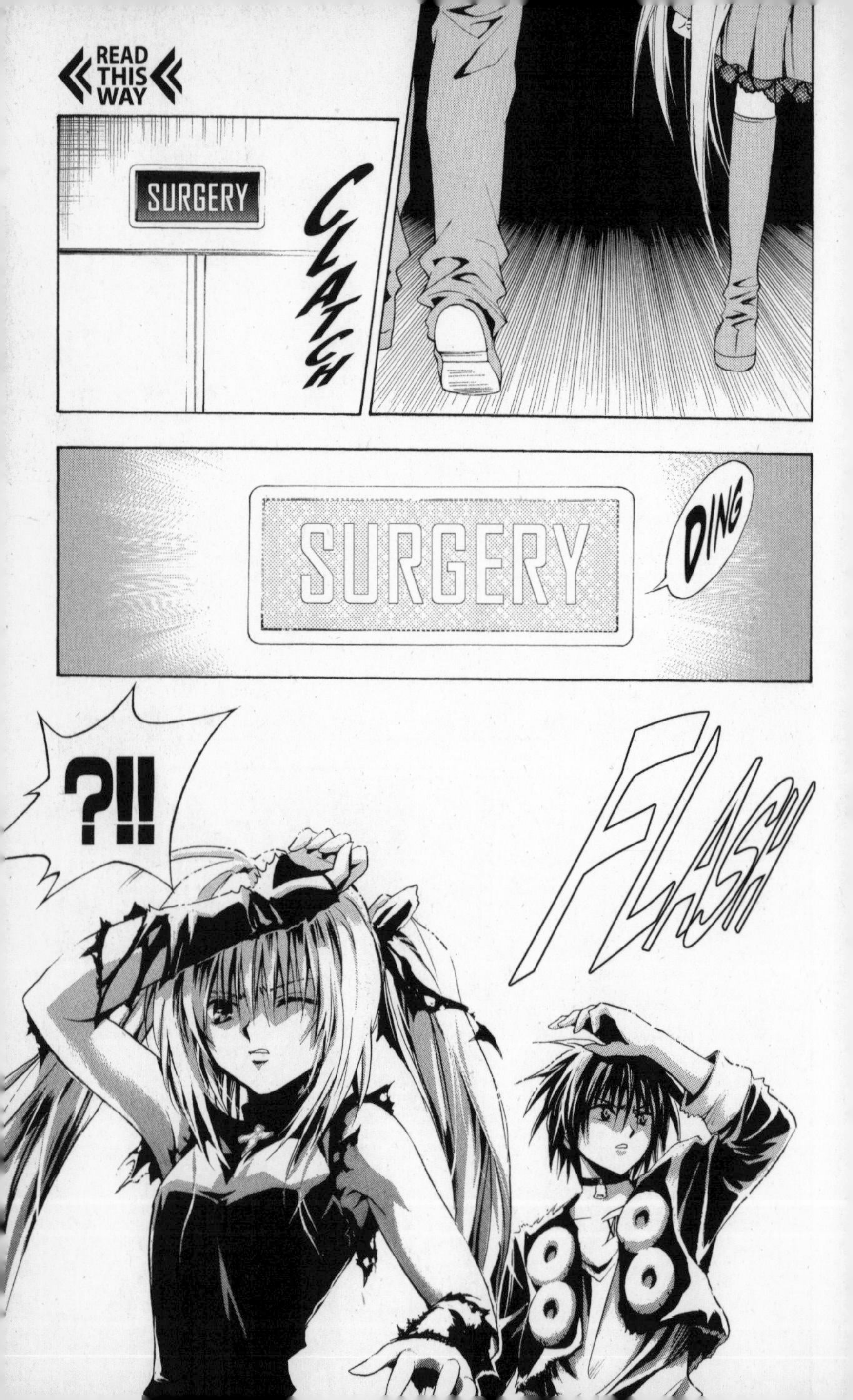
READ THIS WAY
SURGERY
CLATCH
SURGERY
DING
FLASH
?!!

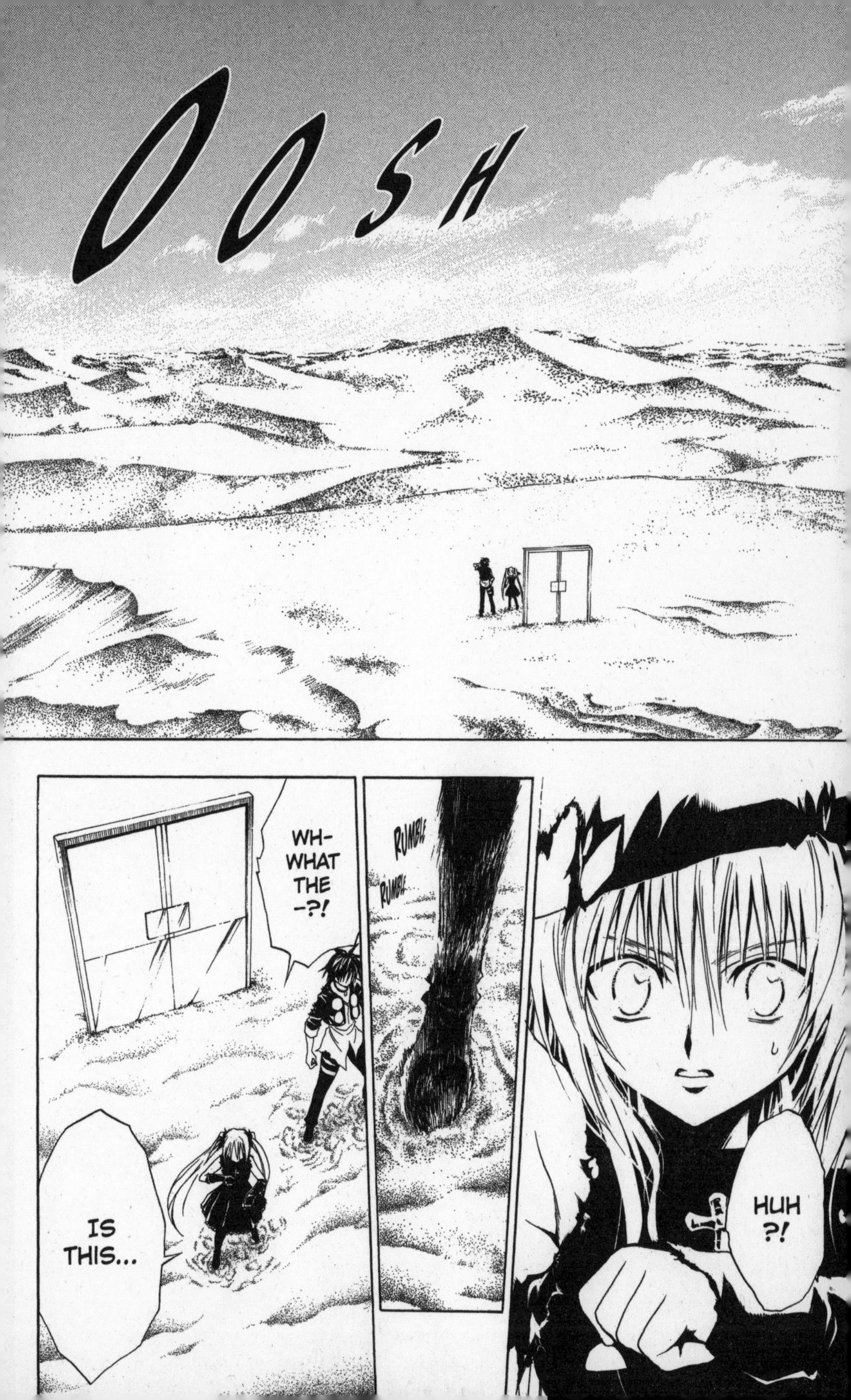
OOSH
HUH ?!
RUMBLE
RUMBLE
WH- WHAT THE -?!
IS THIS...

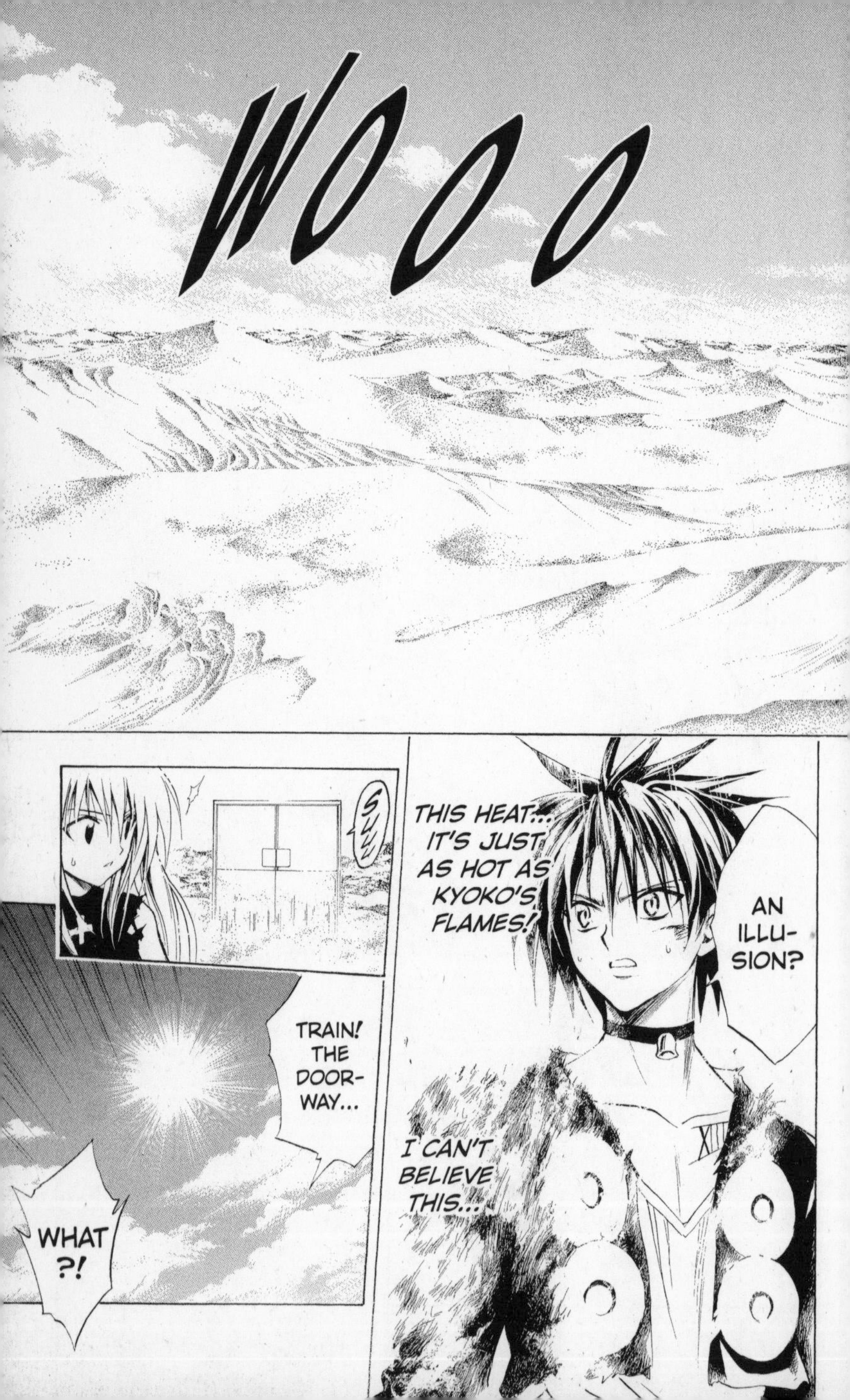
WOOO
AN ILLUSION?
THIS HEAT... IT'S JUST AS HOT AS KYOKO'S FLAMES!
I CAN'T BELIEVE THIS...
TRAIN! THE DOORWAY...
WHAT?!

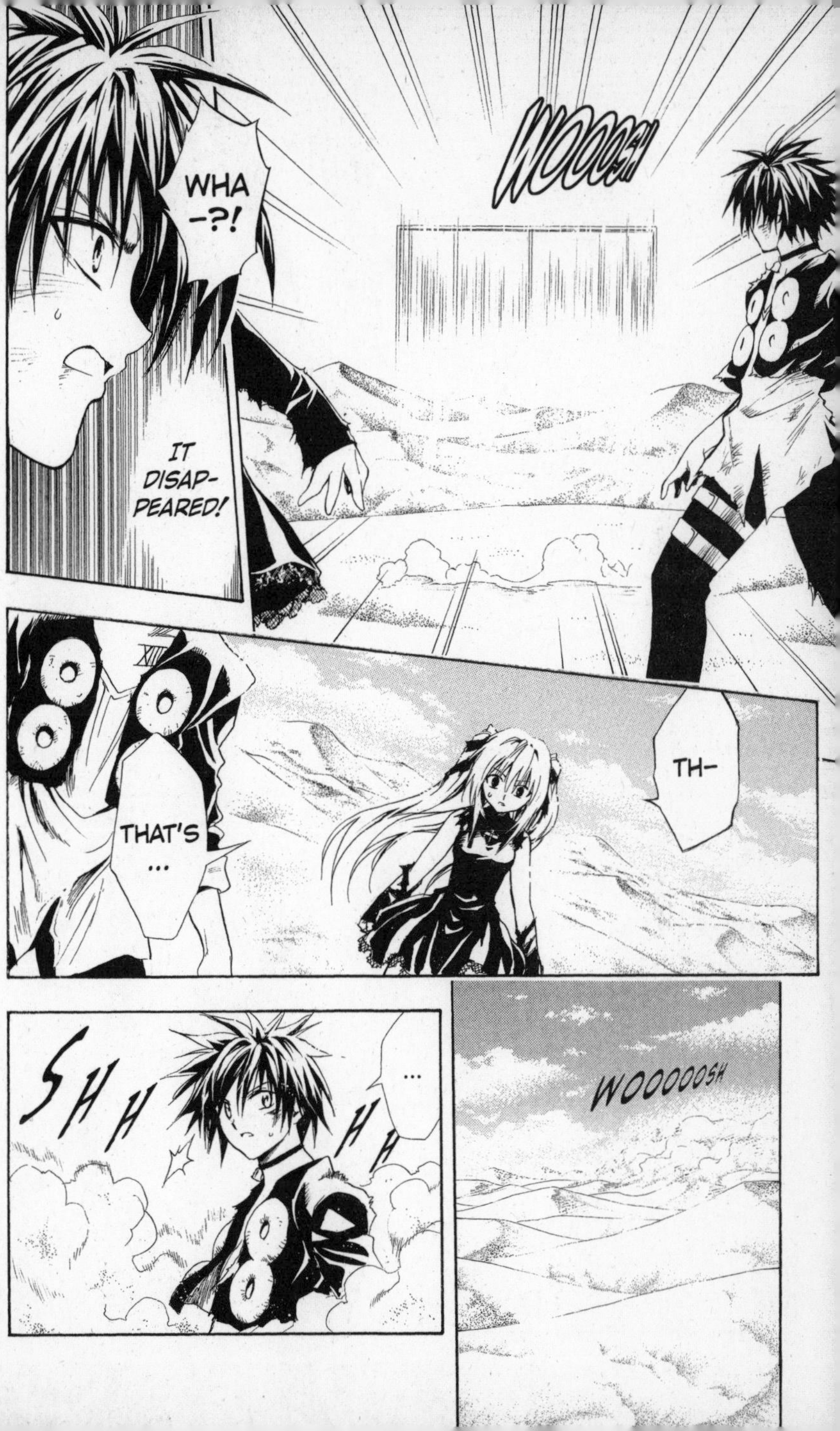
WOOOSH
WHA-?!
IT DISAP-PEARED!
TH-
THAT'S ...
WOOOOSH
...
SHHH

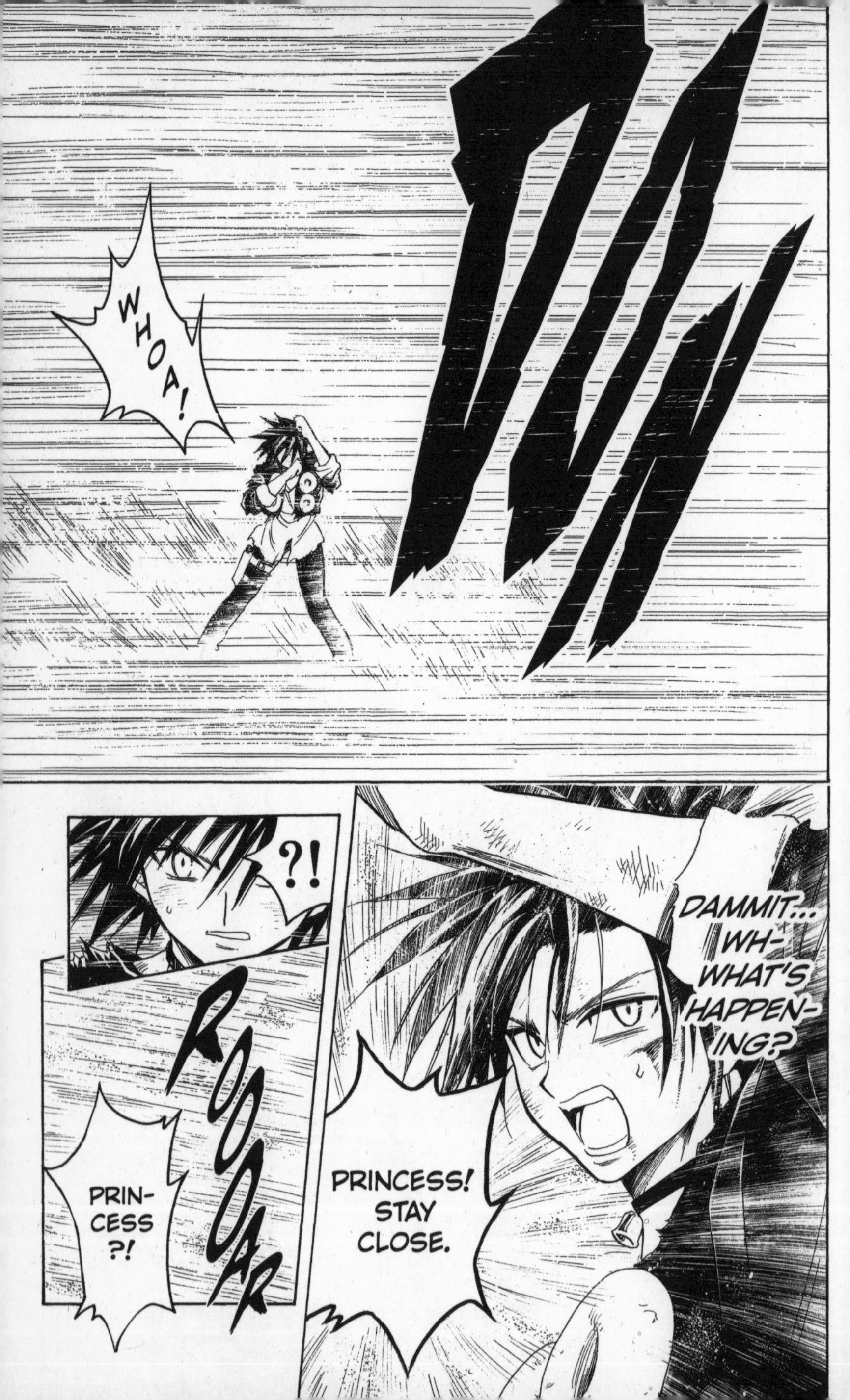
WHOA!
DAMMIT... WH-WHAT'S HAPPENING?
PRINCESS! STAY CLOSE.
?!
ROOOAR
PRINCESS?!

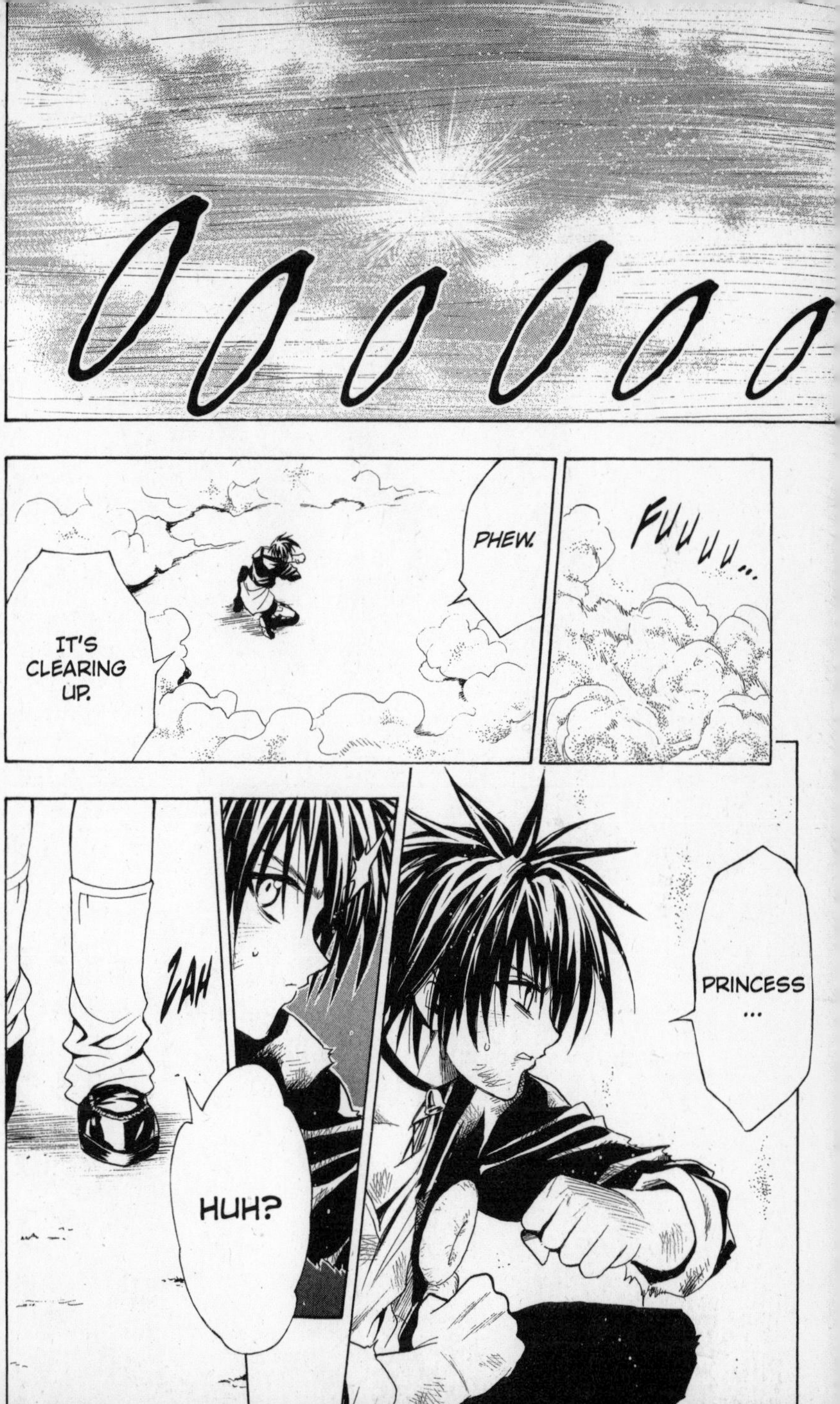
OOOOOO
FUUUU...
PHEW.
IT'S CLEARING UP.
PRINCESS...
ZAH
HUH?

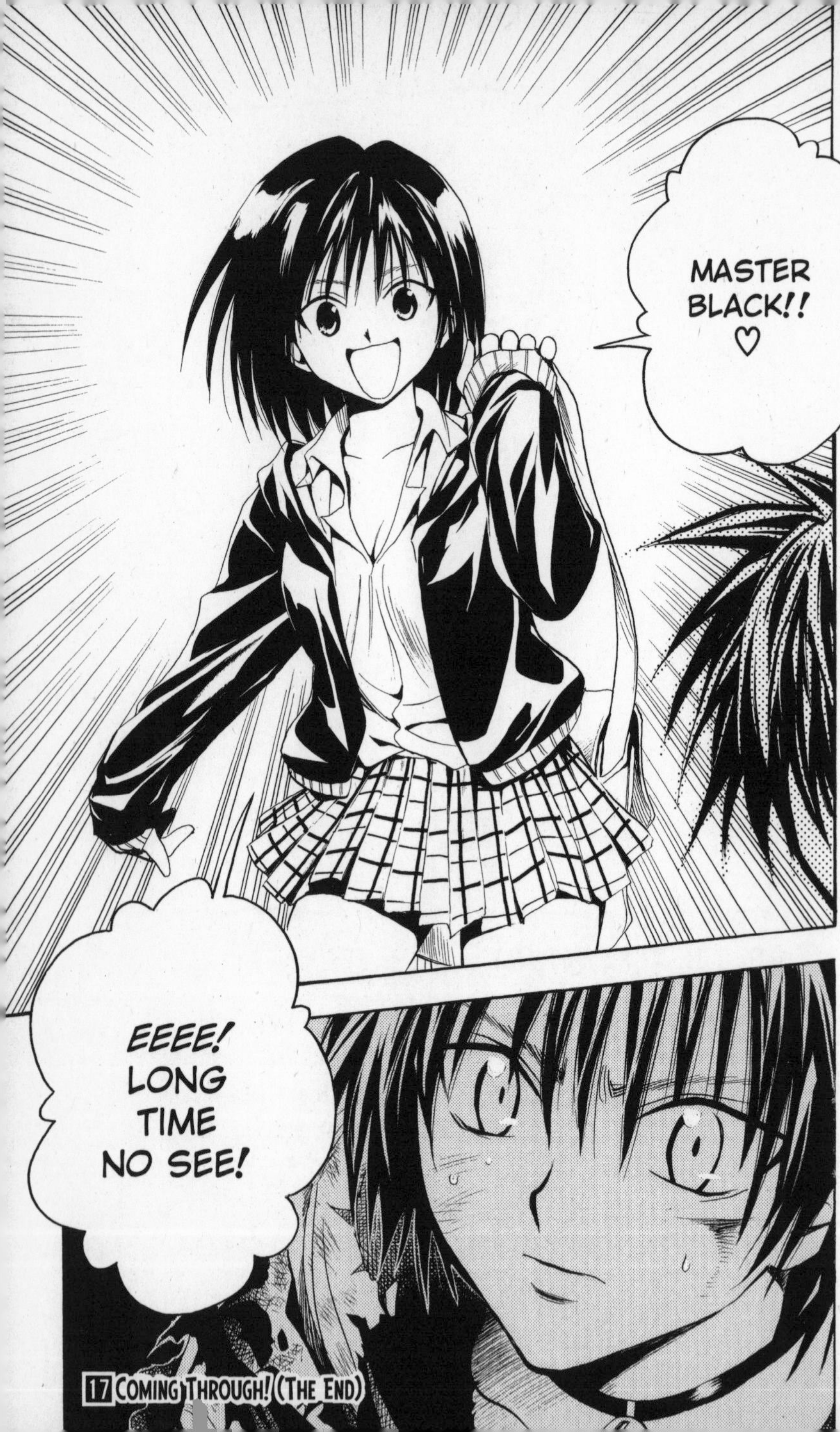
MASTER BLACK!! ♡
EEEE! LONG TIME NO SEE!
17 COMING THROUGH! (THE END)

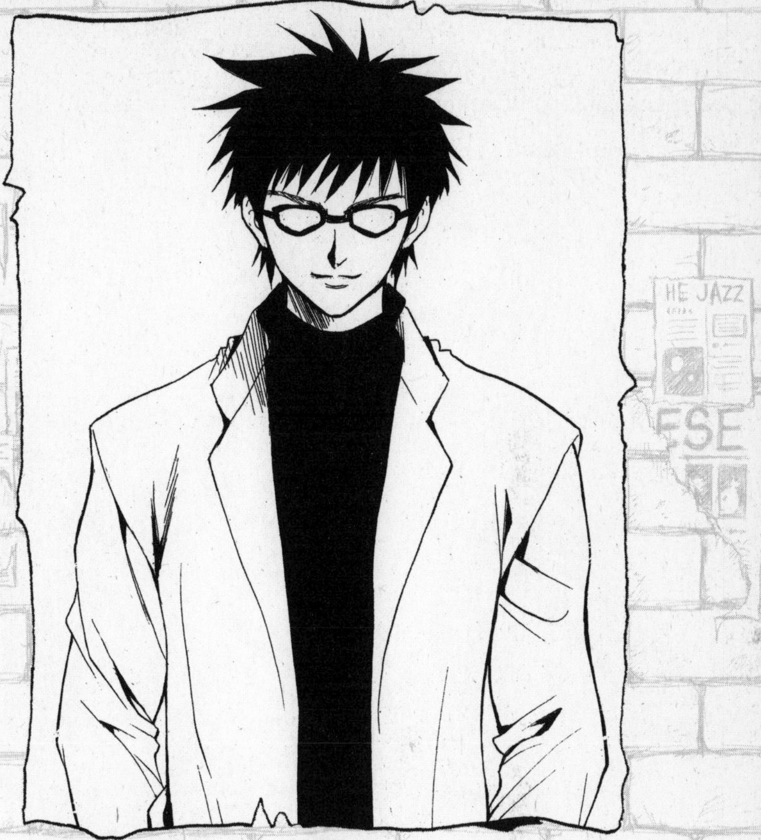
HE JAZZ
ESE

IN THE NEXT VOLUME...

The Doctor traps Train and Eve in his terrible Warp World, where they get separated from each other. As Train searches for an exit, who should he run across but Kyoko, who should be in Jipangu, and Saya, who should be dead! Now Train has to figure out what to believe.

AVAILABLE JANUARY 2008!

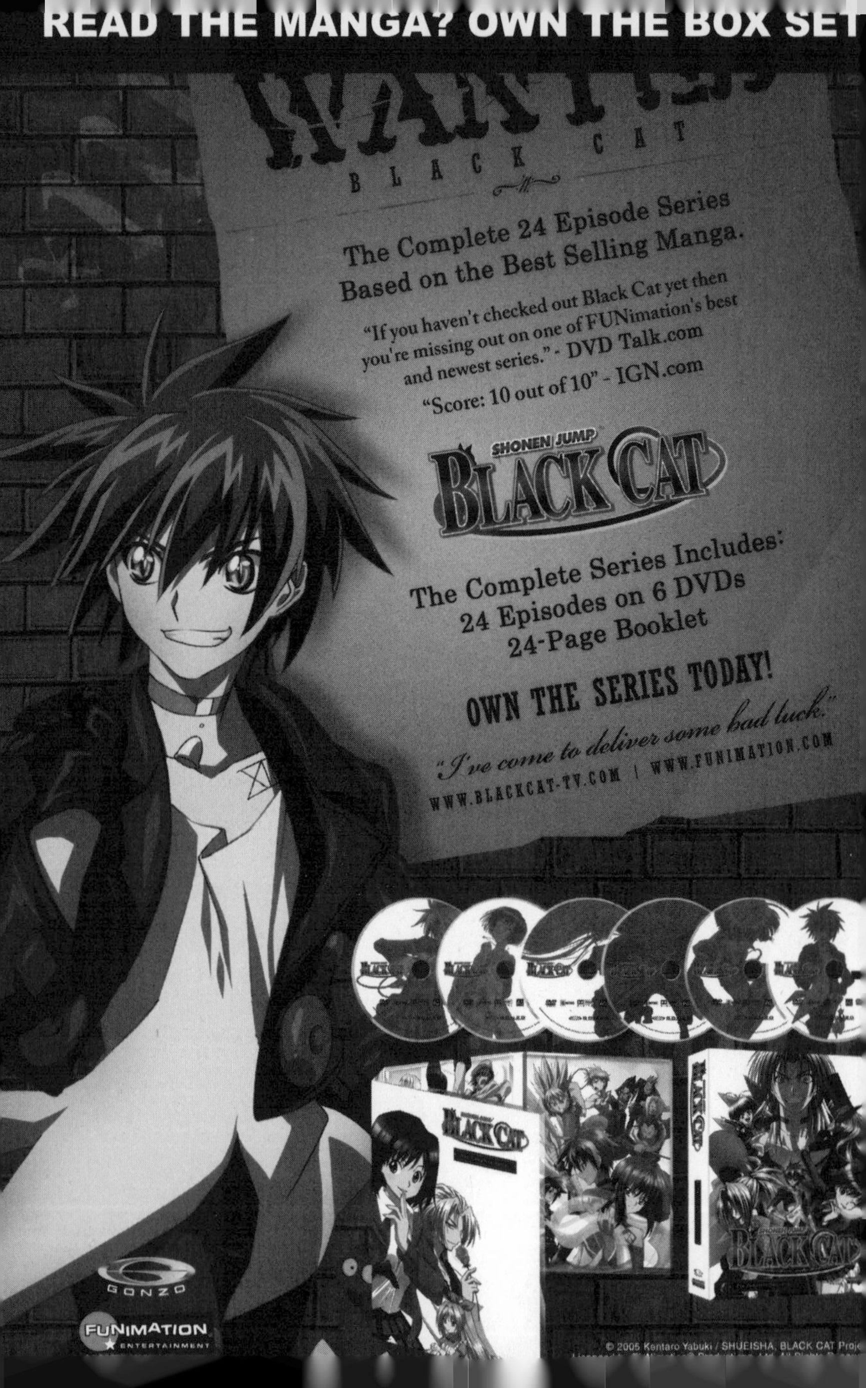
READ THE MANGA? OWN THE BOX SET
WANTED
BLACK CAT
The Complete 24 Episode Series Based on the Best Selling Manga.
"If you haven't checked out Black Cat yet then you're missing out on one of FUNimation's best and newest series." - DVD Talk.com
"Score: 10 out of 10" - IGN.com
SHONEN JUMP
BLACK CAT
The Complete Series Includes:
24 Episodes on 6 DVDs
24-Page Booklet
OWN THE SERIES TODAY!
"I've come to deliver some bad luck."
WWW.BLACKCAT-TV.COM | WWW.FUNIMATION.COM
GONZO
FUNIMATION ENTERTAINMENT
© 2005 Kentaro Yabuki / SHUEISHA, BLACK CAT Proj

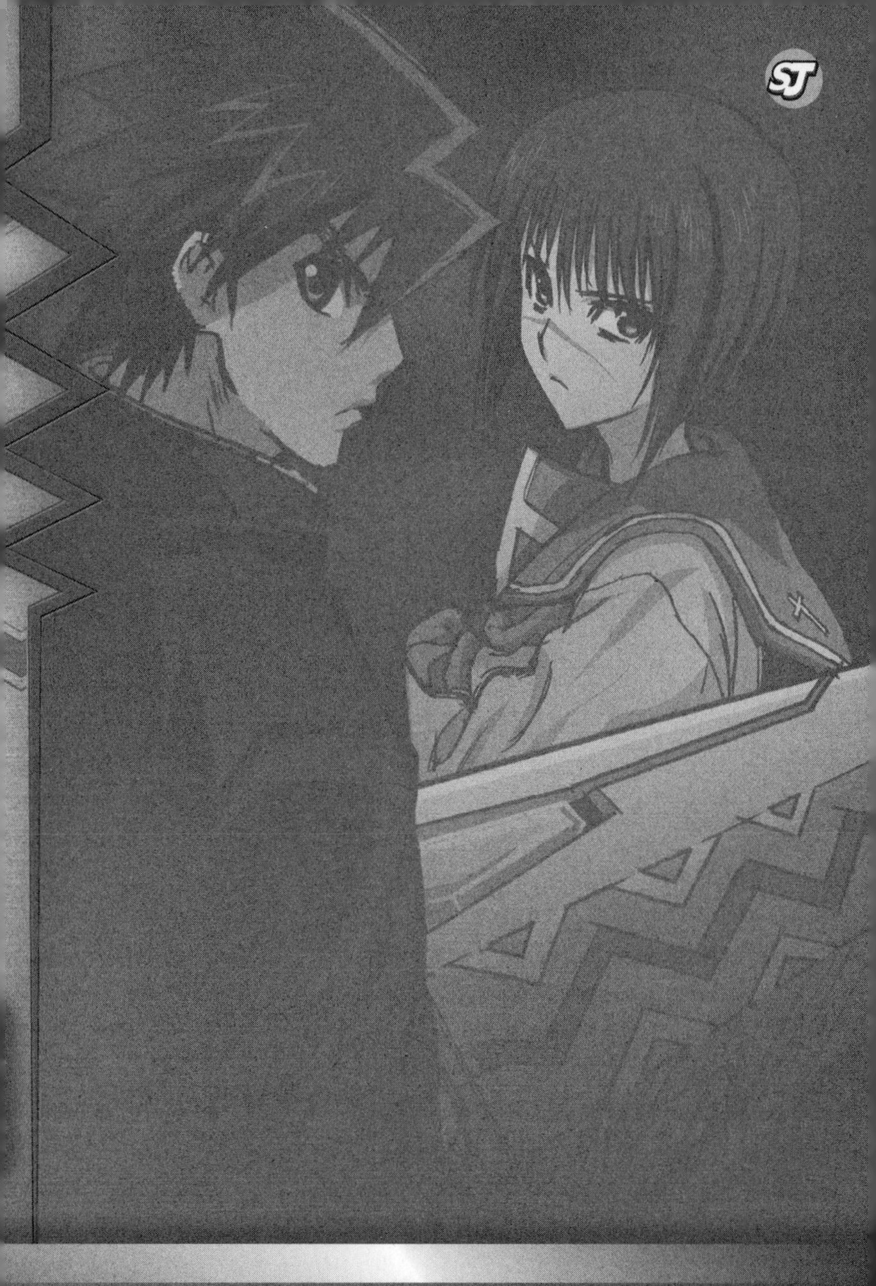
SJ

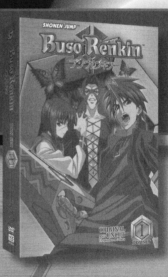

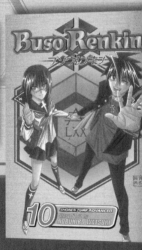

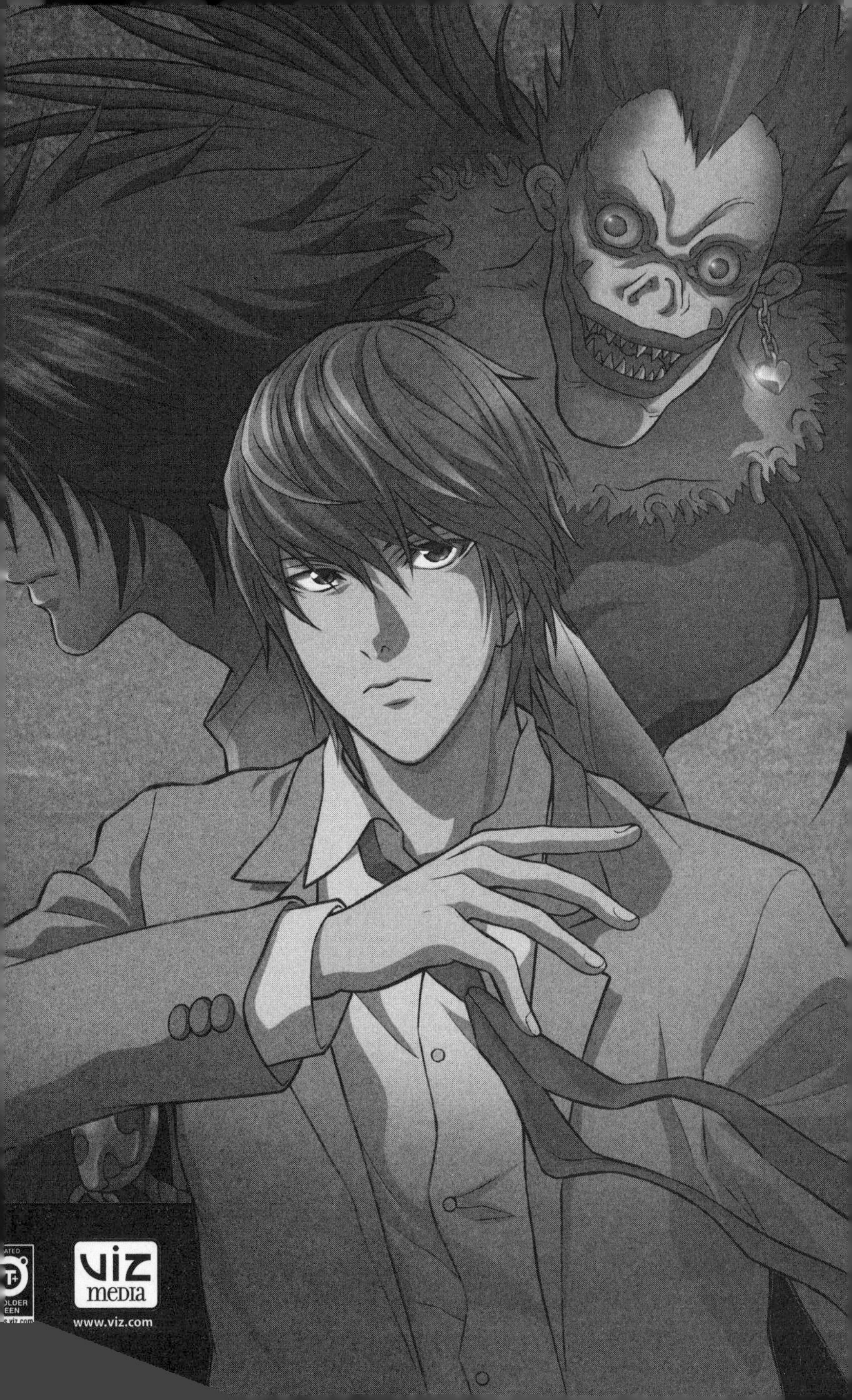
viz media
www.viz.com

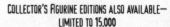
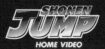

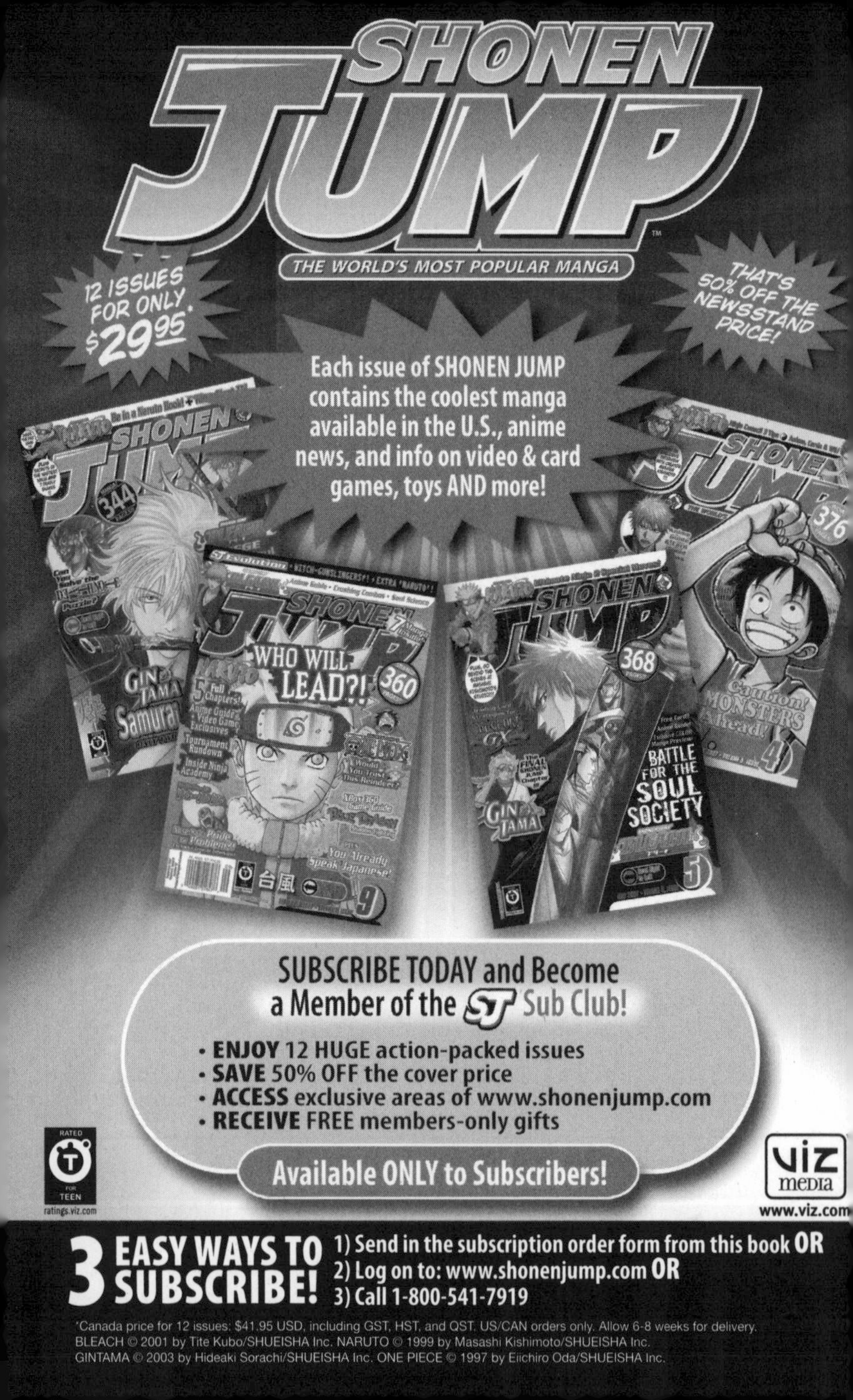
SHONEN JUMP
THE WORLD'S MOST POPULAR MANGA
12 ISSUES FOR ONLY $29.95*
THAT'S 50% OFF THE NEWSSTAND PRICE!
Each issue of SHONEN JUMP contains the coolest manga available in the U.S., anime news, and info on video & card games, toys AND more!
WHO WILL LEAD?!
BATTLE FOR THE SOUL SOCIETY
SUBSCRIBE TODAY and Become a Member of the SJ Sub Club!
• ENJOY 12 HUGE action-packed issues
• SAVE 50% OFF the cover price
• ACCESS exclusive areas of www.shonenjump.com
• RECEIVE FREE members-only gifts
Available ONLY to Subscribers!
RATED T FOR TEEN ratings.viz.com
VIZ media www.viz.com
3 EASY WAYS TO SUBSCRIBE!
1) Send in the subscription order form from this book OR
2) Log on to: www.shonenjump.com OR
3) Call 1-800-541-7919
*Canada price for 12 issues: $41.95 USD, including GST, HST, and QST. US/CAN orders only. Allow 6-8 weeks for delivery.
BLEACH © 2001 by Tite Kubo/SHUEISHA Inc. NARUTO © 1999 by Masashi Kishimoto/SHUEISHA Inc.
GINTAMA © 2003 by Hideaki Sorachi/SHUEISHA Inc. ONE PIECE © 1997 by Eiichiro Oda/SHUEISHA Inc.

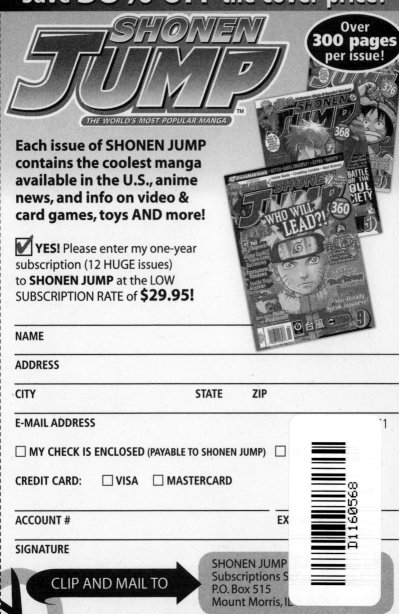